SOMETHING ABOUT THE AUTHOR

ISSN 0276-816X

something ABOUT The AUThOR

**Facts and Pictures about Authors
and Illustrators of Books for Young People**

EDITED BY
ANNE COMMIRE

VOLUME 37

GALE RESEARCH COMPANY
BOOK TOWER
DETROIT, MICHIGAN
48226

Editor: Anne Commire

Associate Editors: Agnes Garrett, Helga P. McCue

Assistant Editors: Dianne H. Anderson, Lori J. Bell, Joyce Nakamura,
Linda Shedd, Cynthia J. Walker

Sketchwriters: Rachel Koenig, Eunice L. Petrini

Researcher: Kathleen Betsko

Editorial Assistants: Lisa Bryon, Carolyn Kline, Marilyn O'Connell,
Susan Pfanner, Elisa Ann Sawchuk

External Production Supervisor: Carol Blanchard

External Production Associate: Mary Beth Trimper

External Production Assistant: Dorothy Kalleberg

Internal Senior Production Assistant: Louise Gagné

Internal Production Assistant: Sandy Rock

Text Layout: Vivian Tannenbaum

Art Director: Arthur Chartow

Special acknowledgment is due to the members of the *Contemporary Authors* staff
who assisted in the preparation of this volume.

Publisher: Frederick G. Ruffner

Executive Vice-President/Editorial: James M. Ethridge

Editorial Director: Dedria Bryfonski

Director, Literature Division: Christine Nasso

Senior Editor, Something about the Author: Adele Sarkissian

Library of Congress Catalog Card Number 72-27107
ISBN 0-8103-0069-9
ISSN 0276-816X

Contents

5

Contents

Introduction

As the only ongoing reference series that deals with the lives and works of authors and illustrators of children's books, *Something about the Author (SATA)* is a unique source of information. The *SATA* series includes not only well-known authors and illustrators whose books are most widely read, but also those less prominent people whose works are just coming to be recognized. *SATA* is often the only readily available information source for less well-known writers or artists. You'll find *SATA* informative and entertaining whether you are:

> —a student in junior high school (or perhaps one to two grades higher or lower) who needs information for a book report or some other assignment for an English class;

> —a children's librarian who is searching for the answer to yet another question from a young reader or collecting background material to use for a story hour;

> —an English teacher who is drawing up an assignment for your students or gathering information for a book talk;

> —a student in a college of education or library science who is studying children's literature and reference sources in the field;

> —a parent who is looking for a new way to interest your child in reading something more than the school curriculum prescribes;

> —an adult who enjoys children's literature for its own sake, knowing that a good children's book has no age limits.

Scope

In *SATA* you will find detailed information about authors and illustrators who span the full time range of children's literature, from early figures like John Newbery and L. Frank Baum to contemporary figures like Judy Blume and Richard Peck. Authors in the series represent primarily English-speaking countries, particularly the United States, Canada, and the United Kingdom. Also included, however, are authors from around the world whose works are available in English translation, for example: from France, Jean and Laurent De Brunhoff; from Italy, Emanuele Luzzati; from the Netherlands, Jaap ter Haar; from Germany, James Krüss; from Norway, Babbis Friis-Baastad; from Japan, Toshiko Kanzawa; from the Soviet Union, Kornei Chukovsky; from Switzerland, Alois Carigiet, to name only a few. Also appearing in *SATA* are Newbery medalists from Hendrik Van Loon (1922) to Beverly Cleary (1984). The writings represented in *SATA* include those created intentionally for children and young adults as well as those written for a general audience and known to interest younger readers. These writings cover the spectrum from picture books, humor, folk and fairy tales, animal stories, mystery and adventure, science fiction and fantasy, historical fiction, poetry and nonsense verse, to drama, biography, and nonfiction.

Information Features

In *SATA* you will find full-length entries for people who are appearing in the series for the first time. This volume, for example, marks the first appearance of Dina Anastasio, Maggie Duff, Annie Fellows Johnston, Ian Ribbons, Marcia Sewall, Bill Sokol, Chris Van Allsburg, and Nancy Willard, among others. Since Volume 25, each *SATA* volume also includes newly revised and updated biographies for a selection of early *SATA* listees who remain of interest to today's readers and who have been active enough to require extensive revision of their earlier entries. The entry for a given biographee may be revised as often as there is substantial new information to provide. In Volume 37 you'll find revised entries for Frank Herbert and Louis Untermeyer.

Brief Entries, first introduced in Volume 27, are another regular feature of *SATA*. Brief Entries present essentially the same types of information found in a full entry but do so in a capsule form and without illustration. These entries are intended to give you useful and timely information while the more time-consuming process of compiling a full-length biography is in progress. In this volume you'll find Brief Entries for Betsy Bang, Joanna Cole, Leonard B. Lubin, Bill Morrison, Paul Neimark, Francine Pascal, Rien Poortvliet, and Walter Wangerin, Jr., among others.

Obituaries have been included in *SATA* since Volume 20. An Obituary is intended not only as a death notice but also as a concise view of a person's life and work. Obituaries may appear for persons who have entries in earlier *SATA* volumes, as well as for people who have not yet appeared in the series. In this volume Obituaries mark the recent deaths of Borghild Dahl, Wolfgang Ecke, Richard Llewellyn, Vanya Oakes, and others.

Each *SATA* volume provides a cumulative index in two parts: first, the Illustrations Index, arranged by the name of the illustrator, gives the number of the volume and page where the illustrator's work appears in the current volume as well as all preceding volumes in the series; second, the Author Index gives the number of the volume in which a person's biographical sketch, Brief Entry, or Obituary appears in the current volume as well as all preceding volumes in the series. These indexes also include references to authors and illustrators who appear in *Yesterday's Authors of Books for Children*. Beginning with Volume 36, the *SATA* Author Index provides cross-references to authors who are included in *Children's Literature Review*.

Illustrations

While the textual information in *SATA* is its primary reason for existing, photographs and illustrations not only enliven the text but are an integral part of the information that *SATA* provides. Illustrations and text are wedded in such a special way in children's literature that artists and their works naturally occupy a prominent place among *SATA*'s listees. The illustrators that you'll find in the series include such past masters of children's book illustration as Randolph Caldecott, Kate Greenaway, Walter Crane, Arthur Rackham, and Ernest L. Shepard, as well as such noted contemporary artists as Maurice Sendak, Edward Gorey, Tomie de Paola, and Margot Zemach. There are Caldecott medalists from Dorothy Lathrop (the first recipient in 1938) to Alice and Martin Provensen (the latest winners in 1984); cartoonists like Charles Schulz, ("Peanuts"), Walt Kelly ("Pogo"), Hank Ketcham ("Dennis the Menace"), and Georges Remi ("Tintin"); photographers like Jill Krementz, Tana Hoban, Bruce McMillan, and Bruce Curtis; and filmmakers like Walt Disney, Alfred Hitchcock, and Steven Spielberg.

In a dozen years of recording the metamorphosis of children's literature from the printed page to other media, *SATA* has become something of a repository of photographs that are unique in themselves and exist nowhere else as a group, particularly many of the classics of motion picture and stage history and photographs that have been specially loaned to us from private collections.

What a *SATA* Entry Provides

Whether you're already familiar with the *SATA* series or just getting acquainted, you will want to be aware of the kind of information that an entry provides. In every *SATA* entry the editors attempt to give as complete a picture of the person's life and work as possible. In some cases that full range of information may simply be unavailable, or a biographee may choose not to reveal complete personal details. The information that the editors attempt to provide in every entry is arranged in the following categories:

1. The "head" of the entry gives

   —the most complete form of the name,
   —any part of the name not commonly used, included in parentheses,
   —birth and death dates, if known; a (?) indicates a discrepancy in published sources,
   —pseudonyms or name variants under which the person has had books published or is publicly known, in parentheses in the second line.

2. "Personal" section gives

   —date and place of birth and death,
   —parents' names and occupations,

—name of spouse, date of marriage, and names of children,
—educational institutions attended, degrees received, and dates,
—religious and political affiliations,
—agent's name and address,
—home and/or office address.

3. "Career" section gives

—name of employer, position, and dates for each career post,
—military service,
—memberships,
—awards and honors.

4. "Writings" section gives

—title, first publisher and date of publication, and illustration information for each book written; revised editions and other significant editions for books with particularly long publishing histories; genre, when known.

5. "Adaptations" section gives

—title, major performers, producer, and date of all known reworkings of an author's material in another medium, like movies, filmstrips, television, recordings, plays, etc.

6. "Sidelights" section gives

—commentary on the life or work of the biographee either directly from the person (and often written specifically for the *SATA* entry), or gathered from biographies, diaries, letters, interviews, or other published sources.

7. "For More Information See" section gives

—books, feature articles, films, plays, and reviews in which the biographee's life or work has been treated.

How a *SATA* Entry Is Compiled

A *SATA* entry progresses through a series of steps. If the biographee is living, the *SATA* editors try to secure information directly from him or her through a questionnaire. From the information that the biographee supplies, the editors prepare an entry, filling in any essential missing details with research. The author or illustrator is then sent a copy of the entry to check for accuracy and completeness.

If the biographee is deceased or cannot be reached by questionnaire, the *SATA* editors examine a wide variety of published sources to gather information for an entry. Biographical sources are searched with the aid of Gale's *Biography and Genealogy Master Index*. Bibliographic sources like the *National Union Catalog*, the *Cumulative Book Index*, *American Book Publishing Record*, and the *British Museum Catalogue* are consulted, as are book reviews, feature articles, published interviews, and material sometimes obtained from the biographee's family, publishers, agent, or other associates.

For each entry presented in *SATA*, the editors also attempt to locate a photograph of the biographee as well as representative illustrations from his or her books. After surveying the available books which the biographee has written and/or illustrated, and then making a selection of appropriate photographs and illustrations, the editors request permission of the current copyright holders to reprint the material. In the case of older books for which the copyright may have passed through several hands, even locating the current copyright holder is often a long and involved process.

We invite you to examine the entire *SATA* series, starting with this volume. Described below are some of the people in Volume 37 that you may find particularly interesting.

Highlights of This Volume

FRANK HERBERT......is best known for his critically acclaimed "Dune" series of novels: *Dune, Dune*

Messiah, Children of Dune, and *God Emperor of Dune.* Highly regarded as the creator of one of science fiction's most compelling fantasy worlds, Herbert has received both the Nebula and Hugo Awards. Although an active campaigner for the conservation of natural resources and an expert on ecology, he believes that "technology isn't bad in and of itself . . . everything depends on how we use it."

DANIEL KEYES......who provided young adults with new insight into the world of the mentally retarded with his touching story *Flowers for Algernon.* First written as a short story and then as a novel, *Flowers for Algernon* won the Nebula and Hugo Awards and has been adapted as a play, television special, and Oscar-winning movie. Keyes finds that he is "fascinated by the complexities of the human mind." He further explores this fascination in *The Minds of Billy Milligan,* a true account of a multiple personality. Surprisingly, it was only after Milligan read *Flowers for Algernon* that several of his twenty-four selves agreed to let Keyes write their story.

WALTER LANTZ......spent many hours as a child copying figures from comic strips. He later founded his own animated cartoon studio and created memorable characters that have delighted generations of children—Wally Walrus, Chilly Willy, Andy Panda, and, of course, Woody Woodpecker. Lantz describes his mischievous bird as "a very fresh, precocious type of character. . . . He does things that all of us would like to, but we don't have the nerve. . . . There's a little bit of Woody in all of us." Lantz's wife, Gracie, is credited with giving Woody his trademark laugh. "Gracie changed the laugh," Lantz remembers. "She put a sort of musical tone in it, like the five notes of a bugle call, 'da-da-da-daaa-da'...." Also an accomplished painter, Lantz has received many honors for his work in animation, including the prestigious Annie Award, a special Oscar, and a permanent home in the Smithsonian Institution for Woody Woodpecker memorabilia.

JOHN R. TUNIS......, well-known author of sports books for young readers, had never really intended to write for children. That decision was made for him early in his career by publisher Alfred Harcourt who labeled *The Iron Duke* a juvenile book. According to Tunis, he was "shocked, rocked, deflated." Because of Harcourt's decision, *The Iron Duke* was successfully published and followed by numerous other books for young people like *The Kid from Tomkinsville, Rookie of the Year,* and *Highpockets.* Toward the end of his career, Tunis expressed great appreciation for his not-so-chosen reading audience. "Youth deserve the best," he declared. "They read for one reason only, they want to."

LOUIS UNTERMEYER......was an inept student who felt imprisoned by mandatory schooling. A voracious reader, he lived in a fantasy world where his companions included D'Artagnan, David Copperfield, Captain Nemo, and Jean Valjean. This reluctant schoolboy went on to become one of the most brilliant anthologists of the twentieth century, compiling volumes of poetry that for years have been considered standard classroom textbooks. He also opened the doors of poetry to young children with books like *This Singing World, Yesterday and Today,* and *Stars to Steer By.* As an editor, poet, biographer, storyteller, and parodist, Untermeyer found the niche in life that had eluded him as a child. "It is in the actual process of writing," he observed, "that I am most myself. . . ."

NANCY WILLARD......remembers reading "books by the arm load" during long childhood summers spent at her family's cottage in Michigan. In her own books, Willard brings her characters to life as she creates them. "If I have a character in my head," she explains, "sometimes I'll make something that belongs to him like his hat. You learn about the characters as you work on things that belong to them." In her dining room is a wooden inn, "filled. . . with furniture and people," that she built while writing her 1981 Newbery Award winner *A Visit to William Blake's Inn.* Also a poet and literary critic, Willard firmly believes that there are two kinds of truth in the world, "the scientific answer and the imaginative answer. And," she adds, "we need both of them." Fantasy and adventure abound in her books for young readers like *The Merry History of a Christmas Pie, Sailing to Cythera,* and *The Marzipan Moon.*

These are only a few of the authors and illustrators that you'll find in this volume. We hope you find all the entries in *SATA* both interesting and useful. Please write and tell us if we can make *SATA* even more helpful to you.

Forthcoming Authors

A Partial List of Authors and Illustrators Who Will Appear
in Forthcoming Volumes of *Something about the Author*

Abels, Harriette S.
Allard, Harry
Allen, Agnes B.   1898-1959
Allen, Jeffrey   1948-
Anders, Rebecca
Andrist, Ralph K.   1914-
Ardley, Neil (Richard)   1937-
Armitage, Ronda
Ashley, Bernard   1935-
Austin, R. G.
Axeman, Lois
Ayme, Marcel   1902-1967
Baker, Olaf
Balderson, Margaret   1935-
Barkin, Carol
Bartlett, Margaret F.   1896-
Batherman, Muriel   1926(?)-
Bauer, Caroline Feller   1935-
Bauer, John Albert   1882-1918
Beckman, Delores
Beim, Jerrold   1910-1957
Beim, Lorraine   1909-1951
Bernheim, Evelyne   1935-
Bernheim, Marc   1924-
Birnbaum, Abe   1899-
Boegehold, Betty   1913-
Boning, Richard A.
Bonners, Susan
Bourke, Linda
Bowden, Joan C.   1925-
Bowen, Gary
Bracken, Carolyn
Brewton, Sara W.
Bridgman, Elizabeth P.   1921-
Broekel, Ray   1923-
Bromley, Dudley   1948-
Bronin, Andrew   1947-
Bronson, Wilfrid   1894-
Brooks, Ron(ald George)   1948-
Brown, Roy Frederick   1921-
Brownmiller, Susan   1935-
Buchanan, William   1930-
Buchenholz, Bruce
Budney, Blossom   1921-
Burchard, Marshall
Burke, David   1927-
Burstein, Chaya M.
Butler, Dorothy   1925-
Butler, Hal   1913-
Calvert, Patricia
Camps, Luis   1928-
Carey, M. V.   1925-
Carley, Wayne
Carlson, Nancy L.

Carrie, Christopher
Carroll, Ruth R.   1899-
Cauley, Lorinda B.   1951-
Chang, Florence C.
Charles, Carole
Charles, Donald   1929-
Chartier, Normand
Chase, Catherine
Cline, Linda   1941-
Cohen, Joel H.
Cole, Brock
Cooper, Elizabeth Keyser   1910-
Cooper, Paulette   1944-
Cosgrove, Margaret   1926-
Coutant, Helen
Dabcovich, Lydia
D'Aulnoy, Marie-Catherine
    1650(?)-1705
David, Jay   1929-
Davies, Peter   1937-
Dawson, Diane
Dean, Leigh
Degens, T.
DeGoscinny, Rene
Deguine, Jean-Claude   1943-
Deweese, Gene   1934-
Dillon, Barbara
Ditmars, Raymond   1876-1942
Duggan, Maurice (Noel)   1922-1975
Dumas, Philippe   1940-
East, Ben
Edelson, Edward   1932-
Edwards, Linda S.
Eisenberg, Lisa
Elder, Lauren
Elgin, Kathleen   1923-
Elwood, Roger   1943-
Endres, Helen
Eriksson, Eva
Erwin, Betty K.
Etter, Les   1904-
Everett-Green, Evelyn   1856-1932
Falkner, John Meade   1858-1932
Farmer, Penelope   1939-
Fender, Kay
Filson, Brent
Fischer, Hans Erich   1909-1958
Flanagan, Geraldine Lux
Flint, Russ
Folch-Ribas, Jacques   1928-
Fox, Thomas C.
Freschet, Berniece   1927-
Frevert, Patricia D(endtler)   1943-
Funai, Mamoru R.   1932-

Gans, Roma   1894-
Garcia Sanchez, J(ose) L(uis)
Gardner, John Champlin, Jr.   1933-1982
Garrison, Christian   1942-
Gathje, Curtis
Gelman, Rita G.   1937-
Gemme, Leila Boyle   1942-
Gerber, Dan   1940-
Gobbato, Imero   1923-
Goldstein, Nathan   1927-
Gordon, Shirley
Gould, Chester   1900-
Grabianski, Janusz   1929(?)-1976
Graeber, Charlotte Towner
Gutman, Bill
Harris, Marilyn   1931-
Hayman, LeRoy   1916-
Healey, Larry   1927-
Heine, Helme   1941-
Henty, George Alfred   1832-1902
Herzig, Alison Cragin
Hicks, Clifford B.   1920-
Hill, Douglas Arthur   1935-
Hirshberg, Albert S.   1909-1973
Hockerman, Dennis
Hollander, Zander   1923-
Hood, Thomas   1779-1845
Howell, Troy
Hull, Jessie Redding
Hunt, Clara Whitehill   1871-1958
Hunt, Robert
Inderieden, Nancy
Irvine, Georgeanne
Jackson, Anita
Jackson, Kathryn   1907-
Jackson, Robert   1941-
Jacobs, Francine   1935-
James, Elizabeth
Jameson, Cynthia
Janssen, Pierre
Jaspersohn, William
Jewell, Nancy   1940-
Johnson, Harper
Johnson, Spencer   1938-
Johnson, Sylvia A.
Kahl, Virginia   1919-
Kahn, Joan   1914-
Kalan, Robert
Kantrowitz, Mildred
Kasuya, Masahiro   1937-
Keith, Eros   1942-
Kelley, True Adelaide   1946-
Kirn, Ann (Minette)   1910-
Klevin, Jill Ross   1935-

Koenig, Marion
Kohl, Herbert   1937-
Kohl, Judith
Kramer, Anthony
Kredenser, Gail   1936-
Krensky, Stephen   1953-
Kurland, Michael   1938-
Laure, Jason   1940-
Lawson, Annetta
Leach, Christopher   1925-
Lebrun, Claude
Leckie, Robert   1920-
Leder, Dora
Le-Tan, Pierre   1950-
Lewis, Naomi
Lindblom, Steve   1946-
Lindman, Maj (Jan)
Lines, Kathleen
Livermore, Elaine
MacKinstry, Elizabeth   (?)-1956
Mali, Jane Lawrence
Manes, Stephen   1949-
Marryat, Frederick   1792-1848
Marxhausen, Joanne G.   1935-
Mayakovsky, Vladimir   1894-1930
McCannon, Dindga
McKim, Audrey Margaret   1909-
McLenighan, Valjean   1947-
McLoughlin, John C.   1949-
McNaughton, Colin   1951-
Melcher, Frederic G.   1879-1963
Mendoza, George   1934-
Michel, Anna   1943-
Miller, J(ohn) P.   1919-
Molesworth, Mary L.   1839(?)-1921
Molly, Anne S.   1907-
Moore, Lilian
Moore, Patrick   1923-
Moskowitz, Stewart
Muntean, Michaela
Murdocca, Sal
Nickl, Peter
Obligado, Lillian Isabel   1931-
Odor, Ruth S.   1926-
Oppenheim, Shulamith (Levey)   1930-
Orr, Frank   1936-
Orton, Helen Fuller   1872-1955

Overbeck, Cynthia
Owens, Gail   1939-
Packard, Edward   1931-
Parenteau, Shirley L.   1935-
Parker, Robert Andrew   1927-
Paterson, A(ndrew) B(arton)   1864-1941
Patterson, Sarah   1959-
Pavey, Peter
Pelgrom, Els
Peretz, Isaac Loeb   1851-1915
Perkins, Lucy Fitch   1865-1937
Peterson, Jeanne Whitehouse   1939-
Phillips, Betty Lou
Plotz, Helen   1913-
Plowden, David   1932-
Plume, Ilse
Poignant, Axel
Pollock, Bruce   1945-
Polushkin, Maria
Porter, Eleanor Hodgman   1868-1920
Poulsson, Emilie   1853-1939
Powers, Richard M.   1921-
Prager, Arthur
Prather, Ray
Preston, Edna Mitchell
Pursell, Margaret S.
Pursell, Thomas F.
Pyle, Katharine   1863-1938
Rabinowitz, Solomon   1859-1916
Rappoport, Ken   1935-
Reich, Hanns
Reid, Alistair   1926-
Reidel, Marlene
Reiff, Tana
Reynolds, Marjorie   1903-
Rockwood, Joyce   1947-
Rosier, Lydia
Ross, Pat
Ross, Wilda   1915-
Roy, Cal
Rudstrom, Lennart
Sargent, Sarah   1937-
Schneider, Leo   1916-
Sebestyen, Ouida   1924-
Seidler, Rosalie
Sewell, Helen   1896-1957
Shea, George   1940-

Shreve, Susan   1939-
Slepian, Jan(ice B.)
Smith, Alison
Smith, Catriona (Mary)   1948-
Smith, Ray(mond Kenneth)   1949-
Smollin, Michael J.
Steiner, Charlotte
Stevens, Leonard A.   1920-
Stine, R. Conrad   1937-
Stubbs, Joanna   1940-
Sullivan, Mary Beth
Suteev, Vladimir Grigor'evich
Sutherland, Robert D.   1937-
Sweet, Ozzie
Thaler, Mike
Thomas, Ianthe
Timmermans, Gommaar   1930-
Todd, Ruthven   1914
Tourneur, Dina K.   1934-
Treadgold, Mary   1910-
Velthuijs, Max   1923-
Villiard, Paul   1910-1974
Waber, Bernard   1924-
Wagner, Jenny
Walker, Charles W.
Walsh, Anne Batterberry
Watts, Franklin   1904-1978
Wayne, Bennett
Werner, Herma   1926-
Weston, Martha
Whelen, Gloria   1923-
White, Wallace   1930-
Wild, Jocelyn
Wild, Robin
Wilson, Edward A.   1886-1970
Winn, Marie   1936(?)-
Winter, Paula   1929-
Winterfeld, Henry   1901-
Wolde, Gunilla   1939-
Wong, Herbert H.
Wormser, Richard   1908-
Wright, Betty R.
Yagawa, Sumiko
Youldon, Gillian
Zistel, Era
Zwerger, Lisbeth

In the interest of making *Something about the Author* as responsive as possible to the needs of its readers, the editor welcomes your suggestions for additional authors and illustrators to be included in the series.

Acknowledgments

Grateful acknowledgment is made to the following publishers, authors, and artists
for their kind permission to reproduce copyrighted material.

ABELARD-SCHUMAN. Photograph by Dr. Archie Carr from *Turtles: Extinction or Survival?* by Sarah R. Riedman and Ross Witham. Copyright © 1974 by Sarah R. Riedman and Ross Witham. Reprinted by permission of Abelard-Schuman.

ACE SCIENCE FICTION. Illustrations by Garcia from *Direct Descent* by Frank Herbert. Text copyright © 1980 by Frank Herbert. Illustrations copyright © 1980 by Garcia. Both reprinted by permission of Ace Science Fiction.

ALLISON & BUSBY LTD. Illustration by Jill Murphy from *The Worst Witch Strikes Again* by Jill Murphy. Copyright © 1980 by Jill Murphy. Reprinted by permission of Allison & Busby Ltd.

ANGUS & ROBERTSON LTD. Illustration by Will Mahony from *The Great Ballagundi Damper Bake* by Christobel Mattingley and Will Mahony. Copyright © 1975 by Christobel Mattingley and Will Mahony. Reprinted by permission of Angus & Robertson Ltd.

ATHENEUM PUBLISHERS, INC. Illustration by Graham Booth from *The Case of the Missing Kittens* by Mark Taylor. Text copyright © 1978 by Mark Taylor. Illustrations copyright © 1978 by Graham Booth./ Illustration by Niki Daly from *Joseph's Other Red Sock* by Niki Daly. Copyright © 1982 by Niki Daly./ Illustration by Velma Ilsley from *Son for a Day* by Corinne Gerson. Text copyright © 1980 by Corinne Gerson. Illustrations copyright © 1980 by Velma Ilsley./ Illustration by Emily Arnold McCully from *How I Found Myself at the Fair* by Pat Rhoads Mauser. Text copyright © 1980 by Pat Rhoads Mauser. Illustrations copyright © 1980 by Atheneum Publishers, Inc./ Illustration by Marcia Sewall from *The Squire's Bride* by P. C. Asbjörnsen. Copyright © 1975 by Marcia Sewall./ Sidelight excerpts from *A Measure of Independence* by John Tunis. Copyright © 1964 by Lucy R. Tunis. All reprinted by permission of Atheneum Publishers, Inc.

AVON BOOKS. Illustration by John Schoenherr from *Rascal* by Sterling North. Text copyright © 1963 by Sterling North. Illustrations copyright © 1963 by E. P. Dutton & Co., Inc. Reprinted by permission of Avon Books.

BERKLEY PUBLISHING GROUP. Cover illustration by Wayne Barlowe from *Soul Catcher* by Frank Herbert. Copyright © 1972 by Frank Herbert./ Cover illustration by Vincent DiFate from *Dune Messiah* by Frank Herbert. Copyright © 1969 by Frank Herbert. Both reprinted by permission of Berkley Publishing Group.

THE BODLEY HEAD LTD. Illustration by Michael Charlton from *The Boy Who Couldn't Hear* by Freddy Bloom. Text copyright © 1977 by Freddy Bloom. Illustrations copyright © 1977 by Michael Charlton. Reprinted by permission of The Bodley Head Ltd.

BROADMAN PRESS. Illustration by Ronnie Hester from *Prayer Is. . .* by Furn L. Kelling. Copyright © 1978 by Broadman Press. Reprinted by permission of Broadman Press.

CAROLRHODA BOOKS, INC. Illustration by Mary Chagnon from *Finist the Falcon Prince: A Russian Folk Tale,* translated by Lydia Regehr. Copyright © 1973 by Carolrhoda Books, Inc. Reprinted by permission of Carolrhoda Books, Inc.

CELESTIAL ARTS. Photographs, illustrations, and Sidelight excerpts from *Uncle Scrooge McDuck: His Life and Times* written and drawn by Carl Barks. Copyright © 1981 by Walt Disney Productions. All reprinted by permission of Celestial Arts.

CHELSEA HOUSE PUBLISHERS. Illustration from *The World Encyclopedia of Comics,* edited by Maurice Horn. Copyright © 1976 by Chelsea House Publishers./ Illustration from *The World Encyclopedia of Cartoons,* edited by Maurice Horn. Copyright © 1980 by Maurice Horn and Chelsea House Publishers. Both reprinted by permission of Chelsea House Publishers.

CHURCHILL PRESS. Sidelight excerpts from *Ross: The Story of a Shared Life* by Norris McWhirter. Reprinted by permission of Churchill Press.

from *The Sea Gull* by Penelope Farmer. Copyright © 1966 by Penelope Farmer./ Illustrations by Jay Hyde Barnum from *The Kid from Tomkinsville* by John R. Tunis. Copyright 1940 by John R. Tunis./ Illustration by Dorothy Bayley from "Who Calls?" by Frances Clarke in *Stars to Steer By*, edited by Louis Untermeyer. Copyright 1941 by Harcourt Brace & Co., Inc./ Illustration by Dorothy Bayley from "The Chart" by Michael Lewis in *Stars to Steer By*, edited by Louis Untermeyer. Copyright 1941 by Harcourt Brace & Co., Inc./ Illustration by Beth and Joe Krush from "The Walrus and the Carpenter" by Lewis Carroll in *The Magic Circle: Stories and People in Poetry*, edited by Louis Untermeyer. Copyright 1952 by Harcourt Brace & World./ Illustration by Reginald Birch from "Little Boy Blue" by Mother Goose in *Rainbow in the Sky*, edited by Louis Untermeyer. Copyright 1935 by Harcourt Brace & World, Inc. Copyright renewed © 1963 by Louis Untermeyer./ Illustration by Reginald Birch from "Jack and Jill" by Mother Goose in *Rainbow in the Sky*, edited by Louis Untermeyer. Copyright 1935 by Harcourt Brace & World, Inc. Copyright renewed © 1963 by Louis Untermeyer./ Sidelight excerpts from *Bygones: The Recollections of Louis Untermeyer* by Louis Untermeyer. Copyright © 1965 by Louis Untermeyer./ Sidelight excerpts from *Angel in the Parlor* by Nancy Willard./ Illustration by David McPhail from *Uncle Terrible* by Nancy Willard. Text copyright © 1982 by Nancy Willard. Illustrations copyright © 1982 by David McPhail./ Illustration by David McPhail from *Uncle Terrible: More Adventures of Anatole* by Nancy Willard. Text copyright © 1982 by Nancy Willard. Illustrations copyright © 1982 by David McPhail./ Illustration by David McPhail from *Strangers' Bread* by Nancy Willard. Text copyright © 1975 by Nancy Willard. Illustrations copyright © 1977 by David McPhail./ Illustration by David McPhail from *The Island of the Grass King* by Nancy Willard. Text copyright © 1979 by Nancy Willard. Illustrations copyright © 1979 by David McPhail./ Illustration by Alice and Martin Provensen from "The Tiger Asks Blake for a Bedtime Story" in *A Visit to William Blake's Inn: Poems for Innocent and Experienced Travelers* by Nancy Willard. Text copyright © 1980, 1981 by Nancy Willard. Illustrations copyright © 1981 by Alice Provensen and Martin Provensen./ Illustration by Alice and Martin Provensen from "A Rabbit Reveals My Room" in *A Visit to William Blake's Inn: Poems for Innocent and Experienced Travelers* by Nancy Willard. Text copyright © 1980, 1981 by Nancy Willard. Illustrations copyright © 1981 by Alice Provensen and Martin Provensen. All reprinted by permission of Harcourt Brace Jovanovich, Inc.

HARPER & ROW, PUBLISHERS INC. Jacket painting by Robert J. Blake from *The Halcyon Island* by Anne Knowles. Copyright © 1980 by Anne Knowles./ Illustration by Dorothy McEntee from "Eagle Boy" in *Nine Tales of Raven* by Fran Martin. Copyright 1951 by Harper & Brothers./ Illustration by Marcia Sewall from *Come Again in the Spring* by Richard Kennedy. Text copyright © 1976 by Richard Kennedy. Illustrations copyright © 1976 by Marcia Sewall. All reprinted by permission of Harper & Row, Publishers Inc.

HASTINGS HOUSE, PUBLISHERS INC. Photograph by Corinne Demas Bliss and Jim Judkis from *That Dog Melly!* by Corinne Demas Bliss and Austin Bliss. Copyright © 1981 by Corinne Demas Bliss. Reprinted by permission of Hastings House, Publishers Inc.

WILLIAM HEINEMANN LTD. Illustration by Joanna Troughton from *The Smallest Man in England* by Julia Dobson. Text copyright © 1977 by Julia Dobson. Illustrations copyright © 1977 by William Heinemann Ltd. Reprinted by permission of William Heinemann Ltd.

HOLT, RINEHART & WINSTON. Illustration by Stow Wengenroth from *The Hudson* by Carl Carmer. Copyright 1939 by Carl Carmer. Copyright renewed © 1967 by Carl Carmer./ Sidelight excerpts from *Tempestuous Petticoat* by Clare Leighton./ Illustration by Ingrid Johnson from *The Story of Life: From the Big Bang to You* by Kim Marshall. Text copyright © 1980 by Kim Marshall. Illustrations copyright © 1980 by Ingrid Johnson./ Illustration by Bill Sokol from *Alvin's Swap Shop* by Clifford B. Hicks. Text copyright © 1976 by Clifford B. Hicks. Illustrations copyright © 1976 by Holt, Rinehart & Winston. All reprinted by permission of Holt, Rinehart & Winston.

THE HORN BOOK, INC. Sidelight excerpts from *Illustrators of Children's Books: 1946-1956*, compiled by Bertha M. Miller and others. Copyright © 1958 by The Horn Book, Inc./ Sidelight excerpts from an article "Caldecott Medal Acceptance," by Chris Van Allsburg, August, 1982 in *The Horn Book Magazine*./ Sidelight excerpts from an article "Nancy Willard," by Barbara Lucas, August, 1982 in *The Horn Book Magazine*. All reprinted by permission of The Horn Book, Inc.

HOUGHTON MIFFLIN CO. Illustration by Chris Van Allsburg from *The Garden of Abdul Gasazi* by Chris Van Allsburg. Copyright © 1979 by Chris Van Allsburg./ Illustration by Chris Van Allsburg from *Jumanji* by Chris Van Allsburg. Copyright © 1981 by Chris Van Allsburg. Both reprinted by permission of Houghton Mifflin Co.

ALFRED A. KNOPF, INC. Illustration by Tracy Sugarman from *I Have a Dream* by Emma Gelders Sterne. Copyright © 1965 by Emma Gelders Sterne./ Jacket painting by Troy Howell from *The Lost Legend of Finn* by Mary Tannen. Copyright © 1982 by Mary Tannen. Jacket painting copyright © 1982 by Troy Howell. Both reprinted by permission of Alfred A. Knopf, Inc.

LITTLE, BROWN AND CO. Illustration by Diane Stanley from *Fiddle-I-Fee: A Traditional American Chant*. Copyright © 1979 by Diane Stanley./ Illustration by John Schoenherr from *Incident at Hawk's Hill* by Allan W. Eckert. Copyright © 1971 by Allan W. Eckert./ Illustration by John Schoenherr from *Otter in the Cove* by Miska Miles. Text copyright © 1974 by Miska Miles. Illustrations copyright © 1974 by John Schoenherr. All reprinted by permission of Little, Brown and Co.

LOTHROP, LEE & SHEPARD BOOKS. Illustration by John Wallner from *Dial Leroi Rupert, D.J.* by Jamie Gilson. Copyright © 1979 by Jamie Gilson./ Illustration courtesy of the U.S. Signal Corps. from *Black Fighting Men in U.S. History* by Edward Wakin. Copyright © 1971 by Edward Wakin. Both reprinted by permission of Lothrop, Lee & Shepard Books.

MACDONALD & CO. LTD. Illustration by Ken Lilly from *The Scandaroon* by Henry Williamson. Copyright © 1972 by Henry Williamson. Reprinted by permission of Macdonald & Co. Ltd.

MACMILLAN, INC. Illustration by Catherine Stock from *The Princess and the Pumpkin* by Maggie Duff. Text copyright © 1980 by Maggie Duff. Illustrations copyright © 1980 by Catherine Stock./ Illustration by Clare Leighton from *The Pinnacled Tower* by Thomas Hardy, edited by Helen Plotz. Copyright © 1975 by Helen Plotz and by Macmillan Publishing Co., Inc. Both reprinted by permission of Macmillan, Inc.

McGRAW-HILL, INC. Photograph and illustration from *Of Mice and Magic: A History of American Animated Cartoons* by Leonard Maltin. Copyright © 1980 by Leonard Maltin./ Illustration by Mildred Waltrip from *Entertaining with Number Tricks* by George Barr. Copyright © 1971 by George Barr and Mildred Waltrip. All reprinted by permission of McGraw-Hill, Inc.

JULIAN MESSNER. Photographs from *No Time For School No, Time For Play* by Rhoda and William Cahn. Copyright © 1972 by Rhoda and William Cahn. Both reprinted by permission of Julian Messner.

WILLIAM MORROW & CO., INC. Jacket illustration from *The Kid Comes Back* by John R. Tunis. Copyright 1946 by Lucy R. Tunis. Reprinted by permission of William Morrow & Co., Inc.

THOMAS NELSON & SONS LTD. Photograph by Leonard Lee Rue III from *Our Wild Animals* by John Bailey. Copyright © 1965 by Rutledge Books, Inc. Reprinted by permission of Thomas Nelson & Sons Ltd.

NOSTALGIA PRESS, INC. Illustration from *The Fleischer Story* by Leslie Cabarga. Copyright © 1976 by Leslie Cabarga. Reprinted by permission of Nostalgia Press, Inc.

PANTHEON BOOKS, INC. Illustration by Marcia Sewall from *The Story of Old Mrs. Brubeck and How She Looked for Trouble and Where She Found Him* by Lore Segal. Text copyright © 1981 by Lore Segal. Illustrations copyright © 1981 by Marcia Sewall. Reprinted by permission of Pantheon Books, Inc.

THE PUTNAM PUBLISHING GROUP. Illustration by Yasuo Ohtomo from *Where's My Daddy?*, adapted from a story by Shigeo Watanabe. Text copyright © 1979 by Shigeo Watanabe. Illustrations copyright © 1979 by Yasuo Ohtomo. American text copyright © 1982 by Philomel Books./ Jacket illustration by Abe Echevarria from *Dune* by Frank Herbert. Copyright © 1965 by Frank Herbert. Both reprinted by permission of The Putnam Publishing Group.

RAINTREE CHILDREN'S BOOKS. Photograph by Peter Ward from *Zebras* by Daphne Machin Goodall. Copyright © 1977 by Wayland Publishers Ltd. American text copyright © 1977 by Raintree Publishers Ltd. Reprinted by permission of Raintree Children's Books.

SCOTT, FORESMAN & CO. Illustration by Charles Mikolaycak from *Children and Books* (sixth edition) by Zena Sutherland, Dianne L. Monson and May Hill Arbuthnot. Copyright 1947, © 1957, 1964, 1972, 1977, 1981 by Scott, Foresman & Co. Illustrations copyright © 1981 by Charles Mikolaycak. Reprinted by permission of Scott, Foresman & Co.

CHARLES SCRIBNER'S SONS. Photograph from *A Carrot for a Nose: The Form of Folk Sculpture on America's City Streets and Country Roads* by M. J. Gladstone. Copyright © 1974 by M. J. Gladstone. Reprinted by permission of Charles Scribner's Sons.

SCROLL PRESS. Illustration by John Watts from *When Sea and Sky Are Blue* by Letitia

Parr. Copyright © 1970 by Letitia Parr and John Watts. Reprinted by permission of Scroll Press.

SIMON & SCHUSTER, INC. Sidelight excerpts from "Wisdom at Cribbs Creek," in *This I Believe: 2,* edited by Raymond Swing. Reprinted by permission of Simon & Schuster, Inc.

STERLING PUBLISHING CO., INC. Photograph from *Guinness Book of World Records,* edited and compiled by Norris and Ross McWhirter. Copyright © 1960 by Guinness Superlatives Ltd./ Illustration by Bill Hinds from *Guinness Book of Dazzling Endeavors* by Norris McWhirter and Ross McWhirter. Copyright © 1980 by Sterling Publishing Co., Inc. Based on the *Guinness Book of World Records.* Revised American edition © 1980, 1979, 1978, 1977, 1976, 1975, 1974, 1973, 1972, 1971, 1970, 1969, 1968, 1967, 1966, 1965, 1964, 1963, 1962 by Sterling Publishing Co., Inc./ Illustration by Bill Hinds from *Guinness Book of Amazing Animals* by Norris McWhirter. Copyright © 1960 by Guinness Superlatives Ltd. Copyright © 1981 by Sterling Publishing Co., Inc. All reprinted by permission of Sterling Publishing Co., Inc.

STUDIO PUBLICATIONS LTD. Sidelight excerpts from *Wood-Engraving and Woodcuts* by Clare Leighton. Reprinted by permission of Studio Publications Ltd.

THE TIMES MIRROR CO. Sidelight excerpts from "The Deer of North America" by Leonard Lee Rue III in *Outdoor Life,* 1978. Reprinted by permission of The Times Mirror Co.

CHARLES E. TUTTLE CO., INC. Illustration by Grace A. Brigham from *Ski Touring: An Introductory Guide* by William E. Osgood and Leslie J. Hurley. Copyright © 1969 by Charles Tuttle Co., Inc. Reprinted by permission of Charles E. Tuttle Co., Inc.

THE VANGUARD PRESS. Illustration by Yeffe Kimball from *Some People Are Indians* by George A. Boyce. Copyright 1955, © 1968, 1974 by George A. Boyce. Illustrations copyright © 1974 by Yeffee Kimball./ Illustration by Ann Blades from *Pettranella* by Betty Waterton. Text copyright © 1980 by Betty Waterton. Illustrations copyright © 1980 by Ann Blades. Both reprinted by permission of The Vanguard Press.

WANDERER BOOKS. Illustration from "The Musical Ghost" in *The Most Famous Ghost of All and Other Ghost Stories* by D. J. Arneson. Copyright © 1971 by Young Readers Press, Inc. Reprinted by permission of Wanderer Books.

FRANKLIN WATTS, INC. Illustration by Manning de V. Lee from "Turn and Turn About" by Rupert Sargent Holland in *Pirates, Pirates, Pirates,* selected by Phyllis R. Fenner. Copyright 1951 by Phyllis R. Fenner./ Illustration by Manning de V. Lee from "Wilderness Road" by Jim Kjelgaard in *Indians, Indians, Indians,* selected by Phyllis R. Fenner. Copyright 1950 by Phyllis R. Fenner. Both reprinted by permission of Franklin Watts, Inc.

WESTERN PUBLISHING CO., INC. Illustration by Joan Walsh Anglund from "Let Others Share" by Edward Anthony in *The Golden Treasury of Poetry,* selected by Louis Untermeyer. Copyright © 1959 by Western Publishing Co., Inc./ Illustration by Joan Walsh Anglund from "Questions at Night" in *The Golden Treasury of Poetry* by Louis Untermeyer. Copyright © 1959 by Western Publishing Co., Inc./ Illustration by Joan Walsh Anglund from "The White Knight's Song" by Lewis Carroll in *The Golden Treasury of Poetry,* selected by Louis Untermeyer. Copyright © 1959 by Western Publishing Co., Inc./ Illustration by Alice and Martin Provensen from "The Great and Little Fishes" in *Aesop's Fables,* selected and adapted by Louis Untermeyer. Copyright © 1965 by Western Publishing Co., Inc. All reprinted by permission of Western Publishing Co., Inc.

THE WESTMINSTER PRESS. Illustration by Ruth Van Sciver from *Melba the Brain* by Ivy Ruckman. Copyright © 1979 by Ivy Ruckman. Reprinted by permission of The Westminster Press.

Sidelight excerpts from an article "How I Made My Book" by Clare Leighton, February, 1955 in *American Artist.* Copyright © 1955 by Billboard Publications, Inc. Reprinted by permission of *American Artist.*/ Sidelight excerpts from an article "John Schoenherr" by Frances Traher in *Artists of the Rockies and the Golden West.* Reprinted by permission of *Artists of the Rockies and the Golden West.*/ Photograph and caricature of Louis Untermeyer from The Bettmann Archive, Inc. Reprinted by permission of The Bettmann Archive, Inc./ Sidelight excerpts from *The Village Book* by Henry Williamson. Copyright 1933, © 1961 by Henry Williamson. Reprinted by permission of Brandt & Brandt Literary Agents, Inc./ Sidelight excerpts from *As the Sun Shines* by Henry Williamson. Copyright 1933, © 1961 by Henry Williamson. Reprinted by permission of Brandt & Brandt Literary Agents, Inc./ Sidelight excerpts from an article "Author Finds Success after Early Rejection," October, 1981 in *Hilltopics.* Reprinted by permission of *Hilltopics.*/ Sidelight excerpts from *A Measure of Independence* by John Tunis. Copyright © 1964 by Lucy R. Tunis. Reprinted by permission of The Sterling Lord Agency,

Inc./ Sidelight excerpts from "In the Studio of Clare Leighton," March, 1937 in *The London Studio.* Reprinted by permission of *The London Studio.*

Sidelight excerpts from an article "Plowboy Interview: Frank Herbert, Science Fiction's 'Yellow Journalist' Is a Homesteading 'Technopeasant,' " May/June, 1981 in *Mother Earth News,* #69. Copyright © 1981 by The Mother Earth News, Inc. Reprinted by permission of *The Mother Earth News.*/ Sidelight excerpts from an article "Talk with Carl Carmer," by Harvey Breit, November 13, 1949 in *The New York Times.* Copyright 1949 by The New York Times Co./ Illustration by David McPhail from *Uncle Terrible* by Nancy Willard. Text copyright © 1982 by Nancy Willard. Illustrations copyright © 1982 by David McPhail. Reprinted by permission of Rita Scott, Inc./ Sidelight excerpts from *Bygones: The Recollection of Louis Untermeyer* by Louis Untermeyer. Copyright © 1965 by Louis Untermeyer. Reprinted by permission of Mrs. Bryna Untermeyer./ Sidelight excerpts from "Newbery Medal Acceptance" by Nancy Willard, August, 1982 in *Horn Book* magazine. Reprinted by permission of Nancy Willard./ Sidelight excerpts from an article "Story behind the Book: The Wreck of the Zephyr" by Selma Lanes, April 9, 1983 in *Publishers Weekly.* Copyright © 1983 by Xerox Corp. Reprinted by permission of Xerox Corp.

Photograph Credits

Corinne D. Bliss: Michael Feinstein; James W. English: Studios of R. L. Giddens II; Corinne Gerson: Shirley Zeiberg; Frank Herbert: George Westbeau; M. P. Kahl: David DeForrest; Anne Knowles: "The Citizen" (Gloucester, England); Norris McWhirter: Ronald A. Chapman; Norris and Ross McWhirter: Ronald A. Chapman; Otto Messmer: (two photographs) *The Record* (Hackensack, N.J.); William E. Osgood: Gail Osherenko; Fred Powledge: Anthony Wolff; Harold Sherman: Marion Parsons; Diane Stanley: Peter Vennema; Mary Tannen: P. Cunningham; John R. Tunis: Lotte Jacobi; Louis Untermeyer (photograph and caricature): The Bettmann Archive; Nancy Willard: Michael Metz.

SOMETHING ABOUT THE AUTHOR

ANASTASIO, Dina   1941-

PERSONAL: First name is pronounced *Die*-nah; born October 9, 1941, in Des Moines, Iowa; daughter of William H. Brown (a sportscaster) and Jean (a writer; maiden name, Stout) Kinney; married Ernest J. Anastasio (a director of research), June 30, 1964 (divorced); children: Kristine, Trey. *Education:* Rutgers University, B.A., 1973. *Home:* 420 E. 55th St., Apt. 6A, New York, N.Y. 10022. *Office:* Children's Television Workshop, 1 Lincoln Pl., New York, N.Y. 10023.

CAREER: Author, 1971—; Sesame Street Publications, New York, N.Y., editor of *Sesame Street* Magazine, 1980—. *Member:* Authors Guild.

*WRITINGS—*All for children: *My Own Book,* Price, Stern, 1975; (editor) *Who Puts the Care in Health Care?* (illustrated by John Freeman), Random House, 1976; (editor) *Who Puts the Plane in the Air?* (illustrated by J. Freeman), Random House, 1976; *My Secret Book,* Price, Stern, 1977; *My Special Book,* Price, Stern, 1978; *A Question of Time* (illustrated by Dale Payson), Dutton, 1978; *Conversation Kickers,* Price, Stern, 1979; *My Private Book,* Price, Stern, 1979; *My Personal Book,* Price, Stern, 1980; *My Own Book, Number Six,* Price, Stern, 1981; *My School Book,* Price, Stern, 1981; *My Wish Book,* Price, Stern, 1981; *My Family Book,* Price, Stern, 1982.

''Write-It-Yourself'' series; published by Price, Stern: *Dear Priscilla, I am Sending You a Pet . . . for Your Birthday,* 1980; *Everybody's Invited to Dudley's Party Except. . .!!,* 1980; *Georgina's Two . . . for Her Own Good, and Someday She's Going to Be Very Sorry!!,* 1980; *Somebody Kidnapped the Mayor and Hid Her in . . . !!,* 1980; *Watch It Sarah!! The . . . Is Right behind You!!,* 1980; *Crazy Freddy's in Trouble Again and His Parents Are Going to . . . !!,* 1981 *Careful*

Melinda, That Footstep Belongs to . . . !!, in press; *Something Weird Is Happening to Matthew, and He's a Little . . . !!,* in press.

Contributor to *Sesame Street Parents Newsletter, Parents Magazine,* and *Ladies' Home Journal.*

SIDELIGHTS: ''I was born in Des Moines, Iowa, where I lived until I was five years old. We then moved to New York and I went away to boarding schools. I returned to Iowa for fifth grade, but basically had all of my schooling in New York State.

''I can't remember writing as a child. My mother is a writer. She was in advertising for most of her life and definitely has a flair for the dramatic. Now she writes 'how-to' columns and books. I don't think there's any question that my facility with ideas, my ability to think up games and stories came from listening to her. The people at Price and Stern, a concept-activity publishing house, told me that most of their writers have been children of people involved in advertising. I think it helps to have had parents who spark creative thinking and who don't kill off any imagination or creativity by saying 'Well, that's dumb . . . that's really stupid.' ''

Received a B.A. from Rutgers University in 1973. ''I was an English major at Rutgers. I love to read, but I've never taken a writing class. I don't know if I believe in them, although I think writing classes can be good in some ways. It's like having an editor who can help you when you already have some talent to think about your work. Of course, it depends on how good the teacher is, and usually, they're not.

Anastasio began free-lance writing as a young mother. ''I started writing in 1971 when my kids were young. I was looking for something to do, went back to school, and then decided to

. . . When she tried to jump a curb, she wiped out and landed on the street. ■ (From *A Question of Time* by Dina Anastasio. Illustrated by Dale Payson.)

invent a game. I sold it but decided to switch to writing because the game market was incredibly hard to break into. I also wrote greeting cards at six dollars a card, but they were very silly.

"Then I began writing textbook stories for children and young adults which varied in length from three to ten pages. I wrote several hundred of these stories, and then edited a series of textbooks for Macmillan. That became very lucrative, but finally, I gave it up because I don't ever want to work with word lists again.

"After the Macmillan textbooks I put together 'My Own Book' series for Price and Stern. The first one was designed to be a fill-in diary that children could write by themselves.

"As my children grew, the characters in my stories grew with them. My first stories featured very young children. When my children were eight or nine, I wrote a children's mystery about children of the same age."

A Question of Time (Dutton, 1978) was Anastasio's first novel-length work. "*A Question of Time* was inspired by my daughter's doll collection. We were in New Orleans and found two dolls that had been modeled after real people who had lived in the French Quarter. One day, I was looking at her collection, saw these two dolls, and decided to write about them.

"I just sat down and started writing. I remember my son was about eight and he would come home every day and want to read it. He'd ask, 'What happened then?' That was great, it was the reason I kept writing. He really had me motivated. When I finished, it was very rough, but I had a good editor who taught me how to revise. I re-wrote it several times.

"If I were to write it again, I think I would do it very differently. Now when I write mystery stories, I think the whole thing out in advance. It was a learning experience. . . .

"I was trying to explain to my assistant at *Sesame Street Magazine* how to make a mystery in, for example, a short story. It's very difficult to explain how a mystery is made and even more difficult to teach. There are many elements. Basically, in any kind of mystery, I think you have to know what the plot is. Then you have to start thinking in terms of clues and finally you must consider character and setting, as you would in any other book. But the mystery plot is different from other kinds of fiction because it's got to have a kicker, and that can't be contrived or thrown in."

Anastasio has been editor of *Sesame Street Magazine* since 1980. "When I knew my children were leaving for college, I decided to look for a job. I was tired of the isolation of writing. I returned primarily to the world of very young children and took a full-time job as editor of *Sesame Street Magazine*. I have always enjoyed creating games and activities, as well as writing, and this job allows me the opportunity to create a wide variety of children's material.

"*Sesame Street Magazine* is twelve years old. It began at the same time as the show, as an adjunct. It is a subscription and newsstand publication, has over a million and a half readers and comes out ten times a year. We also issue a winter book and a summer book.

"The magazine has a curriculum, which means we have to teach something with every story or game. *Sesame Street Magazine* has an audience of pre-readers. In one way, we're lucky because we know there will always be an adult sitting with the

DINA ANASTASIO

child. We have a research staff that goes out into the schools and talks to kids and we eventually get to know what four-year-olds are thinking about.

"I make up all of the games for the magazine and also write the stories, which is similar to inventing games because putting together a game is like putting together a plot. It's cleverness; it's a knack. To write from a cast of characters like the Muppets which I've inherited can sometimes be limiting. Since I've become editor, there's been less of that. We used to have the Sesame Street characters on every page, but now the magazine is changing.

"When I came in, the emphasis was on hard education. The magazine is still concerned with educating, but I've added things like children's poetry, and I think it's softer. I've also tried to encourage more thought questions and problem solving. There is an awareness and encouragement of imagination rather than a focus on school-oriented skills. I think 'Sesame Street' is moving along these lines now. Originally, it was geared toward pre-reading and pre-math skills. The objective was to get kids ready for school. But there's a lot more to learning than knowing letters and numbers as far as I'm concerned.

"Lately I've been writing for adults as well as children. I wrote a column every month for *Sesame Street Parents Newsletter*, based on my own kids, using fictionalized anecdotes. And I've written articles for *Parents Magazine* and *Ladies' Home Journal*."

Of her technique Anastasio admits that "a lot of the things I've written have to do with my children. They have been an enormous source of creativity. Now that they have grown, maybe I can write about some of my own experiences, separate from my children's.

"I always write at the typewriter. I tend to write straight through the first draft. I just *do it*.

"A lot of the books I've written have been novelty books. I think I'm basically an idea person, though I'm changing, hopefully. People ask, 'Where do you get your ideas?' I don't know. Ideas are no problem for me. I'd like to have a little person under the table to carry them out for me.

"If you're writing for kids, and you want feedback, it's more useful to give the book to a child because an adult can often completely destroy your confidence and make you stop writing. I gave my first drafts to my own children. Kids do not say, 'This is badly written.' The point is, are they going to keep reading? If they're bored within the first ten pages, you know something's wrong.

"Now I show the publisher what I write for the magazine. Basically I know when something is weak, and she's always right on target. It's usually because I've rushed it. I just start over and write it again.

"I also think we should encourage children's storytelling and imagination. If children are making up stories, we should ask questions to stimulate them like, 'And then what happened?' and 'What happend next?' That's wrong . . . that's not good.' The best editors do this with writers. They ask questions which are meant to help you with your own thinking, like, 'Why did the character do this?' One should ask questions to inspire a young writer, to help them think in their own way about the things which aren't working. Parents can do that.

"Children are often better at writing than adults because children naturally make things up—cartoons . . . stories. I remember my daughter had a class, and all the kids thought that one girl's story was the best they'd ever read. They thought it was good because she had used enormous words. Not the right words, just big words. Sometimes kids get into flowery language. They think they are romantic poets or something. I feel one should try to find the best word which can also be the most simple word. I don't know how you teach that. I think there is either a knack or there isn't. But kids are naturally creative. Unless it is being killed. And it often is being killed somewhere along the line. I know it is hard to teach writing, but I've always felt there should be a place for it in the schools.

"My advice to children is to *read*. And it's tricky because you can get turned on or off to reading depending on the books you read. I have always felt that as long as kids are reading it doesn't matter what the material is. It's okay to read comics, as long as you're reading other things too. Some kids just like Alfred Hitchcock. That's okay. For kids of eleven or twelve, I can recommend two books guaranteed to put you on to reading. One is *To Kill a Mockingbird* by Harper Lee and the other is *A Tree Grows in Brooklyn* by Betty Smith.

"I'd do almost anything to get a child to read, even bribe them. I remember paying my daughter a dollar to get through the first fifty pages of *Gone with the Wind* when she was twelve. I knew once she got into reading it, she'd finish, and she did.

"I like to read almost anything, all different kinds of material, except detective stories. I love to read biographies of writers and editors. I also like the *New Yorker*.

"As with all children's writers, I've always kept that sense of childishness—a feeling for what kids enjoy. There's still that part of me that is a child. Most of the people I know who are writing for kids have the kind of imagination that works overtime. But I think that's true of adult writers too."

Anastasio's advice to aspiring writers who would like to become published is to begin by writing novels for children. "If they're clever, they can usually get published because there aren't that many people who can do them well. The advice I'd give to those who want to write for children is to go to the library and read, read, read. Read everything that's been written for young people—all the Newbery winners, etc.—and find out why they're winning. Eventually, you'll get it, and then it's time to sit down and *write*."

ANTONACCI, Robert J(oseph)   1916-

BRIEF ENTRY: Born January 21, 1916, in Toluca, Ill. Professor of health and physical education, author, and editor. Antonacci has worked on the staffs of the physical education departments at Oregon State University, University of Chicago, Wayne State University, and Temple University. He has also served as director of health, physical education, and safety for public schools in Gary, Indiana. Along with several co-authors, Antonacci has written seven books in the "Young Champion" series published by McGraw: *Basketball for Young Champions* (with Jene Barr; 1960, 2nd edition, 1979), *Tennis for Young Champions* (with Barbara D. Lockhart; 1982), *Baseball for Young Champions* (with Barr; 1956, 2nd edition, 1977), *Football for Young Champions* (with Barr; 1958, 2nd edition, 1976), *Physical Fitness for Young Champions* (with Barr; 1962, 2nd edition, 1975), *Track and Field for Young Champions* (with Gene Schoor; 1974), and *Soccer for Young Champions* (with Anthony J. Puglisi; 1978). Antonacci is also an editor of health and physical education teaching guides and a contributor to books, professional journals, and newspapers. *Home:* 1508 Elkins Ave., Abington, Pa. 19001. *For More Information See: Michigan Authors*, 2nd edition, Michigan Association for Media in Education, 1980; *Contemporary Authors, New Revision Series*, Volume 9, Gale, 1983.

ARNESON, D(on) J(on)   1935-

PERSONAL: Born August 15, 1935, in Montevideo, Minn.; married wife, Beatrice, in 1958; children: Leif Eric, Marc Anthony. *Education:* Mexico City College, B.A., 1959. *Address:* Box 141, Southbury, Conn. 06488.

CAREER: Author. Dell Publishing Co., Inc., New York, N.Y., editor, 1962-69. *Military service:* U.S. Army, 1954-56, served with counterintelligence.

WRITINGS: (With Jack Sparling) *Instant Candidate '64: Pick Your Politician, Pose, Platform*, Pocket Books, 1964; *The Great Society Comic Book* (illustrated by Tony Tallarico), Parallax Press, 1966; *The Most Famous Ghost of All and Other Ghost Stories* (juvenile), Young Reader's Press, 1971, reprinted, Wanderer Books, 1978; *Secret Places* (juvenile fiction; illustrated with photographs by Peter Arnold), Holt, 1971; *Creature Reader* (juvenile), Young Reader's Press, 1972; *Jokes and Riddles Roundup* (juvenile; illustrated by Jim Kersell), Xerox Education Publications, 1972; *Walk to Survival* (fiction), Ace Books, 1973; *A Friend Indeed: True Tales of Dog Her-*

Downstairs, where no one was supposed to be, somebody was playing their aunt's piano. ∎
(From "The Musical Ghost" in *The Most Famous Ghost of All and Other Ghost Stories* by D. J. Arneson.)

oism, F. Watts, 1981; *The Original Preppy Cookbook,* Dell Trade Paperbacks, 1981; *The Original Preppy Jokebook,* Dell Trade Paperbacks, 1981; *The Official Computer Hater's Handbook,* Dell Trade Paperbacks, 1983; *Sometimes in the Dead of Night* (young adult fiction), Messner, 1983, revised edition, adapted for children by Meg Schneider, Wanderer Books, 1983.

WORK IN PROGRESS: Books for young adults, including *The Night of the Wolves, The Bogman,* and *The Alien Link.*

SIDELIGHTS: Arneson has travelled to twenty-five countries and has lived abroad for extended periods of time. He speaks German, Spanish, Italian, and ''some Russian.''

BANG, Betsy (Garrett)   1912-

BRIEF ENTRY: Born July 9, 1912, in South Carolina. Bang received her B.A. from George Washington University and also attended Johns Hopkins University where she received a diploma in Art as Applied to Medicine in 1937. She went on to become a free-lance surgical illustrator and an illustrator in comparative anatomy at the American Museum of Natural History in New York. Since 1958 Bang has been a research associate in pathobiology at Johns Hopkins University and a summer investigator at the Station Biologique at Roscoff in Brittany and the Marine Biological Laboratory at Woods Hole. She has contributed approximately fifty articles to scientific journals.

Bang has translated and adapted several children's folktales from the Bengali, a language she considers very beautiful. A *Horn Book* reviewer pointed to Bang's ''rich and dynamic language'' in her adaptation of the Bengali tale *The Cucumber Stem,* the story of a little boy who is only two fingers high. Other books by Bang include *The Old Woman and the Red Pumpkin* (Macmillan, 1976), *The Old Woman and the Rice Thief* (Greenwillow, 1977), *Tuntuni, the Tailorbird* (Greenwillow, 1978), and *The Demons of Rajpur* (Greenwillow, 1980). Several of her books have been illustrated by her daughter, Molly Garrett Bang, an award-winning author and illustrator of children's books. *Home:* 3956 Cloverhill Rd., Baltimore, Md. 21218. *For More Information See: Contemporary Authors,* Volume 102, Gale, 1981; *Fifth Book of Junior Authors and Illustrators,* H. W. Wilson, 1983.

BARKS, Carl   1901-

PERSONAL: Born March 27, 1901, near Merrill Oregon; son of William and Arminta (Johnson) Barks; married third wife, Garé Williams (a painter). *Residence:* Grants Pass, Ore.

CAREER: Cartoonist; creator of the Walt Disney character, ''Uncle Scrooge McDuck.'' Held various jobs, including cowboy, logger, steelworker, and carpenter, before becoming a free-lance artist about 1927; Walt Disney Studios, Burbank, Calif., began as apprentice animator, became story outliner, 1935 to 1942; Dell Publishing Co., author and illustrator of ''Donald Duck'' segments in *Walt Disney Comics and Stories* and ''Donald Duck'' feature magazine, 1943-66, and ''Uncle Scrooge'' feature magazine, beginning 1947, retired from active drawing, 1966, contributing scriptwriter, 1965-73.

Carl Barks, wearing two-tone high top shoes, San Francisco, 1920.

WRITINGS—Selected works; all for children; all self-illustrated: (Illustrated with Jack Hannah) *Donald Duck Finds Pirate Gold* (comic book), Dell, 1942; *Donald Duck and the Mummy's Ring* (comic book), Dell, 1943; *Christmas On Bear*

Uncle Scrooge loves his money. He loves the feel of it and the smell of it, and he loves to dive around in it like a porpoise and to burrow through it like a gopher and to toss it up and let it hit him on the head. ■ (From "Go Slowly Sands of Time," in *Uncle Scrooge McDuck: His Life and Times* by Carl Barks. Illustrated by the author.)

(Half-page excerpt from the comic book *Uncle Scrooge: The Seven Cities of Cibola,* Issue #7, Dell Comics, September, 1954.)

Mountain (comic book), Dell, 1947; *Only a Poor Duck* (comic book), Dell, 1952; *Donald Duck and the Magic Hourglass,* Abbeville Press, 1981; *Uncle Scrooge and the Secret of Old Castle,* Abbeville Press, 1981.

Collections: (Editor) *Donald Duck,* Abbeville Press, 1978; (with Piero Zanotto) *Walt Disney's Uncle Scrooge,* edited by Mark Greenberg, Abbeville Press, 1979; *Uncle Scrooge McDuck: His Life and Times,* Celestial Arts, 1981; *The Fine Art of Walt Disney's Donald Duck,* Another Rainbow, 1981; *The Carl Barks Library,* edited by Bruce Hamilton and Russ Cochran, Another Rainbow, 1983; *Limited Edition Lithographs of Disney Duck Subjects,* Another Rainbow, 1983.

WORK IN PROGRESS: (With P. Zanotto) *Huey, Dewey and Louie,* edited by Michael Sonino, publication by Abbeville Press.

SIDELIGHTS: **March 27, 1901.** ''I was born and spent my early years in a homesteader's cabin on the sagebrush plateau country of eastern Oregon, a lonely place for a boy growing up. School was a one-room affair about a mile away. The few hours a day that were spent in school were the only contacts my older brother and I had with other children. The school had a library of thirty (maybe less) books, and those were my

window to the wonders beyond the horizon. I believe that the loneliness was good for me. I had much time to think and to look at animals, plants, birds, the mountains and clouds, and greatest of all, the stars around me. How bright and sparkly the heavens were in those smogless nights of 1908 and thereabouts.

''My parents were stern believers in the rule that work is good for children. We boys had many chores to do. There was wood to cut for the cookstove, and potatoes to grow and dig for the kettle. We hitched mules to the plows and harvesters and worked all day at whatever jobs we were strong enough to handle. No doubt the effects of that way of life showed sometimes in the stories I wrote and drew for the Walt Disney comic books many years later. My characterization of Donald Duck often showed him as a stern disciplinarian and his three nephews as work-bored drudges comically trying to escape their duties.

''The homestead way of life was not all work, however. In winter we made sleds and slid down distant hillsides. We skated on frozen ponds and made snow forts and staged mighty battles at the little schoolyard. We learned how to make kites and shoot firecrackers and ride bucking calves. Donald Duck and his nephews relived many of those experiences again in my stories—always with outrageously disastrous results.

(From the comic book *Uncle Scrooge in The Lemming with the Locket,* Issue #9, Dell Comics, March, 1955.)

"The two years we lived in a city, Santa Rosa, California, when I was ten and eleven broadened my understanding of people and behavior. For the first time I saw moving pictures, and a public library, and attended a school that had swarms of kids. A fellow student in my grade had a talent for cartooning, and I found it very interesting to watch him magically make faces laugh and frown and grow beards on paper with only a pencil and his mind. From then on my whole trust in life was toward the goal of being a cartoonist."

Barks left school at the age of fifteen when he finished the eighth grade. At the end of World War I he moved to San Francisco until, jobless, he was forced to move back to the family ranch.

1923. Moved to a logging camp then to Roseville, California where he worked repairing railroad cars for six years. During this time he began a correspondence course in cartooning which he never finished. "Some of the main people who influenced my drawing style were Winsor McCay, Opper, and Hal Foster. Roy Crane, who drew 'Buzz Sawyer,' also had a direct, simple style. There were a number of real good artists who didn't use much crosshatching or managed to put their story over with good clean lines and just blacks and whites. I knew that I couldn't handle much crosshatching and pen shading or the

benday process they used in comic-book work. A number of guys used processed paper for putting in dots and shading. I knew if I ever got into that, I would just be making myself a mess of trouble and a lot of extra work, so I acted as if I never even knew about it.

"Another influence was a book called *Creative Illustration* by Andrew Loomis. It was an art book, a constructive book with some good pointers in it on illustrating. It explained color balance, drawing and perspective, the handling of groups of people, and drawing individual persons: muscles, hands, heads, and expressions. It was a good book." [Carl Barks, *Uncle Scrooge McDuck: His Life and Times,* Celestial Arts, 1981.[1]]

Late 1920s. Began selling gag cartoons to humor magazines.

1931. Became staff member of the magazine *Eye-Opener* in Minneapolis, where he remained for four years contributing gag cartoons. "I had enough money to send a telegram saying I didn't have enough money to get back there. [The owner of *Eye-Opener*] sent me money to come back thereon, and I closed up my affairs very rapidly and gave away the big stack of joke magazines I had. What I could carry in a valise, I carried with me."[1]

(From the comic book *Uncle Scrooge in Land Beneath the Ground,* Issue #13, Dell Comics, March, 1956.)

(From the comic book *Uncle Scrooge: The Seven Cities of Cibola,* Issue #7, Dell Comics, September, 1954.)

1935. Joined the staff at Walt Disney Studio in California. Became story outliner for the Donald Duck cartoons. "My boyhood gave me a different outlook on life than many of the Disney story men had who grew up in cities. I knew how bad life could be, but I never tried to put it into my stories. Life is wretched enough without trying to dredge up constant reminders. I think I found it natural to satirize yearnings and pomposities and frustrations in the ducks because of my earlier contacts with people in woeful ways of life. Those people had the ability to laugh at the most awesome miseries. If they hadn't had humor in their lives, they would have gone crazy.

"I was never temperamental in any way that I can remember. If you were a _prima donna_ down at the Disney studio, if you went in thinking that you were a genius and then you had to work with a bunch of geniuses, why you soon got the ego knocked out of you. We served an apprenticeship at the Disney story department. You'd come out of there with humility, so you didn't feel that you had to have a grand opera band playing background music before you could get ideas!''[1]

1942. Quit the Disney Studio, moved to a chicken farm near San Jacinto, and began working as a free-lance cartoonist. Barks was hired as a free-lancer to illustrate and write Donald Duck stories for the monthly Disney comic book, "Walt Disney's Comics and Stories." "I had very little editorial supervision. I guess they felt that it was better to leave me alone. In the very beginning—on 'The Mummy's Ring' (1943)—I turned in a script to Eleanor Parker, the editor. She thought that I should change the climax around. I sketched up her

> Ah, spring! Sweet days of love!
> Sweet days when men should take the time
> a money hill to climb, and there
> renew their love affair with their first dime!
>
> —Scrooge McDuck

Illustration from "Go Slowly Sands of Time" a brand new, never published adventure presented in "storybook" style, which is a wide departure from the traditional comic book format of paneled drawings full of dialogue balloons. ■ (From _Uncle Scrooge McDuck: His Life and Times_ by Carl Barks. Illustrated by the author.)

changes and sent in the script. Soon she wrote back and said that my original script was better. From that time on they never monkeyed with my scripts much. If I turned in one that was a turkey, they just paid me for it and put it on the shelf.

"Any time that I wrote a script, when I got through with it, I'd lay it aside, pick it up the next morning, and read it. If it didn't read with a lot of rhythm going right on through, I'd work on it another day or so until I got it to where it sounded good, then start drawing. With the drawing, too, I would pick up sheets that I had done two or three days before and look at them. If the business didn't look right, I didn't mind doing it over. I was after a certain quality. I wasn't thinking of getting a fast buck, and anyway, the bucks in this business were so small that I wasn't throwing much away.

"I worked hard at trying to make something as good as I could possibly make it. When I took the finished art into the office and turned it over to the editor, I was satisfied that I had done the very best I possibly could, and I just dared anybody to see if they could improve it. I had a sourpuss temperament, so when somebody would find some fault with a script, I would blow my marbles in all directions. It actually happened very seldom. If it had happened very many times, I would have gone into another occupation. Once those editors started telling me how to do something, why, I would rather have gone down to the shipyards and gotten a job on a riveting gang.

"I always tried to write a story that I wouldn't mind buying myself. Maybe that's what distinguishes it from the writing of those who only try to get the story past the editors. I was always thinking that other people valued their dimes as much as I did: if I wrote a story that was good enough so that I would want to buy it, then probably a lot of other people would. I wasn't thinking so much of getting it by the editor as I was of getting it by my own critical analysis of value. I think writers should be their own editors and really polish stuff and not fall completely in love with their stuff at first draft."[1]

1943. Began writing longer adventure stories about Donald Duck and his nephews. "I'm not sure of ever committing myself to an absolute formula for writing stories, but basically I always wanted to get a good gag situation and then deal with that. First, I had to think of a good, funny climax gag. Then I would just go back and figure where I could use that climax gag—in a locale in Alaska or wherever—and then from the climax gag would really start from a desire in my system to draw some particular type of scenery, a type of background. If I felt that I could do something with a shipboard story, whether it was a steamer or a sailboat, the desire to draw a sea story would develop. I would start working on gags for a sea story and then come up with something that would make a good, big, powerful gag. Then I'd go back to the beginning and figure out how I would get the ducks into that sea story situation.

"One of the guys who worked down at Western Publishing said, 'Why don't you write your stories the right way? You just start anywhere, say Donald goes out of the house, across the street. Then when you've got him across the street, you say, What can he do when he's over there? So he does something that leads him into going into a grocery store. He meets somebody, and he talks of something, and pretty soon they're out on the desert looking for treasure. You just go from one thing to another, and pretty soon you come up to something big and use that to end the story,' It was a whole different way of working.

Carl Barks, self-portrait, 1939.

"I liked stories that gave me a chance to draw water and ships sailing into storms and big pictorial panels. It helped take the monotony away from drawing just roundheaded ducks all the time. I'd look at pictures of boats or whatever when I was working. While I never copied the layout of any boat, I would always develop one that was so simple I could use it from one scene to another. The reader could always refer to a long-shot view and check it against the close-ups and see where the characters were in relationship to some spot on the boat. . . .

"If my stuff had charm, it could have been that you didn't know when you picked up a story whether you were going to read a hard–boiled one or one that had a bunch of dripping sentiment. I tried to have a wide range of subjects and methods of handling them.

"I did that for several reasons. One is that I couldn't see myself typing each one just alike. I knew that the public liked variety, so I would think back over what I had already done and see if I couldn't come up with something different. That was always one of the first thoughts I had in dreaming up a story: I always looked for plots or formulas that were different, tried to find a different way of doing it, and searched for a different place to stage the business. . . .

"I've always looked at the ducks as caricatured human beings. In rereading the stories, I realized that I had gotten kind of deep in some of them: there was philosophy in there that I hadn't realized I was putting in. It was an added feature that went along with the stories. I think a lot of the philosophy in my stories is conservative—conservative in the sense that I feel

(From the comic book *Uncle Scrooge in Back to the Klondike*, Issue #2, Dell Comics, March, 1953.)

our civilization reached a peak about 1910. Since then we've been going downhill. Much of the older culture had basic qualities that the new stuff that we keep hatching up can never match.

"Look at the magnificent cathedrals and palaces that were built. Nobody can build that kind of thing nowadays. Also, I believe that we should preserve many old ideals and methods of working: honor, honesty, allowing other people to believe their own ideas, not trying to force everyone into one form. The thing I have against the present political system is that it tries to make everybody exactly alike. We should have a million different patterns."[1]

1947. Created "Uncle Scrooge McDuck," the richest duck in the world who seldom spends a cent. ". . . Uncle Scrooge was never a movie star like his noisy nephew Donald. He was a creature of the printed page. He is by any measurements the richest character ever to live in the realm of fiction. He is also the stingiest. He roams the earth and even outer space in search of additional riches to store in his vast money bin. He was a sourdough in the Klondike gold rush, he helped dig the first diamond pits at Kimberley, he found the treasures that escaped Pizarro, Coronado, and Cortez, he cleaned out King Solomon's mines, and he scaled the heights of Asia to find the haunts of the Abominable Snowman.

"To list all of his adventures and feather-rattling battles would take many pages of space. Let it be known that he accomplished his staggering successes without the help of magic or special powers that might have been derived from spider bites or steel corpuscles. He is a web-footed duck who wears spats and a silk hat, which, when you think about it, makes him quite an extraordinary creature, and certainly one blessed with a mystique that transcends human limitations.

"He came into being . . . when I happened to need a rich old uncle as a foil for Donald in a Christmas story. In that first appearance he was only a bit player who forced Donald into a test of courage. His wealth had a very minor role in shaping

Barks in his studio, Hemet, California, 1962.

the action. I might never have used him again, except that about a year later I wanted to write a story about an old Scottish castle on a spooky moor, and Uncle Scrooge's wealth furnished an excuse for Donald and the kids to go there, accompanied of course, by Uncle Scrooge.

"He went on from that spooky tale into other supporting roles, and each new story added more facets to his personality and bulk to the size of his money hoard. In 1952 he was given his own comic, which, under the title of 'Uncle Scrooge,' soon rose to the top of all newsstand comic-book sales.

"A major reason for his rapid rise to stardom was his globe–trotting story roles. I sent him on location to many romantic areas of the world, and I've learned since that kids really liked the geography lessons they absorbed along with the derring-do. Needless to say, in the writing of those tales, I got myself some pleasant hours of armchair trekking, too. Always I tried to make his adventures believable. If Uncle Scrooge voyaged up the Yukon River, the background scenery and the menaces had to be endemic to the Yukon."[1]

Through the years Barks introduced other characters. There was the famous inventor Gyro Gearloose, the lucky Gladstone Gander, and the comic villains, the Beagle Boys.

1952. "The first Uncle Scrooge comic books had been 'Only a Poor Old Man.' Dell Publishing decided they were going to make the book a steady feature, as Scrooge had only been a supporting character before. So 'Back to the Klondike' was the second of Scrooge's own books. In the first issue Scrooge said he had made much of his fortune in the Klondike, so I did a little further buildup on his past to make a whole story about the Klondike years of his life. I used the gimmick of his losing his memory to get him back to the Klondike, where he reviewed some of his former associates and the way he made his money.

"I wasn't sure just how I wanted to make Scrooge—just how much of an old tightwad, how cranky. I was afraid if I got him to be too softhearted, then he would be wishy-washy. So it was difficult to make him do what he did in this story and still keep that whole tightwad personality. In the transition from the old guy in 'Christmas on Bear Mountain'—the very first appearance of Scrooge McDuck, where he was just an invalid and a cranky old guy—to the broadening out of his character, I had to keep an awful lot of that original personality he had, greediness, crankiness, and all. Still, it seemed to me that he had to have some little bit of humanity about him. I was able to do that in 'Back to the Klondike,' to put both elements there, but it really was a story in which I was feeling my way along in every panel.

"Now Uncle Scrooge himself was based on Gould and Harriman and Rockefeller. All those guys made their fortunes in railroads and mines and so on by being just a little bit unscrupulous with the way they eliminated the competition. That's why they were called 'Robber Barons.' Scrooge had to be in that mold, or he couldn't have made it in an era when he was up against all those plutocrats. Since the Klondike era was right at the turn of the century, 1897 through about 1902, the 'Robber Barons' would have been Scrooge's rivals."[1]

1955. Began to paint watercolors. "I had never done painting or sketching on my own until . . . suddenly I was ahead of my deadlines. So I tried to paint some watercolors. But it didn't take me long to find that I was beginning to lose interest in my duck work; I had to go back to concentrating on those

ducks again. The watercolors were too much fun. That's a reason why I never developed my own comic strips. When I got to thinking up material for a strip, I soon realized that it would take months, even years, before I'd get enough polished material to have three weeks of continuity to show to a syndicate. In the meantime, I would have had to have something to buy groceries with. I couldn't leave the ducks for that long, so I decided I'd stick with those ducks and figure that sometime something's going to make the decision for me. I thought, 'It will either be that I go on to the end of my time with the ducks or the ducks lose their publisher or something happens so that there are no longer any duck comic books for me to do.' So I just let fate make the decision for me like old Gladstone Gander.'"[1]

During the years that Barks was drawing his duck stories—over 500 of them—he never received a byline, credit, or royalties for them. "Actually I was expressing myself more freely because I was anonymous than if I had had a lot of fame and a lot of people trying to influence my thinking. Guys like Walt Kelly were surrounded by swarms of people. Of course, he loved it, but it would have stagnated me. I needed privacy and my own little old hole in the earth where I could work in order to be productive and inspired.

"I think I was like a hack horse in a way. I had a bunch of duck characters, and I'd get one story done and go right into doing another. Every story was a challenge as to whether I was going to be able to bring it off. So I dug a little deeper each time."[1]

1966. Retired as free-lance illustrator, but continued to write stories for other artists to illustrate. In reflecting about his long career as a cartoonist, Barks admitted: "That I succeeded [as a cartoonist] to any extent is due, I think, to Walt Disney, and the great industry he built around a stable of squeaking mice and quacking ducks. In the depths of the Great Depression, when my cartooning was barely keeping me in beans and threads, I got hired at the mouse factory in Hollywood, and from then on I have ridden the wings of the Disney ducks to a sort of individual renown that has even gotten an asteroid named for me, 2730 Barks, one of those billions of sparkling objects that I used to see in such awesome splendor in the skies over the lonely homestead long ago."

1971. With his third wife, a highly regarded landscape painter, Barks began to paint. Over a five year period he was allowed by the Disney studio to sell oil paintings of the ducks.

1980. Lives in retirement with his wife in Grants Pass, Oregon. ". . . Ideally, if civilization could keep softening people up, we might have people around who would be so unselfish and kindly that they would never try to take advantage of anyone else. But that's far away in the future.

"I've always wanted to promote a broader understanding of life as well as entertaining. As the world becomes overpopulated, hatreds intensify. People have got to learn to be more patient and liberal about each other's views."[1]

FOR MORE INFORMATION SEE: Charles Beaumont, "The Comic World," *Fortnight,* May, 1955; Michael Barrier, "The Lord of Quackly Hall," *Funnyworld,* June, 1967; M. Barrier, "Interview with Carl Barks," *Comic Art,* 1968; Bill Spicer, "A Visit with Carl Barks," *Graphic Story World,* July, 1971; Dave Wagner, "An Interview with Donald Duck," *Radical America,* 1973; Jack Chalker, *An Informal Biography of Scrooge*

Barks, puttering in his garage workshop, 1974. Photograph by E.B. Boatner.

McDuck, Mirage Press, 1974; M. Barrier, "The Duck Man," *The Comic-Book Book*, 1974; Donald Ault, "Comic Art and How to Read It," *California Monthly*, January-February, 1976; E. B. Boatner, "Carl Barks—From Burbank to Calisota," *The Comic Book Price Book*, 1977; M. Barrier, "Screenwriter for a Duck: Carl Barks at the Disney Studio," *Funnyworld*, fall, 1979; Carl Barks, *Uncle Scrooge McDuck: His Life and Times*, Celestial Arts, 1981; Edward Summer, "Of Ducks and Men: Carl Barks Interviewed," *Panels*, spring, 1981; *Time*, May 17, 1982; *Newsweek*, June 28, 1982.

BISHOP, Bonnie   1943-

PERSONAL: Born August 24, 1943, in Meriden, Conn.; daughter of Welles L. (a birdhouse manufacturer) and Julia (a registered nurse; maiden name, Nettleton) Bishop; married James H. Wells (a laboratory technician), May 21, 1975. *Education:* Skidmore College, B.S., 1965; attended New School for Social Research and Parsons School of Design, 1969-76, and School of Visual Arts, 1974-76. *Residence:* Cornville, Me.

CAREER: Scholastic Magazines, Inc., New York, N.Y., artist, 1966-68, art editor, 1968-72, art director of language arts projects, 1972-76; J.C. Penney & Co., Inc., Skowhegan, Me., merchandise presentation supervisor, 1978-83; Colby College, Waterville, Me., director of publications, 1984—. *Exhibitions:* (Group show) Sam Flax, New York, N.Y., 1976; (one-woman show) Last Unicorn, Waterville, Me., 1979, 1980. *Awards, honors:* Awards from Poster U.S.A. for "Get High on Life" poster; Creativity '73, 1973, for "Garbage Can Poster"; American Institute of Graphic Arts, 1973, for "Getting Together" and "Double Action" learning kits; Creativity '74, 1974, for poster "You Are the American Dream."

*WRITINGS—*For children: *No One Noticed Ralph* (illustrated by Jack Kent), Doubleday, 1979; *Ralph Rides Away* (illustrated by J. Kent), Doubleday, 1979.

*ADAPTATIONS—*Filmstrips: "No One Noticed Ralph," The Westport Group, 1980.

WORK IN PROGRESS: Free-lance design and illustration; children's stories; printmaking.

People heard her, but no one noticed Ralph.

■ (From *No One Noticed Ralph* by Bonnie Bishop. Illustrated by Jack Kent.)

SIDELIGHTS: "Since childhood, I have been fascinated with books. My mother gave me an excellent start by reading to me and encouraging me to draw. I spent many happy hours writing stories and making 'magazines.' With the encouragement of several good teachers, I majored in art and went on to work in publishing. Writing and illustrating children's books was a dream that was half-fulfilled with the publication of the two 'Ralph' books. I say 'half-fulfilled' because I wrote but did not illustrate them. Since I consider myself primarily an artist, that was a disappointment and something I hope to change in the future.

"One of my most difficult problems is finding the time to write and continue my printmaking while earning a living. I have been fortunate in that almost all of the jobs I have had related to art in some way. But not having enough time for my own personal creativity is very frustrating. One solution for me is to continue to take art courses, which not only provide me with scheduled time to work, but also help me to grow as an artist and an individual."

BLISS, Corinne D(emas)   1947-

PERSONAL: Born May 14, 1947, in New York, N.Y.; daughter of Nicholas Constantine and Electra (Guizot) Demas; children: Austin Constantine. *Education:* Tufts University, A.B. (magna cum laude), 1968; Columbia University, M.A. (with highest honors), 1969, M.Phil., 1978, Ph.D., 1980. *Resi-*

I just turned around and walked away and sure enough, Melly followed right behind me. ■ (From *That Dog Melly!* by Corinne Demas Bliss and Austin Bliss. Photograph by Corinne Demas Bliss and Jim Judkis.)

dence: Western Massachusetts. *Agent:* Harriet Wasserman, Harriet Wasserman Literary Agency, 230 East 48th St., New York, N.Y. 10017. *Office:* Department of English, Mount Holyoke College, South Hadley, Mass. 01075.

CAREER: University of Pittsburgh, Pittsburgh, Pa., instructor in English, 1970-78; Mount Holyoke College, South Hadley, Mass., assistant professor of English, 1978—. Lecturer at Chatham College, 1977-78; guest writer at Westfield State College, 1979; visiting writer at Goddard College, spring, 1981; gives readings at colleges. Founder and director of Valley Writers; editor for Author's Registry (literary agency), 1967 and 1968. *Member:* P.E.N., Authors Guild, Bay State Writers Association, Modern Language Association, Society of Children's Book Writers. *Awards, honors:* National Endowment for the Arts fellowship, 1978, 1983; Andrew W. Mellon Foundation fellowship, 1982.

WRITINGS: (With son, Austin Bliss) *That Dog Melly!* (juvenile; with own photographs), Hastings House, 1981; *The Same River Twice,* Atheneum, 1982; *Daffodils or the Death of Love: Short Fiction,* University of Missouri Press, 1983.

Work represented in anthologies, including *Secrets and Other Stories by Women,* 1979. Contributor of about twenty-five stories and poems to magazines, including *Images, Mademoiselle, Ploughshares, Kansas Quarterly, Transatlantic Review,* and *Esquire.*

CORINNE D. BLISS

WORK IN PROGRESS: Matthew's Meadow and *The Magic Whistle Tree*, both children's books; an adult novel; and *Separate Lives*, a collection of short stories.

SIDELIGHTS: "I am most naturally a short story writer and in recent years have turned to the novel. The subject of my doctoral dissertation was the short story—basically it was an inquiry into how writers make readers respond the way they want them to and a study of what makes certain short stories work.

"Certainly writing about literature and teaching it influences my own writing—just as being a writer influences my teaching of literature and writing. My children's books have been written for my own child and his friends, and the age level I write for changes as he does."

HOBBIES AND OTHER INTERESTS: Travel in Greece, music, cross-country skiing.

BLOOM, Freddy 1914-

PERSONAL: Born February 6, 1914, in New York, N.Y.; daughter of Robert (a maritime arbitrator) and Emmy (a journalist; maiden name Schlessing) Wenzel; married Philip M. Bloom (a physician); children: Virginia, William. *Education:* Attended Barnard College and Columbia University, 1931-34; Trinity College, Dublin, B.A. (with honors), 1936. *Home:* 2 Montagu Sq., London, W1H 1RA, England.

CAREER: Free-lance writer. Affiliated with Malaya Tribune Group in Singapore, 1939-41; managing director of Youth Book Club, 1947-48. Member of board of governors of Post Graduate Teaching Hospitals and Special School. *Member:* National Deaf Children's Society (founding chairman, 1956-64), Health Visitors Association (vice-president). *Awards, honors:* Malaya campaign medal, 1947; Member of Order of the British Empire, 1964.

WRITINGS: Our Deaf Children, Heinemann, 1963; *The Boy Who Couldn't Hear* (juvenile; illustrated by Michael Charlton), Merrimack Book Services, 1979, published in England as *The Little Boy Who Could Not Hear*, Bodley Head, 1979; *Our Deaf Children: Into the Eighties*, Gresham, 1979; *Dear Philip*, Bodley Head, 1980; *Care to Help?*, John Clare, 1980; *Face It!*, John Clare, 1981; *101 Questions and Answers about Deaf Children*, John Clare, 1982; *Love Lines and Others* (verse), John Clare, 1983. Editor of National Deaf Children's Society publication, *Talk*, 1955-83.

WORK IN PROGRESS: "A massive book about my mother to be called 'Emmy.' It will probably never be finished."

SIDELIGHTS: "I was working on the Tribune Group of newspapers in Singapore when the Island fell to the Japanese early in 1942. My husband, Philip, was then a doctor in the Royal Army Medical Corps. We were married nine days before Singapore fell. We spent the next three-and-a-half years in separate prisons, he in the military camp and I in the civilian internment camp. We were released late in 1945 and returned to London where he had been in practice. *Dear Philip* is the diary I wrote in Changi Camp. It was in the form of a long letter to Philip, hence the title.

"In September, 1946, our first child was born. Despite the fact that we thought we had fully recovered from the prison years, she was born profoundly deaf. Doctors believe it was due to a delayed vitamin deficiency in me. Sixteen months later our second child was born. We had eaten more by then and there was nothing wrong with him. Both are now very satisfying adults.

"It was through our daughter, Virginia, that I became interested in the development and welfare of deaf children and that, inevitably, led to an interest in other disabilities.

"For no rational reason, I like people and think they should be nicer to each other even if they look or sound different. Since nobody else has ever thought of saying it before, I keep

(From *The Boy Who Couldn't Hear* by Freddy Bloom. Illustrated by Michael Charlton.)

FREDDY BLOOM

repeating that greed, intolerance, and materialism do not pay satisfying dividends. As usual, nobody listens. Shame.''

FOR MORE INFORMATION SEE: Leslie Bell, *Destined Meeting,* Odhams, 1959; Noel Barber, *Sinister Twilight,* Collins, 1968.

BOOTH, Graham (Charles)   1935-

PERSONAL: Born July 24, 1935, in London, England; moved to Canada after World War II; came to the United States in 1955; divorced; children: Kevin, Brendon, Robyn, Nathan. *Education:* Attended East Los Angeles College and University of California, Los Angeles, B.A., 1959; University of Southern California, M.F.A., 1966; Claremont Graduate School, Ph.D., 1984. *Residence:* Fullerton, Calif.

CAREER: Illustrator of children's books. Worked in a plywood mill and at advertising agencies in Canada for five years; taught art at Vancouver School of Art, Vancouver, British Columbia, beginning 1963; Fullerton Junior College, Fullerton, Calif., teacher of art, 1966—. *Member:* Pi Lambda Theta. *Awards,*

honors: Award for significant contributon in the field of illustration from Southern California Council on Literature for Children and Young People, 1971, for *Bobby Shafto's Gone to Sea;* New York Academy of Science Award, 1976, for *Spring Peepers.*

ILLUSTRATOR—All for children: Mark Taylor, *Henry, the Explorer* (Junior Literary Guild selection), Atheneum, 1966; Patricia M. Martin, *Sing, Sailor, Sing,* Golden Gate, 1966; M. Taylor, *The Bold Fisherman,* Golden Gate, 1967; M. Tayor, *A Time for Flowers,* Golden Gate, 1967; M. Taylor, *Henry Explores the Jungle,* Atheneum, 1968; M. Taylor, *The Old Woman and the Pedlar,* Golden Gate, 1969; M. Taylor, *Bobby Shafto's Gone to Sea,* Golden Gate, 1970; M. Taylor, *Henry, the Castaway* (Junior Literary Guild selection), Atheneum, 1972; Franklyn M. Branley, *Think Metric!,* Crowell, 1972; F. M. Branley, *Weight and Weightlessness,* Crowell, 1972; Sara W. Brewton and John E. Brewton, compilers, *My Tang's Tungled, and Other Ridiculous Situations* (humorous poems), Crowell, 1973; M. Taylor, *Henry Explores the Mountains,* Atheneum, 1974; Judy Hawes, *Spring Peepers,* Crowell, 1975; M. Taylor, *The Case of the Missing Kittens,* Atheneum, 1978.

ADAPTATIONS—Filmstrip: ''Henry the Explorer'' (filmstrip with cassette), Weston Woods, 1977.

WORK IN PROGRESS: Illustrating Mark Taylor's *The Case of the Purloined Compass.*

GRAHAM BOOTH

SIDELIGHTS: "Currently, my illustration and design career includes designing and lecturing (especially visiting children in a classroom situation). One of my most recent assignments has been the illustration of American Sign Language for a Tri-Lingual Book (ASL, Spanish, and English) for San Diego State University, to be used in the Clinic for Learning Disabilities at that Institution, a program designed to help children who are hearing impaired and are from Spanish speaking homes. I have also illustrated the covers for the past three years for *Expectations,* an anthology of children's stories published in Braille for blind children throughout the world and is published by The Braille Institute here in Los Angeles."

HOBBIES AND OTHER INTERESTS: "Essentially, my recreational pleasure is spent out on my boat, *The Migrant,* with my two oldest sons fishing and visiting Catalina Island."

FOR MORE INFORMATION SEE: Lee Kingman and others, compilers, *Illustrators of Children's Books: 1957-1966,* Horn Book, 1968.

(From the animated filmstrip "Henry the Explorer." Produced by Weston Woods, 1977.)

Angus barked, and it barked. And then he felt better. . . . ■ (From *The Case of the Missing Kittens* by Mark Taylor. Illustrated by Graham Booth.)

BURBANK, Addison (Buswell)   1895-1961

PERSONAL: Born June 1, 1895, in Los Angeles, Calif.; died October 4, 1961; son of a newspaper editor and publisher and a poetess: married Corvelle Newcomb (an author). *Education:* Attended Santa Clara University, Hopkins Art Institute, San Francisco, Chicago Art Institute, Grand Central Art School, New York, N.Y., Ecole de la Grande Chaumiere, Paris, and Colarros', Paris. *Religion:* Roman Catholic. *Residence:* Port Jefferson, Long Island, N.Y.

CAREER: Author and illustrator beginning in 1938. Worked as a newspaper reporter, columnist, and magazine illustrator; also was president of Sentinel Publishing Co., Winston-Salem, N.C. Has exhibited work at Academia de Bellas Artes, Guatemala City, in Paris, and in a one-man show at Ferargil Gallery, New York, N.Y., 1927. *Awards, honors:* Recipient of First Award from Chicago World's Fair, 1933, for mural painting in oil.

WRITINGS—All self-illustrated: *Guatemala Profile,* Coward, 1939, reprinted, Gordon Press, 1976; *Cedar Deer* (juvenile),

Coward, 1940; *Mexican Frieze,* Coward, 1940; (with wife, Corvelle Newcomb), *Narizona's Holiday* (juvenile), Longmans, Green, 1946.

Illustrator; all written by Corvelle Newcomb; all for young readers: *The Red Hat: A Story of John Henry Cardinal Newman,* Longmans, Green, 1941, reprinted, McKay, 1962; *Vagabond in Velvet: The Story of Miguel de Cervantes,* Longmans, Green, 1942; *Silver Saddles,* Longmans, Green, 1943; *Larger than the Sky: A Story of James Cardinal Gibbons,* Longmans, Green, 1945, published in Australia as *A Story of James Cardinal Gibbons,* Longmans, Green, 1951; *The Secret Door: The Story of Kate Greenaway,* Dodd, 1946; *Running Waters,* Dodd, 1947; *The Broken Sword: The Story of Fray Bartolome de las Casas,* Dodd, 1955; *Brother Zero: A Story of the Life of Saint John of God,* Dodd, 1959; *Christopher Columbus, the Sea Lord,* Dodd, 1963.

Contributor of stories and articles to periodicals, including *Catholic World* and *Travel.*

SIDELIGHTS: "My father being a newspaperman and my mother a poet, I was named Addison as a further inspiration to carry on the literary tradition. While still in my crib, however, I began to draw; and at thirteen I won neighborhood fame and a correspondence art course by a drawing of Mrs. A. Mutt in a 'Directoire gown.' In high school I drew for the school publications, but my first job on leaving was newspaper reporting.

"Wanting to study art, I eventually entered the Chicago Art Institute and, while still a student, began selling my work to national magazines. Before long I came to New York. After a year of study and outdoor painting abroad, I was given my first one-man show at Ferargil's in 1927. I won my first award for a mural for the Florida Building at the Chicago World's Fair.

"Going to Guatemala to paint in 1938, I wrote my first book, *Guatemala Profile,* the record of my experiences among the

Indians, illustrated with pen-and-ink sketches. I drew upon these experiences for *Cedar Deer,* a story for children about an Indian boy who longs to be a sculptor like his Mayan ancestors. Later I visited Mexico, with *Mexican Frieze* and *Narizona's Holiday . . .* resulting from our sojourn below the border." [Bertha M. Miller and others, compilers, *Illustrators of Children's Books: 1946-1956,* Horn Book, 1958.]

FOR MORE INFORMATION SEE: New York Times Book Review, April 23, 1939, September 15, 1940, January 19, 1941; *Saturday Review of Literature,* May 6, 1939, January 4, 1941; *New York Herald Tribune Books,* May 7, 1939, January 5, 1941; *New York Herald Tribune Weekly Book Review,* December 8, 1946; Bertha M. Miller, and others, compilers, *Illustrators of Children's Books: 1946-1956,* Horn Book, 1958.

CAHN, Rhoda 1922-

PERSONAL: Born March 29, 1922; daughter of Israel and Gertrude Lipofsky; married William Cahn (a free-lance writer), 1943 (died October 13, 1976); children: Susan Cahn Krieger, Kathe Cahn Morse, Daniel. *Education:* Southern Connecticut State College, B.S., 1942, M.S., 1971; further study at Bank Street College and Brooklyn College (now of the City University of New York). *Home:* 488 Norton Pkwy., New Haven, Conn. 06511.

Garment workers brought bundles of clothes from factories to work on at home. Here a child is carrying parts of garments to be sewn by the entire family. ■ (From *No Time for School, No Time for Play* by Rhoda and William Cahn.)

. . . Before she was fourteen, she had learned to weave the tribal symbols into her mother's *guipil;* for every girl must learn to weave before she marries. ■ (From *Guatemala Profile* by Addison Burbank. Illustrated by the author.)

CAREER: Affiliated with Cahn Associates (public information service), New Haven, Conn., 1963—. Editor of newsletter and member of board of directors of Connecticut Association of School Psychologists, 1973-76. Founding member of Arts Council of Greater New Haven, 1964—.

WRITINGS—With husband, William Cahn: *The Story of Writings: From Cave Art to Computer,* Harvey House, 1963; *No Time for School, No Time for Play: The Story of Child Labor in America* (juvenile), Messner, 1972; *The Great American Comedy Scene,* Messner, 1978.

WORK IN PROGRESS: A book on the diagnosis, research and treatment of blood diseases; *Blood Lines and Life Lines,* for teenagers; a biography, *Augusta Lewis Troup.*

CAHN, William 1912-1976

PERSONAL: Born May 12, 1912, in New York, N.Y.; died October 13, 1976, in New Haven, Conn.; married Rhoda Lipofsky, 1943; children: Susan, Kathe, Daniel. *Education:* Dartmouth College, B.A., 1934. *Home:* New Haven, Conn.

CAREER: Worked as a newspaperman, and in public relations and advertising; free-lance writer. *Military service:* U.S. Army, 1943-44. *Awards, honors:* Copy Writers Association of New York, Silver Key, 1964, merit citation, 1966; National Conference of Christians and Jews, certificate of recognition, 1964; American Institute of Graphic Arts, certificate of excellence,

1966; Andy Award, Advertising Club of New York, 1967; associate fellow, Calhoun College, Yale University, 1975.

WRITINGS: Guide to Political Action, United Electrical Workers, 1944; (with Herbert Montfort Morais) *Gene Debs: The Story of a Fighting American,* International Publishers, 1948; *Mill Town,* Cameron & Kahn, 1954; *Einstein: A Pictorial Biography,* Citadel, 1955; *Laugh Makers: A Pictorial History of American Comedians,* introduction by Harold Lloyd, Putnam, 1957; *The Union Democracy Built,* Retail Drug Employees Union, 1957; *The Amazing Story of a New American Hero: Van Cliburn,* Ridge Press, 1959; (with Marvin Barrett) *The Jazz Age,* Putnam, 1959.

The Story of Pitney-Bowes, Harper, 1961; *Good Night, Mrs. Calabash: The Secret of Jimmy Durante,* Duell, Sloan & Pearce, 1963; (with wife Rhoda Cahn) *The Story of Writing: From Cave Art to Computer,* Harvey House, 1963; *Harold Lloyd's World of Comedy,* Duell, Sloan & Pearce, 1964; *Signature of 450,000,* Ladies Garment Workers' Union, 1965; *Out of the Cracker Barrel: The Nabisco Story, From Animal Crackers to Zuzus,* Simon & Schuster, 1969; *A Matter of Life and Death: The Connecticut Mutual Story,* Random House, 1970; *A Pictorial History of the Great Comedians,* Grosset, 1970; (with R. Cahn) *No Time for School, No Time for Play: The Story of Child Labor in America* (juvenile), Messner, 1972; *A Pictorial History of American Labor,* Crown, 1972; (with R. Cahn) *The Great American Comedy Scene,* Messner, 1978.

FOR MORE INFORMATION SEE—Obituaries: *New York Times,* October 15, 1976.

Children worked in mines alongside grown men. ■ (From *No Time for School, No Time for Play* by Rhoda and William Cahn. Photograph courtesy of Library of Congress.)

CALMENSON, Stephanie 1952-

BRIEF ENTRY: Born November 28, 1952, in Brookyn, N.Y. Editorial director and author of children's books. After graduating with honors from Brooklyn College of the City University of New York in 1973, Calmenson became an elementary school teacher in Brooklyn. She received her master's degree from New York University in 1976, and went to Doubleday & Co., where she served as an editor until 1980. Since that time, she has been editorial director with Parents Magazine Press. Commenting on children's literature, Calmenson stated, ". . . I enjoy picture books most, particularly those that successfully isolate and explore emotion. . . ," citing as good examples the work by authors such as Maurice Sendak and Dr. Seuss. A member of the Society of Children's Book Writers, Calmenson has written twelve children's books. Among these are *One Little Monkey* (illustrated by Ellen Appleby; Parents Magazine Press, 1982), *Barney's Sand Castle* (illustrated by Sheila Becker; Golden Press, 1983), *The Birthday Hat* (illustrated by Susan Gantner; Grosset & Dunlap, 1983), *The Kindergarten Book* (illustrated by Beth L. Weiner; Grosset & Dunlap, 1983), *Where Is Grandma Potamus* (illustrated by Gantner; Grosset & Dunlap, 1983), and *Where Will the Animals Stay?* (Parents Magazine Press, 1984). She is also the compiler of *Never Take a Pig to Lunch and Other Funny Poems about Animals* (illustrated by Hilary Knight; Doubleday, 1982). *Home:* 150 East 18th St., New York, N.Y. 10003. *For More Information See: Contemporary Authors,* Volume 107, Gale, 1983.

CARL CARMER

CARMER, Carl (Lamson) 1893-1976

PERSONAL: Born October 16, 1893, in Cortland, N.Y.; died September 11, 1976, in Bronxville, N.Y.; son of Willis Griswold (a superintendent of schools) and Mary (Lamson) Carmer; married Elizabeth Black (an artist and illustrator), December 24, 1928. *Education:* Hamilton College, Ph.B., 1914, Ph.M., 1917; Harvard University, M.A., 1915. *Home and office:* Octagon House, Irvington-on-Hudson, N.Y.

CAREER: Syracuse University, Syracuse, N.Y., instructor in English, 1915-16; University of Rochester, Rochester, N.Y., assistant professor of English, 1916-17, 1919-21; Hamilton College, Clinton, N.Y., chairman of public speaking department, 1919; University of Alabama, Tuscaloosa, associate professor, 1921-24, professor of English, 1924-27; *New Orleans Morning Tribune,* New Orleans, La., columnist, 1927; *Vanity Fair,* New York City, assistant editor, 1928-29; *Theatre Arts Monthly,* New York City, associate editor, 1929-33; full-time writer and folklorist, 1933-76. *Military service:* U.S. Army, Field Artillery, World War I; became first lieutenant; served with U.S. Army Air Forces during World War II; received War Department certificate for distinguished service in combat areas.

MEMBER: Society of American Historians (councillor), Authors Guild (former president), Poetry Society of America (former president), American Center P.E.N. (former president), New York State Historical Association (former vice-president of board of trustees), New York State Folklore Society (honorary vice-president), Edward MacDowell Association (former president), Phi Beta Kappa, Psi Upsilon, Pilgrims Club, Century Association. *Awards, honors:* Litt.D., Elmira College, 1937; L.H.D., Hamilton College, 1941; Litt.D., Susquehanna University, 1944; LL.D., University of Buffalo, 1962; *New York Herald Tribune* Spring Book Festival award, 1950, for

Windfall Fiddle; cited for contributions to children's literature by New York State Association for Curriculum Development; adopted by Wolf Clan of the Seneca Nation.

WRITINGS—Juveniles: *Too Many Cherries,* Viking, 1949; *Windfall Fiddle,* Knopf, 1950; (compiler with Cecile Matschat) *American Boy Adventure Stories,* Winston, 1952; (editor) *A Cavalcade of Young Americans,* Lothrop, 1958; *The Boy Drummer of Vincennes,* Harvey House, 1972; *The Pirate Hero of New Orleans,* Harvey House, 1975.

All for children; all with wife, Elizabeth Black Carmer: *Francis Marion: Swamp Fox of the Carolinas* (illustrated by William Plummer), Garrard, 1962; *The Susquehanna: From New York to the Chesapeake* (illustrated by William Hutchinson; maps by Fred Kliem), Garrard, 1964; *Captain Abner and Henry Q.* (illustrated by Ted Schroeder), Garrard, 1965; *Mike Fink and the Big Turkey Shoot* (illustrated by Mimi Korach), Garrard, 1965; *Tony Beaver, Griddle Skater* (illustrated by M. Korach), Garrard, 1965; *Pecos Bill and the Long Lasso* (illustrated by M. Korach), Garrard, 1968.

All for children; all illustrated by wife, E. B. Carmer: *The Hurricane's Children: Tales from Your Neck o' the Woods,* Farrar & Rinehart, 1937, reissued, McKay, 1967; *America Sings: Stories and Songs of Our Country's Growing,* Knopf, 1942; *Wildcat Furs to China: The Cruise of the Sloop Experiment,* Knopf, 1945, reissued, McKay, 1969; *Eagle in the Wind,* Aladdin Books, 1948; *Hurricane Luck,* Aladdin Books, 1949; *A Flag for the Fort,* Messner, 1952; *Henry Hudson: Captain of the Ice-Bound Seas,* Garrard, 1960; *The Hudson River,* Holt, 1962, revised edition, Grosset, 1968.

Other: (With Edwin Francis Shewmake) *College English Composition,* Johnson, 1927; *French Town* (poetry), privately published, 1930, 2nd edition, Pelican, 1968; *Deep South* (poetry), Farrar & Rinehart, 1930; *Stars Fell on Alabama* (Literary Guild selection), Farrar & Rinehart, 1934, 3rd edition, Hill & Wang, 1961; *Listen for a Lonesome Drum,* Farrar & Rinehart, 1936, 2nd edition, Sloane, 1950; *The Hudson* (illustrated by Stow Wegenroth), Farrar & Rinehart, 1939, revised edition, Grosset, 1968.

Gennessee Fever (Literary Guild selection), Farrar & Rinehart, 1941, reprinted, McKay, 1971; (collector and narrator) *America Sings,* Knopf, 1942; (editor) *Songs of the Rivers of America,* Farrar & Rinehart, 1942; (editor, and author of introduction) *The War against God,* Henry Holt, 1943; *The Jesse James of the Java Sea,* Farrar & Rinehart, 1945; *Taps Is Not Enough* (verse drama), Henry Holt, 1945; (editor with C. Van Doren) *American Scriptures,* Boni & Gaer, 1946; *For the Rights of Man,* Hinds, 1947, reprinted, Books for Libraries, 1969; *Dark Trees in the Wind,* Sloane, 1949, reprinted, McKay, 1965.

The Screaming Ghost, and Other Stories, Knopf, 1956; *American Folklore and Its Old-World Backgrounds,* Compton, 1956; (editor) *Cavalcade of America,* Crown, 1956; *Pets at the White House,* Dutton, 1959, revised edition, 1962; (editor) *The Tavern Lamps Are Burning* (anthology), McKay, 1964; *My Kind of Country* (anthology of Carmer's writings about New York State), McKay, 1966; *The Farm Boy and the Angel,* Doubleday, 1970.

Also author of booklet, *The Years of Grace, 1808-1958,* 1958. Writer and narrator of documentary films for motion pictures and television; writer and producer of scripts for radio programs, "Your Neck of the Woods" and "American Scriptures"; adaptor of his own folklore series for Walt Disney's "Melody Time"; collector and editor of four albums of folk songs, Decca Records. Editor, "Rivers of America" series, Holt, and "Regions of America" series, Harper. Contributor to *American Heritage* and other publications.

ADAPTATIONS—Filmstrips: "Captain Abner and Henry Q." (with phonodisc or phonotape, script book, and teacher's guide), Taylor Associates, 1970; "Mike Fink and the Big Turkey Shoot" (with phonodisc or phonotape, script book, and teacher's guide), Taylor Associates, 1970; "Pecos Bill and the Long Lasso" (with phonodisc or phonotape, script book, and teacher's guide), Taylor Associates, 1970; "Tony Beaver, Griddle Skater" (with phonodisc or phonotape, script book, and teacher's guide), Taylor Associates, 1970.

SIDELIGHTS: **October 16, 1893.** Born in Cortland, in upstate New York where Carmer's father was a superintendent of schools. "Out of a chance of great-great-great-grandfathers who fought in the American Revolution (including a soldier of the King) to upstate Yorkers distinguished themselves—one through living to the age of 103 because, as the family said, he was 'too ornery to die,' and the other, (a warrior of many enlistments on sea and shore) through such stirring accounts of his adventures as won him the envied title of 'Biggest Liar in Tompkins County.' From these, if belief in inherited traits is justified, may well have come certain qualities in me.

"I would like to think that others came from my gentle, child-loving school superintendent father, and my schoolteacher mother whose immediate forbears hailed from the whiskey-making tweed-weaving Scottish Isles of Harris and Skye." ["Carl Carmer," *New York Herald Tribune Book Review,* October 11, 1953.[1]]

As a young boy growing up in rural upstate New York, Carmer shared his father's interest in American folklore. "Unsatisfied with formal education, my . . . father had wanted me to know the wisdom of the people—wisdom that had been recognized, sifted, polished, handed down by generations of undistinguished but thoughtful humans. He wanted me to realize that from such succinct, simple folk-proverbs as our Sunday hosts often used, may come such beauty and truth as even our greatest wise men have seldom expressed.

"Each Sunday we visited an old man. One was white-haired Mr. Coan, who had seen bears among the trees in front of the very porch on which we sat, and had known Indian chiefs who still talked of destroying whites who had stolen their lands. Another was town florist, French-born Monsieur Duquette, who had joined the Union Army during the Civil War and whose valor grew ever brighter and more dramatic as he reported it. A third was short, bald and merry Jerry Simpson, editor of the town weekly, who explained as well as he could what a saturnine man named Eugene V. Debs had meant when I had seen him harangue, between trains, a dozen depot idlers on the hardships of the American workingman." [Carl Carmer, "Wisdom at Cribbs Creek," *This I Believe: 2,* edited by Raymond Swing, Simon & Schuster, 1954.[2]]

June, 1910. Graduated from Albion High School and entered Hamilton College. "I was the fourth of seven or eight Carmers to receive a degree from Hamilton College (founded as an academy for Indians) and I needed another year's education (Harvard M.A.) before being able to make a living."[1]

1915. Began teaching English, eventually becoming a professor of English at the University of Alabama. "I taught Anglo-Saxon, pedagogy, creative writing and the other subjects usually assessed a 'general utility' professor for twelve years (the last half-dozen at a state university where the football squad was requested to omit my courses)."[1]

1927. Began career as journalist. "A year in New Orleans as a reporter delighted me but not the *Item-Tribune* and I returned to upstate New York buck-wheat-cakes-for-breakfast from necessity. Through friends I won a job as assistant editor of the regrettably defunct journal, *Vanity Fair.* My salary, however, did not permit that familiarity with the great and the near-great which the magazine demanded, and I was catapulted from my chair in the Graybar Building into that of an assistant editor of *Theatre Arts Monthly.*"[1]

1930. First book of poetry published. Carmer's writing career began with poetry, which had a direct influence on his much later writings for children. "In those days, poetry demanded simplicity, directness of expression and getting away from clichés. They were the essentials. I was influenced by Vachel Lindsay (who was a good friend), Sandburg (who was a good friend), and Sherwood Anderson, by his simplicity and straightforwardness. I strove to write direct, straightforward lyrics. The study of poetry is advantageous to anyone who would write prose, and double so for anyone who would write for children." [Harvey Breit, "Talk with Carl Carmer," *New York Times,* November 13, 1949.[3]]

1934. First best seller, *Stars Fell on Alabama,* was published. "Four years of writing on the theatre and a book of poems, *Deep South,* left me as penniless as a college professor. Then *Stars Fell on Alabama* took me away from editing magazines into the world of authors. Now I produce my books, edit the 'Rivers of America' series and other works for various publishers, collaborate with my illustrator wife, Elizabeth Black

Carmer on stories for children, and live in a fantastic and beautiful dwelling called Octagon House, a pleasure-dome beside the great river of which I have often written—the Hudson. . . ."[1]

1943. Upon the death of co-editor Stephen Vincent Benét, Carmer became editor of the "Rivers in America" series for Holt.

As a specialist in American folklore, Carmer was a radio narrator of American folktales, a radio reporter of Americana, producer of four record albums, and lecturer on the American scene. "People are both a region and a way of life. Landscape becomes a part of them, and they become a part of each other. Generations and institutions enter into this developing pattern, but the pattern, present or past, is always people." [Carl Carmer, "Of Wooden Indians and Iron Dogs," *Craft Horizons*, November/December, 1962.[4]]

1949. *Hurricane Luck*, a book for children, was selected by the Children's Book Club. The following year another children's book, *Windfall Fiddle*, was selected by the *New York Herald Tribune* Spring Book Festival. Carmer was also cited by the New York State Association for Curriculum Develop-

ment for his contributions to children's literature. ". . . I take my writings for kids just as seriously as for adults. I think a great deal of writing for children is bad writing. In an effort to attain simplicity there is a monotony with repetitive structures and without variation in rhythm or style. It is perfectly possible to have both—that is, good writing and simplicity. There have been many books that had them. *The Wind in the Willows* and *Alice*, to name two. There is a whole literature that too few modern writers emulate. There is a considerable difference between writing simply and writing down. Whatever I do, I do not write down. Children are as bright (maybe I ought to say as intelligent) as the author. Children are quite as demanding as adults.

"Children ask for color—not just in pictures but in ideas—they ask for movement, exciting event, writing that gives them a sense of identification with the characters they are reading about. And they like words. I have little or no sympathy for word-list writers.

"I can remember reading and being fascinated by words I didn't know at all. I was fascinated by the sound and color of words. The writer of juveniles should write with style and with prose rhythms. It would be a good thing if children were to become aware of such things as soon as they were able.

. . . **Nature was herself the greatest artist, producing effects that inspired noble contemplation. . . .** ▪ (From *The Hudson* by Carl Carmer. Illustrated by Stow Wengenroth.)

"Children prefer to obtain information in a well-written book that has excitement in it. I try out all my manuscripts on children. In every one of my books, I have made an effort to inform. In my folklore books, for example, I have tried to give the young reader a picture of what America was like in the early days, of the great obstacles Americans had to overcome, of the jobs they had, the variety of landscape they lived in, and the kinds of minds our forebears had."[3]

Many of Carmer's books for children were co-written with his wife who also illustrated several of the children's books.

September 11, 1976. Died in Bronxville, New York. "Often, after a man has reached his mature years, he has experiences that seem, like sudden shafts of sunlight, to illuminate and give meaning to events of his past.

"Such a revelation came to me beside mud-yellow Cribbs Creek when I first saw an Alabama Sunday-baptising. A one-armed Negro in a white robe, waist-deep in the current, was preaching the sermon and I found myself spellbound by a miracle of talk packed with homely but poetic phrasing, with deep and passionately felt wisdom. Somehow the man's words stirred a memory of myself, a small boy on my weekly Sunday afternoon walk with my gentle, child-loving father in upstate New York. The man in the water had suddenly made me understand those walks with my father as I had never understood them.

"Since that Cribbs Creek episode, I have long sought for expressions of the wisdom of the folk, formulated from their own journey through time. Though mountains and deserts have even psychic effects on the man who lives on them, though cattle herding or accounting strongly color a man's mind, it is something more wonderful than these that brings him wisdom."[3]

Carmer's works are included in the Kerlan Collection at the University of Minnesota.

FOR MORE INFORMATION SEE: Saturday Review of Literature, December 6, 1941, January 29, 1955; Gordon Parks, *Camera Portraits,* F. Watts, 1948; *New York Times Book Review,* November 13, 1949, May 17, 1970; *New York Herald Tribune Book Review,* November 20, 1949, October 11, 1953; Raymond Swing, editor, *This I Believe,* Simon & Schuster, 1954; *Craft Horizons,* November/December, 1962; Miriam Blanton Huber, *Story and Verse for Children,* Macmillan, 1965; Martha E. Ward and Dorothy A. Marquardt, *Authors of Books for Young People,* 2nd edition, Scarecrow, 1971.

Obituaries: *New York Times,* September 12, 1976; *Time,* September 27, 1976.

CARTER, Samuel III   1904-

PERSONAL: Born October 6, 1904, in New York, N.Y.; son of Samuel Thomson, Jr. (a lawyer) and Annie (Burnham) Carter; married Justine Smith, September 5, 1929 (died, 1940); married Alison Nott (a writer), March 2, 1940; children: (first marriage) Peter Burnham, Dorothy de Longpre; (second marriage) Margo Alison. *Education:* Princeton University, B.A., 1927; Oxford University, B.A., 1929; Sorbonne, University of Paris, diploma, 1931. *Politics:* "No party affiliation." *Religion:* Presbyterian. *Residence:* Sandy Hook, Conn. *Agent:* Paul R. Reynolds, Inc., 12 East 41st St., New York, N.Y. 10017.

CAREER: J. Walter Thompson Co. (advertising firm), New York, N.Y., radio commercial writer, 1931-40, radio scriptwriter in Hollywood, Calif., 1940-48; National Broadcasting Company, New York, N.Y., editor of television scripts, 1950-55; radio and television scriptwriter and author, 1955—. *Member:* Authors Guild, Princeton Club (New York).

WRITINGS: How to Sail, Leisure League of America, 1936, revised edition, Sentinel Books, 1967; *Kingdom of the Tides,* Hawthorn, 1966; *Cyrus Field: Man of Two Worlds,* Putnam, 1968; *Lightning Beneath the Sea: The Story of the Atlantic Cable* (juvenile), Putnam, 1969; *The Boat Builders of Bristol,* Doubleday, 1970; *The Incredible Great White Fleet,* Crowell-Collier, 1970; *The Gulf Stream Story,* Doubleday, 1970; *The Happy Dolphins* (juvenile), Putnam, 1971; *Blaze of Glory: The Fight for New Orleans, 1814-1815,* St. Martin's, 1971; *Vikings Bold: Their Voyages and Adventures* (juvenile; illustrated by Ted Burwell), Crowell, 1972; *The Siege of Atlanta, 1864,* St. Martin's, 1973; *Cowboy Capital of the World: Dodge City* (juvenile), Doubleday, 1973; *The Riddle of Dr. Mudd,* Putnam, 1974; *Cherokee Sunset,* Doubleday, 1975; *The Last Cavaliers,* St. Martin's, 1979; *The Final Fortress,* St. Martin's, 1980.

Author of screenplays for 20th Century-Fox. Also author of television scripts for "Philco Television Playhouse," "Chevrolet on Broadway," "NBC Masterpiece Theatre," "Believe It or Not," and "Celanese Theatre." Author of radio scripts for "Lux Radio Theatre," "The Tommy Dorsey Show," "Duffy's Tavern," and "The Gracie Fields Show."

Contributor of short stories to *Colliers, Woman's Home Companion,* and others.

CARTLIDGE, Michelle   1950-

BRIEF ENTRY: Born October 13, 1950, in London, England. An author and illustrator of books for children, Cartlidge attended Hornsea College of Art, 1967-68, and Royal College of Art, 1968-70. She began drawing professionally in 1970 and held the first exhibition of her work the same year. In 1979 she received the Mother Goose Award, given to the brightest newcomer to British children's book illustrations, for her first children's book entitled *Pippin and Pod* (Pantheon, 1978). *Publishers Weekly* commented: "Minute details in Cartlidge's soft watercolors should appeal to small boys and girls. . . . The illustrations are the artist's fond representations of her homeplace, Hampstead in London, but the airy story is all her own." *Booklist* added, "The tiny white-faced mice are drawn in dainty line work that contrasts nicely with the bright splashy color of the park and market backgrounds, lending a warm feeling to this simply told tale," In *The Bears' Bazaar* Cartlidge uses a family of bears to demonstrate various projects young readers can do with their own families. In a review of the book, *Publishers Weekly* said, "Cheers for Cartlidge! . . . Colorful, minutely detailed pictures on each page amuse while they show the Bears' house filling up with trinkets fashioned from this and that. . . ." *Booklist* went on to say: "Full-color pen-and-ink drawings are cozy and instructive, picturing steps that the appended directions describe only briefly." Other self–illustrated books by Cartlidge include *A Mouse's Diary* (Lothrop, 1981) and *Teddy Trucks* (Lothrop, 1981).

CAVANAGH, Helen (Carol)   1939-

BRIEF ENTRY: Born December 4, 1939, in Quincy, Mass. Cavanagh attended Bay Path Junior College, 1957-58, and has held a variety of jobs including salesperson, waitress, secretary, teacher, model, newspaper reporter, and columnist. Cavanagh said: "I didn't realize it at the time, but these experiences would be valuable when I began to write steadily." As an author, Cavanagh has written several books for young adults. *Second Best* (Scholastic Book Services, 1979), a novel that deals with the feelings of inferiority in a younger sister, was described by *School Library Journal* as "a neatly done treatment of a common problem." In 1979 both *Second Best* and Cavanagh's second young adult novel, *Honey,* received awards from the New Jersey Institute of Technology. Most of the protagonists in Cavanagh's books are female and as she explains, "All these girls are me, and I feel their pain, but in my books *we* always win and learn a little more about ourselves, and become better people." Cavanagh's other young adult books, all published by Scholastic Book Services, include *Superflirt* (1980), *Wildfire Diary* (1980), *The Easiest Way* (1980), *My Day by Day Diary with Special Poems for Me* (1980), *Angelface* (1981), *A Place for Me* (1981), and *Summer Girl* (1982). She is currently working on three adult novels, *Driftwood, Daughter of Dawn,* and *The Apricot Idea. Home and office:* 29 Burgess Ave., Spotswood, N.J. 08884. *For More Information See: Contemporary Authors,* Volume 104, Gale, 1982.

CHORPENNING, Charlotte (Lee Barrows) 1872-1955

BRIEF ENTRY: Born January 3, 1872; died in January, 1955. Chorpenning is considered by many to be America's first serious and successful children's playwright. She studied the reactions of children in the theatre and then wrote numerous plays with the help of those observations. Chorpenning usually adapted well-known fairy tales for the stage and wrote only a few original plays. Educated at Iowa Agricultural College, she also attended Cornell University where she received her B.L. in 1894 and did her graduate work at Harvard University, 1913-15. Chorpenning worked for the Goodman Memorial Theatre of the Art Institute of Chicago, staging productions and writing and adapting plays. *Three Plays of Adventure* (Coach House, 1954), written for a company at this theatre, was described by *Drama* as "serviceably and well-structured to let out the stories they contain." For adults, Chorpenning wrote *Twenty-One Years with Children's Theatre* in which she revealed what children taught her and how she used what she learned.

Other works adapted by Chorpenning include *The Emperor's New Clothes, Hans Brinker and the Silver Skates, Cinderella, The Adventures of Tom Sawyer, Robinson Crusoe,* and *Hansel and Gretel. For More Information See: Twentieth-Century Children's Writers,* St. Martin's Press, 1978.

CLARKSON, E(dith) Margaret   1915-

PERSONAL: Born June 8, 1915, in Melville, Saskatchewan, Canada; daughter of Frederick Henry (a purchasing agent) and Ethel May (Brown) Clarkson. *Education:* Toronto Teachers College, teacher's certificate, 1935; University of Toronto, sabbatical year's study in English language and literature, 1961-62. *Religion:* Presbyterian. *Home:* 72 Gwendolen Crescent, Willowdale, Ontario, Canada M2N 2L7.

CAREER: Barwick, Ontario, public school teacher, 1935-37; Kirkland Lake, Ontario, supervisor of music in public schools, 1937-42; Toronto, Ontario, public school teacher, 1942-73.

E. MARGARET CLARKSON

Teacher of hymnology courses, Regent College, Vancouver, British Columbia, 1979, 1981. *Member:* Superannuated Teachers of Ontario, Hymn Society of America, Toronto Field Naturalists Club. *Awards, honors: Christianity Today's* hymn competition, first prize, 1982, for "God of the Ages."

WRITINGS: Let's Listen to Music, Gordon V. Thompson, 1944; *The Creative Classroom: A Study in the Teaching of Creative English,* Copp, Clark, 1958; *Susie's Babies* (juvenile), Eerdmans, 1960; *Our Father: The Lord's Prayer for Children* (juvenile), Eerdmans, 1961; *Growing Up* (juvenile), Eerdmans, 1962; *Clear Shining after Rain* (poems), Eerdmans, 1962; *The Wondrous Cross* (pictorial devotional), Moody, 1966; *Rivers among the Rocks* (poems), Moody, 1967; *God's Hedge* (pictorial devotional), Moody, 1967; *Grace Grows Best in Winter,* Zondervan, 1972; *Conversations with a Barred Owl,* Zondervan, 1975, reissued as *They Also Sing His Praises,* Zondervan, 1978; *So You're Single!,* Shaw, 1978; *Destined for Glory: The Meaning of Suffering,* Eerdmans, 1983. Also author of devotional booklets *Hope, God My Help, The Mercies of God,* and *Hurt, but Not Alone* published by Anchor, 1976-79; author of the lyrical text to *Celebration of Discipleship* (contata), Hope, 1976. Hymns (writes words and sometimes music) have been published in hymnals in Canada, the United States, England, Scotland, Ireland, and Asia. Contributor of numerous articles, poems, and stories to anthologies and religious and educational periodicals.

WORK IN PROGRESS: Devotional booklets; new hymns; updating her book on singleness.

SIDELIGHTS: "My mother says I learned to talk in rhyme. I can't remember not writing verses. I published my first poem at ten. . . . My first songs were set to music and sung when I was fourteen. . . . Most of my songs and poems have been religious, though not all of them. Though I have published books of poetry, I am probably best known for my hymns. . . . I don't need any special inspiration; I'm always just full of thoughts that must be expressed. It is a great joy to receive letters from all over the world telling of pleasure and/or help readers have found in my songs, poems, books, and articles. This keeps me going.

"I wrote *Susie's Babies* rather by accident. I was in my twenty-fifth year of elementary school teaching. We had a hamster in the room as a class pet (third and fourth grade), and the children wanted to have baby hamsters. I checked with my principal, we got Susie a little mate, Luke. Before very long Susie was pregnant.

"The children began asking me questions about the whole situation—how I knew she was pregnant, what Luke had done to her to make her pregnant, and so on. They asked me every question in the book and quite a few that never were in any book! I had answered questions of this kind in school before, but never had the whole subject of reproduction come before me in one specific instance as it did here. I have always believed that an honest question deserves an honest answer, so I answered each question honestly and carefully, explaining in children's language all that was happening. It was a holy and beautiful experience. Not once was there a snigger or any 'smart' remark—the children stood in awe before the wonder of life, both animal and human.

"The parents were so impressed with what was happening that a delegation of mothers came to ask me if I wouldn't write a book about it. They had other children, and all would not be in my class. . . . They knew I had already published two books, and that I could accede to their request if I wanted to.

"That summer I wrote *Susie* in three days. The book is almost a stenographic report of what actually took place in the classroom. I used the children's real names, and most of the questions answered in the book were actually asked by the child of that name. I had six doctors in my family of parents, so I asked two of them to check the text for accuracy, then sent it off to Eerdmans. No one was more astonished than I at the success that followed its publication.

"My other writings are the result of my own personal experiences and interests just as this book is. I just happen to have a great many interests—educational, religious, interests in the world of nature, outdoor living, homemaking, teaching, creativity—and all of it feeds into my writing, largely determining the shape of what I write. I have never married, so eventually I wrote a book on singleness. I have had a chronic illness all my life, so two or three books have to do with living with illness. I am profoundly musical, and that comes out in my songs and hymns, and in my first book, which was on the teaching of music. The songs just well up—they are a part of me. So is my personal Christian commitment—the essential 'me' that comes out in all my writing. I haven't an ounce of fiction in me—everything comes from personal experience.

"I spend my retirement in free-lance writing and speaking. [It's the] best job I ever had!"

Clarkson advises aspiring writers: "If you have to write, write. If it's any good, it will find a publisher. Work hard and critically, but don't ever hesitate to send your material out. There is plenty of outlet for anyone who has anything to say. . . . *Somebody* needs it."

FOR MORE INFORMATION SEE: Weekend, March 18, 1961; *Educational Courier,* May-June, 1961; *Decision,* December, 1981; *The Hymn,* July, 1983.

COLE, Joanna 1944-
(Ann Cooke)

BRIEF ENTRY: Born August 11, 1944, in Newark, N.Y. An editor and author, Cole attended the University of Massachusetts and Indiana University before receiving her B.A. from the City College of the City University of New York in 1967. From 1967 to 1968 she worked as an elementary school library teacher in Brooklyn. After spending some time as a letters correspondent at *Newsweek,* she became senior editor of books for young readers at Doubleday & Co. Cole has written over twenty books of fiction and nonfiction for children. Her nonfictional works are the more numerous, focusing on different aspects of the worlds of mammals, insects, and reptiles from a scientific viewpoint. They include titles such as *Cockroaches* (Morrow, 1971), *Giraffes at Home* (Crowell, 1972; written under the pseudonym Ann Cooke), *Twins: The Story of Multiple Births* (Morrow, 1972), *Plants in Winter* (Crowell, 1973), and *Saber-Toothed Tiger and Other Ice-Age Mammals* (Morrow, 1977). In each of her books, Cole attempts to explain the evolution, life cycle, and life style of her particular topic. *Library Journal* has called her work ". . . an invaluable addition to any science collection," while *New York Times Book Review* described her writing as "informative and light-hearted."

Reviewers have taken special note of a series of books written by Cole with photographs by Jerome Wexler. All published by Morrow, these books also incorporate factual observation with simple, concise explanations for young readers. The collection has been described by *Horn Book* as an ". . . outstanding series of books . . . all of which make the reader marvel at the surprising adaptations of animals." The series includes over ten titles such as *A Calf Is Born* (1975), *A Chick Hatches* (1976), *Find the Hidden Insect* (1979), and *A Cat's Body* (1982). Several of the books from this series have received special recognition. *A Chick Hatches* was selected for the Children's Book Showcase in 1977 and was also chosen as an ALA Notable Book along with *A Frog's Body* (1980), *A Horse's Body* (1981), and *A Snake's Body* (1981). In addition, *A Snake's Body* was named an honor book by both *Horn Book* and the New York Academy of Sciences. Cole's fictional books for children include *The Secret Box* (Morrow, 1971), *The Clown-Arounds* (Parent's Magazine Press, 1981). She is also the compiler of two books published by Doubleday, *Best-Loved Folktales of the World* (1982) and *A New Treasury of Children's Poetry* (1983). For adults she has written *Parents Book of Toilet Training* (Ballantine, 1983), first serialized in *Parent's Magazine* to which she is a regular contributor of articles. Cole is currently working on another book for parents dealing with children's manners. *Residence:* New York, N.Y. *For More Information See: Fifth Book of Junior Authors and Illustrators,* H. W. Wilson, 1983.

MARCUS CUNLIFFE

CUNLIFFE, Marcus (Falkner) 1922-

PERSONAL: Born July 5, 1922; son of Keith Harold and Kathleen Eleanor (Falkner) Cunliffe; married Mitzi Solomon, July 3, 1949 (divorced, 1971); children: Antonia, Sharon, Jason. *Education:* Oriel College, Oxford, B.A., 1944, M.A., 1946, B.Litt., 1947; University of Manchester, M.A., 1960. *Home:* 1823 Lamont St. N.W., Washington, D.C. 20010. *Office:* George Washington University, Rm. 102, Bldg. T, 2110 G St. N.W., Washington, D.C. 20052.

CAREER: Yale University, New Haven, Conn., Commonwealth Fund fellow, 1947-49; University of Manchester, Manchester, England, lecturer in American studies, 1949-56, senior lecturer, 1956-60, professor of American history and institutions, 1960-64; University of Sussex, Sussex, England, professor of American studies, 1965-80; George Washington University, Washington, D.C., professor, 1980—. Fellow, Center for Advanced Study in the Behavioral Sciences, Stanford, Calif., 1957-58; visiting professor of American history at Harvard University, 1959-60, City College of the City University of New York, 1970, and at University of Michigan, 1973; fellow, Woodrow Wilson International Center, Washington, D.C., 1977-78. *Military service:* British Army, 1942-46; became lieutenant. *Member:* American Historical Association, Royal Historical Society, American Studies Association, Society of American Historians, Massachusetts Historical Society. *Awards, honors:* D.H.L., University of Pennsylvania, 1976, and New England College, 1979.

WRITINGS: The Royal Irish Fusiliers, 1793-1950, Oxford University Press, 1953; *The Literature of the United States,* Penguin, 1954, revised edition, 1984; *History of the Royal Warwickshire Regiment, 1919-1953,* Clowes, 1957; *George Washington: Man and Monument,* New American Library, 1958, revised edition, 1982; *The Nation Takes Shape, 1789-1837,* University of Chicago Press, 1959; (editor) M. L. Weems, *Life of Washington,* Harvard University Press, 1962; *George Washington and the Making of a Nation* (juvenile), American Heritage Press, 1966; (with the editors of American Heritage) *The American Heritage History of the Presidency,* American Heritage Press, 1968; *Soldiers and Civilians: The Martial Spirit in America, 1775-1865,* Little, Brown, 1968; *American Presidents and the Presidency,* Eyre & Spottiswoode, 1969, McGraw, 1972, revised edition, 1976; (editor with Robin Winks) *Pastmakers: Some Essays on American Historians,* Harper, 1969.

(Editor) *The London Times History of Our Times,* Norton, 1971 (published in England as *The Times History of Our Times,* Weidenfeld & Nicolson, 1971); *The Ages of Man: From Savage to Sew-age,* American Heritage Press, 1971; *The Age of Expansion, 1848-1917,* Weidenfeld & Nicholson, 1974; (editor) *Sphere History of Literature,* Volume VIII and Volume IX: *American Literature,* Sphere Books, 1975; (editor) *The Divided Loyalists: Crèvecoeur's America,* Folio Society, 1978; *Chattel Slavery and Wage Slavery: The Anglo-American Context, 1830-1860,* Univeristy of Georgia Press, 1979. Contributor of articles to periodicals, including *American Heritage, American Quarterly, Commentary, Journal of American Studies, New Republic, Smithsonian* Magazine, and *Washington Post.*

WORK IN PROGRESS: A history of the idea of private property in the United States; a book on republicanism in America.

SIDELIGHTS: ''I am an Englishman who has a lifelong interest in America: its history, literature, and society. By a perhaps inevitable logic, I have moved across the Atlantic to an academic job in Washington, D.C. So far, with return visits to enjoy such British things as skylarks and red pillar boxes, I seem lucky enough to have the best of both worlds.''

HOBBIES AND OTHER INTERESTS: ''In general, the pursuit of happiness.''

DAHL, Borghild 1890-1984

OBITUARY NOTICE—See sketch in *SATA* Volume 7: Born February 5, 1890, in Minneapolis, Minn.; died February 20, 1984. Educator, author, and lecturer. The daughter of immigrants, Dahl reveals in her works the bond she felt with her Norwegian heritage and the struggles she endured with a lifelong eye ailment that eventually led to total blindness. She received her A.B. from the University of Minnesota in 1912, her M.A. from Columbia University in 1923, and, in 1924, was the first woman of a foreign country to be selected Norsk Akademiker at the University of Oslo in Norway. From 1912 to 1922 she taught in several Midwest high schools and was a professor of literature and journalism at Augustana College from 1926 to 1939. Her first book, *Glimpses of Norway,* was privately printed in 1935. It was followed by numerous books of interest to young adults, including the autobiographical books *I Wanted to See* and *Finding My Way,* and those centering on the life of Norwegian Americans, such as *Homecoming, This Precious Year, Under This Roof,* and *The Daughter.* For younger readers she wrote *The Cloud Shoes* and *Rikk of the Rendal Clan,* both based on Norse myths. In honor of her eightieth birthday, E. P. Dutton published *My Window on America* which chronicles the many events and changes that took place during her lifetime. Dahl was the recipient of the St. Olaf Medal, presented by King Haakon of Norway in 1950, for promoting good relations between Norway and the United States. More recently, she received the Outstanding Achievement Award for 1980 from the University of Minnesota. *For More Information See: Third Book of Junior Authors,* H. W. Wilson, 1972; *Contemporary Authors, New Revision Series,* Volume 2, Gale, 1981. *Obituaries:* School Library Journal, April, 1984.

DALY, Kathleen N(orah)

BRIEF ENTRY: Born in London, England. Daly grew up in France, Scotland, and on the island of Mauritius in the Indian Ocean. She received her M.A. from the University of Glasgow in 1951. Daly worked as a children's book editor for Blackie & Son in London, 1952-1953, and for Artists and Writers Press, Inc. in the United States, beginning in 1953. Her books for young children and for young adults have been published both in England and the United States. One of her books, *Body Words: A Dictionary of the Human Body, How It Works, and Some of the Things That Affect It,* has received considerable critical attention as a reference guide to the human body as a unique tool for children. There are approximately 500 terms listed, and Daly defines each carefully and matter-of-factly. Daly not only writes original children's books, but adapts children's stories as well. *Raggedy Ann and Andy,* written for younger readers, is one of her best. *Publishers Weekly* found it "bouncy and full of action, like the movie stills which delight the eye in these pages." Other books by Daly include *Animal Stamps* (Simon & Schuster, 1955), *The Giant Little Golden Book of Dogs* (Simon & Schuster, 1957), *The Cat Book* (Golden Press, 1964), *Ladybug, Ladybug* (American Heritage Press, 1969), *A Child's Book of Animals* (Doubleday, 1975), *Hide and Defend* (Golden Press, 1977), and *Strawberry Shortcake and Pets on Parade* (Parker Brothers, 1983).

DALY, Nicholas   1946- (Niki Daly)

PERSONAL: Born June 13, 1946, in Cape Town, South Africa; son of George (a carpenter) and Sarah (Mathusen) Daly; married Judith Mary Kenny (an artist), July 7, 1973; children: Joseph, Leo. *Education:* Cape Town Technikon, diploma, 1970. *Home and office:* 16 Crescent Rd., Claremont, Cape Province, South Africa. *Agent:* Laura Cecil, 17 Alwyne Villas, London N1 2HG, England.

CAREER: C.B.S. Record Company, London, England, singer and song writer, 1971-73; Advertising Agency, Cape Town, South Africa and London, junior art director, 1973-75; freelance illustrator, London, 1975-79; East Ham Technical College, London, graphics teacher, 1976-79; author and illustrator. *Member:* Association of Illustrators (London). *Awards, honors:* Award for Illustration from the British Arts Council and Provincial Booksellers, 1978.

WRITINGS—All fiction for children; all self-illustrated: *The Little Girl Who Lived Down the Road,* Collins, 1978; *Vim the Rag Mouse,* McElderry Book, 1979; *Joseph's Other Red Sock,*

NICHOLAS DALY

McElderry Book, 1982; *Leo's Christmas Surprise,* Gollancz, 1983.

Illustrator: Kathleen Hersom, *Maybe It's a Tiger,* Macmillan (London), 1981; Louis Baum, *I Want To See the Moon,* Bodley Head, 1984.

WORK IN PROGRESS: No So Fast Songololo has a black urban setting and may be published in English, Afrikaans, and two African languages; board books for preschool children.

SIDELIGHTS: "My interest in illustrating for children started after I settled in London.

"My first book, *The Little Girl Who Lived Down the Road,* was written by myself simply as an excuse to draw the pictures, after realizing that a completed product was more useful to a publisher than trying an unknown illustrator on the work of an established writer.

"I was very encouraged by the favourable reviews I received concerning the writing of *The Little Girl Who Lived Down the Road*—which spurred me on to further books.

"This first book was influenced by the technique and certain simplifying of form seen in the work of Maurice Sendak. I was also drawn to his work because of its emotional content. Nevertheless, I enjoyed working on my first book, very aware that I was using it to cut my teeth on. I do not think it at all a bad thing to allow influences to help you find your way— some illustrators don't need it, perhaps they have a clearer view to start off with. My drawings (that is my natural drawing) had been interfered with by the training I had as a graphic designer, where effects become paramount. Truth and emotion are of no consequence when drawing for advertising. The work I admire most is the work of illustrators who have these qualities—Ardizzone and Harold Jones, also the artists who left such a rich heritage to British illustration, for example, Tenniel, the various Punch Artists, and Ernest Shepard.

"It took about four years for me to pull out of the shadow of people like Edward Ardizzone and Harold Jones—Sendak's was much shorter lived. The very mechanical look of cross hatched drawing seemed to be less appealing or suitable to my temperament, which is more at home with a sketchy style—started in *Joseph's Other Red Sock* and further resolved in *Leo's Christmas Surprise.* I now feel that I'm working from my own source rather than other artists. I'm growing up as an illustrator.

"My work is based on drawing rather than painting. Because I love change I might like to discover a way in which I could illustrate work in a more painterly way. I find that there are two needs to fulfill as an illustrator, one is to develop as an artist and one is to always serve the needs of the text you're illustrating.

"As a writer/illustrator, I'm interested in themes which evolve around young children (one to six years) as they play around the home and on little excursions outside their home, the usual way children observe and interpret things which hold no charm to the adult eye—bath plugs which become telephones when held to the ear, or steering wheels when held firmly between fingers. I'm fascinated by the dual reality children have when playing games. On one level they know the bath plug is 'just a plug' but on another they can transform it into other things by their belief.

"*Maybe It's a Tiger* works beautifully on this level. I thought the writing of that book was really inspired. Unfortunately, I have misgivings over the execution of my illustrations.

"The board books which I'm interested in would make use of this area, a very simple story line revolving around an everyday incident, linked by a few key words. The child's insecurities as they pass from one phase to another is another aspect I find interesting to base ideas on: the reluctance that is felt when leaving things behind, how they need to handle their parents' expectations and that of the greater world outside.

"I find it particularly sad that the world outside the home allows so little freedom for children to retain their belief in fantasy and express themselves so fully. When I take Joseph out to the shops and he takes his 'dolly' with him, we're constantly being bombarded by the prejudices of others, chipping away at our belief that it's O.K. for boys to have dolls, for us to believe in Father Christmas or that pigs can fly for that matter.

"I must not neglect to mention my position as a children's writer/illustrator in South Africa. I returned for quite a few reasons, one being that I thought there would be a place for my work here. I still believe this, but it will take time. Apartheid exists in children's books as it does everywhere else in our lives in South Africa. It's amazing how it actually affects the books I might care to do here. Besides the moral issue, financially and politically, publishers are wary of the books they do for blacks. The black people have other needs which make the needs for children's books seem unimportant. However, I do believe this will not remain the case and soon the joy of having a relevant book must be felt by all children in South Africa. (Perhaps it's time for me to do a lot of ground work

"Joseph!" called Mum. "Are you awake?"
"Almost awake," Joseph yawned.
The sun was shining on the wall, toast was burning and Mum was singing to the music on her transistor radio.

(From *Joseph's Other Red Sock* by Niki Daly. Illustrated by the author.)

and think of earning a living as an illustrator in South Africa later).

"Some remark which was thrown at a white illustrator friend of mine whilst over in the States last year was 'How can you, as a white South African, work for a black market!' I thought this showed a typical lack of insight regarding both the function of an illustrator and as a white South African wanting peaceful change. My answer would be that if children's writers and illustrators can overcome laws of science and make pigs fly, then we can overcome anything our imagination will allow and produce relevant and entertaining books for all children. This is proven already by the way in which children's books can travel and retain their meaning and charm. Of course, not all books, but I think all those which work on a universal truth and emotion, common maybe to children of all races."

DUFF, Margaret K.
(Maggie Duff)

PERSONAL: Born in Walton, Indiana; daughter of Harvey Edward (in the insurance business) and Dulcie (a teacher; maiden name, Crim) Kapp; married Cloyd E. Duff (a musician), October 26, 1940; children: Jonathan, Barbara. *Education:* Butler University, A.B., 1937; Case Western Reserve University, M.L.S., 1966; also studied at Jordan Conservatory (now Butler

MARGARET K. DUFF

University) and Cleveland Institute of Art. *Home:* 1009 Green Mountain Dr., Green Mountain Meadows, Livermore, Colo. 80536.

CAREER: Cuyahoga County Public Library, Cleveland, Ohio, children's librarian in Solon Branch, South Euclid, and Gates Mills, 1966-81, developed and directed Puppet Center, 1975-81. Has exhibited paintings and sculptures in Cleveland and Indiana, and in private exhibits. Member of boards of trustees, Cleveland Orchestra Women's Committee, 1960-65, and Cleveland Institute of Music Women's Committee, 1970-76. Caldecott Committee, 1985. *Member:* American Library Association, International Board on Books for Young People, Mu Phi Epsilon, Pi Beta Phi. *Awards, honors: Rum Pum Pum* was selected one of *School Library Journal's* "Best Books of 1978" and was an International Reading Association's "Children's Choice," 1979; *Dancing Turtle* was selected "Children's Choice" by the International Reading Association, 1982.

WRITINGS—Under name Maggie Duff: *Johnny and His Drum* (juvenile; illustrated by Charles Robinson), Walck, 1972; (reteller) *Rum Pum Pum: A Folk Tale from India* (illustrated by Jose Aruego and Ariane Dewey), Macmillan, 1978; (reteller) *The Princess and the Pumpkin: Adapted from a Majorcan Tale* (illustrated by Catherine Stock), Macmillan, 1980; *Dancing Turtle* (illustrated by Maria Horvath), Macmillan, 1981. Contributor to *Top of the News* and to library journals.

WORK IN PROGRESS: Retelling of several folk tales; junior novel dealing with self-acceptance rather than imitation.

SIDELIGHTS: "I was born and raised in a very small Indiana town (one of three children), where there was not much in the way of 'advantages.' Fortunately, a very gifted young violinist and her family moved into town. There was always an air of mystery about this family, but nonetheless it was our good fortune that they had moved across the street from us. I was captivated by the sound of the violin, and at the age of five began taking lessons. Music became the most important part of my life. My sister and brother, already studying piano, soon started violin lessons also, as did other children in the vicinity. Before long we were all playing together as a Violin Choir— no doubt a forerunner of the Suzuki Violin method presentations. . . . It was a unique experience, and we were in great demand for concerts.

"When this group broke up, our family became a musical unit. Featured as a family group, with mother accompanying on the piano, we played concerts all over the state for service clubs (such as Rotary, Kiwanis and Lions), for churches, for high school commencement exercises, and even for radio. Music opened to us many otherwise closed doors, and enriched our lives immeasurably. Perhaps this is why I am drawn to stories that deal with music in one way or another. As a story-teller, I have always been in search of stories and attracted especially to those that deal with music or musical instruments.

"As a child, I composed stories for my friends, dabbled in watercolor painting, and was very involved in music . . . and so writing, art, and music became an integral part of my life and remain so. These interests have taken me around the world during the past two decades, as I traveled with my husband, a member of the Cleveland Orchestra until his retirement in 1981, on the orchestra's world-wide tours. These tours afforded me the opportunity to explore the literature and art of other countries.

Then Granny's tongue wagged on and on as she told of finding the enormous pumpkin and how she had discovered the great gaping hole. ▪ (From *The Princess and the Pumpkin* by Maggie Duff. Illustrated by Catherine Stock.)

"At the present time, I live with my husband in the mountains of Colorado where we own twenty-seven acres of land. Here, my husband and I live a relaxed and interesting life, and travel at will, both in the United States and in other countries. Writing continues, and there is time also for exploration of various art mediums."

HOBBIES AND OTHER INTERESTS: Music, art, books.

DYER, James (Frederick) 1934-

PERSONAL: Born February 23, 1934, in Luton, England; son of Frederick (a carpenter foreman) and Rose (Stevens) Dyer. *Education:* St. John's College, York, England, teaching certificate, 1958; University of Leicester, M.A., 1964. *Home:* 6 Rogate Rd., Cassel Park, Luton, Bedfordshire LU2 8HR, England.

CAREER: School teacher in Luton, England, 1958-66; Putteridge Bury College of Education, Luton, principal lecturer in archaeology, 1966-75; Harlington Upper School, Bedfordshire, England, teacher of archaeology and head of department, 1975—. Archaeological editor of Shire Publications, Princes Risborough, England, 1968—; governor of Stopsley Infant and Junior Schools, Luton, 1972—. *Military service:* Royal Air Force, 1953-56. *Member:* Society of Antiquaries (fellow), Prehistoric Society (member of council, 1972-76), Royal Archaeological Institute, Society of Authors, Institute of Field Archaeologists.

WRITINGS—All self-illustrated, except as noted: (With J. G. Dony) *The Story of Luton,* White Crescent Press, 1964; *Discovering Archaeology in England and Wales,* Shire Publications, 1969, 4th edition, 1976; *Archaeology in Denmark,* Shire Publications, 1972; *Southern England: An Archaeological Guide,* Noyes Press, 1973; *Your Book of Prehistoric Britain* (juvenile), Merrimack Book Service, 1974; (editor) *From Antiquary to Archaeologist: William Cunnington, 1754-1810,* Shire Publications, 1974; *Penguin Guide to Prehistoric England and Wales* (partly self-illustrated), Penguin, 1981; *Hillforts of England and Wales,* Shire Publications, 1981; *Teaching Archaeology,* Shire Publications, 1982. Editor of *Bedfordshire* Magazine, 1965-73.

WORK IN PROGRESS: A biography of James Wyatt, a Victorian newspaper editor and antiquarian who lived in Bedford, England from 1816 to 1878.

SIDELIGHTS: "I was interested in archaeology as a child and at the age of fifteen was allowed to take part in an excavation

JAMES DYER

in Oxfordshire. As a result I decided to devote my life to archaeological work, especially introducing it to children, by means of books and organizing practical work for them. Now I teach the subject to children, all of whom will take examinations in the subject, but will also, I hope, get a lifetime of interest from it, as I have done.

"I am particularly interested in the upstanding remains of the past in Western Europe and have traveled extensively to examine and record prehistoric material in museums and the countryside from Norway to Austria. I am involved in making my material available to children and in methods of teaching archaeology in English and Danish schools. I believe that I teach more archaeology to young people of fourteen to eighteen years than any other school teacher in Britain. This has made me something of an authority, and I am constantly being asked to lecture and write articles about my methods."

ECKE, Wolfgang   1927-1983

OBITUARY NOTICE: Born in 1927, in Dresden, Germany (now East Germany); died in an automobile accident about November, 1983. Author of literature for young people. A creator of more than one hundred radio plays for children, Ecke wrote mysteries for young people as well. His books, all translated from the German, were compared by some to Donald J. Sobol's "Encyclopedia Brown" series. Two of them, *The Face at the Window* and *The Invisible Witness,* were selected as favorite books by middle school readers in the Children's Choice poll conducted by the International Reading Association/Children's Book Council in 1982 and 1983 respectively. His other works include *The Stolen Paintings, The Bank Holdup, The Castle of the Red Gorillas,* and *The Case of the High Rise Robbery.* He also wrote a children's novel, *Flight toward Home,* which was adapted for television and aired in Europe. *For More Information See: Authors of Books for Young People,* 2nd edition supplement, Scarecrow, 1979. (Obituary information provided by Frank Jacoby-Nelson, foreign rights manager of Otto Maier Verlag, publisher).

ENGLISH, James W(ilson)   1915-

PERSONAL: Born January 13, 1915, in Phoenix, Ariz.; son of James Henderson (a farmer) and Fannie (Briedlove) English; married Dolores V. Hoffelder, December 18, 1948; children: Jamee Dolores, James W., Jr., Diane Marie, Richard Gregory, Stevan Michael, Jeffrey Douglas. *Education:* Phoenix Junior College, A.A., 1935; Vanderbilt University, B.A., 1937. *Politics:* Liberal Republican. *Religion:* Methodist. *Home:* 1046 Beau Brummel Dr., Route 1, Dundee, Ill. 60118.

CAREER: Worked at variety of writing assignments with United Press, *Arizona Highways,* U.S. Social Security Board, and others, 1937-40; *Boys' Life,* New York, N.Y., writer, and later executive editor, 1940-41, 1945-51; D.C. Cook Publishing Co. (religious publisher), Elgin, Ill., 1952-83, began as editorial director, than director of marketing, became director of denominational sales. *Military service:* U.S. Army, Counterintelligence Corps, 1941-45, 1951-52; served in Southwest Pacific; became first lieutenant (field commission). *Member:* Authors Guild, Rotary International.

WRITINGS: The Rin Tin Tin Story, Dodd, 1949; *Border Adventure,* Abelard, 1952; *Tailbone Patrol,* Holiday House, 1955; *Tops in Troop 10* (illustrated by Leonard Shortall), Macmillan,

JAMES W. ENGLISH

1966; *Handyman of the Lord* (biography of William Holmes Borders, a Negro minister), Meredith, 1967; (with Rose Butler Browne) *Love My Children* (Rose Butler Browne's autobiography), Meredith, 1969; *The Prophet of Wheat Street,* David C. Cook, 1973.

WORK IN PROGRESS: Nonfiction; teenage fiction, tentative title, *The Rice Paddy Scientist.*

SIDELIGHTS: "When I was growing up in Phoenix, Arizona, the Southwest was little known, sparse of population, and quite rural. I had to leave Phoenix because of the climate. The hot, dusty summers (except for the mountains) caused my hayfever to flourish into a major illness. Being an only child, saddled with this problem each summer, left me shy, timid, and introspective. Two wonderful men in the Boy Scouts brought me out of this self-pity syndrome.

"When I was a college freshman, my mother sent a short story to *Boys' Life,* the Scout magazine. They took it. I think I was more surprised than my Mom. Anyway, I kept the contact alive and as a result landed a reporter's job on *Boys' Life* in New York City after college. This was a wonderful job. One summer I went north, to the Rockies Cascades and Canada, to climb mountains, glaciers, and canoe; one winter I went camping in the Okefenokee Swamp in Georgia, mountain lion hunting in Arizona with a Zane Grey guide, and rafting down the Colorado's Glen Canyon before Lake Powell spoiled some wonderful scenery and strange history.

"In fact, I traveled so much I had to use three pen names to get all my yarns into the magazine. It was the perfect occupation for a nomad. It forced me into situations where I had to be counted on, and both my knowledge of the outdoors and competence in the wilderness mounted.

"Then came World War II and I was drafted. I landed in the Counterintelligence Corps (CIC), and after work around New York Port, went to the Southwest Pacific, where I earned a field commission. My tour of duty took me to Australia, New Guinea, New Britain, Philippines, and Japan.

"Perhaps my singular childhood taught me to be adaptable and observant. I came home and turned out two books and two *Boys' Life* stories based in part on wartime experiences. Then back to the magazine.

"I have always enjoyed sticking to truths and facts in stories, but I believe in humor and adventure as ingredients in my yarns. I did thirty–six 'Tailbone Patrol' yarns for *Boys' Life* with the above objectives in mind. Each yarn picked up the same group of guys, who were so lazy they invented ways to remain seated on their 'tailbones.' Needless to say, they often wound up doing twice as much work as would have originally been the case. This allows a writer, who enjoys doing dialogue, a golden opportunity to put in barbed and meaningful dialogue.

"This second stint with *Boys' Life* terminated with my being recalled into the Army for the Korean Affair. This time I never got beyond the Golden Gate, being stationed at the Presidio in San Francisco. When I got out I went to work for the David C. Cook Publishing Company in Illinois. The cornfields looked better than the canyons of Manhattan. I still miss the good music and plays.

"With my large family to support, out of necessity, I have been quite work oriented. But now that I am retired, I hope to get back to the typewriter."

FOR MORE INFORMATION SEE: Boys' Life, February, 1967.

FALSTEIN, Louis   1909-

PERSONAL: Born May 1, 1909, in Nemirov, Ukraine, Russia (now U.S.S.R.); came to the United States in 1925, naturalized citizen, 1936; son of Joseph and Bessie (Kammerman) Falstein; married Shirley Gesser (a guidance counselor), April 9, 1949; children: Jessica, Joshua. *Education:* Attended Lewis Institute, Chicago, Ill., 1930-32, and New York University, 1946-48. *Home and office:* 2571 Hubbard St., Brooklyn, N.Y. 11235. *Agent:* Bertha Klausner, International Literary Agency, Inc., 71 Park Ave., New York, N.Y. 10016.

CAREER: Writer, 1945—. Member of faculty at New York University, 1949-50, and City College (now of the City University of New York), 1956. *Military service:* U.S. Army Air Forces, 1943-45; received Purple Heart and Air Medal with three clusters. *Member:* Authors League of America.

WRITINGS: Face of a Hero (novel), Harcourt, 1950; *Slaughter Street* (novel), Lion Press, 1953; *Spring of Desire* (novel), Monarch, 1954; *Sole Survivor* (novel) Dell, 1954; (editor) *The*

LOUIS FALSTEIN

Martyrdom of Jewish Physicians in Poland, Exposition Press, 1963; *Laughter on a Weekday,* Astor–Honor, 1965; *The Man Who Loved Laughter: The Story of Sholom Aleichem* (juvenile), Jewish Publication Society, 1968.

WORK IN PROGRESS: Journey to a Violent Land (tentative title), a novel set in Detroit during the 1930's.

SIDELIGHTS: "I wrote *Face of a Hero* out of my experience as an aerial gunner in World War II. It was such an overwhelming experience that I wished to convey what it was like. Whether I succeeded or not is not for me to judge. *Sole Survivor* is the story of a Holocaust survivor who meets in New York and kills an ex-guard of a death camp. My choice of this theme needs no elaboration; the Holocaust is a subject most Jewish writers wish to write about sooner or later. As for the Sholom Aleichem biography, I wrote it because a publisher asked me to do it and paid me for doing it. As I am a great admirer of Sholom Aleichem, writing this book was for me a labor of love."

FENDERSON, Lewis H.   1907-1983

OBITUARY NOTICE: Born July 22, 1907, in Baltimore, Md.; died of an aortic aneurysm, December 12, 1983, in Washington, D.C. Educator, journalist, and author. Fenderson was a correspondent for the *Pittsburgh Courier* and an associate professor of English at West Virginia State College before joining the faculty of Howard University, where he became a professor of English in 1967 and helped to establish the university's department of journalism. In 1965 he received a grant from the *Washington Evening Star* to develop a book-length epic poem on the American Negro. Fenderson was the author of juvenile biographies on American black leaders, such as *Thurgood Marshall: Fighter for Justice* and *Daniel Hale William: Open-Heart Doctor*. His adult writings include *Modern Journalism* and *Effective Expression: A New Approach to Better Speaking. For More Information See: Directory of American Scholars,* Bowker, 1974; *Contemporary Authors,* Volume 106, Gale, 1982. *Obituaries: Washington Post,* December 16, 1983; *Jet,* January 9, 1984.

FORBES, Bryan   1926-

PERSONAL: Born July 22, 1926, in London, England; son of William Theobald Clarke Forbes and Judith Kate Helen Seaton; married Constance Smith, February 10, 1951 (divorced, 1955); married Nanette Newman, August 27, 1955; children: Sarah Kate Amanda, Emma Katy. *Education:* Attended Royal Academy of Dramatic Art, 1941-42. *Office:* Beaver Film Ltd., Beaver Lodge, The Green, Richmond, Surrey, England; and Bookshop, Virginia Water, Surrey, England.

CAREER: Actor on stage in England, beginning 1942; film actor in London, England, beginning 1948, and in Hollywood,

BRYAN FORBES

(From the movie "Seance on a Wet Afternoon," starring Kim Stanley and Richard Attenborough, original screenplay by Bryan Forbes. Released by Allied Film Makers, 1963.)

Calif., until 1959; Beaver Films, Surrey, England, co-founder, producer, and director, 1959; Associated British Productions Ltd. (now EMI Film & Theatre Corp.), London, head of production and managing director, 1969-71, managing director and chief executive of EMI-MGM Elstree Studios, Boreham Woods, England, 1970-71, executive producer of "The Go-Between," "The Railway Children," and "Tales of Beatrix Potter," all released by EMI, all 1971; director of Capital Radio, 1973—. Director of films by others, including "The Wrong Box," Columbia, 1965, and "The Stepford Wives," Fasdin, 1974; director of British segment of "The Sunday Lovers," MGM, 1980; director of "Macbeth" at The Old Victoria Theatre, London, 1980; director and leading man in "Star Quality" at Theatre Royal, Bath, England, 1982. Also director of "Whistle Down the Wind." Owner and operator of Bookshop, Surrey, British Broadcasting Corp. (BBC), member of general advisory council, 1965–69, member of schools council, 1971-73. *Military service:* British Army, Intelligence Corps, 1943-48. *Member:* British Film Academy (member of experimental film board), British Screenwriters Guild (member of council; council treasurer, 1960-63), British Actors' Equity Association, Writers Guild of Great Britain (trustee), Screen Actors Guild, Writers Guild of America, Directors Guild of America, Association of Cinema Technicians. *Awards, honors:* British Academy awards, 1959, for "The Angry Silence," 1962, for "Only Two Can Play," and 1964, for "Seance on a Wet Afternoon"; award from Writers Guild of Great Britain, 1962, for "Only Two Can Play"; United Nations award, 1962, for "The L-Shaped Room"; Edgar Award from Mystery Writers of America, and best screenplay award from San Sebastian Film Festival, both 1964, for "Seance on a Wet Afternoon."

(From the movie "International Velvet," starring Tatum O'Neal and Anthony Hopkins. Written, produced, and directed by Bryan Forbes. Copyright © 1978 by Metro-Goldwyn-Mayer, Inc.)

(From the movie "The Madwoman of Chaillot," starring Katharine Hepburn with Danny Kaye and Richard Chamberlain, based on the play by Jean Giraudoux. Co-produced and directed by Bryan Forbes. Copyright © 1969 by Warner Brothers-Seven Arts, Inc.)

WRITINGS: Truth Lies Sleeping and Other Stories, Methuen, 1951; *The Distant Laughter* (novel), Harper, 1972; *Notes for a Life* (autobiography), Collins, 1974; *The Slipper and the Rose* (novel), Quartet Books, 1976; *Ned's Girl* (biography of Dame Edith Evans), Little, Brown, 1977; *International Velvet* (based on screenplay), Mayflower Books, 1978; *Familiar Strangers* (novel), Hodder & Stoughton, 1979, published in America as *Stranger,* Doubleday, 1980; *That Despicable Race,* Elm Tree Books, 1980; *The Rewrite Man,* M. Joseph, 1983, Simon & Schuster, in press.

Screenplays: (And co-producer) ''The Angry Silence,'' British Lion, 1960; (and director) ''The L-Shaped Room,'' Columbia, 1962; (and director) ''Seance on a Wet Afternoon,'' Allied Film Makers, 1963; ''King Rat,'' Columbia, 1964; (and director and producer) ''The Whisperers,'' Lopert, 1966; (and director) ''Deadfall,'' Twentieth Century-Fox, 1967; (and co-producer and director) ''The Madwoman of Chaillot,'' Commonwealth United, 1968, Warner Brothers, 1969; (and director) ''The Raging Moon,'' EMI, 1970, released in United States as ''Long Ago Tomorrow,'' EMI, 1970; (co-author and director) ''The Slipper and the Rose,'' (musical), Cinderella Promotions Ltd., 1975, Universal Studios, 1976; (and director and producer) ''International Velvet,'' MGM, 1977; (and director) ''Jessie,'' BBC-TV, 1980; (and director) ''Ménage à Trois,'' Golden Harvest, 1981; ''The Naked Face,'' Cannon Films, 1984.

Author of filmed biography of Dame Edith Evans, released by Yorkshire Television, 1973, and a filmed biography of Elton John, Associated Television, 1974.

Fiction critic for *Spectator,* 1951-52. Contributor to popular British journals.

WORK IN PROGRESS: A novel.

SIDELIGHTS: ''I started writing during World War II, beavering away at very turgid novels which, happily, never saw the light of day. I was heavily influenced by Hemingway (naturally), Aldous Huxley and, most especially, by a great English writer, the late H.E. Bates.

''Much of my work, both literary and on the screen, has been concerned with aspects of love because I am passionately opposed to violence. In my opinion the daily dose of spurious violence spewed out *ad nauseum* by the television networks both in England and in the United States is harmful. I have no doubt that violence can be, and is, sold like any other product and we who are actively engaged in the mass media have a lot to answer for and have not pointed the way for young people, but have systematically invited them to the belief that violence is a normal way of life. I abhore this.

''I like directing young people. The very young have an instinct for portraying truth, for they work from basic principles and without benefit of professional training. Properly handled most children have a talent for acting which may or may not develop, but at a certain age and given the right auspices, I am convinced that I can get a truthful performance out of most young children. I like working with them for that reason. I exclude children who have been dragged onto the stage by Noel Coward's 'Mrs. Worthingtons' and are often a parody of their years. I have directed a number of young people, notably Hayley Mills, Tatum O'Neal and more recently Kimberley Partridge, and they have never disappointed me and have been a pleasure to work with.

(From the movie musical ''The Slipper and the Rose: The Story of Cinderella,'' starring Richard Chamberlain, screenplay co-authored by Bryan Forbes. Released by Universal Studios, 1976.)

''Of course one's personal experiences influence what one writes, for everything is grist to a writer's mill. But it is how he treats experience that matters. Just as there is no such thing as 'naturalistic acting' (acting is acting, not real life, but an impression of real life, and larger than life in most cases) there is no such thing as naturalistic writing. All art is selective and the writer selects from experience, allows the experience to gestate, and then when it is dragged from the sub-conscious and used it has matured in the wood, as it were, and is not just a carbon copy of that original experience, but possesses shades and colours. But writing, like all art, requires enormous discipline.''

HOBBIES AND OTHER INTERESTS: Reading, landscape gardening, photography, collecting books, collecting Napoleonic relics, ''avoiding bores.''

FOR MORE INFORMATION SEE: Bryan Forbes, *Notes for a Life,* Collins, 1974.

I have a little shadow that goes in and out with me,
And what can be the use of him is more than I can see.
He is very, very like me from the heels up to the head;
And I see him jump before me, when I jump into my bed.

—Robert Louis Stevenson

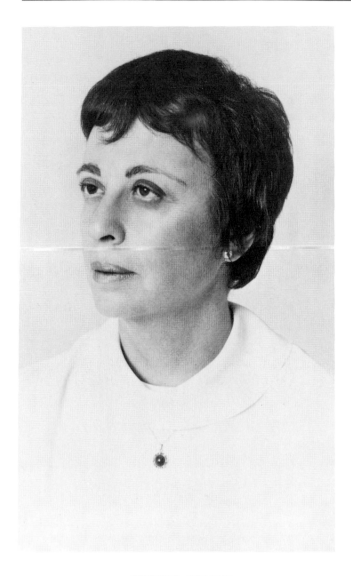

CORINNE GERSON

GERSON, Corinne

PERSONAL: Born in Allentown, Pa.; daughter of Henry and Selma (Deutsch) Schreibstein; children: Risa, Roger. *Education:* Moravian College, B.A. *Home:* Mt. Vernon, N.Y.

CAREER: On editorial staff of magazine and book publishers for eight years; full-time writing thereafter. *Member:* International P.E.N., Forum of Writers for Young People, Authors Guild, Authors League of America, Poets and Writers. *Awards, honors:* Christopher Award, 1981, for *Son for a Day.*

WRITINGS: Like a Sister (teenage novel), Funk, 1954; *The Closed Circle* (juvenile novel), Funk, 1968; *Passing Through* (teenage novel), Dial, 1978; *Tread Softly* (juvenile novel), Dial, 1979; *Son for a Day* (juvenile novel; illustrated by Velma Ilsley; Junior Literary Guild selection), Atheneum, 1980; *Choices* (contemporary adult novel), Tower, 1980; *How I Put My Mother through College* (juvenile novel), Atheneum, 1981; *Oh, Brother!* (juvenile novel), Atheneum, 1982; *Good Dog, Bad Dog* (illustrated by Emily McCully), Atheneum, 1983.

WORK IN PROGRESS: A novel for young people; an adventure story.

SIDELIGHTS: "I have been writing ever since I was in junior high school in Allentown, Pennsylvania. The day after graduation from Moravian College for Women I moved to a 'Y' in New York and found a job in publishing. I continued writing short stories and some were published in women's magazines, but I wasn't planning on doing a novel—not yet. One day while editing someone else's book on hobbies, I thought about my own childhood hobby of having pen pals all over the world and started imagining a situation where a German teenager would come to America after World War II to live with the pen pal's family. The result was my first novel, *Like a Sister.*

"I wrote my next book, *The Closed Circle,* under the hair dryer in a beauty shop. It's about a twelve-year-old girl in a Pennsylvania Dutch setting similar to my hometown. By now I had a daughter, Risa, and a son, Roger, in grade school. I split my time between writing and family pursuits, with a few extra rounds of volunteer work in open housing and supporting political candidates who always seemed to lose. One day I discovered that for some strange reason the best place to write was in the beauty shop, where I went every week with my spiral notebook and pen and scribbled away from the moment the dryer hood was lowered over my rollered hair till it was raised thirty minutes later. I would then rush home, transfer it to the typewriter, and take off from there. It all worked very well, as the momentum carried through till the next week, my hair always looked terrific—and the book got published!

"Nobody in the whole world knows this. You'll be the only one." ■ (From *Son for a Day* by Corinne Gerson. Illustrated by Velma Ilsley.)

"My third novel, *Passing Through,* is about a sixteen-year-old girl and boy who pass through each other's lives at a crucial time and pause for a very special relationship. Next was *Tread Softly,* about twelve-year-old Kitten Tate who was brought up by old-fashioned grandparents after her parents' death and who got into trouble from her need to slip in and out of a make-believe young, modern family.

"It was after this that Danny, my *Son for a Day,* cruised into my imagination. I wrote his story as the result of a casual remark by a man on a radio program about going to the zoo every weekend ever since his divorce because he didn't know what else to do on visiting day with his son. I had so much fun writing the book about Danny and his 'zoodaddies' that I could hardly wait to get to the typewriter each day.

"Most of my published work so far has been books for 'younger readers'—anywhere from eight to sixteen. I dealt with what I considered the important realities in my books for kids before the term 'problem novel' was invented. Now that children's literature seems to have used up that genre I have veered off toward the lighter side of kids' experiences. But they're the same kids, living with the same difficulties that reality hands out indiscriminately. Recently I wondered why my principal success has been with writing for younger people and realized it is because I unconsciously project how they react to particular incidents and situations. I have no idea why I do this; I just know I do it as naturally as I yawn or laugh or cry. For me, the writing itself is something almost organic—something I never learned but just did.

"My next book, *How I Put My Mother through College,* was another funny one about serious things. The following year came *Oh, Brother!,* a sequel to *Son for a Day.* Next was my first book for younger children, *Good Dog, Bad Dog,* which is based on our poodle who is probably smiling over the pages in doggie heaven. I have recently completed a fantasy/reality type novel and am just beginning a new adventure for Danny.

"Writing is a totally solitary—and, thus, lonely—occupation, and sometimes it is hard to bear the isolation, especially for someone who enjoys working with other people. But the rewards—of meeting my readers when I speak to groups, of receiving letters from them about my books—make up for it. And the thrill of seeing my pages transformed into printed, bound books, with beautiful covers, and finding them in libraries and bookstores—well, the thrill never wears off. It is like the thrill of getting that first idea for a story, so compelling that you must drop whatever you're doing and get it down on paper. And then, live with it, and let it drive you wild until it gets done, and you hold in your hands another of your creations."

FOR MORE INFORMATION SEE: Corinne Gerson, "Persist, Persuade, Prevail," *The Writer,* June, 1983.

GILSON, Jamie 1933-

PERSONAL: Born July 4, 1933, in Beardstown, Ill.; daughter of James Noyce (a flour miller) and Sallie (a teacher; maiden name, Wilkinson) Chisam; married Jerome Gilson (a lawyer), June 19, 1955; children: Thomas, Matthew, Anne. *Education:* Attended University of Missouri, 1951-52; Northwestern University, B.S. (honors), 1952-55. *Residence:* Wilmette, Ill. *Office: Chicago Magazine,* 3 Illinois Center, Chicago, Ill. 60601.

JAMIE GILSON

CAREER: Thacker Jr. High School, Des Plaines, Ill., speech and English teacher, 1955-56; Radio Station WBEZ, Chicago, Ill., writer/producer, 1956-59; Radio Station WFMT, Chicago, continuity director, 1959-63; Encyclopaedia Britannica Films, Chicago, writer, 1963-65; *Chicago Magazine,* Chicago, contributing editor and columnist, 1977—. Lecturer and writing workshop teacher, Wilmette Public Schools, 1974—. President, Community Review Committee, 1979-80. *Member:* Society of Children's Book Writers, Children's Reading Round Table, Society of Midland Authors. *Awards, honors:* Merit Award, Friends of American Writers, 1979, for *Harvey, the Beer Can King;* Carl Sandburg Award, Friends of the Chicago Public Library, 1981, and Charlie May Simon Award, 1983, for *Do Bananas Chew Gum?.*

WRITINGS—Juvenile novels; all published by Lothrop: *Harvey, the Beer Can King* (illustrated by John Wallner), 1978; *Dial Leroi Rupert, D. J.* (illustrated by J. Wallner), 1979; *Do Bananas Chew Gum?* (Junior Literary Guild selection), 1980; *Can't Catch Me, I'm the Gingerbread Man* (Junior Literary Guild selection), 1981; *Thirteen Ways to Sink a Sub* (illustrated by Linda Strauss Edwards), 1982; *4-B Goes Wild* (illustrated by L. S. Edwards), 1983. Also author of column, "The Goods," in *Chicago Magazine.* Contributor of articles to *WFMT Guide* and *Perspective* magazine.

WORK IN PROGRESS: A sequel to *Harvey, the Beer Can King* entitled, *Hot Dogs and Cats' Eyes.*

SIDELIGHTS: "My father was a flour miller and I grew up in small towns in Missouri and Illinois, riding the mills' scary, one-man, open elevators called man-lifts, eating handfuls of sweet-smelling wheat, meeting new friends at ice-cream socials, and moving away when a mill burned or my father found

Aaron was carrying his violin in a case, Lenny had the comb in his pocket, but I'd just brought my clarinet along plain, tucked under my arm. ■ (From *Dial Leroi Rupert, D.J.* by Jamie Gilson. Illustrated by John Wallner.)

a better mill job. As small mills closed, we moved to cities—Independence and Chicago.

"In grade school, I studied what was called Expression: Take one step forward, smile, say your piece as loud as possible, take one step back, and bow to polite applause. I loved performing. Even my writing was something to be said aloud—plays, skits, poems, orations. I had, as a senior, a weekly fifteen-minute children's show on radio station WOPA, Oak Park, Illinois.

"At Northwestern University I majored in radio and television education, so that when I started writing professionally it was still words to be spoken. At Chicago's educational radio station WBEZ, I wrote, directed, produced, and acted in dramatizations of the Chicago fire, the Fort Dearborn Massacre, the development of the atom bomb, 'The Bremen Town Musicians,' and 'The Three Little Pigs.' I developed voices with which I was everybody from the Wicked Witch of the West to Timmy Tooth. Then, for some years I was in commercial radio as continuity director of Chicago fine arts radio station WFMT. For a time, too, I wrote films and film strips for Encyclopaedia Britannica Films.

"Perhaps that explains why my books are told in the first person. And why, when I started my first book, *Harvey, the Beer Can King,* it seemed best to take out the tape recorder to interview three neighbor boys who shared a formidable beer-can collection. I still read everything aloud after I write it.

"*Do Bananas Chew Gum?* draws on my first big magazine story, an assignment from *Chicago Magazine* to write about Northwestern University's downstate Illinois archaeological dig. I discovered the real excitement that comes from finding broken arrowheads and shards of once-used clay pots. Sam Mott in *Bananas* shares that enthusiasm. One of the things Sam finds is a piece that was really discovered only a few blocks from my Wilmette, Illinois, home. I hope that children will not only find *Bananas* fun to read, but also revealing of the difficulties that a learning-disabled child faces.

"Before writing books for children, all of my professional writing had been for the voice—radio, TV, films—so that my books, too, are *told,* as a child would tell them. To keep that voice genuine, I work with children a good deal, speaking to them about my writing, teaching writing to sixth graders, sitting in with classes, going with a fifth grade class on a nature study overnight to prepare for *4-B Goes Wild.* My research is a joy."

FOR MORE INFORMATION SEE: Junior Literary Guild Catalog, October, 1980, March, 1981; *Early Years,* January, 1983; *Language Arts,* May, 1983.

GLADSTONE, M(yron) J. 1923-

PERSONAL: Born May 4, 1923. *Education:* Harvard University, S.B., 1944, M.A., 1946. *Home:* 310 East 75th St., New York, N.Y. 10021.

CAREER: Worked as managing editor, *Print* and *Print Collector's Quarterly,* Woodstock, Vt.; art and illustrations editor, G. & C. Merriam Co., Springfield, Mass.; promotion manager and sales representative, Yale University Press, New Haven, Conn.; advertising manager, Seven Arts Book Society, New York, N.Y.; manager of Collector's Book Society of McGraw-

. . .Although in most moderately snowy climates the figure seems to have developed naturally from the available material. There are national differences to be observed. ∎ (From *A Carrot for a Nose: The Form of Folk Sculpture on America's City Streets and Country Roads* by M. J. Gladstone. Photograph courtesy of the Library of Congress.)

Hill Book Co., New York, N.Y.; associate director of publications, Museum of Modern Art, New York, N.Y.; director of publications, Arno Press, New York, N.Y.; director, Museum of American Folk Art, New York, N.Y.; director, Publishing Center for Cultural Resources, New York, N.Y., 1973—.

WRITINGS: A Carrot for a Nose: The Form of Folk Sculpture on America's City Streets and Country Roads (ALA Notable Book), Scribner, 1974.

HALLINAN, P(atrick) K(enneth) 1944-

BRIEF ENTRY: Born November 1, 1944, in Los Angeles, Calif. An author and illustrator of children's books, Hallinan has been writing full-time since 1976. After attending the University of California at Berkeley, Foothill College, and California State University, he worked as a project scheduler for Lockheed Aircraft Corp., a copy writer, and an expediter in aerospace manufacturing. His nine books for young people (eight of which he illustrated) attempt to convey in words and pictures his "completely honest" philosophy. Steering clear of what he terms "impossible, imaginary creatures," he prefers instead to present stories in a realistic or true-to-life way. In *The Looking Book* (Childrens Press, 1973), brothers Mikey and Kenny discover the wonders of outdoor life after their mother shoos them away from the television set, handing each of them a pair of odd spectacles called "lookers." In another of his rhyming stories, *We're Very Good Friends, My Brother and I* (Childrens Press, 1973), a boy relates his pleasure at having a brother with whom to share many experiences. Commenting on the book's text and cartoons, *Publishers Weekly* labeled it "an attractive package," adding that it had "a gentle message." Other books by Hallinan (all published by Childrens Press) are *How Really Great to Walk This Way* (illustrated by Jim Buckley; 1972), *Just Being Alone* (1976), *That's What a Friend Is* (1977), *I'm Glad to Be Me* (1977), *Where's Michael?* (1978), *Just Open a Book* (1981), and *I'm Thankful Each Day* (1981). *For More Information See: Contemporary Authors,* Volumes 69-72, Gale, 1978.

HARRIS, Aurand   1915-

PERSONAL: Born July 4, 1915, in Jamesport, Mo.; son of George Dowe (a physician) and Myrtle (a drama teacher; maiden name, Sebastian) Harris. *Education:* University of Kansas City, A.B., 1936; Northwestern University, M.A., 1939; graduate study at Columbia University, 1945-47. *Agent:* Anchorage Press, Box 8067, New Orleans, La. 70182. *Office:* Department of Drama, University of Texas, Austin, Tex. 78712.

The charm of the play lies in the strengths and foibles of the animal characters who seem very human indeed as they react to disappointments, are frightened, and try to help each other with varying degrees of success. ■ (From "Winnie-the-Pooh" by Kristin Sergel, adapted from A. A. Milne in *Plays Children Love,* edited by Coleman A. Jennings and Aurand Harris. Illustrated by Susan Swan.)

AURAND HARRIS

CAREER: Children's playwright. Teacher of drama at public schools in Gary, Ind., 1939-41; William Woods College, Fulton, Mo., head of drama department, 1942-45; Grace Church School, New York, N.Y., instructor in drama, 1946-77; University of Texas at Austin, lecturer in drama, 1978—. Lecturer at Columbia University Teachers College, summers, 1958-63; lecturer at Western Connecticut State College, summer, 1976; visiting professor and director, University of Kansas, 1980, California State University, 1982. Playwright-in-residence at University of Florida, 1972, Youtheatre in Fort Wayne, Ind., 1979, Young Audiences, Cleveland, Ohio, 1981, and New Orleans Public Schools, 1984. Director and designer at summer theatres in Cape May, N.J., 1946, Bennington, Vt., 1947, Peaks Island, Me., 1948, Harwich, Mass., 1963-75, Youtheatre at Cleveland Playhouse, 1982-83. Member of advisory board of Institute for Advanced Studies in Theatre Arts. *Member:* Children's Theatre Association of America. *Awards, honors:* John Golden Award from Columbia University, 1945, for "Circus Day"; Anderson Award from Stanford University for "Missouri Mural," 1948; Marburg Prize from Johns Hopkins University, 1956; Horatio Alger Newsboy Award, 1967, for "Rags to Riches"; Chorpenning Cup from American Theatre Association, 1967, for "continued contributions to the field of children's drama in the writing of superior plays for young audiences"; creative writing fellowship from National Endowment for the Arts, 1976.

*WRITINGS—*Plays; all juvenile, except as noted: *Once Upon a Clothesline* (four-act; first produced in Fulton, Mo., 1944), Baker, 1945; *Ladies of the Mop* (one-act; adult), Baker, 1945; *The Doughnut Hole* (three-act; adult), Samuel French, 1947; *The Moon Makes Three* (three-act; adult), Samuel French, 1947; *Madam Ada* (three-act; adult), Samuel French, 1948; *Seven League Boots* (three-act; first produced in Cleveland, Ohio, 1947), Baker, 1948; *Circus Day* (three-act; first produced in Seattle, Wash., 1948), Samuel French, 1949, revised edition published as *Circus in the Wind*, 1960; *Pinocchio and the Indians* (three-act; first produced in Seattle, 1949), Samuel French, 1949.

And Never Been Kissed (three-act; adult; adapted from the novel by Sylvia Dee), Samuel French, 1950; *Simple Simon: or, Simon Big-Ears* (three-act; first produced in Washington, D.C., 1952), Children's Theatre Press, 1953; *Buffalo Bill* (three-act; first produced in Seattle, 1953), Children's Theatre Press, 1954; *We Were Young That Year* (three-act; adult), Samuel French, 1954; *The Plain Princess* (three-act; adapted from the book by Phyllis McGinley; first produced in Kalamazoo, Mich., 1954), Children's Theatre Press, 1955; *The Flying Prince* (two-act; first produced in Washington, D.C., 1965), Samuel French, 1958; *Junket: No Dogs Allowed* (three-act; adapted from story by Anne H. White; first produced in Louisville, Ky., 1959), Children's Theatre Press, 1959.

The Brave Little Tailor (three-act; first produced in Charleston, W.Va., 1960), Children's Theatre Press, 1961; *Pocahontas* (two-act; first produced in Birmingham, Ala., 1961), Children's Theatre Press, 1961; *Androcles and the Lion* (two-act; first produced in New York City, 1964), Children's Theatre Press, 1964; *Rags to Riches* (two-act; adapted from stories by Horatio Alger; first produced in Harwich, Mass., 1965), Anchorage Press, 1966; *Pinocchio and the Fire-Eater* (one-act; first produced in Gary, Ind., 1940), McGraw, 1967; *A Doctor in Spite of Himself* (two-act; adapted from a play by Moliere; first produced in New York City, 1966), Anchorage Press, 1968.

The Comical Tragedy or Tragical Comedy of Punch and Judy (two-act; first produced in Atlanta Ga., 1969), Anchorage Press, 1970; *Just So Stories* (three-act; adapted from stories by Rudyard Kipling; first produced in Tallahassee, Fla., 1971), Anchorage Press, 1971; *Ming Lee and the Magic Tree* (one-act), Samuel French, 1971; *Steal Away Home* (two-act; adapted from the story by Jane Kristof; first produced in Louisville, Ky., 1972), Anchorage Press, 1972; *Peck's Bad Boy* (three-act; adapted from the novel by George Wilbur Peck; first produced in Harwich, Mass., 1973), Anchorage Press, 1974; *Yankee Doodle* (two-act; first produced in Austin, Tex., 1975), Anchorage Press, 1975; *Star Spangled Salute* (two-act; first produced in Harwich, 1975), Anchorage Press, 1975; *Six Plays for Children*, edited by Coleman A. Jennings (contains "Androcles and the Lion," "Rags to Riches," "Punch and Judy," "Steal Away Home," "Peck's Bad Boy," and "Yankee Doodle"), University of Texas Press, 1977; *Robin Goodfellow* (two-act; first produced in Harwich, 1974), Anchorage Press, 1977; *A Toby Show* (three-act; first produced in Austin at University of Texas Theatre, 1978), Anchorage Press, 1978; *Ralph Roister Doister* (one-act; adapted from a play by Nicholas Udel), Baker, 1978; *Cyrano de Bergerac* (one-act; adapted from the play by Edmond Rostand), Baker, 1979; *The Romancers* (one-act; adapted from the play by Edmund Rostand), Baker, 1979; *Candida* (one-act; adapted from the play by George Bernard Shaw), Baker, 1979.

The Arkansas Bear (one-act; first produced in Austin, Tex), Anchorage Press, 1980; (with Coleman Jennings) *Plays Children Love: A Treasury of Contemporary and Classic Plays for Children*, Doubleday, 1981. "Treasure Island" (two-act; adapted from the story by Robert Louis Stevenson), first produced in Northridge, Calif., 1982.

Contributor: Dorothy Schwartz, editor, *Give Them Roots and Wings*, American Theatre Association, 1972; Nellie McCaslin, editor, *Children and Drama*, Longman, 1977, revised edition, 1981.

Work represented in six anthologies, including *Twenty Plays for Young People* and *Contemporary Children's Theatre*.

WORK IN PROGRESS: The Magician's Nephew, a dramatization of C. S. Lewis' *Narnia* story.

SIDELIGHTS: "I write plays for youth theatre because I like theatre, I like children, and I like what children like in the theatre—a good story, interesting characters, visual excitement and beauty, suspense, music, and comedy. In youth theatre there is the freedom to write in any style or use any appropriate dramatic form. There is the challenge of breaking new ground. And there is the reward of the spontaneous applause of a young, critical, and appreciative audience. There is also the practical side. Children's theatre is one area in American drama that is growing both in quality and quantity, which means a present and increasing market for good scripts.

"With the exception of a few professional companies, I think the best children's drama is produced in regional theatres across the nation. There is no 'Little Broadway' for a children's playwright, which is healthy. Instead of being bound by the provincial tastes of a New York Broadway, children's theatre is a part of the varied tastes, demands, and mores of the entire country.

"I am proud to be part of a growing movement in American drama and have no regrets about giving up a promising career of writing for adults. I once suggested to the late Pulitzer Prize-winning playwright William Inge that he write a play for youth theatre. Inge replied, 'I have nothing to say to children.' In the same manner, perhaps I have nothing to say to adults. But happily I do have many stories to 'show and tell' to children."

Androcles and the Lion has been translated into six languages and has been performed more than seven thousand times around the world.

HAYNES, Betsy 1937-
(James Betts, a joint pseudonym)

BRIEF ENTRY: Born October 20, 1937, in Benton, Ill. Author of novels for young adults and young readers. Haynes attended the University of Illinois and received a degree in journalism from Southern Illinois University in 1962. She has been employed in a variety of jobs, including switchboard operator, insurance claims examiner, and secretary. In 1978 she was awarded the Journalism Alumnus Award from her alma mater's School of Journalism. Her first novel for young adults, *Cowslip* (Thomas Nelson, 1973), is the story of a thirteen-year-old slave girl and the hardships she endures at the hands of a cruel Kentucky plantation master. Also published in paperback as *Slave Girl* (Scholastic Book Services, 1973), it received the 1974 Book for Brotherhood award from the National Conference of Christians and Jews. Haynes's other young adult novels include *Spies on the Devil's Belt* (Thomas Nelson, 1974), based on an actual American Revolution espionage operation, *The Ghost of the Gravestone Hearth* (Thomas Nelson, 1977), *The Shadows of Jeremy Pimm* (Beaufort Book Co., 1981), and *The Power* (Dell, 1982). Under the joint pseudonym James Betts, she and her husband James Haynes are the authors of another young adult book, *Demon Wheels* (Dell, 1983). For a somewhat younger reading audience, Betsy Haynes has written two books based on the "growing pains" of a pretty, young fifth-grader. They are *The Against Taffy Sinclair Club* (Thomas Nelson, 1976) and *Taffy Sinclair Strikes Again* (Bantam, 1984). *Address:* Route 2, Newton, Iowa 50208. *For More Information See: Contemporary Authors, New Revision Series,* Volume 8, Gale, 1983.

HEMPHILL, Martha Locke   1904-1973

PERSONAL: Born July 25, 1904, in Fort Dodge, Iowa; died October 17, 1973; daughter of Charles Alison (an artist) and Maude Lillian (Preston) Locke; married Lester G. Hemphill (a teacher), October 31, 1925 (deceased); children: Shirley (Mrs. James J. Magarian), Lester, Mary (Mrs. J. R. Swihart), JoEllen. *Education:* Attended Morningside College, 1922-23, University of Chicago, 1923-26, and Colorado State University, summers, 1927-29; National Children's Center, Green Lake, Wis., graduate. *Politics:* Democrat. *Religion:* Protestant. *Residence:* Fort Wayne, Ind. 46805.

CAREER: Ginn & Co., Boston, Mass., member of editorial department, 1923-26; South Wayne Baptist Church, Fort Wayne, Ind., director of nursery school, 1943-47; Crescent Avenue United Methodist Church, Fort Wayne, Ind., director of ministry for children and families, beginning in 1957. Instructor in early childhood education, Fort Wayne Campus, Purdue University, beginning in 1967. National Laboratory School teacher in Chicago, Ill., San Diego, Calif., and Green Lake, Wis. Member of board of directors, Child Care of Allen County; member of Martin Luther King Montessori School Board. *Member:* National Association for the Education of Young Children, Association for Childhood Eudcation International, Midwest Association for the Education of Young Children, Indiana Association for the Education of Young Children.

*WRITINGS—*All published by Judson: *The Three at Vacation Church School* (juvenile), 1953, revised edition, 1963; *Thank You God* (juvenile), 1963; *When Children Worship* (a compilation), 1963; *A Book about Jesus* (juvenile; illustrated by Al Fiorentino), 1969; *Christmas* (juvenile), 1969; *Are You My Friend?* (juvenile; illustrated by Joanne Isaac), 1969; *Partners in Teaching Young Children,* 1972; *Weekday Ministry with Young Children: A Manual for the Church Nursery School,* 1973. Contributor to *Baptist Leader* and other religious magazines.

FOR MORE INFORMATION SEE: Ontario Bible College, June, 1972.

We can never know that a piece of writing is bad unless we have begun by trying to read it as if it was very good and ended by discovering that we were paying the author an undeserved compliment.

—C.S. Lewis

FRANK HERBERT

HERBERT, Frank (Patrick)   1920-

PERSONAL: Born October 8, 1920, in Tacoma, Wash.; son of Frank and Eileen Marie (McCarthy) Herbert; married Flora Parkinson, March, 1941 (divorced, 1945); married Beverly Ann Stuart, June 23, 1946; children: (first marriage) Penelope (Mrs. David R. Merritt), (second marriage) Brian, Bruce. *Education:* University of Washington, Seattle, student, 1946-47. *Residence:* Port Townsend, Wash. *Agent:* Lurton Blassingame, 60 East 42nd St., New York, N.Y. 10017; and Ned Brown, P.O. Box 5020, Beverly Hills, Calif. 90210.

CAREER: Newspaperman with West Coast papers from Los Angeles to Seattle, including more than ten years on staff of San Francisco *Examiner;* novelist specializing in science fiction. Member of national council, World Without War Council, 1970-73, and member of Seattle council, 1972—. Lecturer at University of Washington, Seattle, 1970-72; consultant on social and ecological studies to Lincoln Foundation, 1971. Director-photographer of television show, "The Tillers," 1973. *Awards, honors: Dragon in the Sea* (also variously titled *Under Presser* and *Twentieth Century Sub*) was co-winner of International Fantasy Award, 1956; *Dune* was winner of Nebula Award of Science Fiction Writers of America as best novel, 1965, and co-winner of Hugo Award of World Science Fiction Convention as best novel, 1966; Doctor of Humanities, Seattle University, 1980.

WRITINGS: Dragon in the Sea (originally titled *Under Pressure;* first published in *Amazing Science Fiction,* 1955), Doubleday, 1956, reissued as *Under Pressure,* Ballantine, 1973.

It was as though someone had dropped this ground from space and left it where it smashed. ■
(Jacket illustration by Abe Echevarria from *Dune* by Frank Herbert.)

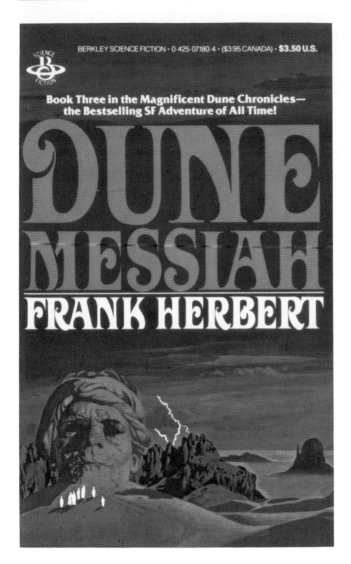

(Cover illustration by Vincent DiFate from *Dune Messiah* by Frank Herbert.)

Dune (first published in *Analog,* December, 1963-February, 1964 and January-May, 1965), Chilton, 1965, reissued, Putnam, 1984; *Great Brain* (first published in *Amazing Stories,* March, 1965), Berkley Publishing, 1966; *Destination: Void* (first published in *Galaxy,* August, 1965), Berkley Publishing, 1966; *Eyes of Heisenberg* (first published in *Galaxy,* June-August, 1966), Berkley Publishing, 1966; *Heaven Makers* (first published in *Amazing Stories,* April-June, 1967), Avon, 1968; *The Santaroga Barrier* (first published in *Amazing Stories,* February, 1968), Berkley Publishing, 1968.

Dune Messiah (first published in *Galaxy,* July-September, 1969), Putnam, 1970; (with others) *Five Fates,* Doubleday, 1970; *Whipping Star* (first published in *If,* January-March, 1970), Putnam, 1970; (editor) *New World or No World,* Ace Books, 1970; *Worlds of Frank Herbert* (anthology), Ace Books, 1971; *The God Makers,* Berkley Publishing, 1971, hardcover edition, Putnam, 1972; *Soul Catcher* (ALA Notable Book), Putnam, 1972; *Book of Frank Herbert,* Daw Books, 1973; *Threshold: The Blue Angels Experience,* Ballantine, 1973; *Hellstrom's Hive* (first published as *Project 40* in *Galaxy,* 1972), Bantam, 1974; *The Best of Frank Herbert,* Sphere Books, 1974; *Chil-*

dren of Dune, Berkley, 1976; *The Dosadi Experiment,* Putnam, 1977; *The Illustrated Dune,* Berkley, 1978; *The Great Dune Trilogy* (contains *Dune, Dune Messiah,* and *Children of Dune*), Gollancz, 1979; (with Bill Ransom) *The Jesus Incident,* Berkley, 1979, reissued, 1984.

Direct Descent, Ace Books, 1980; *Priests of Psi,* Gollancz, 1980; (with Max Barnard) *Without Me You're Nothing: The Essential Guide to Home Computers* (nonfiction), Simon & Schuster, 1981; *God Emperor of Dune* (Literary Guild selection), 1981; (editor) *Nebula Awards Fifteen* (anthology), Harper, 1981; *The White Plague,* Putnam, 1982; *Heretics of Dune,* Putnam, 1984; *The Dune Encyclopedia,* Putnam, 1984; *The Lazarus Effect,* Berkley, 1984.

Recordings: "Sandworms of Dune," Caedmon, 1978; "The Truths of Dune," Caedmon, 1979; "The Battles of Dune," Caedmon, 1979. Contributor of fiction to *Esquire, Galaxy, Amazing Stories,* and other magazines.

ADAPTATIONS—Motion pictures: "Dune" (screenplay by David Lynch), Universal, 1984.

Books: Joan Vinge, *The Dune Storybook* (adapted from the screenplay by David Lynch, which is based on the book *Dune*), Putnam, 1984; *Dune: The Making of Dune* (based on the making of the movie "Dune"; reported by Ed Naha), Berkley, 1984; *The Art of Dune* (includes artwork from the film and the complete screenplay), Berkley, 1984.

Teaching kits: "The World of Dune" (teaching kit for junior and senior high school teachers), Life-time Learning Systems, Inc., 1984.

SIDELIGHTS: **October 20, 1920.** Born in Tacoma, Washington. ". . . I developed *all* of my basic ideas during my childhood years on our family's farm. I milked cows—by hand—for over half of my early childhood years . . . on a small subsistence farm in Kitsap County, Washington. And I can still clench my hands like you wouldn't believe.

". . . There were pigs to feed, and I had corn and such to hoe. I once even reared and canned 500 chickens as a 4-H project. We raised all our own food, so—although I grew up during the Depression—I never had to worry about being hungry. In fact, I remember those 'bad years' as marvelous times, because I spent them in the company of a kind of large, extended family. My father had six brothers, so I never lived far from aunts and uncles. . . .

". . . I knew what I wanted to do with my life even when I was quite young. In fact, on my eighth birthday I told my family, 'I'm going to be an author.'" ["Plowboy Interviews: Frank Herbert: Science Fiction's 'Yellow Journalist' is a Homesteading 'Technopeasant'," *Mother Earth News,* number 69, May/June, 1981.[1]]

1946-1947. Attended the University of Washington.

Over the years Herbert had many jobs, including work as a professional photographer and television cameraman, radio news commentator, oyster diver, and jungle survival instructor, although his first ambition to become a writer never left him. ". . . I've never really strayed far from that goal. I was employed as a newspaper writer for many years, and I took those jobs because I saw the field as a training ground that would financially support my own writing while helping me learn to use the tools of my trade. In addition, I put in some time as a radio and television commentator. And I've done a lot of photojournalism work . . . I was picture editor of the San Francisco *Examiner* for quite a few years.''[1]

1950. Began to write science fiction stories. ''. . . I had been writing adventure fiction and pulp stuff. I had sold to *Esquire*, and I started looking around for a field that really would catch my interest and that I could grow in. I looked at science fiction, and it struck me that there was a lot of elbow room in it, that you had fewer literary restrictions in what you did, and I liked the imaginative room this allowed.''

1956. Published *The Dragon in the Sea*, his first work of science fiction to appear in book form. This first novel won the International Fantasy Award and established Herbert's reputation in science fiction writing. ''. . . I approach a writing project pretty straightforwardly. I research the scientific information I need, I build the characters in my mind and on paper, set up the situation to fit the idea around which I'm constructing a story, and then sit down and write the story.

''My wife is my best critic; she takes a critical look at everything I do and is extremely helpful.''

1965. Second major novel, *Dune*, published. In *Dune* and its sequels, *Dune Messiah*, *Children of Dune*, and *God Emperor of Dune*, Herbert portrays life and government on a harsh desert planet. In an effort to create a better life for its citizens, the government works to increase the water supply in their environment. ''Dune was so arid that the very idea of water coming down from the skies in rain, and of great rivers flowing over the land, conjured up visions of paradise. But when that one change was *made*, it had a regular 'domino theory' series of consequences that hadn't been anticipated. Indeed, by the time Dune reached the state described in my fourth desert planet book—*God Emperor of Dune*—the changes had pretty well eliminated individualism!

A speculative look spread over the PN's face. "That's pretty big trouble you'd be stirring up there, son." ■ (From *Direct Descent* by Frank Herbert. Illustrated by Garcia.)

Anger boiled in Sil-Chan.... "He's selling us out," **Sil-Chan muttered.** ■ (From *Direct Descent* by Frank Herbert. Illustrated by Garcia.)

''I feel that the historical interrelationship between the native Fremen and their desert planet had created what amounted to a religion. They had learned not to question the way to behave in their environment, but to act in certain ways on faith. They were locked into their system. So, even when the environment changed, the people didn't change their social mythology, their values, or their ways of relating to one another.

''. . . I think there are such things as psychological ecology, religious ecology, economic ecology, etc. And none of them can exist in a vacuum. They're all interrelated. So whenever we make decisions and put them into effect, we ought to review and assess *all* the potential results.

''The people I distrust most are those who *want* to improve our lives but have only *one* course of action in mind.

''Too many ecologically concerned individuals seem to think that simply getting rid of *one* noxious environmental pollu-

He heard the message of Tamanawis, the greatest of spirits, as a drumbeat matching the beat of his heart. ■ (Cover illustration by Wayne Barlowe from *Soul Catcher* by Frank Herbert.)

tant—whether that 'culprit' be nuclear power, commercial pesticides, or whatever—will solve all our problems.''[1]

1970-1972. Taught at the University of Washington. ''I actually don't think you can teach writing. People learn to write by writing. What you can do is teach them the plumbing, the care and feeding of editors, how to know when you're being badly screwed on a contract, that kind of thing. You can show them techniques that have been used and let them try them on, like trying on Grandma's clothing. But the whole idea is to write and develop your own style. I have always been right up front with people about that.''

''. . . I once taught a course, at the University of Washington, that was called Utopia/Dystopia. It was billed as an examination of the current state of our country and our myths of the 'better life' . . . only I had trouble getting my students to really investigate their own premises about technology and lifestyle.

''So I hit on the idea of taking them out for a long weekend hike in the Olympic mountains . . . in the early spring when

I *knew* the weather was going to be cold and rainy. All I told my class was, 'We'll be out in the Olympics for two nights. It's going to rain. Bring your gear, food, and paper and pencils for taking notes. I'll meet you at the trail's head.'

''Now, I'm a hedonist in the wilderness. I own a good down sleeping bag and a fine one-man tent with a fly, and carry a very light pack stocked with trail food and the like. Naturally, my gear is pretty much a *product* of high technology.

''Once we all got up to our campsite—at a place called the Flats—I set up my tent, dug a drain trench, stashed some firewood under the canopy for the morning, and helped organize the evening meal. We ate and hit the sack . . . and *then* the rain came. Well, I was quite dry and comfortable in my tent, but a lot of my students weren't so well prepared. During the night I heard voices crying, 'My sleeping bag's all wet!' or 'God, it's cold!' I simply rolled over and went back to sleep.

''The next morning, I got up early and built a big fire. The shivering students soon gathered round, we scrounged together something to eat, and afterward I told them to get their note pads. Then I said, 'OK, the bomb just dropped and we're all that's left. How much of our former technology do we try to reconstitute?' Well, let me tell you . . . those cold, wet people who had eaten an inadequate breakfast looked at society's technology a good bit more closely than they had when sitting in a comfortable university classroom. Students who'd been saying things like 'Oh sure, I could do without all this stuff' began to ask some basic questions, and to comprehend that technology isn't bad in and of itself . . . everything depends on how we use it.''[1]

1971. A recognized expert on ecology, Herbert served as a consultant in social and ecological studies to the countries of Vietnam and Pakistan. ''It was on land reclamation and land reform. Pakistan, for example, has a social, semireligious— that is, ritual—use of goats. They sacrifice them, eat them, count them as wealth. Goats are browsers. We estimated that goats were making desert in Pakistan at the rate of about one hundred thousand acres a year. But the entire subcontinent, including Pakistan right up to the Northwest Territory—up around the Kyber Pass—has a long tradition of water management, of having communal water systems and distributing water equitably. They also have an enormous reservoir of artesian water coming down from the Himalayas; they can get this water with tube wells drilled six hundred to fifteen hundred feet deep. We surveyed areas such as the Soan Valley there and projected a land-use policy and a redistribution policy to create more landowners, more land parcels a little bit better than subsistence farm holdings. Now what they're going to do with it I don't know. They do have now a reclamation project going on in the Soan Valley but I haven't been in touch with it for more than three years.''

Herbert is an active campaigner for the conservation of natural resources. One of his major ecological experiments has been to turn his own six-acre wooded tract in Port Townsend, Washington, into an ecological demonstration project to show how a maximum of quality life can be maintained with a minimal energy drain.

''What I did there was take an existing house, and work out a few things that could be done to reduce the demand on existing energy. We built a solar space heater for the house, for example. It went right on the roof and was a convection pumping system to heat air in the house—very easily adaptable, by the way, to A-frame-type structures. This is not an A-frame struc-

(From the forthcoming movie "Dune," starring Sting and Kyle MacLachlan. Copyright © 1983 by Universal City Studios, Inc.)

ture, but it is like an A-frame in that it has high ceilings. There are a lot of those around, and a great deal of energy is used up to heat them. I devised a system that would heat the air in the house, even on cloudy days, and redistribute it throughout the house with an existing furnace system, just by running a fan.

"In addition, we developed a wind machine, which we've patented. . . . We've designed a wind machine that will run in a fifty-mile-an-hour wind. Our thought is to pump salt water up into large reservoirs and run it down on demand through turbines to generate electricity. . . . It is a state-of-the-art way of using wind energy. It won't take up all of the slack on the electrical-energy demand, but it will certainly take up a large chunk of it. That's the sort of thinking we have to use. John Oppenheimer, my partner in the wind machine, and I decided that there had not been any really new thinking on the wind machine since the Dutch windmill. But we know a great deal more now about movement of air, the use of airfoils, that sort of thing."

1973. Writer, director, and photographer of television special, *The Tillers*.

1984. Herbert's book, *Dune,* was adapted into a movie by Universal Studios. About contemporary science-fiction movies that have been produced, Herbert said: ". . . The production has not all been bad. Neville Shute's *On the Beach* set in Australia; *Who Goes There?* was a good one, and *The Day of the Triffids*. There have been any number of really good movies that have been done on a science-fiction base and that could only be done as science fiction. But the current crop doesn't have much to say for it; it's kind of catering to several denominators, including the lowest common one. But I enjoyed the television series 'Star Trek,' for example, and I think it did a great service for science fiction in general. There are a lot of clichés in science fiction. 'Star Trek' on TV educated the general public to these clichés, and in doing so broadened the audience enormously. It was a control-room drama, designed to keep down production costs but to tell these stories anyway. It did very well. Roddenberry deserves kudos for what he did."

As winner of both the Nebula and Hugo Awards, Herbert's *Dune* remains a classic in science fiction writing, and the ideas proposed in it have been discussed in various university courses. ". . . There's a list of about fifteen different kinds of courses that are using *Dune,* for example, as a textbook, including

Director David Lynch with *Dune's* author, Frank Herbert, on the first day of shooting.

architecture, philosophy, psychology, English, a spatial design course, and that sort of thing. I've always said that as long as it's enjoyable reading, then that's great, go ahead and use this kind of contemporary fiction. Science fiction lends itself to that because we're dealing with ideas a great deal of the time—but don't take the enjoyment out of it, don't make it an academic hassle.''

When pressed to comment about his latest work in progress, Herbert responded: ''I don't like to talk about work in progress, because you use the same energy to talk about it as you do to write it. I would give that advice to anybody who wants to write. Don't talk about it, write it. That's the best single piece of advice I had as a young writer. I took it to heart and I'm sure it's true. I've seen any number of young writers who talk their stories out and then you never see the stories. I would really like to see a log of young, innovative writers coming on. I personally would help as much as I can. I don't read copy, I don't read people's stories, but I am available for advice on the plumbing, on the technicalities of the field, the things that writers usually have to learn the hard way.

''I'd like to see more young writers coming on. A lot of them feel that the markets are closing down because the main writers are being published by big publishing houses as kind of a sure thing. Some names will sell a certain number of books, and the big-name publishers believe that's the only investment that's safe to make. Some of them, though, are gambling on young

writers, and there's always the magazine market and there's always the regional press market. A lot of young writers don't know about that, and I think it would help if they got the word. There are about twenty good regional presses around the United States, like the Copper Canyon Press at Port Townsend, Washington. They don't pay very much—sometimes they pay in books which you have to sell yourself—but they are a way to get your self published and to get feedback. And that's the important thing, that feedback from readers.''

Universal Pictures was responsible for creating a Dune fan club in 1984, which boasted 2,000 members shortly after its inception. The company also collaborated with Life-time Learning Systems, Inc. to create a teaching kit, ''The World of Dune,'' for distribution to over 4,000 senior and junior high schools.

Among the licensed products which were distributed by the Berkley and Putnam Publishing Groups in connection with the film ''Dune'' were a 1985 ''Dune'' calendar and several activity books for young readers, including *The Dune Activity Book, The Dune Coloring Book,* and *The Dune Pop-Up Panorama Book.*

The Library of the California State University at Fullerton has a large collection of Herbert's papers.

FOR MORE INFORMATION SEE: New York Times Book Review, March 11, 1956, September 8, 1974, August 1, 1976,

November 27, 1977, May 17, 1981; *Amazing Stories,* July, 1956; *Analog,* July, 1956, April, 1966, June, 1970; *Magazine of Fantasy and Science Fiction,* March, 1966, April 1969, May, 1971, February, 1977; *Galaxy,* April, 1966, September, 1976, August, 1977; *New Worlds,* October, 1966.

Science Fiction Review, August, 1970, August, 1979; *Time,* March 29, 1971, November 15, 1982; *Extrapolation,* December, 1971, May, 1974, December, 1974, May, 1976; *America,* June 10, 1972, June 26, 1976; Brian W. Aldiss, *Billion Year Spree: The True History of Science Fiction,* Doubleday, 1973; *School Library Journal,* March, 1973; *Psychology Today,* August, 1974; Louis David Allen, *Herbert's 'Dune' and Other Works,* Cliff's Notes, 1975; Robert Scholes, *Structural Fabulation: An Essay on Fiction of the Future,* University of Notre Dame Press, 1975; Harold L. Berger, *Science Fiction and the New Dark Age,* Popular Press, 1976; *Booklist,* May 1, 1976; *Washington Post Book World,* May 9, 1976, May 24, 1981; *Observer,* October 3, 1976; Scholes and Eric S. Rabkin, *Science Fiction: History, Science, Vision,* Oxford University Press, 1977; *Times Literary Supplement,* January 14, 1977; *National Observer,* May 23, 1977; *New York Times,* September 2, 1977, April 27, 1981; Dick Riley, editor, *Critical Encounters: Writers and Themes in Science Fiction,* Ungar, 1978; *Spectator,* August 26, 1978; *Future Life,* #14, 1979; *World Authors 1970-1975,* H. W. Wilson, 1980; *Contemporary Literary Criticism,* Volume XII, Gale, 1980, Volume XXIII, 1983; Charles Platt, *Dream Makers: The Uncommon People Who Write Science Fiction,* Berkley Publishing, 1980; *Mother Earth News,* number 69, May/June, 1981; *Chicago Tribune Book World,* June 14, 1981; *Publishers Weekly,* May 4, 1984; *People,* June 25, 1984.

JACKSON, Anne   1896(?)-1984

OBITUARY NOTICE: Born about 1896; died January 4, 1984. Librarian. Jackson was considered a pioneer in the training of children's librarians and was well-known for her expertise in the field of children's and young adult literature. She received her degree from the Ontario Library School in Canada and was employed by the Brooklyn Public Library in New York for thirty-three years. During that time she served as branch librarian of the Brownsville Children's Branch and later as head of the Central Children's Room. Following her retirement in 1960, Jackson continued to work as a part-time curator of the children's literature collection until 1968. *Obituaries: School Library Journal,* March, 1984; *Horn Book,* April, 1984.

JAFFEE, Al(lan)   1921-

BRIEF ENTRY: Cartoonist. Born March 13, 1921, in Savannah, Ga. Jaffee attended New York's High School of Art and Design and began his comic book career in 1941 as a writer and artist of Quality's *Inferior Man* feature. He later worked for Marvel doing humor features. He has worked for *Mad* magazine as well as in advertising and illustrating children's books. The creator of the "Mad Fold-In," a feature that called for "reader participation," Jaffee has been associated with numerous *Mad* paperbacks. In 1973 he was awarded a plaque for best advertising and illustration artist by the National Cartoonist Society. His work has made him one of the leading satirists for children as well as adults. Jaffee's books include *Al Jaffee Gags* (NAL, 1974), *Still More Snappy Answers to Stupid Questions* (Warner, 1976), *Al Jaffee Sinks to a New*

Low (NAL, 1978), *Al Jaffee Meets His Ends* (NAL, 1979), *Al Jaffee Goes Bananas* (NAL, 1982), and *Mad's Vastly Overrated Al Jaffee* (Warner, 1983). *For More Information See:* Nick Meglin, *Art of Humorous Illustration,* Watson-Guptill, 1973; *The World Encyclopedia of Comics,* Chelsea House Publishing, 1976.

JOHNSTON, Annie Fellows   1863-1931

PERSONAL: Born May 15, 1863, in Evansville, Ind.; died October 5, 1931, in Pewee Valley, Ky.; buried at Oak Hill Cemetery, Evansville, Ind.; daughter of Albion (a Methodist minister) and Mary (Erskine) Fellows; married William L. Johnston, October 11, 1888 (died, 1892); stepchildren: John, Mary, Rena. *Religion:* Methodist. *Education:* Attended University of Iowa, 1881-82. *Residence:* Pewee Valley, Ky.

CAREER: Early in career, taught in public schools in Evansville, Ind., and worked as a private secretary; turned to full-time writing after the death of her husband in order to support his three children. She is best known as the author of the popular "Little Colonel" series of books for children. *Member:* Authors Club of Louisville (co-founder), Lyceum Club (London), Authors' League, Woman's Club of Louisville.

Annie Fellows Johnston at age nineteen.

...Presently Eugenia sat up in the hammock and gave her pillow an impatient thump.

"Whew! how deadly stupid it is here!" she exclaimed.

■ (From *The Little Colonel's House Party* by Annie Fellows Johnston. Illustrated by Louis Meynell.)

WRITINGS—"Little Colonel" series; all for children; all published by L. C. Page, unless otherwise indicated: *The Little Colonel* (illustrated by Etheldred B. Barry; also see below), J. Knight, 1896 [other editions include one illustrated by Harold M. Brett, 1905; a Shirley Temple edition, illustrated with photographs from the motion picture, Grosset, 1935; an edition illustrated by James Rice, Pelican, 1974; and has been reprinted in Laura E. Richards' *Captain January*, Random House, 1959, and with Thomas N. Page's *Two Little Confederates*, Garland Publishing, 1976]; *Two Little Knights of Kentucky Who Were the Little Colonel's Neighbours* (illustrated by E. B. Barry; also see below), 1899 [another edition illustrated by H. M. Brett, 1906]; *The Little Colonel's House Party* (illustrated by Louis Meynell), 1901, new edition, 1938 [two stories have been published separately as *The Legend of the Bleeding Heart*, 1907, and *The Road of Loving Heart* (illustrated by Winifred Bromhall), 1922]; *The Little Colonel's Holidays* (illustrated by L. J. Bridgman), 1901, new edition, 1938; *The Little Colonel's Hero* (illustrated by E. B. Barry; music by sister, Albion Fellows Bacon), 1903, new edition, 1938 [two stories have been published separately as *The Story of the Red Cross as Told to the Little Colonel* (illustrated by John Goss), 1918, and *The Rescue of the Princess Winsome: A Fairy Play for Old and*

Young, 1908]; *The Little Colonel Stories* (illustrated by E. B. Barry; includes *The Little Colonel, The Giant Scissors,* and *The Little Knights of Kentucky*), 1904, *The Little Colonel at Boarding School* (illustrated by E. B. Barry), 1904; *The Little Colonel in Arizona* (illustrated by E. B. Barry), 1905.

The Little Colonel: Maid of Honor (illustrated by E. B. Barry), 1906; *The Little Colonel's Christmas Vacation* (illustrated by E. B. Barry), 1906; *The Little Colonel's Knight Comes Riding* (illustrated by E. B. Barry), 1907; *Mary Ware, the Little Colonel's Chum* (illustrated by E. B. Barry), 1908; *The Little Colonel's Good Times Book* (illustrated by P. Verburg), 1909; *The Little Colonel Doll Book, Representing Characters and Costumes from the Books of the Little Colonel Series* (illustrated by stepdaughter, Mary G. Johnston), 1910; *Mary Ware in Texas* (illustrated by Frank T. Merrill), 1910; *Mary Ware's Promised Land* (illustrated by John Goss), 1912; *The Mary Ware Doll Book*, 1914; *Georgina of the Rainbows*, Britton Publishing, 1916; *Georgina's Service Stars* (illustrated by Thelma Gooch), Britton Publishing, 1918; *The Little Colonel Stories: Second Series* (illustrated by Harold Cue; includes *Ole Mammy's Torment, The Three Tremonts* and *The Little Colonel in Switzerland*), 1931.

Other works; all for children unless otherwise indicated; all published by L. C. Page, unless otherwise indicated: *Big Brother*, J. Knight, 1894 [another edition illustrated by Frank T. Merrill, 1907]; *Joel, a Boy of Galilee* (illustrated by Victor A. Searles), Roberts Brothers, 1895, new edition, illustrated by L. J. Bridgman, 1904, reprinted, 1928; *In League with Israel: A Tale of the Chattanooga Conference*, Curts & Jennings, 1896; (with Albion Fellows Bacon), *Songs Ysame* (poems for adults), 1897; *Ole Mammy's Torment* (illustrated by M. G. Johnston and Amy M. Sacker), 1897; *The Gates of the Giant Scissors* (illustrated by E. B. Barry), 1898, new edition published as *The Giant Scissors* (illustrated by F. T. Merrill), 1906; *The Story of Dago* (illustrated by E. B. Barry), 1900; *Asa Holmes; or, At the Cross-Roads*, 1902; *Cicely, and Other Stories* (illustrated by Sears Gallagher and others), 1903; *Aunt 'Liza's Hero, and Other Stories* (illustrated by W. L. Taylor and others), 1904; *Flip's "Islands of Providence"* (illustrated by E. F. Bonsall), 1904; *In The Desert of Waiting: The Legend of Camelback Mountain*, 1905; *The Quilt That Jack Built [and] How He Won the Bicycle* (illustrated by E. B. Barry), 1905; *The Three Weavers: A Fairy Tale for Fathers and Mothers as Well as for Their Daughters*, 1905.

Keeping Tryst: A Tale of King Arthur's Time, 1906; *Mildred's Inheritance, Just Her Way, [and] Ann's Own Way* (illustrated by Diantha W. Horne), 1906; *The Jester's Sword: How Aldebaran, the King's Son, Wore the Sheathed Sword of Conquest*, 1909; *Travelers Five along Life's Highway: Jimmy, Gideon Wiggan, the Clown, Wexley Snathers, Bap. Sloan*, 1911; *Miss Santa Claus of the Pullman* (illustrated by Reginald B. Birch), Century, 1913, reprinted, L. C. Page, 1931; *The Little Man in Motley* (illustrated by Emily B. Waite), 1918; *It Was the Road to Jericho* (poems; illustrated by John R. Neill), Britton Publishing, 1919; *The Land of the Little Colonel: Reminiscence and Autobiography* (adult) 1929; *For Pierre's Sake, and Other Stories* (illustrated by Billie Chapman), 1934.

Contributor to *Youth's Companion, Munsey's, McClure's,* and *Century.*

ADAPTATIONS—Movies and filmstrips: "The Little Colonel" (motion picture), starring Shirley Temple and Lionel Barrymore, Fox Film Corp., 1935.

SIDELIGHTS: **May 15, 1863.** Born and reared in Evansville, Indiana; daughter of Albion and Mary Erskine Fellows. ". . . My earlier recollections are singularly happy. They are of the house in the country to which we moved when I was two years old, after the death of my father, a young minister; of lying on the grass looking up at the sky through boughs of pink peach blossoms; of lullabies in the summer dusk with one tiny waxen taper on the high mantel-shelf and fireflies flashing past the open door.

"This house was on my grandfather's farm, not far from Evansville. We lived there two years, returning to the city when I was nine. Then my mother decided to locate permanently in the country, and built a house within a stone's throw of the old homestead, where her eldest brother was living and just across the lane from another brother. So with my two sisters and myself there were eight of us cousins to visit back and forth. . . .

"My mother taught me to read when I was five. I have only one recollection of these lessons, and that was given one busy morning because I followed her around insisting upon it. She stopped sweeping, and taking me on her lap pointed out the words with her scissors.

"When I reached the point where I could read the simple lessons in my First Reader, I was so proud of the accomplishment that I insisted upon following her about the house to practise it. With one hand holding the book and the other tightly clutching her skirts lest she elude me, I was whisked upstairs and downstairs and in my lady's chamber, for she never paused in her tasks at such times and I was fain to prove the truth of Scripture, that 'he may run that readeth.'" [Annie Fellows Johnston, *The Land of the Little Colonel: Reminiscence and Autobiography,* L. C. Page, 1929.']

Johnston was greatly influenced by her mother's belief in education for women and her father's theological library. "It was about that time that my ambition to write was vaguely aroused. . . .

". . . I had been encouraged to subscribe for a tiny magazine called *The Children's Hour,* and it was always a proud moment when I climbed up and fetched down a little inlaid workbox in which I kept my savings to pay for the magazine each month.

"It was always understood between my mother and myself that some day I was to write stories for *The Children's Hour.*

"After that magazine we had the *Little Corporal,* and the *St. Nicholas* and the *Youth's Companion.* But we had few children's books, so we were forced to turn to the periodicals of our elders, *The American Agriculturist, Harper's Weekly, The Monthly* and *The Christian Advocate.* In that last named there was always a page of children's stories which I devoured eagerly, and then read the column of obituaries, taking a lively interest in its record of last words and funeral texts.

"We gathered much from my father's theological library, for amid such dry picking as *Harmony and Exposition* were *Foxe's Book of Martyrs,* Aesop's Fables, Pilgrims Progress, and many bound volumes of *The Ladies' Repository.* Here, too, we came for the poets, yards and yards of whose verse we learned to repeat around our daily tasks. Later, many copies of Godey's lady books found their way into the house. They were given to us that we might cut out the colored illustrations for paper dolls, but we discovered the sentimental love stories and read them eagerly.

After that all her home lessons were learned on the stairs, where no out-door sights and sounds could arrest her attention. ■ (From *The Little Colonel's Holiday* by Annie Fellows Johnston. Illustrated by L. J. Bridgman.)

"There was one more source of literature, and that was some two score volumes in a little red bookcase in one corner of the church. It is the same library that Betty read in the *Little Colonel's House Party.*

"It held all that was left of a scattered Sunday School library in use a generation before. Queer little books they were, time-yellowed and musty-smelling, but to us story-loving children, hungry for something new, they seemed a veritable gold mine.

"The church, a bare wooden structure, stood in a grove of locusts and cedars, just beyond the end of our lane. Many an afternoon I spent reading in its straight hard pews with nothing to break the stillness but the cooing of a distant dove. Never was such stillness as that which wrapped that old meeting-house. I think of it when I hear the words, 'The peace of God which passeth understanding.'"'

1879. First published work, a poem titled "The Harvest," appeared in *Gems of Poetry.* "When I was sixteen, a publication fell into my hands called *Gems of Poetry.* Scott's longer poems ran serially in it, and it had selections from all the old poets and a page devoted to some brand new ones who had not yet arrived. Albion [Johnston's sister] and I each sent some

Annie Fellows Johnston, from an oil painting by Herbert Ross.

verses to it. Hers were called 'Rain' and mine 'The Harvest.' But as weeks went by without our hearing from them we concluded that they had found their way into the waste-basket.

"Then one July day, one never-to-be-forgotten Thursday afternoon, as I went slowly home from the post-office, reading as I walked, I came upon both her verses and mine. Never again do I expect to feel such a thrill as the one that shot through me then. Hers had a footnote to the effect that they were written by a young lady of fourteen. Mine had 'aged 16' in parentheses after my name.

"We walked on air the rest of that day. To see our verses side by side with such gems as 'Marmion,' 'The Landing of the Pilgrims,' and selections from Milton made us feel that ours were of the few 'immortal names that were not born to die.' The intoxication of actually seeing our verses in print sent us about with our heads in the stars for days.

"It seems strange that after that little touch of success we did not try again; but although we made great plans for what we intended to do in the future, and scribbled continually, we did not seek a publisher for anything else for several years. At school and at the Literary, however, all that next year we

redoubled our efforts, practising verse-making constantly. Many an autograph album is now in existence that bears testimony to that period, in our acrostics and poems of a highly didactic and sentimental nature."[1]

1880. Began teaching at the district school she had attended. "The summer that I was sixteen I successfully passed the examination for a teacher's license. But sixteen was below the age limit and no license could be issued to me. At seventeen I tried it again and proceeded to get myself a school. Ignoring the proverb about the prophet in his own country, I applied for the primary room in the same district school that I had attended all my life.

"The pupils were obedient and tractable, and I enjoyed teaching. Not until long afterward did I realize what an important part it was playing in my preparation for writing.

"The following year I went away to school. My father's brother, Stephen Fellows, was a professor in the State University of Iowa. He was also my guardian and I made my home with his family while in Iowa City.

"The next year [I] went to Evansville, where Albion entered high school and I began teaching in the public schools. I had short hair which made me look much younger than my eighteen years.

"Living just across the street from us were two sisters who were also ambitious to write. The four of us formed a club called the Crambo Club, and we met once a week to play Crambo.

"We also wrote a novel 'by Alma,' the word which our initials spelled. Each member wrote a chapter in turn. Our only restriction was that we could not kill off each other's characters. The effect was spoiled somewhat by our all shying away from the chapter containing the love scenes. When my turn came I introduced an accident in order to postpone them to the next chapter.

"Two of the boys who came to see us frequently were embryo writers and kept us screwed up to heights of enthusiasm. One of them asked for a copy of my poem 'Apple Blossoms.' He sent it to a high school paper in the East which paid for contributions, and shortly after brought me the munificent sum of seventy-five cents, my first literary earnings.

". . . I continued teaching for three years; then the nervous wear and tear became evident, and I saw that it was necessary to change my occupation. I was teaching in my sleep harder than when I was awake. I dreamed continually of ineffectual discipline and disorder, although my classes were in reality very well behaved. The vacation after my third year of teaching I spent travelling through New England with one of my great-uncles and his wife. I had my first glimpse of the mountains and the sea. It was a wonderful experience.

". . . I started in as private secretary for a second cousin of mine. He was in the insurance business. I took up stenography in office hours. When I had mastered it sufficiently to take his dictation, my work extended to the writing of policies and the keeping of the records. Even then there was time to scribble, and I wrote a poem called 'Bob White' and sent it to _Harper's Weekly_. I thought I was on the road to fame and fortune when the acceptance came and a check for ten dollars.

"Three years of office work was fine preparation for the work I was to do later. . . ."[1]

October 11, 1888. Married Will Johnston, her mother's cousin, a widower with three children. "On the 11th of October we were married at Trinity Church. It was the church my father had built the last year of his life. As soon as we were established in our new home, the children came to us from Kentucky where they had been in the home of an aunt for five years. They brought with them an ardent love for Kentucky. Pewee Valley to them was only another name for Paradise. They were all three bright, beautiful children with golden curls. John, the youngest, was only seven. Through them the Land of the Little Colonel was drawing closer to me, although I did not know it then.

"I had a proper audience now for the short stories I wrote about that time. I always tried them out on John and his sisters. If they squirmed during the reading, I knew the story must be changed; if they listened quietly, I knew editors would find it acceptable. The short stories I was writing then were for the *Youth's Companion*. I intended them just for practice. It was my ambition to write the 'great American novel' some day, but it seemed as if everything conspired to keep me writing nothing but children's stories.

"There wasn't much time for writing, however. I had many social duties and used to stop for all sorts of things, like going duck hunting with Mr. Johnston on the Ohio River. But he was a most discriminating critic, always stimulating and encouraging me. He took the greatest interest in my plots or my search for the right word.

"For three years we had the happiest companionship, although the last one was a year of illness. He died in 1892. I cannot write of this time and the hard and desolate months which followed. There was a tangle of business to straighten out, caused by the long illness. When it was settled there was little left, which was a good thing in some ways. It forced me to take an interest in my surroundings and it drove me to write in real earnest.

"The children at that time were the greatest comfort. To keep them with me I busied myself in all sorts of ways. I did tutoring for several years, preparing a boy and his sister for college. I also did typewriting at home."[1]

In **1893** I published my first book, basing it on an experience of one summer when Albion and I had gone out to Iowa. We had met a carload of orphans being taken to homes in Kansas. Among them were two like Big Brother and Robin. I called the book *Big Brother*.

"The book was a disappointment. It was so small and it was a child's story. Then a neighbor sent a note one day telling about a prize-offer of a thousand dollars for the story of a child living in the time of Christ. It was to be a sort of 'Ben Hur' for children. I had a most particular use for that thousand dollars, the element of chance appealed to me, and even while I was reading the note the character of a boy whom I afterward called 'Joel' flashed across my mind; a cripple healed of his lameness, who witnessed the miracle from a boy's viewpoint.

"The story did not take the prize, but after the first few minutes of keen disappointment, I tied up the manuscript and started it off again. This time it was accepted immediately. Several years later, when I went to Rome, one of the first things I saw was a translation of *Joel* into Italian. It was being used in a mission school.

"The careful writing of that story was an invaluable part of my apprenticeship."[1]

The walk was over so soon. The Little Colonel's heart beat fast as they came in sight of the gate. ■ (From *The Little Colonel* by Annie Fellows Johnston. Illustrated by Etheldred B. Barry.)

1895. Visited Pewee Valley, Kentucky, from which her "Little Colonel" series developed. First book of series, *The Little Colonel*, was published. "Ever since the children had first come back from Kentucky they had talked so much of Pewee Valley that I felt acquainted with the place and the people. The girls went back every summer, and just after finishing *Joel* I went after John for a visit. It appealed to me as a most picturesque place, full of interesting characters.

"I felt as if I had stepped back into a beautiful story of antebellum days. Back into the times when people had leisure to make hospitality their chief business in life, and could afford for every day to be a holiday; when there were always guests under the spreading rooftree of the great house, and laughter and singing in the servants' quarters.

"The old Colonel came often to the house, and I saw much of his little granddaughter. She had a dreadful temper and would sometimes bang on a tree with a broom until she was red in the face, if the parrot objected to riding in her doll buggy or if any little thing displeased her. But on the other hand, she was grace and gentleness itself, as she tiptoed around singing to the flowers and stringing words together that pleased her fancy with their beauty.

"After my return to Evansville I kept thinking of her attractive little ways and of the suggestion of my hostess to put her into a story, until finally I began it. Little did I dream that it would expand into twelve volumes.

"After that I was almost ready to begin my real life work— as I then regarded it—to write a 'grown-up' novel. . . ."[1]

(From "The Little Colonel," the first of several movies in which Shirley Temple danced with Bill "Bojangles" Robinson. Copyright 1935 by Fox Film Corp.)

1899. Stepdaughter Rena died. Travelled with stepson, John, because of his frail health. ''September brought us a great sadness. Rena was taken very ill on the sixth with appendicitis. She died on the twelfth after an operation. Her death made us all the more anxious about John's health.

''A visit from Cousin Olin, who was located in New York, resulted in John's going to Walton, New York, for a year, where he had a position which kept him out of doors, driving around the country. Just before Christmas I joined him in Walton and stayed with him till the following autumn. Then we went back to Kentucky again and the specialist who examined him said he must go immediately to Arizona.

''So once more I packed my truck and started West with him. We went to Lee's ranch near Phoenix where we lived in tents all winter. The ranch was devoted to the care of invalid borders. John was so much better that he could go hunting. I rented a little shack on the edge of the desert, just across the alfalfa field from the rows of tents, and fitted it up for my workshop. There I went every morning to write. I wrote the *Little Colonel at Boarding School* that winter.

''In May it was so hot that we had to make a change, so we went first to California, then to Comfort, Texas, and out to another ranch for invalid borders. My chief diversion that summer was poling a flat-bottomed boat up and down the creek.

''In the fall Mary [stepdaughter] came out to take my place and I went to Evansville for the winter. While there I wrote the *Little Colonel in Arizona,* which includes *In the Desert of Waiting.* That allegory of old Camelback Mountain was suggested by a remark of one of the boys at Lee's ranch: 'It's just like us, broken down and left to die on the sands.' But it seemed to me it must have some message of hopefulness and I began a search for a legend about it. I finally made up an allegory to suit myself.

''When I found that teachers down in Mexico had translated it into Spanish for their classes, that it has been done in Braille for the blind, and that it has been translated into Japanese and brought out over there in a little book, I was glad that I had taken that liberty with old Camelback Mountain. . . .

''We lived nearly eight years in Texas, and I wrote a book each year. Much of my writing was done at John's bedside. I thought of him whenever I wrote of Jack Weare, and he was my inspiration for *The Jester's Sword.*''[1]

1910. Stepson died. Returned to her home in Pewee Valley. ''After John's death . . . we came back to Kentucky to live. We have been back in the valley now for seventeen years. Life is intensely interesting wherever Mary is, because she makes it so. She is an artist, a wonderful gardener, and the dearest daughter anybody ever had.

''She made some of the illustrations in the original *Little Colonel* book and designed the first 'Paper Doll book.' It is through her unselfishness that I have had leisure to write. I drew upon some of her experiences in creating Joyce Ware.

''The greatest thing, of course, that my work has brought me is the friendship of such a host of children and young people. The dear little letters! Hundreds come drifting in from all parts of the country till it is impossible to send personal replies. I can send only a printed slip in answer, although I long to let each one know how much it means to me to be counted in as a 'real sure enough friend,' as one girl expressed it, 'who knows just how we feel about things.'

''The young folks have shared their own good times with me so loyally that my letter-box reminds me of the swineherd's magic kettle. Looking into it I cannot tell what everybody in the kingdom is having for breakfast, but I can tell what they found in their Christmas stockings, and how they spent their vacations at seashore and mountain resorts, in farmhouses or inland villages. And I know what per cent many of them made in their examinations, what their ambitions are, and what good times they are having from kindergarten to high school, not only in this country but sometimes in India and Japan, and some of the islands of the sea.

''Sometimes it seems as if the whole world must be full of happy, ambitious young people, who not only work and play with a zest but who even 'dream valiantly.' To feel that one has a part in making such conditions, in starting these ripples which go on and on in ever widening circles, is a happiness that cannot be estimated. It was a delightful surprise to me when I heard of the first club formed as a result of the Little Colonel's 'Order of Hildegarde.' Now they are scattered all over the United States, and I often receive letters from those who say they have been saved from some girlish foolishness by the warning of the Three Weavers, and are making their standards those of the Silver Yardstick.

''And the Tusitala rings! I wish I might see in one long row all the little hands from New England to the Philippines that have written me that they are wearing a ring like Betty's and Lloyd's as a reminder of the road of the loving heart they are trying to leave behind in the world's memory. Some of them belong to college girls, and some of them to tiny folk not yet 'allowed to use ink.'

''. . . I have never found the time to begin on what was always my dream, the grown-up novel. I have ceased to care about that, however, and this is the reason:

''One day on the street-car a lady introduced herself to me and said: 'I want you to know about my little daughter. I thought it might be an inspiration to you. She was playing about the excavations for a new building one day, and fell between the timbers. In falling she cut the tip of her tongue almost off and it had to have several stitches taken in it. Her nose had been injured also, so that she could not take an anesthetic, so we had to think of some way to induce her to sit perfectly still. When asked what she would take to do that she said: ''The new 'Little Colonel' book and all the others of the set that I haven't got yet.'' And when we brought them, she sat through that painful operation without a whimper—like a little stoic.'

''When I heard that, I asked myself: 'Would any grown person have sat through that painful operation comforted by any of the six best sellers, or by anything written by Thackeray, George Eliot, or Dickens? You'd better stick to your audience of loyal, loving children, than fly to others that you know not of.' ''[1]

October 5, 1931. Died of cancer at the age of sixty-eight at her home in Pewee Valley, Kentucky. She was buried at Oak Hill Cemetery in Evansville, Indiana. At the time of her death, Johnston's books had sold over one million copies.

FOR MORE INFORMATION SEE: Bookman, June, 1909; *New York Times Book Review,* November 16, 1913, November 12, 1916; *St. Nicholas,* December, 1913; *Publishers Weekly,* September 26, 1916, October 24, 1931; Annie Fellows Johnston, *The Land of the Little Colonel: Reminiscence and Autobiography,* L. C. Page, 1929; *Saturday Review of Literature,* November 15, 1930; Stanley J. Kunitz and Howard Haycraft,

(From the movie "The Little Colonel," starring Shirley Temple and Lionel Barrymore. Copyright 1935 by Fox Film Corp.)

editors, *The Junior Book of Authors,* H. W. Wilson, 1934; *Sewanee Review,* April-June, 1936; *Indiana Authors and Their Books, 1816-1916,* Wabash College, 1949; Kate Matthews, *Kate Matthews and the Little Colonel,* Lithocraft, 1963; Ray B. Browne and others, editors, *Challenges in American Culture,* Bowling Green University Popular Press, 1970; Edward T. James, editor, *Notable American Women,* Volume II, Belknap Press, 1971; Linda Mainiero, editor, *American Women Writers,* Volume II, Frederick Ungar, 1980. *Obituaries: Publishers Weekly,* October 10, 1931.

JONES, Jessie Mae Orton   1887(?)-1983

OBITUARY NOTICE: Born about 1887 in Lacon, Ill,; died October 6, 1983, in Wilmette, Ill. Educator, administrator, and author. During the late 1930s and early 1940s, Jones worked as a nursery and grammar school teacher in Illinois. She also directed the Highland Park Community Center for two years. Her books for children, most of them religious, include *Small Rain, Secrets, A Little Child, Many Mansions,* and *This Is the Way.* Jones was cited for her distinguished service to literature

in 1964. *For More Information See: Chicago School Journal,* May, 1951; *Who's Who of American Women,* 4th edition, Marquis, 1966. *Obituaries: Chicago Tribune,* October 12, 1983.

KAHL, M(arvin) P(hilip)   1934-

PERSONAL: Born September 28, 1934, in Indianapolis, Ind.; son of Marvin P. (a certified public accountant) and Kathryn (Black) Kahl; married second wife, Lindsay B. Scott, May 29, 1981; children (first marriage) Robert Allen. *Education:* Butler University, B.S., 1956; University of Georgia, M.S., 1961, Ph.D., 1963. *Address:* P.O. Box 2263, Sedona, Ariz. 86336.

CAREER: Zoologist and wildlife photographer. Research biologist with National Audubon Society, 1959-63; Makerere University College, Makerere, Uganda, National Science Foundation fellow, 1963-65; independent researcher on storks, National Geographic Society grant, 1966-69; Chapman fellow at American Museum of Natural History, 1970-71; independent researcher on flamingos, National Geographic Society grant, 1972-74; research associate with Rare Animal Relief Effort,

A nestling Asian Openbill Stork — about thirty days old — does not yet show the gap in the bill that is characteristic of the adults. ■ (From *Wonders of Storks* by M. P. Kahl. Photograph by the author.)

M. P. KAHL

ROGER KAHN

1974-77. *Member:* American Ornithologists Union (fellow, 1979), British Ornithologists Union.

WRITINGS: Wonders of Storks (juvenile; self-illustrated with photographs), Dodd, 1978. Contributor of scientific articles to periodicals, including *National Wildlife, National Geographic, International Wildlife,* and *Audubon.*

WORK IN PROGRESS: Research on the ecology and behavior of spoonbills.

HOBBIES AND OTHER INTERESTS: Music (classical and modern jazz), photography, travel.

KAHN, Roger   1927-

PERSONAL: Born October 31, 1927, in Brooklyn, N.Y.; son of Gordon Jacques (a teacher and editor) and Olga (Rockow) Kahn; married Joan Rappaport, July 14, 1950; married second wife, Alice Lippincott Russell, November 27, 1964 (divorced); married Wendy Meeker, September 28, 1974; children (first marriage) Gordon J., Roger L.; (second marriage) Alissa A. *Education:* New York University, student, 1944-47. *Home:* 234 Pine Rd., Briarcliff Manor, N.Y. 10510. *Agent:* Jay Acton, 928 Broadway, New York, N.Y. 10010.

CAREER: Writer. *New York Herald Tribune,* New York, N.Y. reporter, 1948-54; *Sports Illustrated,* New York, N.Y., con-

tributing writer, 1955; *Newsweek,* New York, N.Y., sports editor, 1956-60; *Saturday Evening Post,* New York, N.Y., editor-at-large, 1963-68; columnist for *Esquire,* 1970-75, *Time,* 1976—, and *New York Times,* 1978-79. Professor of creative writing, Colorado College, 1972; director of nonfiction, University of Rochester Writers Workshop, 1973, 1974, 1976. *Member:* Society of Journalists and Authors, Authors League of America. *Awards, honors:* E. P. Dutton Award for best magazine sports article, 1960, 1969, 1970, 1980, 1982.

WRITINGS: (Editor and author of epilogue) *The World of John Lardner,* Simon & Schuster, 1961; *Inside Big League Baseball* (juvenile), Macmillan, 1962; *The Passionate People: What It Means to Be a Jew in America,* Morrow, 1968; *The Battle for Morningside Heights: Why Students Rebel,* Morrow, 1970; *The Boys of Summer* (illustrated with photographs), Harper, 1972; *How the Weather Was,* Harper, 1973; *A Season in the Sun,* Harper, 1977; *But Not to Keep,* Harper, 1979; *The Seventh Game,* New American Library, 1982. Contributor to *Nation, American Scholar, Reader's Digest* and other magazines.

What are you able to build with your blocks?
Castles and palaces, temples and docks.
Rain may keep raining, and others go roam,
But I can be happy and building at home.

Let the sofa be mountains, the carpet be sea,
There I'll establish a city for me:
A kirk and a mill and a palace beside,
And a harbor as well where my vessels may ride.
          —Robert Louis Stevenson

KELLING, Furn L.   1914-

PERSONAL: Born September 11, 1914, in Shawnee, Okla.; daughter of William E. (a railroad engineer) and Grace L. (Craig) Kelling. *Education:* Southwestern Baptist Theological Seminary, Certificate in Elementary Education, 1949; also studied at George Peabody College for Teachers, 1949-50. *Politics:* "Vote for the best man." *Home:* 768 Holcomb Ave., Reno, Nev. 89502.

CAREER: Owner and operator of beauty shops, St. Louis, Mo., 1933-47; Knoxville (Tenn) public schools, kindergarten teacher, 1950; director of children's work at Central Park Baptist church in Birmingham, Ala., 1951-54; Arizona Southern Baptist General Convention, Phoenix, director of children's work, 1954-55; Southern Baptist Convention of California, director of children's activities, 1956-60; director of children's work at churches in Kansas, Oklahoma, and director of Day Care Centers in southern California, 1960-69 and in Houston, Tex., 1969-75. *Member:* National Association for Nursery Education, National Education Association. *Awards, honors: Listen to the Night* was included in U.S. cultural exhibit in Moscow, 1958.

WRITINGS: Listen to the Night (picture book for children), Broadman, 1957; *This Is My Family* (picture book for children), Broadman, 1963; *Prayer Is . . .* (juvenile), Broadman, 1979. Contributor of articles to newspapers and magazines including Southern Baptist and Methodist periodicals.

FURN L. KELLING

Prayer is...
talking to God.

■ (From *Prayer Is. . .* by Furn L. Kelling. Illustrated by Ronnie Hester.)

WORK IN PROGRESS: Recreation for Young Children; Parents and Teachers; poetry for young children.

SIDELIGHTS: "My parents' families were early settlers in Missouri, Grandfather Kelling coming from Germany at the age of six. He married Elizabeth Trail who was a teacher and whose family did much for early education in Missouri. They are all listed in Missouri history books.

"When my parents were divorced, I felt a deep responsibility for my younger brother and sister. My one desire was to make happy homes for children everywhere. My mother lived with me and I never married, but spent my time with all kinds of projects, helping other children.

"Early in my career I owned and operated beauty shops in Missouri, but in 1945 I dedicated my life to the religious education of young children. After completing school in 1950 I taught kindergarten in Knoxville, Tennessee, then turned to directing children's work in large churches and state and convention-wide conferences until I retired. During these years, many summers were spent in demonstration lab schools and in demonstration teaching with preschool children.

"As a result of seeing a great need for love in southern California homes where so many children had their own psychiatrists, I wrote *This Is My Family. Listen to the Night* was published to help young children overcome nighttime fears. Realizing a need for early prayer experiences in the lives of children and parents of young children, I wrote *Prayer Is. . . .*

I have two books at publishers—one to help the single parents and their children, and another on life in the forest.''

HOBBIES AND OTHER INTERESTS: Music, traveling, art, nature, sports, collections, recreation, libraries, public speaking, architecture—''just about anything that is of interest to children.''

KELLY, Martha Rose 1914-1983
(Marty Kelly)

PERSONAL: Born November 14, 1914, in Fort Benton, Mont.; died August 19, 1983, of a heart attack; daughter of Charles (a retail merchandiser) and Grace (Carroll) Houck; married Mike Cinker, 1936 (deceased); married Earle Reynolds, 1943 (deceased); married Robert Kelly, 1954 (deceased, 1971); children: Grace, Margaret. *Home:* 1714 Fourth Avenue, Great Falls, Mont. 59401.

CAREER: Writer. Has worked as a store detective, firefighter, electrician, waitress, and practical nurse. *Member:* American Heritage Society, Ancient Order of Hibernians, Montana Institute of Arts, Humane Society of Great Falls.

*WRITINGS—*All children's books: *Green-Up: The Story of a Buffalo,* America Heritage Press, 1971; *The House on Deer-Track Trail* (illustrated by Ronald Himler), McGraw, 1976. Contributor of short stories to *Ladies Home Journal, Majestic Montana, Playgrounds of the Rockies, True West,* and other periodicals.

WORK IN PROGRESS: The Poet in the Country House, a book of poems; *Mouse Tracks,* a children's book; and ''Crickets under the Walk,'' a children's story.

SIDELIGHTS: Kelly commented on her early career as a writer: ''I didn't know how to type, but I made a deal with a merchant for a second-hand Corona, and my career began, one peck at a time. I hadn't found my style yet. There were miles of love stories which didn't sell, sheets of poetry, adventure, fantasy, mystery—you name it, I wrote them all. And then one day *True West Magazine* bought 'The Door Stop Skull.' I didn't realize that this publication was factual. My story was a combination of two different tales, dovetailed together into a hell-roaring saga of the old West.

''I believe I have been writing for a thousand years. When I wasn't putting it down on paper, I was writing it in the air. I do a great deal of reading and I still love children's books.''

KESSLER, Ethel 1922-

BRIEF ENTRY: Born January 7, 1922, in Pittsburg, Pa. An author of books for children, Kessler received her B.A. from Carnegie-Mellon University in 1944. She has worked in children's summer camps as a counselor and in supervisory positions. Kessler went on to write, collaborating with her husband, author and illustrator Leonard Kessler, on more than twenty books for infants and pre-schoolers. Their first book, *Plink, Plink! Goes the Water in My Sink,* was published in 1954. Thirty years later their collaboration continues. More recent books by the Kesslers include *What's Inside the Box?* (Dodd, 1976), *Two, Four, Six, Eight: A Book about Legs* (Dodd, 1980), *Pig's New Hat* (Garrard, 1981), *Pig's Orange*

House (Garrard, 1981), and *Night Story* (Macmillan, 1981). Two of their books, *Peek-a-Boo* and *The Big Mile Race,* were Junior Literary Guild selections. *Residence:* New City, N.Y. *For More Information See: Fifth Book of Junior Authors and Illustrators,* H. W. Wilson, 1983.

KEYES, Daniel 1927-

PERSONAL: Born August 9, 1927, in Brooklyn, N.Y.; son of William and Betty (Alicke) Keyes; married Aurea Vazquez (a fashion stylist, photographer, and artist), October 14, 1952; children: Hillary Ann, Leslie Joan. *Education:* Brooklyn College (now Brooklyn College of the City University of New York), A.B., 1950, A.M., 1961. *Residence:* Athens, Ohio. *Office:* Department of English, Ohio University, Athens, Ohio 45701.

CAREER: Stadium Publishing Co., New York City, associate editor, 1951-52; Fenko & Keyes Photography, Inc., New York City, co-owner, 1953; high school teacher of English, Brooklyn, N.Y., 1954-55, 1957-62; Wayne State University, Detroit, Mich., instructor in English, 1962-66; Ohio University, Athens, lecturer, 1966-72, professor of English, 1972—, director of creative writing center, 1973-74, 1977-78. *Wartime service:* U.S. Maritime Service, senior assistant purser, 1945-47. *Mem-*

DANIEL KEYES

(From the movie "Charly," starring Claire Bloom and Cliff Robertson, who won the Academy Award as best actor for his role, based on the novel *Flowers for Algernon* by Daniel Keyes. Released by Cinerama, 1968.)

ber: Associated Writers Program, Dramatists Guild, Authors League of America, P.E.N. *Awards, honors:* Hugo Award, World Science Fiction Convention, 1959, for "Flowers for Algernon" (short story); Nebula Award, Science Fiction Writers of America, 1966, for *Flowers for Algernon* (novel); Mystery Writers of America special award for *The Minds of Billy Milligan.*

WRITINGS—Novels, except as indicated: *Flowers for Algernon,* Harcourt, 1966; *The Touch,* Harcourt, 1968; *The Fifth Sally,* Houghton, 1980; *The Minds of Billy Milligan* (nonfiction), Random House, 1981; *Claudia* (nonfiction novel), Bantam, in press. Short story "Flowers for Algernon" included in anthology, *Ten Top Stories,* edited by David A. Sohn, Bantam, 1964. Contributor of fiction to periodicals. Contributor to fifty anthologies. Associate editor, *Marvel Science Fiction,* 1951.

ADAPTATIONS: "The Two Worlds of Charlie Gordon" (television play; based on short story "Flowers for Algernon"), CBS Playhouse, February 22, 1961; "Charly" (film; based on novel *Flowers for Algernon),* starring Cliff Robertson, Cinerama, 1968; "Flowers for Algernon" (two-act play based on

novel), Dramatic Publishing, 1969; "Flowers for Algernon" (stage musical; based on novel), first produced at The Citadel Theatre, Alberta, Canada, December 12, 1978; first produced as "Charlie and Algernon" at the Queens Theatre, London, England, June 14, 1979, first American production by Folger Theatre Group, under title "Charly and Algernon" at the Terrace Theater, Kennedy Center, Washington, D.C., March 8, 1980; and later produced on Broadway at Helen Hayes Theater, September 4, 1980.

WORK IN PROGRESS: "The Mix-Up Time of Billy Milligan," a play adapted from *The Minds of Billy Milligan;* a nonfiction novel.

SIDELIGHTS: "I was born in Brooklyn, New York, and attended New York City Public schools. At seventeen, after a year of college, I joined the U.S. Maritime Service and went to sea as ship's purser on oil tankers carrying cargo to Europe and the Middle East.

"After leaving the sea, I went back to school and received a B.A. in psychology from Brooklyn College in 1950, and the following month accepted a position as associate fiction editor with a magazine publishing firm in New York. Here I began to learn the craft of writing. I left editing to go into the fashion photography business, and then left that business to go into teaching—coming full circle to teach at the high school from which I had graduated ten years earlier.

"In the years that followed I combined a life of teaching and writing; I went back to Brooklyn College to work nights for a Master's degree in English and American literature, while teaching days and writing weekends. One of my first short stories 'Flowers for Algernon' was widely anthologized, and I developed the short story into a novel which has been widely translated. The novel was made into the film 'Charly,' for which Cliff Robertson received an Oscar, as well as a dramatic musical.

"In 1966, I joined the English faculty at Ohio University in Athens, Ohio, to teach writing and American literature."

The author of several books focusing on psychological themes, Keyes stated that he is "fascinated by the complexities of the human mind."

"In connection with my book, *The Minds of Billy Milligan,* I have been lecturing at universities across the country." The circumstances under which Keyes was contracted to write the story proved unusual: It was only after several of Milligan's selves read *Flowers for Algernon* that they agreed among themselves to work with the author.

FOR MORE INFORMATION SEE: Saturday Review, March 26, 1966; *Times Literary Supplement,* July 21, 1966; Robert Scholes, *Structural Fabulation,* University of Notre Dame Press, 1975; *Los Angeles Times,* December 12, 1980; *Village Voice Literary Supplement,* October, 1981; *Chicago Tribune,* November 11, 1981; *New York Times Book Review,* November 15, 1981; *Washington Post Book World,* November 29, 1981; *Los Angeles Times Book Review,* January 3, 1982; *Contemporary Authors New Revision Series,* Volume 10, Gale, 1983.

KIMBALL, Yeffe   1914-1978

PERSONAL: Born March 30, 1914, in Mountain Park, Okla.; died in 1978; daughter of Other Star Good Man and Martha Clementine Smith; married Harvey L. Slatin. *Education:* Attended Art Students League, 1935-39; studied art in France and Italy, 1936-39. *Residence:* New York, N.Y. *Agent:* (Paintings) Frank Rehn Gallery, 655 Madison Ave., New York, N.Y. 10021.

CAREER: Painter, sculptor, illustrator, and expert on American Indian art. Portland Art Museum, Portland, Ore., cataloger of art objects of Pacific Northwest Coast Indians, 1949; Mattuck Museum, Waterbury, Conn., American Indian Exhibition, arranger of collection, 1950; Brooklyn Museum, Brooklyn, N.Y., Northwest Indian Art Exhibit, assistant, 1951; Americana Foundation, New York, N.Y., technical advisor, 1951-56; se-

They went past all the stores . . .to the edge of an arroyo, where a man and a woman could sit, shoulder to shoulder. . . . ■ (From *Some People Are Indians* by George A. Boyce. Illustrated by Yeffe Kimball.)

lected American Indian art objects for U.S. Department of State American Indian Art Tour Abroad, 1953; Isaac Delgado Museum, New Orleans, La., American Indian Exhibit, assistant, 1964; Institute of American Indian Arts, Santa Fe, N.M., teacher, American Forum International Study, Special American Indian Program, 1970. Director, juror, Brotherhood Children's Annual Exhibition of Art, Brooklyn High School, 1950-60; juror, National American Indian Exhibition, Scottsdale, Ariz., 1970, Center for Arts of Indian American Exhibition, U.S. Department of Interior, 1970, and National Exhibition of American Indian Art, Philbrook Art Center, 1975; member of panel, Convocation of American Indian Scholars, Princeton University, 1970; consultant and advisor to several museums and publishers, and to U.S. Government, on American Indian history and art. Work has been included in many group exhibitions and one-woman shows including National Gallery of Art, Washington, D.C., 1970, Smithsonian Institution, Washington, D.C., 1970, Princeton University, Princeton, N.J., 1970, Northern Virginia Fine Arts Exhibition, Alexandria, 1971, and Trinity College, Hartford, Conn., 1971. Work is represented in numerous permanent collections, including National Gallery of Art, Washington, D.C., Boston Museum of Fine Arts, Boston, Mass., Dayton Art Institute, Dayton, Ohio, Portland Art Museum, Portland, Ore., Norfolk, Museum of Arts and Sciences, Norfolk, Va., and many private collections. *Member:* Artists Equity Association, Audubon Artists, National Academy of Design, National Congress of American Indians, Native North American Artists. *Awards, honors:* First prize, National Indian Exhibition, Philbrook Art Center, 1959.

WRITINGS: (With Jean Anderson) *The Art of American Indian Cooking* (self-illustrated; foreword by Will Rogers, Jr.), Doubleday, 1965.

Illustrator: Ruth Brindze, *The Story of the Totem Pole* (juvenile; American Indian folk tales), Vanguard, 1951; Thomas B. Leekley, *The World of Manabozho: Tales of the Chippewa Indians* (juvenile), Vanguard, 1965; Wilcomb E. Washburn, compiler, *The American Indian and the United States* (nonfiction), Random House, 1973; George A. Boyce, *Some People Are Indians* (juvenile), Vanguard, 1974.

FOR MORE INFORMATION SEE: Lee Kingman and others, compilers, *Illustrators of Children's Books: 1957-1966,* Horn Book, 1968; Marion E. Gridley, editor, *Indians of Today,* I.C.F.P., 1971; L. E. Oxendine, "Contemporary Indian Artists," *American Artist,* July, 1972.

KNOWLES, Anne 1933-

PERSONAL: Born November 25, 1933, in Oxford, England; daughter of Walter (an army major) and Winifred (Dixon) Coleman; married Adam Knowles, December 21, 1957 (divorced January, 1979); children: Rachel, Simon, Matthew, Hannah, Gideon. *Education:* Bedford College, London, B.A. (with honors), 1956. *Politics:* "Not committed." *Religion:* Church of England. *Home and Office:* Clissold Farm, Sheepscombe, Stroud, Gloucestershire, England. *Agent:* Gina Pollinger, Murray Pollinger, 4 Garrick St., London, WC 2E 9BH, England.

CAREER: Oswestry Girls High School, Oswestry, Shropshire, England, teacher of English literature and language, 1956-58; Richmond Road School, Richmond, Surrey, England, teacher of English literature and language, 1958-59; Holmewood House Preparatory School, Langton Green, Kent, England, extra-

ANNE KNOWLES

mural general tutor, 1966-70; School of Russian Ballet, Tunbridge Wells, Kent, England, teacher, 1970-72; writer. Riding instructor, painter of landscapes.

WRITINGS: Flag (juvenile; illustrated by M. Dinsdale), Blackie & Son, 1976; *Sea Change* (juvenile), Blackie & Son, 1979; *Matthew Ratton* (adult novel), Eyre Methuen, 1980, St. Martin's, 1981; *The Halcyon Island* (juvenile; illustrated by Gavin Rowe), Blackie & Son, 1980, Harper, 1981; *The Raven Tree* (adult novel), Eyre Methuen, 1981; *Under the Shadow* (juvenile), Harper, 1983 (published in England as *The Stirrup and the Ground,* Granada, 1983); *The Work of Her Hands* (adult), St. Martin's, 1983 (published in England as *Single in the Field,* Methuen, 1983). Contributor to *Cotswold Life* and *Home and Country.*

...Ken and Giles were on and around the river from the first early mist trails to late evening, when reflections of upside-down clouds, sunset pink, glided across the water, looking as tangible as cotton candy.
■ (Jacket painting by Robert J. Blake from *The Halcyon Island* by Anne Knowles.)

WORK IN PROGRESS: A book on the Cotswolds; two novels.

SIDELIGHTS: "I run a small farm, and ride, and paint. I write because I can't stop writing, which I would do even without prospect of publication. I re-educate naughty ponies, have children stay for riding holidays, and enjoy myself exploring the Cotswold countryside.

"I have enjoyed playing around with words from a very young age, when I used to write excruciating poems about gnomes. I write, as far as possible, from my own knowledge and experience, but because these are limited, I must also see, with imaginative comparison, into the minds and lives of other people, in order to create believable characters whose whole existence is credible, so that the reader feels that although the books are fiction—a pretence of reality—things could and do happen in just such a way. I think out my stories, plan plots, and build up characters in my mind while I do my other work. That way, when I work at my writing, I have plenty of material to draw upon. It was such a bad winter one year, however, that I shelved the story I had been planning, and wrote instead about the hot, idle summer days on the river, to keep my mind off the cold. It worked, and *The Halcyon Island* was the result!

"When I write for children, I like to write a story that will tempt them to read, and then make them stretch to understand, because stretching makes you grow and that's what reading is for. I do not 'write down' to children, or limit the vocabulary I use. Words are worth reading for themselves, and if the meaning of one is unknown, it can easily be discovered by asking someone or using the dictionary.

"I write what I enjoy writing. If I don't, the magic goes, and the whole thing fails; which is not to say the writing itself isn't very hard work, demanding, sometimes disappointing, constantly in need of drastic revision and painful pruning. It makes a full day on the farm seem easy by comparison!"

Although she has not illustrated her own books, Knowles does pastel portraits of animals in her spare time and has contributed illustrations to local magazines.

HOBBIES AND OTHER INTERESTS: Painting, music, drama.

LANTZ, Walter   1900-

PERSONAL: Born April 27, 1900, in New Rochelle, N.Y.; married Grace Stafford, 1941. *Education:* Attended Art Students League. *Address:* c/o Walter Lantz Productions, Inc., 6311 Romaine St., Hollywood, Calif. 90038.

CAREER: Animated cartoon producer. Hearst's International Film Service, animator of the cartoon series "Katzenjammer Kids," "Krazy Kat," and "Happy Hooligan," 1916-18; John Randolf Bray Studios, animator and producer of "Colonel Heeza Liar," beginning 1922, creator of "Pete the Pup" and "Dinky Doodle;" gag writer, Mack Sennet Studio, California, 1927; Walter Lantz Productions, Inc., Hollywood, Calif., founder

ANDY PANDA

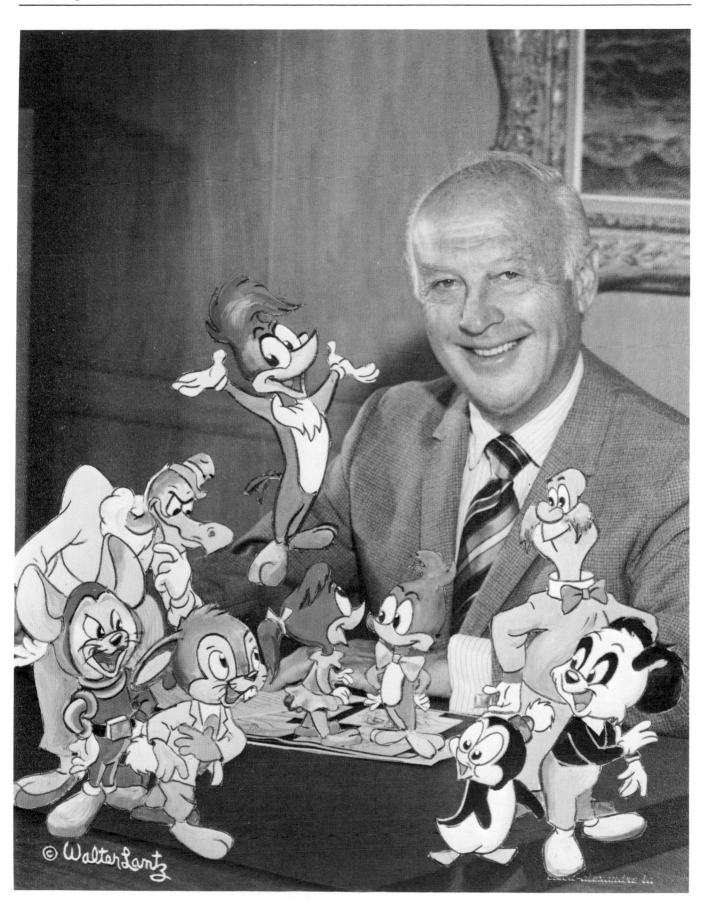

Walter Lantz surrounded by some of his creations.

Woody Woodpecker makes his entrance at the Macy's Thanksgiving Day Parade, 1980.

and president; Universal Pictures, Hollywood, producer of "Oswald the Rabbit" series, 1928-38, creator of "Woody Woodpecker," 1941; producer, "The Woody Woodpecker Show," 1957—. *Awards, honors:* Golden Globe Award; Association Internationale du Film d'Animation Award; Academy Award, Academy of Motion Picture Arts and Sciences, 1979, for achievement in the field of animation.

ILLUSTRATOR—All under the name Walter Lantz Studio: Riley Thomson and Sam Armstrong, adaptors, *Woody Woodpecker Shoots the Works* (from the story "Now Everybody Loves Waldo" by Mabel Watts), Whitman Publishing, 1951; Annie North Bedford (pseudonym of Jane Werner Watson), *Woody Woodpecker Joins the Circus* (adapted by R. Thomson), Simon & Schuster, 1952; Alfred Abranz and John Knight, adaptors, *Woody Woodpecker's Pogo Stick Adventures,* Whitman Publishing, 1954; Frank McSavage and Samuel Armstrong, adaptors, *Woody Woodpecker Shoots the Works,* Whitman Publishing, 1955.

Films—All animated short subjects, except as indicated (selected): "Barnyard Rivals," Bray Productions, 1928; "Cold Turkey," Universal, 1929; "Hurdy Gurdy," Universal, 1930; "Farmer," Universal, 1931; "Crowd Snores," Universal, 1932; "Pin Feathers," Universal, 1933; "Toyland Premiere," Snappy, 1934; "Candyland," Snappy, 1935; "Beach Combers," Universal Productions, 1936; "Sailor Mouse," Universal, 1938; "Life Begins for Andy Panda," Universal, and Walter Lantz Productions, 1939; "Woody Woodpecker," Universal, Walter Lantz Productions, 1941; "Mother Goose on the Loose," Universal, and Walter Lantz Productions, 1942; "Meatless Tuesday," Universal, and Walter Lantz Productions, 1943; "Pied Piper of Basin Street," Universal, and Walter Lantz Productions, 1944; "Woody Woodpecker in Woody Dines Out," Universal, and Walter Lantz Productions, 1945.

Gracie and Walter Lantz.

"Poet and Peasant," Walter Lantz Productions, and Universal, 1946; "Overture to William Tell," Walter Lantz Productions, 1947; "Playful Pelican," Walter Lantz Publications, 1948; "Mountain Flower," Walter Lantz Productions, 1949; "Scalp Treatment," Universal, 1952; "Mouse and the Lion," Universal, 1953; "Alley to Bali," Universal, 1954; "Tree Medic," Universal, 1955; "Woody Meets Davy Crewcut," Universal, 1956; "Big Snooze," Universal, 1957; "Chilly Reception," Universal International, 1958; "Yukon Have It," Universal International, 1959; "Clash and Carry" (feature-length animated film), Walter Lantz Productions, 1961; "Science Friction," Walter Lantz Productions, 1963; "Woody's Clip Joint," Castle Films, 1964.

Also producer of the first technicolor cartoon, for the opening scenes of the motion picture "King of Jazz," Universal, 1930. Producer of cartoons for the Army and Navy, and of educational and commercial films.

ADAPTATIONS—Books based on Lantz cartoons: *Andy Panda Goes Fishing,* adapted by Paul T. Gilbert, Rand McNally, 1940; *Life Begins for Andy Pandy,* adapted by Gilbert, Rand McNally, 1940.

SIDELIGHTS: Born in New Rochelle, New York, on **April 27, 1900.** "I wanted to be an artist for as long as I can remember. My aunt tells me I was drawing when I was six years

CHILLY WILLY

WOODY WOODPECKER

old. I was always copying pictures out of the newspapers, the comic books, comic sheets, comic strips.

"I went to work at a very early age. When I was nine years old my mother passed away with the birth of my younger brother, Michael, who's now a very famous sculptor. When my father became an invalid I went to work at thirteen to partly support the family. My father set up a grocery store at one of the quarries in Middletown, Connecticut, and I ran the grocery store. While I was doing that, I was taking correspondence school courses in cartoons and that's how I learned, really, to draw. I started when I was thirteen years old."

1914. Worked as a copyboy for the *New York American Newspaper* in New York City. Morrell Goddard, the paper's editor and the originator of the first Sunday newspaper color comic section, recommended the young Lantz to Gregory LaCava (later a famous director), who was opening a cartoon studio in New York for William Randolph Hearst, owner of the *American.* "I was working on the newspaper and studying art at the Art Students League in New York in 1914. I took a dramatic course in drawing—drawing from a nude model. I did have good academic training, though I never finished high school.

"While I was in New York, working as an office boy, I saw the animated cartoon, 'Gertie,' which was made by Winsor McCay. He was the first to produce an animated cartoon, and it was also the first time a cartoon had played in a theater to a paying audience. I knew, then, that it was something I wanted to do.

"About 1916, Mr. Randolph Hearst wanted to start his own cartoon studio to promote characters that were famous in his newspapers, like the 'Katzenjammer Kids,' 'Happy Hooligan,'

'Krazy Kat,' and 'Bringing Up Father.' Gregory LaCava was to head this studio, and he put me to work. I would say that he was a great influence on my career, because he gave me my first start in animation. I didn't begin with a comic strip, like some animators. I really started in animated cartoons, which we started producing in 1916, and I've been in the business ever since. Of course, later on, I had comic books by the millions—drawing books, paint books, puzzles, but my main work has always been animated cartoons."

1922-1935. Lantz, whose animated characters include, in addition to Woody, Wally Walrus, Buzz Buzzard, Charlie Beary, Charlie Beary, Jr., Gabby Gator, Chilly Willy, Smedly, Sugarfoot, Andy Panda and many others, produced and directed his first cartoon series in New York in 1922. It was called "Col. Heeza Liar," was produced at the pioneer J. R. Bray Studios, and was one of the most famous of all silent cartoons. "When I was twenty-two years old I produced a series of cartoons for the Bray studios in New York. I used the characters of Dinky Doodle and his little dog Pete the Pup. I did something different in those days, which is called combination animated cartoon and live action. I made over a hundred of those for Bray. Then, in 1926 when Mr. Bray discontinued the department, I went out to Los Angeles and began working for Universal studios where I set up a cartoon department. I've been releasing cartoons for them for about fifty-six years now."

Universal Studio's Carl Laemmle assigned Lantz to produce the popular Oswald Rabbit cartoons, which he did for ten years. Lantz also produced the first technicolor cartoon, "The King of Jazz."

OSWALD *The Rabbit*

Walter Lantz, circa 1924.

In **1935,** Lantz formed his own company, but continued (and still continues) to release his cartoons through Universal Pictures, making this the longest producer-studio relationship in the annals of show business. ''The first color cartoon I made was even before my friend Walt Disney had made his. It was a feature by Universal about the life of Paul Whiteman. Universal wanted a five minute animated segment showing how Whiteman became the 'King of Jazz.' Bing Crosby did the voice of the lion, and that was the first time he had ever recorded his voice on film. This was also the first cartoon to be produced in technicolor.''

Of his peers in the cartoon animated business, Lantz commented, ''I knew Disney only as a personal friend. We never worked together, but we had lunches and dinners and everything else over the years. Disney used to love to tell people that I started in the business six years before he did—even though we're about the same age. He used to project my early cartoons to see how we animated. He was a wonderful person, and he did more for the animated cartoon industry than anybody because he put a lot of money in his pictures. I wasn't able to borrow money as he did, so I worked on salary at Universal for ten years before going independent and producing on my

own. Now I own all of my pictures. I just release them through Universal.

''Disney and Max Fleischer were very famous. They were my idols in the field of animation. It's funny, but all the other people who were big in the business were really employees of the studios. Disney, Max Fleischer, and I were the only ones that owned our own studios and owned our own characters.''

1941. Married Broadway and screen actress, Grace Stafford. It was on their honeymoon that the character of Woody Woodpecker came into being. ''Woody really started when my wife Grace and I were married. We had a cottage at Sherwood Lake, California. There are woodpeckers in the area and one in particular picked my roof to drill holes in. He became quite a nuisance, but he did make me realize that no one had ever used a woodpecker in a cartoon. Rather than featuring him, I decided to put him in a picture with Andy Panda, who was quite a famous character at the time. Woody gave such a wonderful performance, and got so many laughs from the audience, that the artists and myself realized that we had the making of a new character. We starred him in the second picture, and Woody's been a star ever since.

animated character. We learned an awful lot from the early Chaplin pictures.

Lantz's cartoons are dubbed in many languages, but not Woody's famous laugh, which remains the exclusive rendition of his wife, Gracie. "From the beginning I knew I wanted a peculiar type of laugh. The first laugh, which was more like a cackle, was done by the famous voice artist, Mel Blanc. He worked on the first four pictures, and then left because Warner Brothers signed him to do the voice of Bugs Bunny.

"I tried several voice artists, but I could never get the right type of laugh. After about ten years, my wife Gracie did a very sneaky trick. I was having an audition for a new voice for Woody Woodpecker, and, unknown to me, she went to the studio where we were doing the audition and slipped her recording in with the others. When the tracks were played back, and I picked number seven, the director said, 'You know who that is? That's Gracie!'

"Gracie changed the laugh. She put a sort of musical tone in it, like the five notes of a bugle call, 'da-da-da-daaa-da,' and we now have a musical laugh, different from Mel Blanc and the others. She's been doing it for thirty-four years now.

"Gracie has helped me in other ways. She's had so much experience in the theater—working in theater and feature pictures since she was twelve years old. I discuss everything about

HOMER PIGEON

"I think Woody became so famous because he is a very fresh, precocious type of character with a lot of nerve. He does things that all of us would like to, but we don't have the nerve. He never does anything to hurt anybody, though he does get a little rough at times. I think there's a little bit of Woody in all of us.

"Before he existed, we used to make 'good deed' characters, like Oswald Rabbit and Mickey Mouse. Woody came along and threw all that out. He did things that were active, physical. I always felt that children love to see physical gags. I depend mostly on physical humour to get laughs in the theater. Because these cartoons play all over the world, it's important not to have to depend on dialogue for humour. Let live actors do that.

"Charlie Chaplin didn't depend on dialogue. He never spoke a word. It was all physical humor—pie in the face, slipping on a banana peel, falling into a manhole. In fact, in the early days, when I was learning to animate, I used to run the old Chaplin films. I ran them on the wall, projected each frame of the film onto a piece of paper, and made tracings. Then I'd flip the drawings made from each traced frame to see how he moved. His action was always so broad. He moved like an

WALLY WALRUS

WALTER LANTZ

the cartoons with Gracie. She's given many good suggestions, and we've done many personal appearances together. We've been on practically every well known talk show on the air and have given hundreds of phone interviews with disc jockeys all over the United States. We've had a lot of fun with this.''

Fall, 1969. The Lantzes set out on a USO-sponsored "handshake tour," which was inspired by a magazine article Gracie had read about the need for entertaining servicemen wounded in Viet Nam. Gracie had had fifteen years of nursing experience as a Red Cross Gray Lady in Los Angeles, and was eager to make the trip. They visited every one of the twenty-four hospitals in the U.S. Pacific Naval command—in Japan, and Philippines, Guam, Okinawa, Korea, and other Pacific outposts. Gracie did the Woody laugh an estimated 5,000 times during the thirty-one day tour, which totaled over 30,000 flight miles. With the departure of U.S. troops from Viet Nam, the Lantzes turned their attention to soldiers and veterans hospitalized in domestic facilities. "Visiting the five or six thousand young men at their bedsides in hospitals throughout the entire Pacific was an honor. We'd go and spend the day visiting them— Gracie would talk to them as Woody Woodpecker, and they'd tape her laugh. I made drawings for them on their casts, post cards, photographs. That was a fine experience; I think one of

the most rewarding. Bringing joy to people who are isolated or in pain is very rewarding.''

1970. The celebration of Woody Woodpecker's thirtieth birthday was marked by a number of activities including a six-week exhibit on the art of animation at the California Museum of Science and Industry in Los Angeles, as well as on-the-air tributes to the Lantzes and Woody by leading personalities.

In **1972,** the Lantzes were given another tribute as guests of honor at the Animated Film Festival held in Zagreb, Yugoslavia.

In **1973,** Lantz received the Annie Award—animation's equivalent of the Oscar—from the Association International du Film d'Animation, the animation industry's worldwide organization. The Museum of Modern Art in New York City honored Lantz in a special three-day program which featured a retrospective of his cartoons in **June, 1977.** A year later, another tribute was paid to the artist when Filmex '78, the Los Angeles Film Festival, honored Lantz personally and presented several of his films as part of the scheduled activities. Woody Woodpecker is also featured in permanent exhibits at the Smithsonian Institution in Washington, D.C., and at the Universal Entertainment Center, at Universal Studios in Hollywood, California.

Lantz spoofed Norman Rockwell's "Triple Self-Portrait" in this design for a collector plate.

1979. Awarded a special Oscar for his sixty years of outstanding service to the motion picture industry by the Academy of Motion Pictures. "I was surprised by the Oscar for achievement in the industry because it is voted by the Board of Governors, not by the industry itself. I've received the Golden Globe, the Oscar and all sorts of other awards, but I think the most cherished honor right now is to be in the Smithsonian, because it is known world-wide, and millions of people can go to see the memorabilia of Woody Woodpecker. That, to me, was the greatest accomplishment."

1980. Traveled to New York City for the Macy's Thanksgiving Day Parade which featured a 125-foot-high Woody Woodpecker balloon. "Next would be the Macy's Thanksgiving Day Parade. They say 130 million people see that around the world. The Oscar sits on the piano, the other awards are in my office—but 130 million people—that's what I call hitting the jackpot!"

In his eighties, Lantz is recognized for his ability as an artist, and his paintings are in great demand in a worldwide market. His works are sold exclusively at the Center Art Galleries in Honolulu, Hawaii, the largest art gallery in the world. "I'm the only cartoon producer who is also a professional painter.

"My dedication to painting High Sierra landscapes began years ago when I met the famed seascape artist Robert Wood. I had a home up in the High Sierras on Silver Lake. Robert Wood had a studio south of there in a town called Bishop. During the summer months, which I spent at my cottage, I used to drive sixty miles every Thursday to study with him. I hadn't done any seascapes before that. After a while, I learned the art of painting both seascapes and landscapes.

"The gallery in Hawaii which has been handling my paintings sells everything.

"In the last five or six years I have placed my cartoon characters in every painting. As soon as I did that, the prices of the paintings quadrupled."

Since Lantz's favorite character, "Woody," was so close to his thoughts, it was not surprising that one day, after he had finished a particularly beautiful still life of apples in a Steuben bowl, he added Woody holding up one of the apples. Reactions from friends and the public alike stimulated the creation of a concept for this painting, called "Happy Art," which is now trademarked. The oil paintings differ—Woody serenading Winnie Woodpecker on the beach of Waikiki, Woody seen as part of

Mount Rushmore—but the distinctive character of Woody Woodpecker is always included.

Lantz has also created a series of 10,000 numbered Woody Woodpecker collectors' plates, which were shown for the first time at the Plate Collectors' Convention in South Bend, Indiana. In 1981, 1982, and 1983, the Lantzes were guests of honor at the Collectors' Convention, and in 1983 they promoted a new line at another convention held in Anaheim, California. "The series of plates evolved from a painting I had done of Woody called 'Woody's Triple Portrait,' which sold for $30,000 in a gallery. A plate collector who had seen it there said, 'Walter, would you give us the rights to make a plate of this painting?' I agreed, and two years ago we showed the plate at the Plate Collectors' Convention in South Bend, Indiana. The numbered series of 10,000 was brought up by the dealers in two days. You can't get this plate anymore, unless you buy it privately. That first set we issued sold for about $40 a plate. Today that same issue would sell for $2,000, because they've become very scarce."

Lantz offers the following advice to young people who aspire to be artists. "Young peole who want to be artists should know that there are no shortcuts. I'd advise them to get good academic training, to learn to draw a human being in every possible position. That became very important to me. I could already draw when I got the opportunity to go into cartoon animation. I had taken cartoon correspondence courses, and had a knowledge of drawing so that animation came a lot easier than it would have if I hadn't had that early start. All of the famous abstract painters had a wonderful background in realistic painting before they ever went the abstract way. But, I'm a realist. I don't go for the abstract.

"Younger children can copy the pictures in the comic strips they like—as I did, but I suggest they copy the well-drawn strips—not the distorted comics. When they become older, fifteen or sixteen years old, I suggest they take a correspondence course in art, so that they can work at home, and still keep up with school. Don't drop out of school just to become an artist. I dropped out because I had to. There was no other way. Later they can continue with academic courses, then there is illustration for magazines, and if they have a sense of humour, they can become cartoonists. You never know what's going to happen. That's why it's never boring."

FOR MORE INFORMATION SEE: Films in Review, April, 1971; Martin M. Cooper, *Academy Awards 1979 Oscar Annual,* ESE California, 1979; Danny Peary, "Reminiscing with Walter Lantz," in *An American Animated Cartoon,* Dutton, 1980.

Golden volumes! richest treasures,
Objects of delicious pleasures!
You my eyes rejoicing please,
You my hands in rapture seize!
Brilliant wits and musing sages,
Lights who beam'd through many ages!
Left to your conscious leaves their story,
And dared to trust you with their glory;
And now their hope of fame achiev'd
Dear volumes! you have not deceived!
          —Isaac D'Israeli
    (From *Curiosities of Literature*)

BETSY LEE

LEE, Betsy 1949-

PERSONAL: Born June 4, 1949, in Bayshore, N.Y.; daughter of James Weir (an educational administrator) and Betty (a teacher, maiden name, Crowder) Colmey; married Lawrence Lee (an assistant city manager), December 31, 1972; children: Brenna Elizabeth. *Education:* Attended University of New Mexico, 1967-68, and Chapman College's World Campus Afloat, 1969; University of Wyoming, B.A., 1971. *Politics:* Democrat. *Religion:* Christian. *Home and office:* 8 East Minnehaha Parkway, Minneapolis, Minn. 55419.

CAREER: Chapman College, Orange, Calif., publications adviser for World Campus Afloat, 1972; free-lance photographer and consultant, 1973; Open University, Milton Keynes, England, assistant publications and information officer, 1974-76; consultant, 1976-77; free-lance writer and photographer, 1978—. *Member:* Authors Guild.

WRITINGS: No Man to Himself (poems and photographs), Post Press, 1971; (editor) *This Place Has Its Ups and Downs* (juvenile), People's Press, 1977; *Charles A. Eastman: The Story of an American Indian* (juvenile biography), Dillon, 1979; *Mother Teresa: Caring for All God's Children* (juvenile biography), Dillon, 1980; *Judy Blume's Story,* Dillon, 1981; *Miracle in the Making,* Augsburg, 1983.

Contributor of articles and photographs (including covers) to magazines and newspapers, including *Easy Living, Carte Blanche, Cross-Country, New York Times, St. Louis Post-Dispatch, Republic Scene, Living Trends, Corporate Report, Nuestro, Minnesota Monthly, Alaska, Scope, Moody Monthly, Marriage Encounter,* and *Maryknoll.*

More and more people began to hear about Mother Teresa's good works. ■ (From *Mother Teresa: Caring for All God's Children* by Betsy Lee. Illustrated by Robert Kilbride.)

WORK IN PROGRESS: The Loving Tree, an exploration of intimacy in various relationships: married love, the love between parent and child, the love between friends, and Christian love for others and for God.

SIDELIGHTS: ''I've always wanted to be a writer. When I was in the third grade, my teacher let me sit in the back of the classroom and put my first books together: a combination of pictures and writing done on construction paper. I am grateful to that teacher for encouraging my creativity.

''Throughout high school and college I kept a journal of private thoughts. Writing these thoughts down allowed me to understand myself better and to make some sense of the world, which can be awfully confusing at times. Writing still does that for me; it is a method of problem-solving.

''I landed my first writing assignment when I was nineteen—a book chapter, 'How to Teach Creative Writing in Elementary Schools,' for Southeastern Educational Laboratory in Atlanta, Georgia. I was so excited when I received the check, I wanted to frame it! I couldn't believe that anyone would actually pay me to do something I enjoyed so much.

''When I was twenty, I sailed around the world on *World Campus Afloat,* a university on an ocean liner. I met my husband, Larry, on that boat and together we published a book of poems and photographs from our travels in forty countries.

''We liked traveling so much that we decided to live in a foreign country after we were married. For five years we lived in England. During that time, I worked in public relations for the Open University, the largest university in Britain.

''It was an exciting job, but I found that working for an institution did not allow me the creativity I needed to develop as a writer. I wanted to be my own boss. When I came back to the United States, I became a freelancer, writing articles for newspapers and magazines. Most of my articles were illustrated with my own photographs.

''Then an educational publisher in Minneapolis asked me to write my first juvenile biography. I liked writing biographies so I wrote two more: one about Judy Blume and the other about Mother Teresa. As a biographer, I write best if I feel a sense of personal involvement with my subject.

''I found I had much in common with Judy Blume. She was born in New Jersey; I was born in New York. Her favorite book, *Starring Sally J. Freedman as Herself,* was written about her experiences in Miami, Florida when she was ten years old. I also lived in Miami when I was ten. I interviewed Judy at her home in Santa Fe, New Mexico, an area I knew well because I has attended the University of New Mexico in Albuquerque.

''I discovered that our childhoods were alike too. She had a tremendous imagination and liked to act out her fantasies. Both of us were great pretenders as all creative people are, especially writers. 'Writing for me is just a continuation of a game of pretend,' she told me. 'I was a very big pretender and still am, except now I act it out on paper.'

''When I wrote my biography about Mother Teresa, I also felt personally involved with her. I had been to India during my travels as a student and I had seen the terrible slums where Mother Teresa worked. I remembered seeing people digging for scraps of food in garbage cans and sleeping in the streets.

As a Christian, I understand Mother Teresa's deep desire to share God's love with the hungry and homeless.

"While I was writing Mother Teresa's biography, some friends adopted a child from one of her orphanages. In their honor, I donated my writing fee from the book to Mother Teresa's orphanage work. That made her biography very special to me.

"I realize now that telling Mother Teresa's story was a turning point in my career. I grew to love the 'little nun' while I was researching her life; her faith was a great inspiration to me. I asked myself, 'What is my mission in life? Is there something that I am uniquely called to do?'

"My next book was an answer to that question. Instead of writing a biography about someone else's life, I wrote a book about my own life. The biggest thing that happened to me at the time was becoming a mother. I wrote about that experience in *Miracle in the Making*.

"The book tells the story of my change of heart from an ambitious, professional woman to a new parent who discovers the unexpected joys of parenthood. Like many women today, I had a difficult time deciding to give up my independence and carefree lifestyle to become a mother. But I didn't realize how much I would gain.

"My career is still important to me. Becoming a mother hasn't changed that. It has simply enhanced other areas of my life. I am more well-rounded, more compassionate, more open—a more giving person. I learned that the liberated life is not measured by how much of yourself you keep intact, but how much you give away.

"While I was writing *Miracle in the Making*, my daughter Brenna played close by. Often I would hear her banging away at her toy typewriter, just as intent as I was. 'Oh, no,' my husband sighed, 'another writer in the house!'

"I learned a lot about myself through the writing of that book. *Miracle in the Making* was my first Christian book, the first time I shared my faith through my writing. I enjoyed writing it so much that it made me want to write more books with a Christian focus.

"Writing is more than mastering a craft and learning technique; you have to have something to say. For years I tried different kinds of writing, searching for my 'voice,' that absolute sense a writer feels when he expresses his deepest self and his own unique vision of the world.

"Now I believe I've found where I belong as a writer. The quality that distinguishes Christian books, says Madeleine L'Engle, is their 'ultimately affirmative view of life.' They say yes to life. That is what I want my writing to do."

Twinkle, twinkle, little star,
How I wonder what you are,
Up above the world so high,
Like a diamond in the sky.

As your bright and tiny spark
Lights the traveler in the dark,
Though I know not what you are,
Twinkle, twinkle, little star.

—Jane Taylor

MANNING de V. LEE

LEE, Manning de V(illeneuve)   1894-1980

PERSONAL: Born March 15, 1894, in Summerville, S.C.; died March 31, 1980, in Chestnut Hill, Pa.; son of Joseph and Gertrude Marie (Sweeny) Lee; married Eunice Celeste Sandoval (an author under name Tina Lee), April 8, 1922; children: Richard Sandoval. *Education:* Attended Pennsylvania Academy of Fine Arts, 1914-15, 1919-22; studied art in Europe, 1921. *Politics:* Democrat. *Religion:* Episcopalian. *Home:* The Kenilworth, Alden Park Manor, Philadelphia, Pa. 19144.

CAREER: Artist and illustrator. Work hangs in a number of public buildings, including the U.S. Mint, Philadelphia, Pa., U.S. Naval Academy, Annapolis, Md., Cranbrook Academy, Bloomfield Hills, Mich., County Court House, Bel Air, Md., and the Presidential Palace, Monrovia, Liberia; work is represented in numerous private collections. Exhibitions include: Gibbs Art Gallery, Charleston, S.C., 1920; Pennsylvania Academy of Fine Arts Watercolor Show, Philadelphia, 1931; N. W. Ayer & Co., Philadelphia, 1945. Also instructor of illustration at the Pennsylvania Academy of Fine Arts, summer, 1947. *Military service:* Served with First Virginia Field Artillery at the Mexican border, 1916; U.S. Army, 1917-19, served in field artillery in France; became second lieutenant. *Member:* Philadelphia Art Alliance, Royal Society of Arts (fellow), Southern States Art League, Society of Mayflower Descendents, Order of Foreign Wars. *Awards, honors:* Recipient of gold medal from the Charleston Exposition, 1907.

(From *The Beckoning Road* by Caroline Dale Snedeker. Illustrated by Manning de V. Lee.)

ILLUSTRATOR—All for young people: Reginald W. Kauffman, *Spanish Dollars*, Penn Publishing, 1925; Thomas A. Mawhinney, *The Sword of the House of de Marillac*, Penn Publishing, 1925; Andrew Lang, editor, *The Blue Fairy Book*, Macrae, 1926; T. A. Mawhinney, *English Oak and Spanish Gold*, Penn Publishing, 1926, reprinted, McKay, 1943; Rupert S. Holland, *Historic Ships*, Macrae, 1926; R. S. Holland, *Historic Railroads*, Macrae, 1927; R. W. Kauffman, *The Overland Trail*, Penn Publishing, 1927; A. Lang, editor, *The Red Fairy Book*, Macrae, 1927; R. S. Holland, *Historic Airships*, Macrae, 1928; T. A. Mawhinney, *The Messenger of the Black Prince*, Penn Publishing, 1928; Caroline D. Snedeker, *The Beckoning Road*, Doubleday, Doran, 1929; Rose B. Knox, *The Boys and Sally Down on a Plantation*, Doubleday, Doran, 1930; C. D. Snedeker, *The Town of the Fearless*, Doubleday, Doran, 1931; R. B. Knox, *Gray Caps*, Doubleday, Doran, 1932; Robert Louis Stevenson, *Kidnapped*, Garden City Publishing, 1932; Eleanor Roosevelt, *When You Grow Up to Vote*, Houghton, 1932; C. D. Snedeker, *Uncharted Ways*, Doubleday, Doran, 1935.

R. B. Knox, *Cousins' Luck in Louisiana Bayou Country*, Macmillan, 1940; *Knight of the Revolution*, Macrae, 1941; Eric P. Kelly, *From Star to Star: A Story of Krakow in 1943*, Lippincott, 1944; Marjorie Hayes, *Green Peace*, Lippincott, 1945; Marjorie H. Allee, *Smoke Jumper*, Houghton, 1945; Margaret Leighton, *The Singing Cave* (Junior Literary Guild selection), Houghton, 1945; Florence Hayes, *Burro Tamer*, Random House, 1946; Watson, *High Stepper*, Houghton, 1946; Evelyn C. Nevin, *Lost Children of the Shoshones*, Ryerson Press, 1946; Tina Lee (pseudonym of wife, Eunice Lee), *What to Do Now*, Dou-

bleday, 1946; Russell Emery, *Adventure North*, Macrae, 1947; T. Lee, *How to Make Dolls and Doll Houses*, Doubleday, 1948; Walter D. Edmonds, *Cadmus Henry*, Dodd, 1949; T. Lee, *Fun with Paper Dolls*, Doubleday, 1949; Marjorie Medary, *Prairie Printer*, Longmans, Green, 1949.

Alida S. Malkus, *Colt of Destiny: A Story of the California Missions*, Winston, 1950; Wirt, *Pirate Brig*, Scribner, 1950; Phyllis R. Fenner, *Cowboys, Cowboys, Cowboys: Stories of Roundups, and Rodeos, Branding and Broncobusting*, F. Watts, 1950; L. Pannell and F. Cavanah, editors, *Holiday Round Up*, Macrae, 1950; P. R. Fenner, *Indians, Indians, Indians: Stories of Tepees and Tomahawks, Wampum Belts and War Bonnets, Peace Pipes and Papooses*, F. Watts, 1950; P. R. Fenner, *Dogs, Dogs, Dogs: Stories of Challengers and Champions, Heroes and Hunters, Warriors and Workers*, F. Watts, 1951; P. R. Fenner, editor, *Pirates, Pirates, Pirates: Stories of Cutlasses and Corsairs, Buried Treasure and Buccaneers, Ships and Swashbucklers*, F. Watts, 1951; Elizabeth Pack, *Saddle for Hoskie*, Abingdon-Cokesbury, 1951; Kenneth C. Randall, *Wild Hunter*, F. Watts, 1951; Mary Alice Jones, *Bible Stories*, Rand McNally, 1952, reprinted as *Bible Stories for Children*, 1974; Elizabeth Jane Coatsworth, *Boston Bells*, Macmillan, 1952; W. D. Edmonds, *Corporal Bess: The Story of a Boy and a Dog*, Dodd, 1952; P. R. Fenner, *Elephants, Elephants, Elephants: Stories of Rogues, and Workers, Tuskers and Trekkers, Jungle Trails and Circus Tanbark*, F. Watts, 1952; Harold Coy, *First Book of Presidents*, Heath, 1952; P. R. Fenner, editor, *Ghosts, Ghosts, Ghosts: Stories of Spooks and Spirits, Haunts and Hobgoblins, Werewolves and Will-o-the Wisp*, F. Watts, 1952; Isabelle Lawrence, *The Night Watch: Adventure with Rembrandt,* Rand McNally, 1952; Anne Emery, *Scarlet Royal,* Macrae, 1952.

E. J. Coatsworth, *Aunt Flora,* Macmillan, 1953; Margaret Hill, *Goal in the Sky,* Little, Brown, 1953; E. J. Coatsworth, *Old Whirlwind: A Story of Davy Crockett,* Macmillan, 1953; Irvin Block, *Real Book about Ships,* Garden City Publishing, 1953; Mary Elting, *Ships at Work,* Garden City Publishing, 1953; Elsie Ball, *George Washington, First President,* Abingdon, 1954; E. J. Coatsworth, *The Sod House,* Macmillan, 1954; Virginia L. Eifert, *The Buffalo Trace,* Dodd, 1955; E. J. Coatsworth, *Cherry Ann and the Dragon Horse,* Macmillan, 1955; M. Hill, *Hostess in the Sky,* Little, Brown, 1955; T. Lee, *Manners to Grow On: A How-To-Do Book for Boys and Girls,* Doubleday, 1955; I. Lawrence, *A Spy in Williamsburg,* Rand McNally, 1955.

V. L. Eifert, *Out of the Wilderness: Young Abe Lincoln Grows Up,* Dodd, 1956; A. S. Malkus, *Sidi, Boy of the Desert,* Winston, 1956; S. North, *Son of the Lamp Maker: The Story of a Boy Who Knew Jesus,* Rand McNally, 1956; V.L. Eifert, *Mis-*

The canoes that were not already kindling-wood were dashing madly for shore. ■ (From "Turn and Turn About" by Rupert Sargent Holland in *Pirates, Pirates, Pirates,* selected by Phyllis R. Fenner. Illustrated by Manning de V. Lee.)

An inch at a time, he slunk around the trees and through the brush that hemmed them in. He was Crawling Cat, the warrior.... ■ (From "Wilderness Road" by Jim Kjelgaard in *Indians, Indians, Indians,* selected by Phyllis R. Fenner. Illustrated by Manning de V. Lee.)

sissippi Calling, Dodd, 1957; Jo Sykes, *Stubborn Mare,* Winston, 1957; M. Hill, *Senior Hostess,* Little, Brown, 1958; Jakob Grimm, *The Elves and the Shoemaker,* Rand McNally, 1959; V. L. Eifert, *New Birth of Freedom: Abraham Lincoln in the White House,* Dodd, 1959; V. L. Eifert, *Delta Queen: The Story of a Steamboat,* Dodd, 1960; M. Hill, *Really, Miss Hillsbro,* Little, Brown, 1960; V. L. Eifert, *George Shannon, Young Explorer with Lewis and Clark,* Dodd, 1968; Mary Alice Jones, *The Twenty-Third Psalm,* Rand McNally, 1964; I. Lawrence, *Drumbeats in Williamsburg: A Story of Washington, Lafayette and Yorktown,* Rand McNally, 1965; M. A. Jones, *The Story of Joseph,* Rand McNally, 1965; T. Lee, *Things to Do,* Doubleday, 1965; V. L. Eifert, *With a Task before Me: Abraham Lincoln Leaves Springfield,* Dodd, 1966.

Also illustrator of over 120 other books, mostly for young people. Work appeared in magazines, including *Ladies' Home Journal, Country Life, Redbook,* and *Maclean's;* also created educational filmstrips, and a series of commemorative postage stamps designed for Guinea, Liberia, and Indonesia.

SIDELIGHTS: "I was born near Charleston, South Carolina, March 15, 1894. Attended public and private schools. Spent

(From *Historic Ships* by Rupert Sargent Holland. Illustrated by Manning de V. Lee.)

much of my youth in the country and at an early age learned to love books, horses and the sea.'' [Bertha E. Mahony and Elinor Whitney, compilers, *Contemporary Illustrators of Children's Books,* The Bookshop for Boys and Girls, 1930.[1]]

"One of my earliest and most vivid memories is of blue-clad soldiers marching past our front gate. The war with Spain was on then and near our place in South Carolina was an army camp. My father being a general in the National Guard, the house was often full of clanking sabres and gold braid. All this made a deep impression on a four-year-old and for years afterward the fly-leaves and margins of school books were embellished with rearing horses, waving flags and all the gory detail of a battlefield.

"In 1914 I entered the Pennsylvania Academy but left it two years later to go to the Mexican border with the Virginia Field Artillery. Pancho Villa attended to, we were sent back to Virginia only to find ourselves in the First World War. A year and a half in France as an artillery lieutenant, then back to school. Two years later I was again sent to Europe on an Academy Traveling Scholarship—England, France, Switzerland and Italy. Won the 2nd Toppan Prize on my return.

"I still like battle scenes, but since there are no glittering sabres and charging steeds in modern warfare, most of these subjects now are drawn from the past. Historical subjects of all kinds interest me. They enable me to hobnob with quaint characters from a bygone era while enjoying at the same time all the modern gadgets and conveniences. A highly satisfactory arrangement.'' [Bertha E. Mahony and others, compilers, *Illustrators of Children's Books: 1744-1945,* Horn Book, 1947.[2]]

Lee's career in illustration began with drawings for periodicals. Throughout his career, he illustrated over two hundred books dealing with adventure in all parts of the world and every period in history. He has illustrated books by Phyllis R. Fenner, Elizabeth Coatsworth, Virginia Eifert, and Carol Snedeker as well as many other authors including his wife, Tina.

Lee died March 31, 1980, at his home in Chestnut Hill, Pennsylvania.

FOR MORE INFORMATION SEE: Bertha E. Mahony and Elinor Whitney, compilers, *Contemporary Illustrators of Children's Books,* The Bookshop for Boys and Girls, 1930, Gale, 1978; Bertha E. Mahony and others, compilers, *Illustrators of Children's Books: 1744-1945,* Horn Book, 1947; B. M. Miller and others, compilers, *Illustrators of Children's Books: 1946-1956,* Horn Book, 1958; Walt Reed, compiler, *The Illustrator in America 1900-1960's,* Reinhold, 1966; *Illustrators of Books for Young People,* 2nd edition, Scarecrow, 1975. *Obituaries: Publishers Weekly,* May 30, 1980.

LEIGHTON, Clare (Veronica Hope) 1900(?)-

PERSONAL: Born April 12, about 1900, in London, England; came to United States in 1939; naturalized U.S. citizen, 1945; daughter of Robert (a writer) and Marie (a writer; maiden name, Connor) Leighton; married Henry Noel Brailsford. *Education:* Attended Brighton School of Art, Slade School of Fine Art, University of London, 1921-23, and London County Council Central School of Arts and Crafts. *Residence:* Woodbury, Conn. 06798.

(From "Both Man and Bird and Beast" in *Imagination's Other Place,* compiled by Helen Plotz. Wood engraving by Clare Leighton.)

CAREER: Artist, illustrator, engraver, and author. Has lectured at Duke University. Commissions include stained glass windows for St. Paul's Cathedral, Worcester, Mass., the Lutheran Church, Waterbury, Conn., the Methodist Church, Wellfleet, Mass.; a mosaic for Convent Holy Family of Nazareth Church, Monroe, Conn.; twelve plates for Josiah Wedgwood & Sons Ltd.; and design work for Steuben Glass Co. *Exhibitions:* Art Center, New York, N.Y., February, 1929. Work is represented in the permanent collections of the Victoria and Albert Museum and the British Museum, London; the National Gallery, Stockholm, Sweden; the National Gallery of Canada, Ottawa; Metropolitan Museum of Art, New York, N.Y.; Boston Fine Arts Museum, Boston, Mass.; and the Baltimore Museum, Baltimore, Md.

MEMBER: Society of Wood Engravers, National Academy of Design (fellow), Society of American Graphic Artists (former vice-president), Royal Society of Painters, Etchers and Engravers (fellow), National Institute of Arts and Letters (former vice-president). *Awards, honors:* First prize, International Engravers Exhibition, Art Institute of Chicago, 1930; represented England in wood engraving at the International Exhibition in Venice, Italy, 1934; D.F.A., Colby College, 1940.

(From "Charm Me Asleep" in *The Singing and the Gold: Poems Translated from World Literature,* selected by Elinor Parker. Wood engraving by Clare Leighton.)

WRITINGS—Self-illustrated: *Woodcuts: Examples of the Work of Clare Leighton,* introduction by Hilaire Belloc, Longmans, Green, 1930; *The Musical Box* (juvenile), Longmans, Green, 1932; *How to Do Wood-Engraving and Woodcuts,* The Studio, 1932, reprinted, Branford, 1960; *The Farmer's Year: A Calendar of English Husbandry,* Longmans, Green, 1933; *The Wood That Came Back* (juvenile), Nicholson & Watson, 1934, Artists and Writers Guild, 1935; *Four Hedges: A Gardner's Chronicle,* Macmillan, 1935, reprinted, Gollancz, 1970; *Wood Engraving of the 1930s,* The Studio, 1936; *Country Matters,* Macmillan, 1937; *Sometime-Never,* Macmillan, 1939.

Southern Harvest, Macmillan, 1942; *Give Us This Day,* Reynal, 1943, reprinted, Books for Libraries, 1971; *Tempestuous Petticoat: The Story of an Invincible Edwardian* (biography of mother, Marie Connor Leighton), Rinehart, 1947; *Where Land Meets Sea: The Tide Line of Cape Cod,* Rinehart, 1954, reprinted as *Where Land Meets Sea: The Enduring Cape Cod,* Chatham Press, 1973; *Growing New Roots: An Essay,* Book Club of California, 1976.

Illustrator: Robert Nathan, *The Fiddler in Barty,* Heinemann, 1927; Alan E. Mulgan, *Home: A New Zealander's Adventure in England,* Longmans, 1927; Thornton Wilder, *The Bridge of San Luis Rey,* Longmans, 1929; Joseph Auslander, *Letters to Women,* Harper & Brothers, 1929; Thomas Hardy, *The Return of the Native,* Macmillan, 1929; Henry M. Tomlinson, *The Sea and the Jungle,* Duckworth, 1930; Emily Brontë, *Wuthering Heights,* Duckworth, 1931; Eleanor Farjeon, *Perkin in Pedlar,* Faber, 1932; Constance Holme, *The Trumpet in the Dust,* Nicholson & Watson, 1934; T. Hardy, *Under the Greenwood Tree; or, The Mellstock Quire: A Rural Painting of the Dutch School,* Macmillan, 1940, reprinted, St. Martin's, 1968; Elsie H.J. Symington, *By Light of Sun,* Putnam, 1941; Bertha C. Damon, *Sense of Humus,* Simon & Schuster, 1943; Elizabeth M. Robert, *The Time of Man,* Viking, 1945.

Josephine Y. Case, *Freedom's Farm,* Houghton, 1946; Bertha L. Pope, *Green Corners,* M. Joseph, 1947; *The Book of Psalms*

[and] *The First Psalm of David, the Book of Proverbs* [and] *The Book of Ecclesiastes,* Doubleday, 1952; *North Carolina Folk Lore,* compiled by Frank C. Brown and others, edited by Newman I. White, Duke University Press, 1952; *Imagination's Other Place: Poems of Science and Mathematics* (young adult), edited by Helen Plotz, Crowell, 1955; *Untune the Sky: Poems of Music and the Dance* (ALA Notable Book), edited by H. Poltz, Crowell, 1957; *I Was Just Thinking: A Book of Essays,* edited by Elinor Parker, Crowell, 1959; *The Singing and the Gold: Poems Translated from World Literature* (Horn Book honor list), edited by E. Parker, Crowell, 1962; *The Earth Is the Lord's: Poems of the Spirit,* edited by H. Plotz, Crowell, 1965; T. Hardy, *The Pinnacled Tower: Selected Poems of Thomas Hardy* (young adult), edited by H. Poltz, Macmillan, 1975.

Contributor of woodcuts to periodicals, including *Forum* and *Living Age.*

SIDELIGHTS: Leighton was born in London, England, about 1900. "My mother and father were both writers. My mother wrote the melodramatic serials that appeared in the English newspapers owned by Lord Northcliffe, and my father wrote boys' adventure stories. The entire household revolved around my mother's writing, for it was the large sums of money she earned that supported us. My father's work was not supposed to matter nearly as much, because he earned far less.

"The melodrama of my mother's stories seeped into our daily life, and even upstairs in the seclusion of the nursery we three children were made aware of the urgency of her work.

"My mother was proud of the fact that during the months of her pregnancies she was writing instalments each week of three separate serial stories.

"'I shall never forget how I had to rush to get my heroine married to my hero just as the first labor pains were beginning,' she laughed. 'It's all nonsense—this morning sickness and such. Leave that to the women with no work to do.'

"Hearing this, I remembered how Grandmamma had once told me that I was almost born into the inkwell, and that it was

(From *The Pinnacled Tower* by Thomas Hardy, edited by Helen Plotz. Illustrated by Clare Leighton.)

only because the nurse practically carried my mother upstairs that I first saw the light of day as a self-respecting human being should, from the comfort of a double bed.

"Because Mother and Father were always working, the most important room in the house was the study. It was filled with the material for her stories and for my father's boys' books. The enormous table in the middle of the room was cleared one day a year, so that on Christmas Day it might be used for a family party, as the dining room would be too small. . . .

"Our mother was not the only one to use this study table. To her left, past a barricade of books, sat our father. His was no world of heroes and villains. He lived among Wild West Indians and Northwest Mounted Police, boys' schools and dogs. Walled in, ever since I could remember, by deafness, he was able to write his adventure stories within touch of my mother; for he could not hear her as she dictated her melodramas across the study table to Miss Walmisley, the secretary. This suited him well, as he worshipped my mother so much that he was never happy when she was out of sight. With his minute, copperplate handwriting, so different from my mother's enormous quill-pen scrawl, he covered sheet after sheet with blood-curdling tales about Sargeant Silk of the Northwest Mounted Police, and Kiddie of the Camp of Australia, and sea battles of the days of Nelson.

"My father's part of the table was piled high with the history books and accounts of Indians and cowboys he needed for his stories. Innumerable pencil scribbles of canoes and Indian chiefs and dogs also lay around. For deep within my father was the yearning to be an artist. Finding that my mother expected him to go on with his writing, to help in earning the family income, he had tried to satisfy this urge by encouraging me in my earliest enthusiasms.

"'You've got to be an artist when you grow up,' he would tell me. 'It's what I've always wanted to be myself—more that anything else. I shan't feel so bad about it, though, if I see you painting pictures.'

"And while I was still a very small child he bought me my first oil paints. I was never given much chance to use them, for he was so often up in the nursery with them himself, painting from memory the little brown-sailed fishing smacks we watched in the summer on the North Sea, or heads of dogs, or even, when he felt particularly ambitious, scenes from his own Wild West stories.

"Then the seat at the study table beside Mother was vacant for hours at a time, and when Father returned to work Mother would look at him with a cold stare, as though he were a malingerer. He always supposed Mother had not noticed his absence. But he was not really able to slip away unobserved, for this study table was so crowded that any empty space showed up conspicuously.

"Unfortunately, the things I wanted to paint didn't coincide with what he wished. About this time, when I was six years old, I had a passion for mythological subjects. My father wanted me to paint landscapes or dogs or pretty faces, whereas I struggled stubbornly with a design of Andromeda chained to a rock. Soon he must have realized there wasn't much satisfaction to be found in vicarious painting, for he returned to his writing in the study. Once again that room in St. John's Wood was normal, with its full congestion of workers and bundles, undergarments, aspidistra, gramophone, easel, and dogs.

"We lived in a part of London called St. John's Wood. The actual neighborhood can still be found on the map, just beyond Baker Street and Regent's Park; but its spirit vanished many years ago. For St. John's Wood belonged to the age of Romance.

"'You have to be worthy of living here,' our mother used always to say. 'And that is not a question of money or fame. I can think of many very rich and important people who would be incapable of understanding the spirit of the place. They might have heaps of money, but nothing on earth could ever make them belong.'

"It was a world of individual seclusion. Houses stood hidden behind high garden walls. Garden walls were dwarfed by massive trees. Whatever might take place within these walls was shielded from the eyes of the public. . . .

"Our house, which had the romantic name of Vallombrosa, was satisfactorily invisible from the road. The solid garden gate and the high brick wall were topped with pieces of broken glass bottles to prevent burglars from scaling them. Against the entire length of this wall grew a row of linden trees. We were proof against the vulgar gaze of passersby. Nobody could know of our thirty-six lilac bushes or the apple tree in the back garden that blossomed each spring, or the straggly grapevine that draped the wall at the fat end of Vallombrosa.

"'But then, nobody has any right to know what goes on inside one's garden gate.' Our mother said. 'I have no patience with people who need to live in public. You can always tell them by a certain flat look in their eyes. They have no magic about them. It's as though their outlines end where they end, instead of being surrounded by an aura of glow.'

"In the St. John's Wood of my childhood most of our neighbors had this 'glow.' For we lived in the sacred innermost circle, which housed the writers and painters, the actresses and singers, and a few romantic minded but impecunious retired Army officers.

"Our sheltered, secure world was dominated by class feeling. But because both of our parents were writers, it was a very special, peculiar class feeling. It had none of the rigid standards of the 'huntin' and shootin' aristocracy, even though that had been our Grandpapa's background. It was a snobbishness that included the celebrated poet or the knighted sculptor. For these were the days when Art was highly paid and romantic, and so long as the artists were successful, the doors of Society were flung open wide to receive them. . . .

"Each spring the family moved to a house in East Anglia. This annual migration had an Old Testament flavor to it, as though we moved out of Ur of the Chaldees into Canaan. It ought never to have been negotiated in a modern conveyance like a railway train. There should have been camels as beasts of burden, and rivers and deserts to cross.

"The first few years of my life we had rented a furnished house for two or three months each summer on the South Coast. It had been exciting to go to a different resort every season, and later on, when we went always to the same place, we often hankered after this change of scene, as over the years of our childhood we grew to know each bush and stone near Lowestoft. For the time came when the Leighton family decided it should have a permanent seaside home, and we bought a half-built house in East Anglia, on a cliff overlooking the North Sea.

(From "Reading, Writing, and Talking" in *I Was Just Thinking: A Book of Essays,* selected by Elinor Parker. Wood engraving by Clare Leighton.)

"'Of course,' my mother said, 'if we could have found a suitable house for sale that had been lived in and mellowed, it might have been better—though then we'd have had to spend quite a time getting rid of the mental atmosphere left behind by the people who'd lived there before. But as things are, the fact that The Red Croft was only half-built when we bought it ought to make everything pretty safe.'

"My mother had a deep superstition against building a house. Nothing on earth could have persuaded her to do so.

"The migration started a week or two before we actually took the journey by train, for there was so much to be packed. Countless linen chests and trunks appeared on the landings, and in odd corners of all the rooms. I never knew where these were kept over the rest of the year, because there were depths in that St. John's Wood house which we were not allowed to penetrate. Two staircases in Vallombrosa were forbidden to us: the pitch black stairs to the basement, and the equally dark stairway, shut off by a door, that led to the servants' bedrooms in the attic. Between these two floors lay our world; but the outer darknesses were the unknown. Sounds came to us from these regions. The ring of the alarm clock that wakened the servants before sunrise on winter mornings broke into our sleep in the night nursery. As we walked through the hall on our way out, we could hear Dolly stoking the kitchen range, and could imagine the glow of the great banked fire that cooked our dinner. But it never worried us to realize that the servants lived in perpetual gaslight and saw no sun. . . ." [Clare Leighton, *Tempestuous Petticoat: The Story of an Invincible Edwardian,* Reinhart & Co., 1947.[1]]

Leighton was privately educated at home. "This schooling took place in the dining room in St. John's Wood, and often we had to wait until the breakfast table had been cleared before we could start. The smell of bacon and toast hung in the air and seemed to rest upon my school books. Every day at about eleven o'clock my mother entered the room to fetch her un-

varying refreshment of a glass of Burgundy and two Osborne biscuits—seeming to forget the cold bacon on toast that had been saved from the breakfast table for this occasion.

"'It's useless for you to think you need any serious schooling,' my mother would remind me. 'I disapprove of education for women. Never forget that a blue stocking is a woman who has failed in her sex, and that the few females who find their way to a university are inevitably far from being the well-bred women of England. A career woman never belongs to the aristocracy. A woman is meant for marriage, and once she is married she has lost all chance to pursue her career.'

"And without a glance at Father who was idly drawing a little fishing boat, Mother would turn round to Walmy and go on dictating the instalment of one of her serial stories which was to feed and clothe the three children."'[1]

According to Leighton, her early education by governesses was far from adequate. She later studied at the Brighton School of Art and at the Slade School of Art. It was at the Central School of Arts and Crafts in England that Leighton learned the art of wood-engraving. "Wood-cuts have one great advantage over any other form of art. They are the cheapest to produce. Unlike the etcher's more delicate copper plate, innumerable reproductions can be taken from a boxwood block. People who never dreamt of being able to afford an original work of art before, find that they can buy one for a guinea. This means that a whole new public can be introduced to the possession of art.

"This popularisation of art should be the wood-cutter's aim and ambition. I have no patience with the attempt that is being made by some dealers . . . to limit output so as to appeal to the snobbishness of collectors. With etchings that cannot be reproduced indefinitely there is a reason. With woodcuts there is definitely no excuse for the limiting of editions and numbering of prints. Not only is it a far more moral attitude for an artist to sell his prints at the lowest price and in the largest quantities possible, but I am sure that it will also be to his advantage in the long run. A wide following is so much safer than the whims of a few well-to-do collectors.

"Definitely there is a huge new public awaiting a form of art like wood-cutting that is within their reach. Moreover the precision of engraving has a special appeal today. It fits in so well with the present scientific spirit. The wood-cutter's absorption with shapes and movements, rather than detail, is also all part of the modern age.

"Another point on which I feel strongly is that painting and woodcutting should go hand in hand instead of being separate arts. Wood-engraving is such an excellent training for a young painter. The two chief faults in painting today are lack of design and carelessness. Woodcutting will cure them both. First of all when you are working in a small framework it is impossible to neglect design. Unless the whole thing is well planned out in advance it will be a complete mess. Wood-engraving also teaches great precision. You have to think before each stroke. Not only is there no chance of getting away with bad work, it cannot even be covered up.

"There is absolutely nothing in wood-engraving that can harm a young painter and much that can do him good. Above all in these days it provides him with something that he can sell and a young artist does have a terribly difficult time nowadays. I don't think that the temptation to make an easy living by wood–cutting will ever keep him from painting if he has real talent. You can't go on working in miniature without eventually wanting to do something bigger. I've even got an ambition that way, although up till now wood-engraving has always been my real work. I want to do big mural decorations, go to the opposite extreme in size for a change. For working on a large scale can teach the wood-cutter many things, just as working in miniature can help a painter.'' ["In the Studio of Clare Leighton,'' *The London Studio,* March, 1937.[2]]

From the onset of her career as a wood-engraver, Leighton won numerous awards. She won first prize at the 1938 International Engravers Exhibition at the Art Institute of Chicago. She was also chosen as the English representative in wood-engraving at the International Exhibition in Italy, and has had her work exhibited in the permanent collections at the British Museum, the National Galleries of Stockholm and Canada, and in museums in Boston, Baltimore, and New York. "Of all media, wood-engraving is the one in which there is the least to be taught and the most to be learnt. The principle of the modern woodcut is that of a white chalk drawing on a blackboard, while the principle of etching is that of a black line drawing on white paper. Every cut made on a wood block prints white, so that one is always working up from the black towards the light. If the new, unengraved block were printed, it would be but a rectangle of black ink.

"The technique of the wood block has changed radically since the days of the pioneers. The early prints, which should be called woodcuts rather than wood-engravings, nearly always gave the effect of black lines on white, but the white line on a black background is the natural and more direct method. . . .

"The wood-engraving appeals to any artist who loves strong, clean, deliberate drawing, for it is impossible on the wood block to 'codge' or re-state. The thinking must be done before the engraving, and whereas in the etched plate accidents or uncertainties—or even poor draughtsmanship—can be hidden by a stronger bath of acid, there is in the wood block no way out except a new start.

"Wood-engraving is a dangerous craft, inasmuch as it is possible so easily to get a showy effect. The modern creative engraver has discovered that he can use the wood block as a direct means of self-expression. This is a new development, for in the last century the old professional engraver, before the invention of mechanical methods of reproduction, merely translated the artist's drawing into a wood-engraving. This has had its danger, for whereas the good artist realises that the best work is that which uses the medium to the uttermost, never abusing it, the indifferent artist is apt to excuse his careless, slovenly cutting, by saying that he is getting a 'woody quality' into his work. . . . Only when the artist realises that he must also be a craftsman, and the craftsman aspires to be an artist, shall we preserve and develop the outstanding school of wood-engraving that is our glory to-day." [Clare Leighton, *Wood-Engraving and Woodcuts,* Studio Publications Ltd., 1932.[3]]

Besides exhibiting woodcuts, Leighton has illustrated numerous books with wood-engravings, such as Brontë's *Wuthering Heights,* Hardy's *The Return of the Native,* and Wilder's *The Bridge of San Luis Ray.* She has also written and self-illustrated several books, including two books for children, *The Musical Box* and *The Wood That Came Back.* "There is something exacting about producing a book entirely by yourself. Be an author, and somebody else carries the responsibility of illustrating and designing the book. Be an artist, and all you need to do is to sink yourself into the entity and the world of the author whom you are interpreting. Combine the two, and you have no alibi.

(From "All Creatures Here Below" in *The Earth Is the Lord's: Poems of the Spirit,* compiled by Helen Plotz. Illustrated by Clare Leighton.)

"But the dual role is rewarding, for thereby you are able to make a true work of art out of the book you have planned. In addition, you can manage to turn your prose, somehow or other, into the channels of whatsoever subject you wish to draw: thus, to be fantastic, should I have yearned all my life to do a wood engraving of a hippopotamus, I am at liberty, in my writing, to introduce the subject of the hippopotamus—however obscurely—and so justify myself in making a wood block of the ridiculous creature.

"More seriously, the main pleasure lies in being the sole arbiter of the shape of the book, of the choice of the type face, of the size and proportions of the type area, of the entire mood of the book, including the design of the jacket and the cover and the conscious control over the rhythm of the book as a whole. Only thus can an illustrated, decorated book become a complete work of art.

"It was many years ago that I wrote my first book. Ever since leaving art school in London, I had been illustrating the books of others; but, though I was able to delight in this, and could identify myself fairly completely with the world of the author— a rich experience, when it takes one to Peru or the Amazon, and opens up unknown worlds—yet I seemed never to feel I had fully realized myself. It happened that I had been wanting to do a series of large wood engravings, based upon the twelve months on an English farm. I discussed this with my publisher, wondering whom we could find who best might write the accompanying prose. And it was then that he suggested I write my own text and design the entire volume.

"It is strange, being both writer and artist, for I never quite know on which side of the cultural curtain I the more belong. Reviewers write of my prose; art critics devote themselves to my engravings. Sometimes I have a disquieting fear lest I be diluting my forces. But then I recollect such giants as William Blake and Rossetti, who felt no concern over their dual role, and I get a comforting sense of unity of purpose, and an awareness of the one medium being a kind of recreating holiday from the other. As a wood engraver, dealing always with form, and unavoidably with symbols—for the graphic artist must depend upon lines, and tones built up of lines, to show texture and color, and is deprived of the sensuous facility of the palette—it has always seemed to me as though I escape into my writing and become a verbal painter. In my prose I am freed from the arbitrary demands of black-and-white form, and can revel in all possible richness of color.

"One of the first questions I am always asked is: Which do you do first—the writing or the engraving? This is difficult to answer, for I work upon the entire book by stages. The first stage, naturally, is the planning. Into this must come an awareness of the actual shape of the book, with a determined page size and type area. One could not, else, design the chapter headings, which must—or generally should, though license is permitted—be the width, somewhere in the outermost points of their surface, of the type area. For a well-designed book must have a good shape to the page. It can have no unintentional looseness.

"The next, the very essential, stage, is to decide what type face will balance best the weight of my engravings. Wood engravings are, by nature, rich, thick, definite blacks and whites. They demand an entirely different type face from—say—the gray-toned lithograph or the thinner, grayer, finer copper or steel engraving. This choice of type face is an important thing in the designing of a book. If one is fortunate in one's choice of publisher, one will have a few pages set up in the selected type, so as to get the required balance into the weight of the wood blocks.

"The following stage is the harvesting of the written matter. For this must hold its own in value against the decorating engravings. And here a most interesting element enters in. While I must, unavoidably and inevitably, assemble my material from reality—trolling for the bluefish in the Bay of Cape Cod, gathering high bush blueberries in the pond-fringed swamps, partaking of the annual festival of the Blessing of the Fleet in Provincetown, wandering across the mud flats at low tide to learn the magic of all those tiny ocean events that in their due season occur—while I am doing this I am aware of the imminence of yet another element: the fructifying force of nostalgia.

"Nostalgia is a mighty power. It has begotten many of the world's best ballads and songs. From this fierce force of loneliness comes a great surge of creating. And so, if I am wise, at that moment when I am sodden with something, I leave it. Thereby, suddenly, with a strange clarity I am aware of what I have left, and fully understand it. Thus, when I had accumulated much of my material for 'Where Land Meets Sea,' I forsook Cape Cod and returned to Connecticut in order that I might become homesick for the ocean. In this way, also, I get

away from any possibility of too factual and photographic representation. The creative side functions more fully.

"When it comes to the writing of the text, I do the first draft rapidly and very sloppily, content just to get down upon paper the ideas that tumble over each other, and willing to rewrite it many times over. It is when this first draft is done that I design all my blocks, roughing them in on odd bits of paper the size of the book itself, and planning them against the boundaries of the type area.

"Now comes the real labor: months upon months of tedious engraving follow. If you are lucky in your deadline you can let the designs get 'cold' before you start actually to engrave, for only thus can you be certain of their quality. . . . Your endgrain boxwood blocks stand ready. Your tools have been sharpened. Excitedly you want to begin.

"Being normally human, I start on the easiest and the simplest blocks. There are two main ways of putting the design upon the wood: Either you can blacken the surface with india ink and transfer the drawing with light tracing paper, or you can coat it with a thin layer of white watercolor paint and then draw your design on with pencil. The first way is, in theory, the better, for the whole principle of wood engraving is that of cutting white upon a black surface. I happen to use the second method only because I was trained that way.

"Finally, two or three months later, the book appears. Am I interested and excited? No. I even dread looking at it. I assume interest, because the author is supposed to feel it. And perhaps tepidly I await the first reviews. But even the reviews fail to elate me. I only know that I would feel unhappy if they were bad ones. The book no longer belongs to me. I have finished with it. And somewhere within me, after I have recovered from the fatigue of doing this one, somewhere deep down I am aware of a queer sort of unrest, as the next ideas begin, already, to form." [Clare Leighton, "How I Made My Book," *American Artist,* February, 1955.[4]]

Leighton became a United States citizen in 1945, making her home in Woodbury, Connecticut. After settling in New England, Leighton did a set of twelve engravings depicting New England industries for Wedgewood plates. She has also designed for Steuben Glass and has designed stained glass windows and mosaics. In 1950 Leighton was elected to the National Institute of Arts and Letters.

FOR MORE INFORMATION SEE: New York Times, February 10, 1929; *Saturday Review of Literature,* October 14, 1939, January 23, 1943, May 17, 1947; *New York Herald Tribune Books,* December 20, 1942, December 12, 1943, March 2, 1947, August 15, 1954; *New York Times Book Review,* December 20, 1942, December 19, 1943, February 23, 1947, August 15, 1954; *Book Week,* December 26, 1943; *Time,* March 3, 1947; *Christian Science Monitor,* October 21, 1950; *American Artist,* November, 1954, February, 1955; Loring Holmes Dodd, *A Generation of Illustrators and Etchers,* Chapman & Grimes, 1960.

Three wise men of Gotham
Went to sea in a bowl;
If the bowl had been stronger
My story had been longer.

—Mother Goose

LEVOY, Myron

BRIEF ENTRY: Born in New York, N.Y. Levoy, who received his M.Sc. from Purdue University, has worked as a chemical engineer and was once involved in a scientific project for a manned space flight to Mars. As an author, he has written children's books, novels for young adults, plays, poetry, and short stories. In 1973 *The Witch of Fourth Street, and Other Stories* (Harper, 1972), was selected for the Children's Book Showcase. This book, a collection of stories for children about immigrants in New York during the 1920s, has been praised by authors and critics alike. *Horn Book* noted that the "tales and characters are highly original, sometimes humorous, sometimes poignant, and often profound." *Library Journal* added, "Levoy's descriptions of these people's hopes [and] fears . . . evoke empathy and successfully convey the feeling of the period."

Levoy again uses an immigrant theme in his young adult novel *Alan and Naomi* (Harper, 1977), in which he unfolds the relationship that develops between an American-Jewish boy and a twelve-year-old World War II refugee from France. In a review of the book, *Horn Book* commented that "the story not only skillfully evokes the effect of the Nazi horror on a Jewish family in America but presents the crisis in terms of the understanding and the emotions of a sensitive well-intentioned schoolboy." It was an American Book Award finalist in the paperback fiction category and was selected as an honor book for the Boston Globe-Horn Book Award in 1978. Translated into Dutch and German, *Alan and Naomi* also received the Buxtehuder Bulle Award as well as other European prizes. Other books by Levoy include *A Necktie in Greenwich Village* (Vanguard, 1968), an adult novel; *Penny Tunes and Princesses* (Harper, 1972), for children; and *A Shadow Like a Leopard* (Harper, 1981), a novel for young adults. Levoy has also written numerous plays that have been produced in New York, such as "Eli and Emily," 1969, "Footsteps," 1970, and "Smudge," 1971. *Residence:* Rockaway, N.J. *For More Information See: Fifth Book of Junior Authors and Illustrators,* H. W. Wilson, 1983.

LEYLAND, Eric (Arthur) 1911-

PERSONAL: Born in 1911, in Ilford, Essex, England; children: Two. *Education:* Attended Brentwood School and University College, London. *Residence:* Woodford Green, Essex, England.

CAREER: Author and editor of numerous books for children, beginning 1939. Chief librarian of Chingford Borough, London, England, 1938-46; chief librarian and curator of Walthamstow Borough, London, 1946-49; Noryanhurst School, London, principal, beginning 1949. Lecturer on books and the English language; literary advisor to publishing firms. *Member:* Library Association (fellow).

*WRITINGS—*Fiction; all for young people: *Mystery Trail,* Blackie & Son, 1942; *Treasure in Devon,* Blackie & Son, 1943; *Coming Shortly,* Hutchinson, 1944; *Gentleman of Sussex,* Hutchinson, 1944; *Hazard Royal,* Hutchinson, 1945; *All Fares Please!,* Hutchinson, 1946; *Eagles from the South,* Hutchinson, 1946; *The Silver Skein,* Hutchinson, 1946; *Skeleton in the Cupboard,* Macdonald & Co., 1946; *The Scorpion Strikes,* Hutchinson, 1946; *Dead Man's Gold,* Hutchinson, 1947; *Little World,* Macdonald & Co., 1947; *Long Odds,* Hutchinson, 1947; *The*

Mandeville Mystery, Hutchinson, 1947; *The Valiant Quest,* Hutchinson, 1947; *Faint Shadow,* Macdonald & Co., 1948; *Jackdaw's Hoard* (illustrated by M. Mackinlay), Hutchinson, 1948; *The Adventure Omnibus,* Odhams, 1949; *The Colorado Kid* (illustrated by W. G. Gale), Hutchinson, 1949; *Flame of the Sierras* (illustrated by A. Berkeley), Hutchinson, 1949.

The Captain Rides Again, Jenkins, 1950; *The Cricket Week Mystery,* Ward, Lock, 1950; *Discovery on the Thames* (illustrated by Leslie Atkinson), University of London Press, 1950; *Exercise Commando,* Museum Press, 1950; *Flame Takes Over* (illustrated by Maben), Hodder & Stoughton, 1950; *Mystery Moor,* Museum Press, 1950; *Versus the Shadow,* Hutchinson, 1950; *Arizona Round-Up* (illustrated by Douglas Relf), Brockhampton Press, 1951; *The Captain Intervenes,* Jenkins, 1951; *Case for Red Lawson,* Hutchinson, 1951; *The Counterfeit Mystery,* Museum Press, 1951; *Flame Over Africa* (illustrated by Maben), Hodder & Stoughton, 1951; *Full Steam Ahead!* (illustrated by Leslie Otway), Brockhampton Press, 1951; *Knock-Out,* Ward, Lock, 1951; *The Million Pound Island,* P. Garnett, 1951; *Monsieur Debonair,* Hutchinson, 1951; *The Mystery of the Pig's Nose* (illustrated by John Woods), Brockhampton Press, 1951; *No Quarter!,* Hutchinson, 1951; *Rustler's Trail,* Brockhampton Press, 1951.

All Hands on Deck (illustrated by J. Woods), Brockhampton Press, 1952; *Calling Red Lawson,* Hutchinson, 1952; *The Captain on Guard,* Jenkins, 1952; *The Captain Strikes Back,* Jenkins, 1952; *Challenge!,* Hutchinson, 1952; *Crash Landing* (illustrated by Jack Matthew), Brockhampton Press, 1952; *Flame of the Amazon,* Hodder & Stoughton, 1952; *Outlaw Gulch* (illustrated by D. Relf), Brockhampton Press, 1952; *The Abbotsbury Case,* Ward, Lock, 1953; *Counter Attack,* Hutchinson, 1953; *Flame Takes a Chance,* Hodder & Stoughton, 1953; *Flame Wins Through,* Hodder & Stoughton, 1953; *Indian Range* (illustrated by D. Relf), Brockhampton, 1953, reprinted, White Lion, 1975; *Sabotage,* Hutchinson, 1953; *Village under the Water* (illustrated by J. Woods), Brockhampton Press, 1953.

Danger Below (illustrated by J. Woods), Brockhampton Press, 1954; *Flame Hits Back* (illustrated by Wardill), Hodder & Stoughton, 1954; *Flame Hits the Trail,* Hodder & Stoughton, 1954; *Jolly Roger, Buccaneer* (illustrated by Annette Allcock), Hutchinson, 1954; *Madman's Peak,* Hutchinson, 1954; *Operation Treasure Trove,* Hutchinson, 1954; *Flame and the King's Ransom,* Hodder & Stoughton, 1955; *Flame of the Sahara,* Hodder & Stoughton, 1955; *Jolly Roger Sails Again* (illustrated by A. Allcock), Hutchinson, 1955; *Man Overboard* (illustrated by J. Woods), Brockhampton Press, 1955; *Red Lawson and the Sons of the Desert,* Hutchinson, 1955; *Well Done, Skinny!,* Hutchinson, 1955.

Abbey Sees It Through (illustrated by Jack Harman), Thomas Nelson, 1956; *Fire over London,* Hutchinson, 1956; *Flame on the Treasurer Trail,* Hodder & Stoughton, 1956; *Rip Randall and the Pharoah's Tomb,* Hutchinson, 1956; *Skinny on the Warpath,* Hutchinson, 1956; *To Arms for the Queen!* (illustrated by Biro), Brockhampton Press, 1956; *White Fury* (illustrated by J. Woods), Brockhampton Press, 1956; *Conspiracy at Abbey* (illustrated by Eric Tansley), Thomas Nelson, 1957; *Flame Makes the Grade,* Hodder & Stoughton, 1957; *Flame Takes Command,* Hodder & Stoughton, 1957; *Forest Feud* (illustrated by J. Woods), Brockhampton Press, 1957; (with Trevor E. S. Chard) *Hunter Hawk, Skyway Detective,* Edmund Ward, 1957; *Rebellion at Prior's* (illustrated by E. Tansley), Thomas Nelson, 1957; *Six Gun Gauntlet Gets His Man* (illustrated by Stanley Smith), Hutchinson, 1957; *Six Gun*

Gauntlet Rides Again (illustrated by S. Smith), Hutchinson, 1957; *Six Gun Gauntlet Strikes the Trail* (illustrated by S. Smith), Hutchinson, 1957; *Skinny's Christmas Eve,* Hutchinson, 1957; *Stop Thief* (illustrated by E. Tansley), Thomas Nelson, 1957.

Abbey on the Warpath (illustrated by George Lane), Thomas Nelson, 1958; *Emergency Call,* Thomas Nelson, 1958; *Flame, Secret Agent,* Hodder & Stoughton, 1958; *Half-Term Adventure* (illustrated by G. Lane), Thomas Nelson, 1958; *Mystery at Mardale* (illustrated by Geoffrey Whittam), Thomas Nelson, 1958; *Scotland Yard Detective* (illustrated by Eric Wade), Edmund Ward, 1958; *Ship's Captain* (illustrated by R. Barnard Way), Edmund Ward, 1958; *Wings over the Outback* (illustrated by J. Woods), Brockhampton Press, 1958; *Abbey Turns the Tables* (illustrated by Robert Johnston), Thomas Nelson, 1959; *Flame and the League of Fire,* Hodder & Stoughton, 1959; *Oll Mun* (illustrated by B. Gerry), Edmund Ward, 1959; *Six Gun Gauntlet Hits Back* (illustrated by S. Smith), Hutchinson, 1959; *Tall Timber Trail* (illustrated by J. Woods), Brockhampton Press, 1959.

Abbey Makes the Grade (illustrated by R. Johnston), Thomas Nelson, 1960; *Crisis at Black Creek,* Thomas Nelson, 1960; *Dangerous Waters,* Oldbourne, 1960; *Rustlers of the Fells* (illustrated by Robert Hodgson), Thomas Nelson, 1960; *Six Gun Gauntlet Wins Through* (illustrated by S. Smith), Hutchinson, 1960; *Smuggler's Trail,* Thomas Nelson, 1960; *Calling Steven Gale,* Muller, 1961; *Crash Dive* (illustrated by B. Gerry), Edmund Ward, 1961; *Gale Hits the Headlines,* Muller, 1961; *Going Concern* (illustrated by R. Hodgson), Thomas Nelson, 1961; *Odd Man Out at Abbey,* Thomas Nelson, 1961; (with T.E.S. Chard) *Bandit Gold* (illustrated by N. Dear), Edmund Ward, 1962; *Gale and the Sword of Mars,* Muller, 1962; *Scoop for Steven Gale,* Muller, 1962; *Treasure Trove at Abbey,* Thomas Nelson, 1963; *The Eagles Flew Straight* (illustrated by D. Relf), Harrap, 1965.

Nonfiction: *The Public Library: Its History, Organization, and Functions,* Pitman, 1937; *The Public Library and the Adolescent,* Grafton & Co., 1937; *The Wider Public Library,* Grafton & Co., 1938; (with Maurice J. Wrigley) *The Cinema,* Grafton & Co., 1939; *Librarianship as a Career* (juvenile), Vawser & Wiles, 1944; *Thrills and Spills: A Book of High-Speed Sports* (juvenile), Ward, Lock, 1951; *Budgerigars for Pleasure and Profit* (juvenile), English Universities Press, 1954; *Pet Birds for Boys and Girls* (juvenile), Nicholas Vane, 1954; *Wild Animals* (juvenile; illustrated by John T. Kenney), Edmund Ward, 1955; *Seabirds* (juvenile; illustrated by J. T. Kenney), Edmund Ward, 1956; *Dogs* (juvenile; illustrated by J. T. Kenney), Edmund Ward, 1957; *For Valour: The Story of the Victoria Cross* (juvenile history; illustrated by J. T. Kenney), Edmund Ward, 1960, Roy, 1961; *The Open Air Is My Hobby,* Wheaton, 1960; *Libraries in Schools,* Oldbourne, 1961, Philosophical Library, 1964; *The Farmer in the Mechanical Age* (juvenile), Edmund Ward, 1962.

Editor; all for young people: *Best Adventure Stories,* Youth Book Club, 1950; *The Boys' Book of Adventure,* Evans Brothers, 1950; *Boys' Book of Scouting and the Open Air,* Edmund Ward, 1956; (with T.E.S. Chard) *Boys' Book of the Air* (illustrated by R. B. Way and J. T. Kenney), Edmund Ward, 1957, Roy, 1958; *The Modern Boys' Book of Achievement,* Edmund Ward, 1958; *Boys' Book of the Seas,* Roy, 1959; *Meet Your Authors,* Harrap, 1963.

Contributor of short stories to *Boys' Own Paper* and *Eagle,* and of book reviews to various publications. Also author of numerous television scripts.

SIDELIGHTS: Leyland has written and/or edited more than 200 books for boys during his writing career. Hailed as one of the most popular writers of light boys' fiction in England, he has written several series of interest to boys. Included in the list of books he has written are the ''David Flame'' series, the ''Steven Gale'' series, the ''Abbey School'' series, the ''Max and Scrap'' series, the ''Huster Hawk'' series and the ''Boys' Book of . . .'' series. During his long writing career, which began in 1939, he has written television scripts, contributed to British boys' magazines, lectured throughout England on books and the English language, worked as literary adviser to publishing firms, edited series of books, and reviewed books for various publications.

FOR MORE INFORMATION SEE: Brian Doyle, *The Who's Who of Children's Literature,* Schocken Books, 1968.

LIERS, Emil E(rnest) 1890-1975

PERSONAL: Born in 1890, in Clayton, Iowa; died October 17, 1975. *Education:* Graduated from State Normal School (now University of Wisconsin, La Crosse), 1920.

CAREER: Authority on wildlife, author of wildlife books for children. Taught early in career before becoming full-time author; created an otter sanctuary in Minnesota. Walt Disney Studios, Burbank, Calif., technical advisor for Academy Award-winning film, ''Beaver Valley.'' *Awards, honors:* Aurianne Award from the American Library Association, 1964, for *A Black Bear's Story.*

WRITINGS—All for children: *An Otter's Story* (Junior Literary Guild selection; ALA Notable Book; illustrated by Tony Palazzo), Viking, 1953; *A Beaver's Story* (Junior Literary Guild selection; illustrated by Ray Sherin), Viking, 1958; *A Black Bear's Story (Horn Book* honor list; illustrated by R. Sherin), Viking, 1962; *A Groundhog's Story* (illustrated by Bill McPheeters), Southern Publishing, 1976; *A Mink's Story,* Southern Publishing, 1979.

SIDELIGHTS: A wildlife enthusiast and nature lover, Liers had the distinction of being the first man to breed and raise otters in this country. At his farm in Homer, Minnesota, Liers raised over fifteen otters in the hope that the world would learn about them and protect them from indiscriminate and ruthless hunting. His study of otters led to his first book for youngsters, *An Otter's Story.*

''I was born on July 2, 1890, at Clayton, Iowa, a little village nestling among the hills along the Mississippi River, ten miles downstream from where the Wisconsin River merges with the Father of Waters. I always loved to play along the shore and fell in the river several times. But, like a cat, I scrambled out of the water faster than I fell into it.

''My parents loved the outdoors and took me with them for walks along the river. They taught me to observe the habits of birds and animals and flowers. One day we saw some animals playing in the water and on land. They were having a great time as they slid down the bank into the water. My first otters! They were probably a family that had migrated down the Wisconsin River from northern Wisconsin. Their antics intrigued me. Every day while fishing for sunfish or bass, I would watch for my otters.

''Since much of my boyhood was spent on farms, my interest in nature increased as I grew up. With my dogs and Uncle

George, I spent all the time I could in the woods or along the river.

"When I was twelve, we moved to Dubuque, Iowa, where my father followed his trade as a barber. I attended school there—grade and high school. Though I used to go out early in the morning to fish and hunt, I was seldom late for my classes. I played football although I hated missing time from my beloved outdoors. Whenever I could, I would go off to spend a week end or several days at a fisherman's camp, helping him trap and fish.

"In 1912 I married a girl who had also lived all her life on the river. For three years we made our home on an island above La Crosse, Wisconsin. I fished and trapped and dug mussel shells for pearls and button. Then we bought a houseboat and traveled up and down the Mississippi River, camping on the islands and the mainland. In 1914 our little daughter Patricia was born. A few years later, I attended the Wisconsin Teacher's College in La Crosse. I moved our houseboat to a nearby island and earned my way through college by trapping and fishing.

"For a time I had a mink farm. Then . . . I caught my first baby or cub otter. I became so intrigued with him that I discontinued the minks and made a business of the otters. My pets have been filmed for the movies and written up in national and international magazines. I have shown the otters at schools and clubs. For two summers I showed them at the Bronx Zoo. The interst everyone showed in my pets led me to write. . . ."

FOR MORE INFORMATION SEE: Patricia Marr, "Emil Liers, the Otter Man," *Nature Magazine,* March, 1950; Martha E. Ward and D. A. Marquardt, *Authors of Books for Young People,* Scarecrow, 1967.

LIGNELL, Lois 1911-

PERSONAL: Born June 4, 1911, in Duluth,, Minn.; daughter of Werner (an architect) and Eva (Strasberger) Lignell; married Ryerson Johnson (a writer), May 10, 1938; children: Jennifer. *Education:* Attended Parsons School of Design, Traphagen School of Fashion, Massachusetts School of Art, School of the Art Institute of Chicago, Chicago School of Design, Denison University, and Columbia University. *Home:* 35 School St., Lubec, Maine 04652.

CAREER: Free-lance illustrator of children's books. Worked with sculptor Gozo Kawamura, 1933-38; has executed free-lance graphic arts and advertising jobs for such magazines as *Charm* and *Glamour,* and for such companies as Shulton, for whom she designed Old Spice and Friendship Garden toiletry packages, 1943-50. *Awards, honors:* Jane Addams Award from the Woman's International League for Peace and Freedom, 1963, for *The Monkey and the Wild, Wild Wind.*

WRITINGS: (With Betz Princehorn) *Three Japanese Mice and Their Whiskers* (self-illustrated; juvenile), Farrar & Rinehart, 1934.

Illustrator; all for children; all written by husband, Ryerson Johnson, except as indicated: *Gozo's Wonderful Kite,* Crowell, 1951; Clyde R. Bulla, *A Tree Is a Plant,* Crowell, 1960, reprinted, 1973; *The Monkey and the Wild, Wild Wind,* Abelard, 1961; *The Mouse and the Moon,* E.M. Hale, 1968; *Let's Play Dinosaur,* Front Row Experience, 1978.

LOIS LIGNELL

WORK IN PROGRESS: Illustrating her own book, tentatively titled, *Pocket Bear.*

SIDELIGHTS: "As a child I felt a warm interest in what little Japanese art I was exposed to, and as I grew older my sympathy and identification with it increased. I think this was because of the simplicity and directness the Japanese have for getting at the essence of an idea or feeling. In 1934 I illustrated my first children's book, *Three Japanese Mice and Their Whiskers.* It won a book jacket prize and was included in an exhibit of outstanding illustrated books.

"From 1933 to 1938 I assisted Gozo Kawamura, a Japanese sculptor who invented an enlarging machine, and enlarged the statues in and outside of the new Supreme Court Building in Washington, D.C., Prometheus at Rockefeller Center, New York, and many others all over the country. While studying painting and calligraphy with Mr. Kawamura, I married a writer, Ryerson Johnson, in 1938, and free-lanced finished art for *Charm* magazine, *Parents* publications and *Glamour.*

"From 1943 to 1950 I designed Shulton's packages for Old Spice and Friendship Garden Toiletries as well as displays and ads for national magazines. The Art Directors Show exhibited one of these ads. In 1950 I had a baby girl, and devoted myself to motherhood and free-lancing. I illustrated *Gozo's Wonderful Kite* which my husband wrote, using some of Gozo

(From *Let's Play Dinosaur* by Ryerson Johnson. Illustrated by Lois Lignell.)

Kawamura's actual boyhood background.'' [Bertha M. Miller and others, compilers, *Illustrators of Children's Books: 1946-1956*, Horn Book, 1958.]

''I've been doing canvas painting lately, and illustrating a book of mine in progress: working title, *Pocket Bear*.''

FOR MORE INFORMATION SEE: Bertha M. Miller and others, compilers, *Illustrators of Children's Books: 1946-1956*, Horn Book, 1958.

LLEWELLYN LLOYD, Richard Dafydd Vyvyan 1906-1983 (Richard Llewellyn)

OBITUARY NOTICE—See sketch in *SATA* Volume 11: Born December 8, 1906, in St. David's, Pembrokeshire, Wales; died of a heart attack, November 30, 1983, in Dublin, Ireland. Playwright and novelist. Best known as Richard Llewellyn, he received the National Book Award in 1940 for his novel, *How Green Was My Valley*. The book sold 50,000 copies in Great Britain in only four months and went over the 100,000 mark in the United States. The book was the basis for the film of the same name, which won six Academy Awards in 1941. *None But the Lonely Heart*, a story about a young boy who becomes a criminal, was also adapted to film. Many critics hailed the book for its depth of characterization, comparing it to Dickens. A prolific writer, Llewellyn produced a large collection of books, including *The Witch of Merthyn*, 1954, *A Man in a Mirror*, 1961, *The End of the Rug*, 1968, and *At Sunrise, the Rough Music*, 1976. *For More Information See: Twentieth-Century Authors*, H. W. Wilson, 1942, supplement, 1945; *Contemporary Authors, New Revision Series*, Volume 7, Gale, 1982; *Dictionary of Literary Biography*, Volume 15: *British Novelists, 1930-1959*, Gale, 1983. *Obituaries: London Times*, December 1, 1983; *New York Times*, December 2, 1983; *Washington Post*, December 2, 1983; *Los Angeles Times*, December 2, 1983; *Chicago Tribune*, December 3, 1983; *Time*, December 12, 1983; *Newsweek*, December 12, 1983; *Publishers Weekly*, December 16, 1983; *Current Biography*, January, 1984; *School Library Journal*, March, 1984.

Reading furnishes our mind only with materials of knowledge; it is thinking makes what we read ours.
—John Locke
(From *An Essay Concerning Human Understanding*)

LUBIN, Leonard B.

BRIEF ENTRY: Author and illustrator. Lubin was born in Detroit, Mich. and attended the John Herron School of Art in Indianapolis, Ind. He made his debut as an illustrator in a new edition of Lewis Carroll's *The Pig-Tale* (Little, Brown, 1975), which was one of the *New York Times* best illustrated children's books of the year in 1975 and was selected for the Children's Book Showcase in 1976. Lubin has since illustrated several books for children, including Sheila Fox's *The Little Swineherd and Other Tales* (Dutton, 1978), a National Book Award finalist. The *New York Times Book Review* called Lubin's black-and-white illustrations "graphic and elegant," and the book earned a place in the American Institute of Graphic Art Books Show in 1979. Lubin has adapted and illustrated two books for children, Marie d'Aulnoy's *The White Cat* (Little, Brown, 1978) and *Aladdin and His Wonderful Lamp* (Delacorte, 1982). The latter tale is heightened by what *Booklist* described as "intricate blue-and-white drawings in the French Chinoiserie style. . . ."

Lubin is also the author and illustrator of *The Elegant Beast* (Viking, 1981), a history of costume for older readers in which he used various animals to model clothes from past centuries. Described by *New York Times Book Review* as "delightfully amusing," this book won an American Book Award for illustration in 1980. *School Library Journal* praised the writing of *The Elegant Beast:* "Although the concise text is not the real point of the book, it is so astute and clever that one hopes the artist will turn his hand again to writing." Other children's books illustrated by Lubin include *Henny Penny* (Little, 1976) by Veronica S. Hutchinson, *The Perfect Peach* (Little, 1977) by Stephen Schwartz, and *The Birthday of the Infanta* (Viking, 1979) by Oscar Wilde. He is also the illustrator of *Gilbert Without Sullivan* (Viking, 1981), a selection of libretti from their well-known operettas.

LYNDS, Dennis   1924-
(William Arden, Nick Carter, Michael Collins, John Crowe, Carl Dekker, Maxwell Grant, Mark Sadler)

BRIEF ENTRY: Born January 15, 1924, in St. Louis, Mo. Editor and author, under his own name and various pseudonyms, of novels, short stories, mysteries, science fiction, crime novels, and children's fiction. In addition to writing freelance since the 1960s, Lynds has also held editorial posts on the trade journals *Chemical Week, Chemical Engineering Progress,* and *Chemical Equipment.* He has been editor of *International Instrumentation* since 1975. Under pseudonym William Arden, he wrote several juvenile mysteries for the "Alfred Hitchcock and the Three Investigators" series. All published by Random House, they include *The Mystery of the Moaning Cave* (1968), *The Secret of the Crooked Cat* (1970), *The Mystery of the Dead Man's Riddle* (1974), *The Secret of Shark Reef* (1979), and *The Mystery of the Purple Pirate* (1982). *School Library Journal* noted that these fast-paced stories are "ideal for reluctant readers, since the momentum keeps them going." Other books by Lynds include crime novels featuring series characters such as Dan Fortune, The Shadow, and Kane Jackson. Lynds is a member of the Authors Guild, Authors League of America, Mystery Writers of America, and Crime Writers Association of Great Britain. He received a Mystery Writers of America Edgar Allan Poe Award for best first mystery novel in 1967, for *Act of Fear,* and a Special Award in 1968, for the short story "Success of a Mission." *Home:* 633

Chelham Way, Santa Barbara, Calif. 93108. *For More Information See: Encyclopedia of Mystery and Detection,* McGraw, 1976; *Twentieth-Century Crime and Mystery Writers,* St. Martin's, 1980; *Contemporary Authors, New Revision Series,* Volume 6, Gale, 1982.

MACHIN GOODALL, Daphne (Edith)

PERSONAL: Surname sometimes indexed under Goodall; born in Chilton, Sudbury, Suffolk, England; daughter of Vernon and Edith Mary (Stebbing) Machin Goodall. *Education:* Educated privately and at schools in England, France, and Germany. *Politics:* Conservative. *Religion:* Church of England. *Home:* Sparrows House, Gt. Henny, Nr. Sudbury, Suffolk, England.

CAREER: Writer, photographer. Worked with her sister, Mrs. V.I. Boon, breeding and training show jumpers and event horses; served as judge for British Show-Jumping Association prior to 1962, and British Show Hack and Cob Association; breeder of pedigree poll Hereford cattle; lecturer on horses. *Military service:* Women's Transport Service, 1940-45. *Member:* Wild Horse Specialist Group.

WRITINGS: Successful Show-Jumping, Scribner, 1951, revised edition, A. S. Barnes, 1964; *Know Your Pony,* Hart–Davis, 1955, revised edition, Pelham Books, 1972, A. S. Barnes, 1973; *Huntsmen of the Golden Age: Stephen Goodall, 1757-1823, William Goodall, 1817-1859,* Witherby, 1956; *Silver Spring and Other Stories,* Witherby, 1958; *Die Pferde mit der Elchschaufel,* Paul Parey (Berlin), 1960, 4th edition, 1974, English translation by the author published as *The Flight of the East Prussian Horses,* Arco, 1973; (with Anthony A. Dent) *The Foals of Epona,* Galley Press, 1962; (self–illustrated) *British Native Ponies,* Country Life, 1963, published as *Ponies,* A. S. Barnes, 1967; (editor) J. Nissen, *The Young Specialist Looks at Horses,* Ambassador, 1963; (translator) W. Schmalenbach, *The Noble Horse,* J. A. Allen, 1963; *Horses of the World,* Macmillan, 1965, 3rd edition, David & Charles, 1973, Macmillan, 1974; (editor) J. Nissen, *The Young Horseman's Guide,* A. S. Barnes, 1965; (translator) *The Long Way Home,* Heinemann, 1965, published in America as *The Quest,* Little, Brown, 1966; (translator from the German) Hans Mueller, *The Pocket Dictionary of Horseman's Terms,* Country Life, 1969; (translator from the German) Reiner Klimke, *Cavaletti: The Schooling of Horse and Rider over Ground Rails,* J. A. Allen, 1969; *The Seventh Continent,* Priory Press, 1969.

(Translator) Erna Moehr, *The Asiatic Wild Horse,* J. A. Allen, 1972; (translator) Harold Lange, *The Horse Today—and Tomorrow?,* Kaye & Ward, 1972; *A History of Horse Breeding,* R. Hale, 1974; (translator) *The Language of the Horse,* Kaye & Ward, 1975; *Horses and Their World,* David & Charles, 1976; (editor) *Horses and Jumping,* Pelham Books, 1976; *Zebras,* Raintree, 1977; (editor) Regional Sherriff Summerhays, *The Observer's Book of Horses and Ponies,* revised edition (Machin Goodall was not associated with earlier edition), Warne (London), 1978; *How to Ride,* Warne, 1980; (translator) R. Klimke, *Horse Trials,* J. A. Allen, 1984.

Contributor to numerous books on horses, including *The World's Finest Horses and Ponies, The Complete Book of the Horse,* and *The Horse.* Contributor to *Encyclopedia Americana, International Encyclopedia of the Horse,* and contributor to periodicals, including *Country Life, Riding, Horse and Hound,* and *Chronicle of the Horse.*

A Burchell zebra foal is born after 371 days. ■ (From *Zebras* by Daphne Machin Goodall. Photograph by Peter Ward.)

SIDELIGHTS: "I live in a sixteenth-century farm house on ninety acres of land which has been in my mother's family since 1622. The chimney of a house which stood on this site in the fourteenth century is incorporated in the present house. Three of the paddocks belonged to the fourteenth–century farm. All of the buildings, including a double tithe barn, are also very old. Thus, there is an atmosphere of peace and timelessness for myself, horses, Hereford cattle and dogs—a Weimaraner and a Lakeland terrier.

"I have travelled as far as the Falkland Islands and then on to Antarctica. The journey is described in *The Seventh Continent.* I have also visited a number of European countries including Austria, home of the Lipizzaner horses, and to Poland and the very beautiful Mazuren lake and forest district which was once part of pre–war Germany, France, Spain and also to Argentina and Chile.

"As my books are all factual about horses, I have to spend a lot of time researching and my latest, *A History of Horse Breeding,* took three years research before I started writing the book. It is now to be published in German as *Welt Geschichte der Pferde.*"

HOBBIES AND OTHER INTERESTS: Traveling, photography, riding, driving harness ponies, anything to do with the country.

Read not to contradict and confute, nor yet to believe and take for granted, nor to find talk and discourse, but to weigh and consider.

—Francis Bacon
(From *Of Studies*)

MAKIE, Pam 1943-

PERSONAL: Born August 17, 1943, in Ithaca, N.Y.; daughter of Ted (a craftsman) and Margaret (Northrup) Makie. *Education:* Mohawk Valley Community College, Utica, N.Y., A.A.S., 1962; attended School of Visual Arts, Cooper Union, Columbia University, and International Center of Photography. *Home:* 227 East 21st St., New York, N.Y. 10010.

CAREER: Art director; graphic designer. Eastman Advertising, Ithaca, N.Y., design and production, part time, 1960-61; Osrow Products, Glen Cove, N.Y., graphic design and production, 1962-64; Abner Kohn Associates, New York, N.Y., art director, 1964-66; GAF Corporation, New York, N.Y. assistant art director, 1966-70; James Ward, Inc., New York, N.Y.,

partner in graphic design firm, 1972-76; Makie Graphics, New York, N.Y., owner, 1976-78, 1981; Leber Katz Partners, Inc., New York, N.Y., permanent free–lance art director, 1979-80; art director for Celebrity, Inc., 1981-82. *Awards, honors:* First prize, packaging, Chicago Hobby and Crafts Show, 1974; first prize, packaging, Chicago Hardware Show, 1976; PIA award, 1982; award for Art Directors 62 annual show, 1983.

ILLUSTRATOR: Mindel Sitomer and Harry Sitomer, *Spirals,* Crowell, 1974; Phillip Balstrino, *Fat and Skinny,* Crowell, 1975.

SIDELIGHTS: ''As an art director/graphic designer, I consult with top management to define the nature of the work to be done; then, deciding on a course of action, I am responsible

A skinny person might eat more than a fat person. ■ (From *Fat and Skinny* by Philip Balestrino. Illustrated by Pam Makie.)

for the project through the various stages of concept, design, art production, and printing. This includes coordinating the talent of individuals and using my own talents and creative abilities.''

Makie has designed award–winning packaging, promotional materials, posters, book jackets, and catalogues. She has also illustrated two children's books. ''My children's book illustration was done in line with ruby overlays, but I prefer watercolor.

''My father, a craftsman, was a big influence in the development of my art career. Other artists have also influenced me. Actually, everything I see influences me, but my most motivating drive and influence has been my spiritual development. I meditate daily.''

MARSHALL, Michael (Kimbrough) 1948-
(Kim Marshall)

PERSONAL: Born March 11, 1948, in Oakland, Calif.; son of Randolph Laughlin and Anne (Grant) Marshall; married Rhoda Schneider (a lawyer), May 25, 1973. *Education:* Harvard University, B.A., (magna cum laude), 1969; Harvard University, Ed.M., 1981. *Politics:* Independent. *Home:* 222 Clark Rd., Brookline, Mass. 02146. *Agent:* Donald Cutler, Sterling Lord Agency, Inc., 660 Madison Ave., New York,

MICHAEL MARSHALL

The dinosaurs became extinct about 65 million years ago. ■ (From *The Story of Life: From the Big Bang to You* by Kim Marshall. Illustrated by Ingrid Johnson.)

N.Y. 10021. *Office:* Boston Public Schools, 26 Court St., Boston, Mass. 02108.

CAREER: Martin Luther King School, Boston, Mass., sixth grade teacher, 1969-80; Boston Public Schools, special assistant to the superintendent, 1981-82, director, curriculum objectives unit, 1982-83, manager of instructional services department, 1983—. Lecturer, Cambridge Educational Associates, 1974-76. *Member:* Common Cause, Boston Teachers' Union. *Awards, honors:* Calvert Smith Award, *Harvard Magazine,* 1970 and 1971.

WRITINGS—All under name Kim Marshall: *Law and Order in Grade 6-E,* Little, Brown, 1972; *Opening Your Class with Learning Stations,* Education Today, 1974; *The Story of Life: From the Big Bang to You* (illustated by Ingrid Johnson; Junior Literary Guild selection), Holt, 1980.

Also author of four books in ''Kim Marshall'' text/workbook series, *Math, English, Vocabulary,* and *Reading,* Educators Publishing Service, 1980-81. Contributor to professional journals. Contributing editor, *Learning.*

SIDELIGHTS: Marshall's interest in writing was encouraged by his teachers. "The British school put great emphasis on writing, and I built up self-confidence and fluency. But perhaps the best training was the constant stream of long letters I wrote to my father in Nigeria and my mother in Boston.

"The inspiration for my writing has come from my eleven years of work in an inner city Boston public school. I got bitten by the teaching bug and got deeper and deeper into education. After a very rocky year in which everything went wrong, I devised a successful classroom system and became a happy, innovative teacher with something to say to other teachers. And that's when I started writing again—two articles on my classroom for the *Harvard Bulletin.* These turned into a book called *Law and Order in Grade 6-E.*

"Meanwhile, my most important writing was taking place every night for my students. I found the available textbooks boring and unsuitable for my eager, bright, below-grade-level, street–wise students. So I wrote my own curriculum. One of the most difficult areas was the history of life on Earth. Haltingly, I began to write worksheets for my students. From the first conception to publication, *The Story of Life* was subjected to constant criticism and rewriting and rethinking. It was a six-year project.

"I have become fascinated with classroom organization, kids, and curriculum, and have been anxious to share my experiences with others. The material I have published for teachers was originally written for my own students and subjected to their very critical scrutiny as they worked their way through it.

"Although I am most interested in being a school principal, I have recently spent almost all my time writing a new curriculum for the Boston Public Schools. I miss being away from the real world of schools, but feel very good about providing a structure for teachers throughout the city—one that still leaves great flexibility for each teacher to decide on the methods and materials best for their setting. In other words, I'm writing the kind of curriculum I would have wanted as a teacher."

FOR MORE INFORMATION SEE: Christian Science Monitor, June 30, 1973.

MATTINGLEY, Christobel (Rosemary) 1931-

PERSONAL: Born October 26, 1931, in Abelaide, Australia; daughter of Arthur Raymond (a civil engineer) and Isabelle Margaret (Provis) Shepley; married Cecil David Mattingley (a teacher), December 17, 1953; children: Rosemary Christobel, Christopher Jonathan David, Stephen Michael. *Education:* University of Tasmania, B.A. (with honors), 1951; Public Library of Victoria Training College, certificate (associate), 1971. *Religion:* Anglican. *Home:* 18 Allendale Grove, Stonyfell, South Australia 5066, Australia. *Agent:* A.P. Watt & Son, 26-28 Bedford Row, London WC1R 4HL, England.

CAREER: Department of Immigration, Canberra, Australia, librarian, 1951; Latrobe Valley Libraries, Latrobe Valley, Australia, regional librarian, 1953; teacher and librarian in England, 1954-55; librarian at private schools in Adelaide, Australia, 1956-57, and 1966-70; Wattle Park Teachers College, Adelaide, acquisitions librarian, 1971, reader services librarian, 1972; Murray Park College of Advanced Education, Abelaide, lecturer and reader education librarian, 1973-74; writer,

CHRISTOBEL MATTINGLEY

1974—. Presented "Children's Books to Enjoy," a weekly television program, 1973-74. Co-founder of South Australian section of Community Aid Abroad, 1964; citizen member of Burnside City Council Library, 1971—; South Australia chairman of National Book Council of Australia, 1979-83; writer-in-residence, Churchlands Campus, West Australian College of Advanced Education, 1981.

MEMBER: Australian Society of Authors, Australian Writers Guild, Australian Conservation Foundation, National Trust, Library Association of Australia, Children's Book Council of Australia, Indo-China Refugee Association, Oral History Association. *Awards, honors:* Children's Book Council of Australia commendations, 1972, for *Windmill at Magpie Creek* and *Worm Weather,* 1982, for *Rummage;* Australian Council Literature Board fellowship, 1975 and 1983; International Youth Library scholarship for study in Munich, West Germany, 1976-77; Australian Book Publishers Award, 1980, for *Black Dog;* first recipient of Children's Book Council Medal for Junior Readers, 1982; National Parks and Wildlife Services of New South Wales Writers Award, 1983.

*WRITINGS—*Children's books: *The Picnic Dog* (illustrated by Carolyn Dinan), Hamish Hamilton, 1970; *Windmill at Magpie Creek* (illustrated by Gavin Rowe), Brockhampton Press, 1971; *Worm Weather* (illustrated by C. Dinan), Hamish Hamilton, 1971; *Emu Kite* (illustrated by G. Rowe), Hamish Hamilton, 1972; *Queen of the Wheat Castles* (illustrated by G. Rowe), Brockhampton Press, 1973, two-part abridgment, *Cricket* magazine, 1977; *The Surprise Mouse* (illustrated by C. Dinan),

Outback 'Arry headed westwards, across the black soil plain, glad to leave the troubles of the town behind. ■ (From *The Great Ballagundi Damper Bake* by Christobel Mattingley. Illustrated by Will Mahony.)

Hamish Hamilton, 1974; *Tiger's Milk* (illustrated by Anne Ferguson), Angus & Robertson, 1974; *The Battle of the Galah Trees* (illustrated by Gareth Floyd), Brockhampton Press, 1974; *Show and Tell* (illustrated by Helen Sallis), Hodder & Stoughton, 1974; *Lizard Log* (illustrated by H. Sallis), Hodder & Stoughton, 1975; *The Great Ballagundi Damper Bake* (illustrated by Will Mahony), Angus & Robertson, 1975; *The Long Walk* (illustrated by H. Sallis), T. Nelson, 1976; *New Patches for Old*, Hodder & Stoughton, 1977; *The Special Present and Other Stories* (illustrated by Noela Young), Collins, 1977; *The Big Swim* (illustrated by Elizabeth Honey), T. Nelson, 1977; *Budgerigar Blue* (illustrated by Tony Oliver), Hodder & Stoughton, 1978; *The Jetty* (illustrated by G. Rowe), Hodder & Stoughton, 1978; *Black Dog* (illustrated by Craig Smith), Collins, 1979; *Rummage* (illustrated by Patricia Mullins), Angus & Robertson, 1981; *Brave with Ben* (illustrated by E. Honey), T. Nelson, 1982; *Lexl and the Lion Party* (illustrated by Astra Lacis), Hodder & Stoughton, 1982; *The Magic Saddle* (illustrated by P. Mullins), Hodder & Stoughton, 1983; *Duck Boy* (illustrated by P. Mullins), Angus & Robertson, 1983; *Southerly Buster*, Hodder & Stoughton, 1983; *The Angel with a Mouth Organ* (illustrated by A. Lacis), Hodder & Stoughton, 1984; *Ghost Sitter*, Patrick Hardy Books, 1984; *McGruer and the Goat*, Angus & Robertson, in press.

Screenplays; all released by South Australian Film Corp.: "Women Artists of Australia," 1981; "Come to the Party!: Children's Libraries," 1981.

Work represented in anthologies, including *A Swag of Australian Stories*, edited by Leon Garfield, Ward, Lock, 1977; *Spooks and Spirits*, Hodder & Stoughton, 1978; *Early Dreaming*, edited by Michael Dugan, Jacaranda Press, 1979. Contributor of stories, articles, and poems to library journals and literary magazines for adults and children, including *Orana, Pivot, Reading Time, Cricket,* and *Landfall*.

WORK IN PROGRESS: Poems; articles; an historical novel; a picture book text; a screenplay, "Social Development Series: For Junior Primary Schools"; an adolescent novel; biographical memoirs; a photographic and documentary volume on Aboriginal experience in South Australia since 1836.

SIDELIGHTS: "I was born within the sound of the sea at Brighton, South Australia and lived the first eight years of my life in a house perched on a sandhill. The freedom of the sandhills, the mystery of the sea, and the joys of a freshwashed beach with new possibilities of discoveries each day contributed, I now believe, to my evolution as a writer.

"Our home was well supplied with books of all kinds, and my parents always read and made up stories for my sister and me, so that by the time I went to school it was natural for me to write my own. I wrote poems in my mother's recipe book, and some of my first story pieces were published in the children's pages of newspapers and the nature magazine, *Wild Life*. When some of my contributions were rejected by the school magazine, I compiled a magazine for my family instead.

"As well as reading, my sister, my friends, and I loved pencil and paper word games of all kinds. We also spent many hours dressing up, dramatizing our favorite fairy tales and other stories, and playing charades. Radio was a great pleasure to us and we followed certain serials very keenly, which must have helped to develop my ear for the cadence of the spoken word and my sense of story. Now I always hear the words I write, and I read my work aloud to my family first, because I believe that if stories read aloud easily, they will also read well silently.

"The power of language caught my imagination very early and before I was eight I had begun teaching myself Latin and French. By the time I was twelve I was trying German and Swedish, also self–taught, I went on to major in German and French at university and to enjoy some of the riches of these literatures in the original.

"My father's work involved our family in several moves. When I was eight we went to Sydney. I missed the beach, but the bush near our home gave plenty of scope for my growing interest in nature study. An enlightened teacher introduced me to the concept of ecology, so that from the age of nine I was a conservationist. Five years later we moved to Tasmania where wonderful opportunities for sailing, skiing, and bush walking in the wilderness areas strengthened the affinity I had always felt with nature. At the same time a growing understanding of my father's work as a civil engineer led me to appreciate the need for man's harmony with his environment. This has since come through, quite subconsciously, in my writing. Animals and birds feature in almost all of my books, not because I set out to write stories about animals, but because for me they have always been a natural part of life.

"In my profession I worked with many children in public and school libraries. When I had children of my own, the sense of childhood, which had always remained strong in me, gained a new perspective. I perceived vividly the drama and conflict in the world of the child and the stories which are all around us in everyday things, events, and places. I wrote . . . *The Special Present* after our daughter lost her first tooth. *The Picnic Dog* was written because our dog was run over. An onion growing in a glass of water gave me the idea for *Show and Tell*, and our older son's jar of pet worms started me on *Worm Weather*. When our younger son gave me a mouse in a box for a surprise early birthday present he also gave me two stories, *The Surprise Mouse* and *The Budgerigar Blue*.

"Other stories, such as *Windmill at Magpie Creek, Tiger's Milk, New Patches for Old*, and *The Jetty*, are even more deeply rooted in my own childhood, but have been sparked to life by observation of contemporary situations. In all my stories feelings are very important, especially fear, loneliness, and the feeling of being an outsider, feelings which we all know, but which we may have reservations about expressing.

"When I was about the age of Cathy in "The Cat Stowaway" [short story published in *Cricket*], we had a beautiful gray cat called Smoky. But now we haven't a cat, because of all the birds in our garden. Our garden is very large, rather wild and overgrown, full of secret corners and hiding places where our three children have built cubby houses and our dog has buried hundreds of bones. We often take our meals outside, and sometimes we can hardly hear ourselves talk for the noise of the parrots.

"They come flying as swift as arrows, in flocks of fifty and more, to feed on the nectar in the blossoms of the tall eucalyptus trees, or to feast on our loquats, apricots, and apples. Their brilliant green and yellow feathers are as gay as any clown's costume, and they have bright red checks and a purple patch over their beaks. They hang upside down twisting and turning to feed, like acrobats swinging and swaying on a trapeze, and all the while they shriek and shrill, chatter and call, as excited as a circus crowd.

"The problem of minority groups and disadvantaged individuals have always moved me deeply. My own childhood experiences, moving from state to state and changing houses, friends, and schools perhaps contributed to the empathy I have felt for migrants, and provided the basis of my novel, *New Patches for Old*. I joined the Department of Immigration when the post-World War II wave of displaced persons arriving in Australia was at its height. Early in the sixties, my husband and I founded Community Aid Abroad in South Australia, an organization encouraging self–help projects in developing countries on a community–to–community basis. More recently I have become involved with resettlement of Indo–Chinese refugees and with the social injustices suffered by the most deprived sector of Australian society; aborigines. These and other issues are coming through in my current writing, particularly in the film scripts and poetry.

"Since 1975 I have spent several months each year touring and lecturing on books, and reading and writing at schools, tertiary institutions, and organizations, for teachers, parents, and librarians. I see this as an important extension of my communication as a writer, particularly in assisting children to realize the link between books and people, between books and life."

Mattingley's books have been published in Danish, German, and French. They have been transcribed in Braille, recorded on tape, and serialized on radio and television programs in Australia and abroad.

HOBBIES AND OTHER INTERESTS: Nature study (especially bird-watching), reading, music, gardening, exploring the Australian bush (especially in wilderness areas), camping, swimming, beachcombing, travel (New Zealand, England, Europe, Papua New Guinea, Japan, Korea), flying in light aircraft.

FOR MORE INFORMATION SEE: Reading Time, April, 1977, October, 1979; D. L. Kirkpatrick, editor, *Twentieth-Century Children's Writers,* St. Martin's Press, 1978; *New Zealand Libraries,* December, 1979; *Contemporary Authors,* Volumes 97-100, Gale, 1981.

MAUSER, Patricia Rhoads   1943-

PERSONAL: Surname is pronounced *Mah-zer;* born January 14, 1943, in Sacramento, Calif.; daughter of Kenneth C. (a real estate broker) and Betty Jane (Arnold) Rhoads; married Richard Lewis Mauser (a national account manager for American Telephone and Telegraph), June 5, 1965; children; Laura Elaine, Peter Brent. *Education:* Attended Washington State University, 1961-63 and 1964-65, and University of Oregon, 1963-64. *Home and office:* 5111 26th St. N.E. Puyallup, Wash. 98371. *Agent:* Amy Berkower, Writer's House, Inc., 21 West 26th St., New York, N.Y. 10010.

CAREER: Writer, 1955—. *Member:* Pacific Northwest Writer's conference. *Awards, honors:* Washington State Governor's Award for Children's Literature, 1983, for *A Bundle of Sticks.*

WRITINGS: How I Found Myself at the Fair (juvenile novel; illustrated by Emily A. McCully), Atheneum, 1980; *A Bundle of Sticks* (juvenile novel), Atheneum, 1982. Author of "Broadview," a weekly column in *Federal Way.* Contributor to local magazines.

WORK IN PROGRESS: Rip–Off (tentative title), a novel for junior high school students, about a girl involved in shoplifting; another novel, about a girl and her horse, for high school students; *I'd Rather Be Dead,* a teen romance in which a high school girl attempts suicide.

SIDELIGHTS: "I sent my first story off (in a Big–10 tablet) to *Ladies' Home Journal* when I was 12. They rejected it, but I was hooked into writing." ["Author Finds Success after Early Rejection," *Washington State University Hilltopics,* October, 1981.']

"As a child I couldn't read because of an eye problem. Books, therefore, represented a threat to me. I was the kid who stayed in from recess because I hadn't finished my assignments. I wanted my first book, *How I Found Myself at the Fair,* to be non-threatening; lots of white space. One chapter, for instance, has only two pages.

"I was also painfully shy. If I wanted to say anything I had to put it on paper, and I learned right away that the worlds I created in stories were much nicer and more fun than my real world. My heroines always had canopy beds and went to exciting places. I got the same vicarious thrills from writing that most kids got from reading. It wasn't until much later that I developed a passion for reading other people's works."

"Most of what I produced in the early years was pretty bad, but I did get a start at learning the craft. Herb Arntson [Mauser's

If only I could stop this thing, I thought, or jump off just as it gets to the bottom. When would the ride be over? ▪ (From *How I Found Myself at the Fair* by Pat Rhoads Mauser. Illustrated by Emily Arnold McCully.)

PATRICIA RHOADS MAUSER

creative writing professor at Washington State University] has been a big influence over the years, first by giving me A's in his writing classes and convincing me that I had something to offer, and second by doing critiques on lots of my manuscripts."[1]

How I Found Myself at the Fair won a contest judged by her present editor, Jean Karl. "Book publishing is incredibly hard to crack. . . . I was lucky. She (and all New York editors) receive thousands of manuscripts a year. She agreed to take a second look at the book because she like the length. Nothing more. She sent it back to me four times, each time suggesting revisions.

"I had made up my mind to revise as many times as she could stand. By the time it was published, I had the feeling *Fair* was an awful book, marginal at best. I couldn't believe the reviews. Mostly they were good!. . . In this game perseverance is the magic ingredient."[1]

"The kind, gentle kids who work for good grades often find themselves isolated and miserable, at conflict with the values their parents have taught them. Without having planned to do so, I seem to write for that group, the decent kids who need to know they are not alone. In my books the 'good guys' emerge victorious over difficult odds. I don't waste type feeling sorry for the 'bad guys.' They are disposed of neatly and fairly."

FOR MORE INFORMATION SEE: *Pierce County Herald*, September 16, 1980; *Washington State University Hilltopics*, October, 1981.

McENTEE, Dorothy (Layng) 1902-

PERSONAL: Born September 21, 1902, in Brooklyn, N.Y.; daughter of Thomas Lockley and Frances (Layng) McEntee. *Education:* Graduated from Pratt Institute, 1923; attended Pennsylvania Academy of Fine Arts, 1928-31, and Art Students League.

CAREER: Teacher of art at public high schools in New York, N.Y., 1923-1960; illustrator of children's books. Work is represented in permanent collections of Reading Museum, Reading, Pa., and Brooklyn Museum, Brooklyn N.Y. and in private collections. *Member:* Art Students League, (life member), American Watercolor Society of New York (life member), Philadelphia Watercolor Club.

*ILLUSTRATOR—*All written by sister, Frances M. Martin: *Knuckles Down,* Harper, 1942; *No School Friday,* Harper, 1945; *Sea Room,* Harper, 1947; *Nine Tales of Coyote,* Harper, 1950; *Nine Tales of Raven,* Harper, 1951, revised edition pub-

When he and his young brother came in from fishing, they would dump their salmon on the sandbar, and let the Eagles have a share. ▪ (From "Eagle Boy" in *Nine Tales of Raven* by Fran Martin. Illustrated by Dorothy McEntee.)

lished as *Raven-Who-Sets-Things-Right: Indian Tales of the Northwest Coast,* 1975; *Pirate Island,* Harper, 1955.

SIDELIGHTS: McEntee, who has illustrated all of the children's books written by her sister, Frances Martin, was also an art teacher for many years. In addition to her work as a teacher and illustrator, she has exhibited her watercolors in museums and art shows for 50 years.

She received her art training from Pratt Institute and the Art Students League. ". . . Science might well have been my field if family plans for sending me to Wellesley had been fulfilled. But my father's severe illness prevented that. Art school was a happy solution. After Pratt I began to teach in a big city high school, intending to stop and illustrate books as soon as possible. A combination of economic necessity and a real love for teaching kept me going for the next seven years. Then I did stop for two wonderful years in the country, drawing and painting in the Old Chester Springs Country School of the Pennsylvania Academy. We were outdoors from dawn to dark. Afternoons we listened to symphonic music from a loud speaker strung up in a huge sycamore tree on the lawn. There were long walks, painting expeditions to New Hope or Newcastle, Delaware, and museum and theater trips to Philadelphia.

"After all that I went back to teaching in the same Brooklyn high school where a three-hour-a-day art course for talented students had been instituted. Many of the girls were excep-

tional, and it all interested me too much to leave. In those years I did some water-color painting, exhibited regularly, joined the two big water-color clubs and did some wood engraving. In 1942 my sister, Fran Martin, had her first boys' book accepted by Harper's. [We became] . . . a team, not a very prolific one, since she had a full-time job raising a family, and I a full-time one in teaching." [Bertha M. Miller, and others, compilers, *Illustrators of Children's Books: 1946-1956,* Horn Book, 1958.]

"When I retired at the beginning of the sixties it was obvious that one form or another of abstraction would take over the art field in the U.S. and that realism would at least temporarily be dead. I continued to paint in my own way but I stopped exhibiting. In the late seventies I saw that the tide had turned. Since I had a great backlog of good work I was given a solo showing on East 70th Street, a maiden show at age eighty, entitled 'Skyscrapers.' The Whitney Museum included me in its show, 'Visions of New York City,' at the Tokyo Museum. The Brooklyn Museum used one of my watercolors in their centennial salute to the Brooklyn Bridge. I showed in many small group exhibitions here and in Connecticut from 1980 until the present.

"I found time to make nine trips to Europe beginning in 1958 and saw the great museums, churches, and monuments for the first time in my life. Life has been very rewarding."

McWHIRTER, Norris (Dewar)   1925-

PERSONAL: Born August 12, 1925, in London, England; son of William Allan (former editor, _London Daily Mail_) and Margaret (Williamson) McWhirter; married Carole Eckert, December 28, 1957; children: Jane, Alasdair. _Education:_ Trinity College, Oxford, B.A., and M.A., 1948. _Politics:_ Conservative. _Religion:_ Church of England. _Office:_ Guinness Superlatives Ltd., 2 Cecil Court, London Rd., Enfield, Middlesex EN2 6DJ, England.

CAREER: McWhirter Twins Ltd., London, England, co-founder with twin brother, Ross, 1950; _Athletics World_ (magazine), publisher, 1951-57; Guinness Superlatives Ltd., London, England, managing director, beginning, 1954, vice-president of New York branch, 1956-58. Track and field correspondent for London _Star_, 1951-60, and London _Sunday Observer_, 1951-67; British Broadcasting Corp., sports commentator, 1951-72 (announced first-minute mile by Roger Bannister, 1954), radio commentator of Olympic track and field events, 1952-56, television commentator of Olympic track and field events, 1960-72, co-presenter with Roy Castle of BBC-TV series "Record Breakers" as "memory man" on facts and figures, on other radio and television programs. William McWhirter & Son, Electrical Engineers, Glasgow, Scotland, chairman, 1955; Redwood Press Ltd., Printers, co-founder and chairman, 1966-72; The Freedom Association, co-founder, 1975, and chairman, 1983. Contested 1964 and 1966 general election for Conservatives. _Military service:_ Royal Naval Volunteer Reserve, 1943-46; became sub-lieutenant. _Member:_ Royal Institution, Association of Track and Field Statisticians, Society of Geneaologists, Achilles Club, Vincent's Club (Oxford).

WRITINGS—With twin brother, Ross McWhirter: _Get to Your Marks_, Kaye, 1950; (compilers) _Guinness Book of Records_, Guinness Superlatives, 1955, 31st edition, 1984, published as _Guinness Book of World Records_, Sterling, 1961, 21st edition, 1982; (editors) _Guinness Book of Olympic Records_, Sterling, 1963-84; (compilers) _Dunlop Book of Facts_, Dreghorn Publications, 1964, 2nd edition, 1966; _The 1966 Guinness Book of British Empire and Commonwealth Games Records_, Guinness Superlatives, 1966; (compilers) _Dunlop Illustrated Encyclopedia of Facts_, Doubleday, 1969; _Guinness Sports Record Book_, Sterling, 1972, 7th edition, 1980; _Surprising Facts about Kings and Rulers_, F. Watts (London), 1973; _Guinness Book of Answers_, Sterling, 1976, 4th edition, 1983; _Guinness Book of Essential Facts_, Sterling, 1979; _Guinness Book of Sports Records, Winners, and Champions_, Sterling, 1980, revised edition, 1982; _Guinness Illustrated Encyclopedia of Facts_, Sterling, 1981.

Books written by Norris McWhirter only, except as noted: _Ross: The Story of a Shared Life_ (adult memoir), Churchill, 1977; (with Norvin Pallas) _Guinness Game Book_, Sterling, 1978; (with Peter Cardozo) _The Guinness Record Keeper_, Bantam, 1979; _Guinness Book of Amazing Animals_ (illustrated by Bill Hinds), Sterling, 1981; _Guinness: The Stories behind the Records_, Sterling, 1982; _Guinness Book of Sports Spectaculars_, Sterling, 1982; _Guinness Book of Discovery and Invention_, Guinness Superlatives, 1984. Contributor to _Encyclopaedia Britannica, Encyclopaedia Britannica Year Book, Modern Athletics, Encyclopaedia of Sport, Sport International, News of World Almanac_ (1950-57), _Evening News London Year Book_ (1953-54), _Kenyon's Gold Coins of England_ (1969), _In Defence of Freedom_ (1978), _Proceedings of the Royal Institution of Great Britain_, Volume 53, 1981, _Dictionary of National Biography_, Oxford University Press, in press.

NORRIS McWHIRTER

WORK IN PROGRESS: A book on the British Islands.

SIDELIGHTS: **August 12, 1925.** Born in London, England, the twin brother of Ross and son of editor, William Allan McWhirter. "At the age of 19 our father began a career as a journalist in Glasgow, which led him to Fleet Street and to become the first man to edit three national newspapers (_Sunday Pictorial, Sunday Dispatch_ and _Daily Mail_). He started 11 newspapers from scratch in the provinces and was managing director of both Northcliffe Newspapers, which he virtually founded, and the Associated Newspapers." [Norris McWhirter, _Ross: The Story of a Shared Life_, Churchill Press, 1977.[1]]

1928. By the age of three, Norris and his identical twin brother, Ross, began to exhibit a personality bond which continued throughout their lives. ". . . Ross and I developed our twin language, which though unintelligible to anyone else, was demonstrably understood between ourselves. This phase, unfortunately before the era of tape-recorders, was short–lived and we relapsed after a few months into English. Doting adults always asked the same question and they always got the same answer. 'How does your Mummy tell you apart?' was the eternal question. We were in fact uncommonly alike and during our first six months the easiest way to identify the elder [Norris, by twenty minutes] was to search through his silvery blond hair for a tiny mole-like spot on his scalp. Thus any enquirer received a standard reply according to which twin was the spokesman of the day. . . ."[1]

1939. Attended Marlborough School with Ross. "Marlborough was a strongly religious school with the Archbishop of Can-

The largest known litter for a dog is 23 puppies. Two dogs share this record. One was a foxhound named "Lena.". . .The other dog was a St. Bernard named "Careless Ann." ∎ (From *Guinness Book of World Records,* edited and compiled by Norris and Ross McWhirter.)

terbury as *ex officio* visitor and sometimes up to eight other Bishops, many of them Old Marlburians, on the School's Council. Sons of clergy enjoyed reduced fees and virtually everyone worked hard, played hard and, when they left for the war, fought hard. The death roll was appalling. The roll of honour for World War I was in excess of 600 killed and in World War II 391.

"Life was vigorous from waking to sleeping. The dormitory sport in Upcot was blanket-tossing in which the tossed, if there was some over-zealous coordination, would occasionally brush with the ceiling. Some found the experience disconcerting or even frightening, while others found it exhilarating. Another activity was raiding rival dormitories armed with well-knotted towels used as cudgels. When one dormitory has established an ascendancy over another, the curious stability of a pecking order reigned and peace broke out. Disarmament consisted of unknotting the towels—something easier said than done in the case of a well soaked and hardened figure-of-eight knot.

"After four terms at Upcot, Ross and I were due in May 1940 to join Kennedy [their older brother] at our senior house called Cotton House. . . . In the 97-year history of the School, it was seemingly unique to have three brothers in one house simultaneously. We had however contracted mumps and before we were able to return, the Low Countries and France joined Denmark and Norway in falling before the all-conquering Nazi *Wehrmacht*. The evacuation of Dunkirk had just been pulled off and Britain awaited invasion with a national solidarity. . . ."[1]

1940. "At the age of fifteen years and one month, in September . . . Ross and I joined the Officers' Training Corps. Of the three arms of His Majesty's Forces it was the naval arm which, however, most commanded our attention, although I also joined the Air Training Corps. . . ."[1]

1942. "Our twelfth term at Marlborough and our first as 17-year-olds ran from 22 September to 18 December 1942. It was the term in which we learnt the real value of *esprit de corps*. We had joined the Home Guard. . . ."[1]

1943. Following graduation from Marlborough, Norris and Ross joined the Royal Navy at the age of seventeen.

During active duty, Norris served at the sinking of four U-boats in the Battle of the Atlantic and later on a minesweeper

in the Pacific. "Ross and I did not part until 8 October 1944 when I was sent on a navigation course at the Royal Naval College, Greenwich, and he to North Shields. . . . Ross was to specialise in the always grinding and often dangerous work of minesweeping while I was to be sent on an anti-submarine course at HMS *Osprey* in Dunoon, Scotland, and to HMS *Nimrod* at Campbeltown. Thus at the age of 19 we were parted for the first time and our weekly letters to each other, if preserved, would have read very laconically. Our brief and infrequent leaves did not coincide. Ross moved to HMS *Granton* on the east side of Scotland while I was on the west side. Ross was appointed as a midshipman and as a 4th officer of the 545 ton fleet dan-laying trawler HMS *Shillay*. She was an Isles Class trawler called after one of the two outer Hebridean islands, so named and used for laying the dan buoys which flagged the boundaries between swept and unswept waters in a minesweeping operation. I was meanwhile appointed as the most junior officer of nine on the American built frigate HMS *Labuan* at Gladstone Dock, Liverpool."[1]

1947. Returned to Oxford University, where he majored in economics and international relations, while Ross majored in jurisprudence. In athletics the twins held the distinction of being the only twins ever to be members of a title-winning AAA relay team.

1950. Established own business with Ross. ". . . The business was to supply facts and figures to newspapers, year books, encyclopaedias and advertisers and we called it a Press and Periodical Features Service. It seemed that there was no other such concern in the country, but that did not daunt us: in fact it encouraged us. We had found what we believed to be the formula which best suited us; the thing which we would be both best at and which we would most enjoy. We debated what we should call our new company. Since companies are often called 'and Sons' or 'Bros' or even sometimes 'and Nephew,' why shouldn't we call our company 'McWhirter Twins Ltd'— and that is precisely what we did. We set up our office on what would nowadays seem a derisory capitalisation of £300 each and acquired the unexpired portion of a lease on two small rooms, one back and one front, on the third and top floor of 15 Great James Street in Holborn. This was part of a terraced row of houses built in the early eighteenth century, probably just in the reign of Queen Anne. The property was on its last legs and our part of it had clearly been used in palmier days as accommodations for living-in servants.

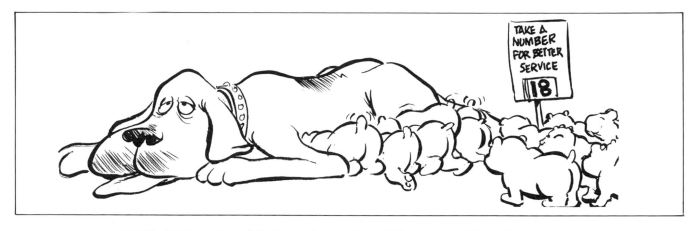

Bill Hinds' illustration of the largest known litter of 23 puppies. ■ (From *Guinness Book of Amazing Animals* by Norris McWhiter. Illustrated by Bill Hinds.)

"On the very first day we opened for business we had a lucky break. I had taken the bus down Kingsway to visit His Majesty's Stationery Office to see what I could procure in the way of a few basic reference sources for our bare bookcase. While I was looking around the main counter, an assistant came through from the back and slapped down a small pile of a new publication by the cash register. I glanced at this and saw it was the latest edition of the daily evidence of the Gowers Royal Commission then deliberating on capital punishment. On the contents page, I noticed the name of A. Pierrepoint. I was rather surprised that this Home Office functionary (who—as public hangman—was prevented from giving interviews to the press or of disclosing any details on how the most infamous murderers met their end) should be revealing, if not all, at least something. I made an immediate investment of a few coppers and caught the bus back to the office to find a note saying that Ross had gone to the Holborn reference library. I read Pierrepoint's evidence and wrote three or four pithy paragraphs about the way in which he said none of his 'clients' (433 male and 17 female) caused him any trouble except one German spy, who had caused a 'punch-up' on the scaffold.

"Not knowing the ropes on how a newspaper operated, I phoned my three paragraphs through to the *Star* newspaper, which had the middle circulation of London's trio of evening papers. The copytaker took it all down and asked me for my name and phone number in case the newsroom wished to contact me—something which from his tone of voice he indicated would be highly unlikely. It was rather in the modern idiom of 'Don't call us we'll call you.' Minutes later, however, the telephone rang and someone asked for me saying he was the Editor's secretary. 'Do you think you could come round and see the Editor about the story you have just sent in abut the hangman?,' the voice said, adding 'Mr. Cranfield would like to see you about it.' The six flights of stairs seemed as one as I cavorted down them and in the euphoria of the moment and hailed a cab to take me to Bouverie Street on the south side of Fleet Street where the *Star* shared an office with the *News Chronicle*.

"I was very unimpressed with the dinginess of the *Star's* offices but was conducted into the presence of the great 'Cran' himself. 'That was a damn good story you gave us about the fight on the scaffold,' he said, 'I can't understand it. Somehow we missed it and I only hope the opposition missed it too. How did you come to pick it up?' I replied that I had been standing in the right place at the right time—the moment it was put on sale at the Stationary Office. 'Cran' turned to his male secretary and said rather sharply 'You had better look into it and see why our coverage failed.' Then he picked up a piece of scrap paper and scribbled a few hieroglyphics in pencil, handed it to me and said, 'See the cashier on your way out and come back and see me with your twin brother in a few days, because I have got something to discuss.'"[1] The McWhirter brothers covered track and field and rugby football as correspondents for the *Star* for nine years.

1952. "In our Holborn garret Ross and I worked to build up our practice. Two new interesting assignments were the *News of the World Almanac,* for which we were commissioned to provide all the data for the general 150-page information section, and the provision of information for panels on the Shredded Wheat breakfast food boxes. The theme we sold to them was artist's impressions of superlative objects and people—a theme which we were later to develop.

"However, our main new activity in 1952 was to launch a specialist monthly publication called *Athletics World.* This was a ten-page typescript publication printed by photo-lithography of which the first issue was in March 1952 in which, in December 1955, we converted to a 16-page type-set monthly. The magazine involved an intensely personal effect and built up a devoted readership of connoisseurs. Before the end of the year we had subscribers in 54 countries, many of them members of the Association of Track and Field Statisticians. . . ."[1]

Served as radio commentator for the Olympic Games in Helsinki. Later became the television, as well as the radio, commentator for the Olympic games. "In 1952 Ross and I worked on the Helsinki Olympic Games in a way which may have irritated our fellow correspondents but certainly delighted the *Star's* accountants. The system was that since we both knew everything that the other one knew, the man on the spot (which on this occasion was me) merely had to confine himself to the eye-witness points. Thus, for instance, in the case of the women's Olympic long-jump finals, all that I would send by cable would be that Yvette Williams was wearing two track suits against the cold plus blue gloves. I did not have to mention her age, her New Zealand nationality, her previous personal best performance, previous titles or her appearance, because Ross sitting in London knew all that. Thus it was that the *Star's* cable bill for the entire 16 days of Olympic coverage from me was less than that of the rival *Evening News'* correspondent for the first night of the Games.''[1]

1955. Compiled the first *Guinness Book of Records* with Ross. ''The first three versions of the *Guinness Book* were anonymously compiled, namely those for 1955, 1956 and 1958. The facsimile signature of Ross and myself did not appear inside for the first time until 1960. . . .

''In all later editions Ross and I established a tradition, maintained to this day, of listing all the people in the office who, over the years, had helped in their various ways in the enterprise. . . .''[1]

''The work on the book could be summed up as extracting '-ests' (i.e. highests, oldests, richests, heaviests, fastests, etc.) from 'ists' (dendrochronologists, helminthologists, ichthyologists, palaeontologists, and vulcanologists, etc.).

''Ross and I soon learnt some rather important rules about acquiring information quite apart from leads which could be culled from other reference works and from newspaper cuttings. When writing to an expert, it is fatal to ask point-blank for a piece of information such as the fastest anyone has been made a saint, or the greatest recorded amount of milk yielded by one cow or the greatest weight lifted by a woman. It is much more effective to find what you believe may be about the right answer, then ask the expert for advice in correcting your submission. We found that people who have a total resistance to giving information often have an irresistible desire to correct other people's impressions. Another rule we soon found was that the enthusiastic amateur is often a far better source than the rather bored over-published professional who suffers almost from a surfeit of self-expression. Later we found also that people who were not answering enquiries from within their own country would answer the same enquiry if it came from overseas. Additionally it seemed that while a Frenchman would not reply to a letter in English, a German often regards it as an insult to receive a letter translated into German from a Briton.

''Compiling a reference book thus is something which we soon discovered entails not only an expenditure of energy far beyond that called for by any fiction writer, but also the deployment of some measure of psychology. The work went on ceaselessly and came to a climax mercifully when the nights were shortest during June and July. The stream of letters sent out to experts all over the world had begun to yield a useful harvest. . . . It was arranged for the East London firm of F. Howard Doulton and Co. of Stratford, East London, to carry out the printing.

''The great day arrived on 27 August 1955 when Peter Page walked into the office bearing the first bound copy of the book. It had a plain green cover gold blocked with the words 'The Guinness Book of Records' above the Guinness trade mark of a harp. Extraordinary to relate in the intervening era of hyperinflation, it was decided that the published price of this crown quarto volume of more than 200 pages with illustrations and line blocks and a full colour frontispiece should be five shillings. The first copy was sent by registered post to the man who commissioned it, Sir Hugh Beaver. . . .''[1]

1956-1958. Became vice-president of the New York branch of Superlatives, Inc. ''As it turned out, the problems in New York were greater than those in London because of the fundamental difference in commercial outlook. While the Britain people

tend to be resistant to products which are advertised because they think that if they were really good they could sell without advertising, in the United States people will not buy anything unless it is advertised because they think that the manufacturer cannot really believe in the product unless he spends a lot of money 'pushing' it. In New York we were not prepared to advertise our pioneer edition which was unwisely entitled *The Guinness Book of Superlatives,* and in addition we had no distribution set-up.''[1]

1957. Married Carole Eckert. ''We bought a 20-year-old house, not dissimilar from Ross's in Kingswood Warren, north of Reigate in Surrey. We changed its name from 'Durley Dene' to the more appropriate 'Carrick' after the Carrick province of Ayrshire from which our immediate paternal forbears had come. Thus after more than 30 years, Ross and I were living under different roofs and even on different sides of the Thames. However we still met almost every day in Temple Gardens where we had two third-floor rooms in what must be the closest approach in London to an Oxford or Cambridge quadrangle. Particularly in the autumn and winter, there was something almost Dickensian about the scene with all the formally-dressed barristers and their clerks beavering away under the rather brighter illumination afforded by the electricity, which had just 'recently' replaced the candles and gaslight.''[1]

1966-1972. Co-founder and president of Redwood Press Ltd. From 1963 until 1976, McWhirter completed 400 radio and television shows in the United States on publishing promotion tours. He has also served as the ''memory man'' on the BBC-TV series ''Record Breakers'' since 1972 in more than 100 shows.

1975. Twin brother Ross died of gunshot wounds suffered during an Irish Republican Army terrorist attack. ''Looking back on Ross's crowded and abbreviated life, I feel forced to the conclusion that in the apparently rare cases in which twins work closely together there is a multiplier factor which determines how much they can get done. This is because Ross and I could always rely on having a deputy who was genetically the same person, and thus tended to operate singly in the knowledge that if some insoluble double commitment arose the other one could always stand in. However, there were times when even this latitude was not sufficient and we had a notional triplet called 'Horace' whom we would dearly have liked to press into service on increasingly frequent occasions. Ross and I could never understand how non-twins managed to get through the week. The answer, of course, is that they just have to take on half as much.

''The last joint operation on which we embarked was a round-the-world promotional visit to Australia and the United States to tie in the publication of an Australian supplement to the *Guinness Book of Records* and to a new U.S. hard back edition of what in America is called *The Guinness Book of World Records.* The intensity of this tour can be reflected in the figure of 71 radio and television shows in 12 working days with 23 flights.''[1]

1977. Wrote *Ross: The Story of a Shared Life,* the joint biography of McWhirter and his brother.

Sales of *The Guinness Book of Records* surpassed 45 million in 1982 and the book has been translated into twenty-three languages. In 1980 McWhirter was appointed commander of Most Excellent Order of the British Empire (CBE).

FOR MORE INFORMATION SEE: Time, January 19, 1963; *Sports Illustrated*, February 8, 1965, July 15, 1974, July 30, 1979; *Reader's Digest*, May 1965; London *Observer*, March 21, 1971; London Sunday *Times* magazine, January 16, 1972; London Sunday *Telegraph*, July 21, 1972; *Los Angeles Times*, December 9, 1974; Norris McWhirter, *Ross: The Story of a Shared Life*, Churchill, 1973; London *Daily Telegraph*, October 29, 1977; *People*, September 16, 1979; *Contemporary Biography*, November, 1979; *International Herald Tribune*, October 18-19, 1980; *Proceedings of the Royal Institution of Great Britain*, Volume 53, 1981.

McWHIRTER, (Alan) Ross   1925-1975

PERSONAL: Born August 12, 1925, in London, England; died of gunshot wounds suffered during an Irish Republican Army terrorist attack on November 27, 1975, in Enfield, London, England; son of William Allen (former editor of *London Daily Mail*) and Margaret (Williamson) McWhirter; married Rosemary J. Hamilton Grice, May 18, 1957; children: Ian Charles Hamilton, Andrew James Kennedy. *Education:* Trinity College, Oxford, B.A., and M.A., 1948. *Politics:* Conservative. *Religion:* Church of England. *Residence:* London, England. *Office:* Guinness Superlatives Ltd., 2 Cecil Court, London Rd., Enfield, Middlesex EN2 6DJ, England.

CAREER: McWhirter Twins Ltd., London, England, co–founder with twin brother, Norris, 1950; *Athletics World* (magazine), publisher, 1951-57; *Star*, London, staff sports writer, 1951-60; Guinness Superlatives Ltd., London, co–director, beginning 1954; *Evening News*, London, staff sports writer, 1960–62; Dreghorn Publications Ltd., London, director, beginning, 1962. Conservative candidate for Parliament for Edmonton constituency in 1964 general election (his twin also stood in the same election). Member of British Olympic and Empire Games Appeal Committees, 1964-72. *Military service:* Royal Navy, 1943-46. *Member:* Sports Writers Association (chairman, 1959), Vincents' Club (Oxford University; committee, beginning 1964), Achilles Club (Oxford and Cambridge; committee, beginning 1952).

WRITINGS—With twin brother, Norris D. McWhirter: *Get to Your Marks*, Kaye, 1950; (compilers) *Guinness Book of Records*, Guinness Superlatives, 1955, 31st edition, 1984, published as *Guinness Book of World Records*, Sterling, 1961, 21st edition, 1982; (editors) *Guinness Book of Olympic Records*, Sterling, 1963-84; (compilers) *Dunlop Book of Facts*, Dreghorn Publications, 1964, 2nd edition, 1966; *The 1966 Guinness Book of British Empire and Commonwealth Games Records*, Guinness Superlatives, 1966; (compilers) *Dunlop Illustrated Encyclopedia of Facts*, Doubleday, 1969; *Guinness Sports Record Book*, Sterling, 1972, 7th edition, 1980; *Surprising Facts about Kings and Rulers*, F. Watts (London), 1973; *Guinness Book of Answers*, Sterling, 1976, 4th edition, 1983; *Guinness Book of Essential Facts*, Sterling, 1979; *Guinness Book of Sports Records, Winners, and Champions*, Sterling, 1980, revised edition, 1982; *Guinness Illustrated Encyclopedia of Facts*, Sterling, 1981.

Books written with other authors: (With Sir Andrew Nobel) *Centenary History of Oxford University Rugby Football Club*, Oxford University Rugby Football Club, 1969; (with U. A. Titley) *Centenary History of the Rugby Football Union*, Rugby Football Union, 1970. Weekly columnist, "World of Sport," in *Observer*, 1956-67.

Norris and Ross McWhirter.

SIDELIGHTS: Ross McWhirter was born on August 12, 1925, the "younger" twin of Norris McWhirter. Since the age of ten, the McWhirter twins collected reference materials as a hobby. During their youth the twins were inseparable—they attended the same preparatory school, Marlborough, as had their older brother, Kennedy.

Their first separation came during World War II, when, at the age of nineteen, Ross was appointed midshipman and a fourth officer to the trawler HMS *Shillay*, and Norris was appointed a junior officer on the HMS *Labuan*. The two young seamen met only once during their war service, when Norris' ship, HMS *Scaravay*, owing to engine failure, collided with Ross' ship, HMS *Shillay*, coming alongside in Malta. The crews of the two ships were unable to tell the two brothers apart.

After the war Ross and Norris returned to Oxford University where Ross graduated with a degree in jurisprudence.

Following graduation from Oxford, the brothers opened a fact–finding business supplying editors, writers, and newspapers with answers to queries. This business eventually led to the compilation of the *Guinness Book of Records*. Its immediate success was recalled by brother Norris: "Ross and I had long had the suspicion that our own fascination for records and superlatives may not have been as quirkish as some of our closer friends thought, but . . . there had been no confirmation that it would arouse such a widespread enthusiasm among others." [Norris McWhirter, *Ross: The Story of a Shared Life*, Churchill, 1977.[1]]

Not a cheap cheep: A Japanese fancier . . . laid out the most money ever paid for a bird—about $48,000 to Georges Desender (Belgium) for a pigeon in October, 1978. ■ (From *Guinness Book of Dazzling Endeavors* by Norris McWhirter and Ross McWhirter. Illustrated by Bill Hinds.)

Ross published *Athletics World* from 1951 to 1957 and was a sports writer for the London *Star* from 1951 to 1960 and for the London *Evening News* from 1960 to 1962. As lawn tennis and rugby football correspondent for the *Star,* he covered 85 rugby internationals and eleven Wimbledons single-handedly. Norris recalled: "Ross used to cover Wimbledon every year lone-handed and even had the zeal to study the terminology of women's fashions so that he could describe the various tennis dresses accurately. In anything so hopelessly saturated by press coverage as Wimbledon, scoops were a virtual impossibility; but Ross achieved one on the strike of the British players over the matter of concessionary tickets and other privileges, with which the *Star* led the paper. His newsy paragraphs pervaded the diary page as well as the sports' pages and included even an interview with a beribboned veteran commissionaire who had fought the fuzzy-wuzzies in the Sudan, the story behind the supply of strawberries, and pieces about the referee, the umpires, the linesmen and even the ballboys. During the fortnight of the eleven Wimbledons which he covered there was no precedent or record which escaped him on the outside courts or on the Centre Court. He even reported that rare meteorological phenomenon serein—rain from a cloudless sky—but the telephonist censored it because he throught Ross was pulling his leg.

"In the winter Ross covered Rugby Union football and witnessed, in all, more than 85 international matches."[1]

In 1957, Ross married Rosemary Hamilton Grice. Norris, still unmarried at the time, recalled the event: "His wedding day was on 18 May 1957 with the service arranged at Christ Church, Old Southgate, a noble edifice in Waterfall Lane (now Road) overlooking the playing fields of the renowned Southgate cricket and hockey clubs. Rosemary, an only child, lived in her parents' house literally next door to the church and was thus able to walk with her father Leslie to reach her wedding on time. 'Aberfoyle' [the McWhirter family home] was however a mile distant and as 'best man' I had to get my man to the starting line from there. At that time we shared a car which was a Mercedes 220, registration number RXN 630, or, as mother used to say 'Ross & Norris, 6.30' (the time at which we aimed but rarely succeeded in leaving the office together). Thinking that I had better spruce it up a bit, I drove across to the nearest car-wash. So far so good, until I found the exit was jammed by another car whose driver (and keys) could not be found. The minutes towards the vital 11 o'clock ticked by. At about 10.54 the errant driver who had been shopping turned up. I was back at Aberfoyle where Ross was standing in the road at 10.57. We got to the church simultaneously with Rosemary at 11.01. However, luckily there was some fuss with her headdress and we sat side by side composing ourselves for a few minutes in the front right pew of the packed church. An instant before Mendelssohn struck up, I was enabled to say to Ross: 'If there is one thing I cannot stand it's unpunctuality.' He was only slightly amused and merely replied: 'Did you remember the ring?' "[1]

The couple had two sons, Ian and Andrew James.

Throughout his career, Ross McWhirter was greatly interested in sports, especially track, rugby football, and lawn tennis. He was widely traveled, and had visited about forty countries, mostly in connection with sports. He once said that he was "pro United States and a detester of extreme right or left wing politics on scientific grounds."

In 1964 Ross was the conservative candidate for Parliament for the Edmonton constituency in the general election. Besides being actively involved in politics, journalism, and publishing, he was also a frequent guest on a number of BBC-TV children's programs.

Ross McWhirter was assassinated in an Irish Republican Army terrorist attack at his home in Village Road, Enfield, London, on November 27, 1975. Norris explained the possible motives behind the terrorist attack: ". . . Any revolutionary body had a hostility insofar as my brother was a declared opponent of what he regarded as the unlawful usurpation of legislative power by trade unions in general and of the attempts to impose a 'closed shop' (compulsory unionism) in Fleet Street in particular. His activities in trying to resist what he called the brain–washing proposition that the general public had meekly to accept any amount of inconvenience provided this 'convenienced,' by way of blackmailing leverage, those using the strike weapon were, of course, anathema to potentially violent militants of several kinds.

"The nature of his death seemed to prick many people's conscience. He had set a standard that was an implied criticism of the inertia of Government, particularly of the Home Office in defending the Queen's Peace. He saw earlier and saw more clearly than others the threat of anarchy. He was a freedom fighter in the less fashionable but surely truer sense of that term. It was all a repetition of the story of our late father who, as an editor, had seen earlier and more clearly than others the folly of the reluctant rearmers in the 1930s. To understand Ross one has to understand his roots.

"One of the many projects on which Ross was working at the time of his death was a monograph entitled 'Deceived in Her Grant,' which set out in icily clear terms the total illegality of the *method* of Britain's entry into Europe. He maintained that the national referendum was a farrago: The Treaty of Rome required any new entrant to accede strictly in accordance with their constitutional requirements. Since the requirements had not been fulfilled the nation was being asked to vote on a nullity. When the day comes that this country is compelled to have a written constitution, his manuscript is something which might be studied with rather more than passing interest."[1]

"On August 13, 1981, over five years after his death, twenty-one judges of the European Court of Justice voted 18-3 in favor of his proposition that the United Kingdom had violated the European Convention of Human Rights by legalizing compulsory unionism. New laws were formed in 1982 as a result of this test case in the British Rail 'closed shop.' I went to the Strasbourg Court to witness the vindication of the seven-year legal battle."

In 1977 *Ross: the Story of a Shared Life,* a personal account of the McWhirters' lives and careers together, was written by Norris McWhirter as a tribute to his brother's memory.

The famous *Guinness Book of World Records,* which the McWhirter twins compiled, has sold over forty-eight million copies and has been translated into such diverse languages as Czechoslovak, Hebrew, Indinesian, Japanese, Croat, and Slovene.

FOR MORE INFORMATION SEE: Sports Illustrated, February 8, 1965 (an article by J. A. Maxtone Graham, condensed as "Last Word in Books," *Reader's Digest,* May, 1965); *Publishers Weekly,* April 15, 1968; *Contemporary Authors,* Volumes 17-20, reivsed, Gale, 1976; Norris McWhirter, *Ross: The Story of a Shared Life,* Churchill, 1977.

OBITUARIES: Washington Post, November 28, 1975, November 29, 1975; *New York Times,* November 29, 1975; *Newsweek,* December 8, 1975; *Publishers Weekly,* December 8, 1975; *Time,* December 8, 1975; *AB Bookman's Weekly,* December 22, 1975; *Bookseller,* January 17, 1976.

MESSMER, Otto   1892(?)-1983

PERSONAL: Born about 1892, in West Hoboken, N.J.; died of a heart attack, October 28, 1983, in Teaneck, N.J.; children: two daughters. *Education:* Attended Thomas School of Art. *Residence:* Fort Lee, N.J.

CAREER: Cartoonist and animator. First cartoons published in 1914; worked as animator, advertising artist, and scenery painter, 1914-16; joined staff of Pat Sullivan Studios as artist and animator, 1916; created with Pat Sullivan, the cartoon character "Felix the Cat," who first appeared in the 1916 animated film "Tail of Thomas Cat" and was renamed "Felix" in subsequent films directed by Messmer during the 1920s; credited with drawing "Felix the Cat" daily comic strip in *New Journal American* between 1923 and 1954, and in Toby Press comic books during the 1940s; Douglas Leigh Corp., New York, N.Y., animator for giant electrical ad board in Times Square, 1940-72; animator for films "Popeye," "Little Lulu," "Snuffy Smith," and others, 1944-45; retired, about 1973.

WRITINGS: Felix, Cinematheque Canadienne (Montreal), 1967.

"Felix the Cat." ■ (From *The World Encyclopedia of Comics,* edited by Maurice Horn.)

Otto Messmer draws "Felix" for two youngsters at a comic book convention.

Starting in 1948, Dell published "Felix the Cat" as a monthly comic book. Above is a page from an early edition. Copyright 1949 by King Features Syndicate, Inc.

Pat Sullivan (far left), next to him Otto Messmer with the entire "Felix" staff at the Sullivan Studios, 1925.

FILMS—All produced by Pat Sullivan, except as noted; all animated short subjects (selected): "Motor Matt and His Fliv," Universal Film Manufacturing, 1916; "Felix Gets in Wrong," Universal Film Manufacturing, 1916; "Felix on the Job," Universal Film Manufacturing, 1916; "Fearless Freddie in the Wooly West," Universal Film Manufacturing, 1917; "20,000 Laughs under the Sea," Universal Film Manufacturing, 1917; "Felix the Cat at the Rainbow's End," 1925; "Felix the Cat on the Farm," 1925; "Felix the Cat Braves the Briny," 1926; "Felix the Cat in Reverse English," 1926; "Felix the Cat Seeks Solitude," 1926; "Felix the Cat Weathers the Weather," 1926; "Felix the Cat in No Fuelin'," 1927; "Felix the Cat in Icy Eyes," 1927; "Felix the Cat as Roameo," 1927; "Felix the Cat in Art for Heart's Sake," 1927; "Felix the Cat in the Last Life," 1928; "Felix the Cat in In and Out Laws," 1928; "Felix the Cat in Futuritzy," 1928; "Felix the Cat in Sure-Locked Homes," 1928; "Pat Sullivan's Felix the Cat" (collection), Felix the Cat Productions, 1959-61.

ADAPTATIONS: Various films, recordings, comic books, and sheet music, all based on "Felix the Cat."

Television: "Felix the Cat" (animated cartoons), Joe Oriolio Productions, syndicated, beginning 1960.

SIDELIGHTS: **1892.** Born in West Hoboken, New Jersey. "I was from a poor family. My father was a hard working ma-chinist and iron worker. He didn't make much money, but it was a pleasure, a pleasure to live.

"In those days, West Hoboken was united with Union Hill, which later became Union City. It was not like today—now-adays children watch television—they don't seem to play in the streets very much. But when I was young, girls and boys played lots of games outside. The streets were our playground. In winter we went sledding down the hills together; in summer we played 'hide and seek,' or 'hare and hound,' where one would try to find a hidden object by following little clues. We played stick ball and baseball and had a lot of outdoor fun. I read a lot; everybody did. I loved Charles Dickens.

"Cars hadn't been invented. It was difficult to shop because the stores were so far away, but everything came to us on wheels. Horses and wagons paraded through the streets and on Fridays, the fishermen would blow their horns and people would come out and buy the day's fresh catch.

"In grammar school there was a section in which drawing was taught, I was pretty good. The teachers noticed that I had a little ability, so, with their encouragement I followed up and went to art school.

Messmer attended the Thomas School of Art in New Jersey. "At Thomas I developed my talent. I did a little scenery work after I graduated, then I took a job with an advertising agency."

A vivid model sheet which captures the essence of Felix. ■ (From *Of Mice and Magic: A History of American Animated Cartoons* by Leonard Maltin.)

1921   TODAY

"Felix" changed physically over the years. ■ (From *The Fleischer Story* by Leslie Cabarga.)

1913-14. Submitted cartoons to various newspapers and magazines. "While working in advertising, I made comics on the side. I sent a few to *The New York Sunday World,* a big newspaper that had a special magazine section called 'Fun.' They accepted all ten of my comics, saying 'Very good, send us some more.' I was surprised. Then I sent some to *Life* magazine—I felt marvelous when they said 'yes.' It gives you a great feeling when that happens."

1916. Intrigued by the new field of animation, Messmer made a one-minute test cartoon for Universal Studios called "Motor Matt and His Fliv." He was hired and assigned to German cartoonist, Hy Mayer, who was then doing newsreel films. Mayer and Messmer collaborated on "The Travels of Teddy." During this time, Messmer also worked in advertising for Auerbach Chocolates. "It was just the beginning of animation. Movies hadn't been invented, but someone had invented a way to animate a drawing. I applied to Universal Films in Fort Lee, New Jersey, which was the center of movies before Hollywood. I made a sample for them and they hired me. I worked with some of the great cartoonists of those days, who were just starting to animate."

When Paramount fell behind schedule, the extra work was sub–contracted to Sullivan's Studio. During this time, Messmer created "Feline Follies," a probable forerunner of "Felix the

Cat." "Paramount movies put out a newsreel every week which also featured a cartoon. Because they wanted a new cartoon each week, they ran short and asked Pat Sullivan to help them out. Sullivan's was one of the only studios around. Pat Sullivan was very busy so he asked me to see what I could come up with in my spare time. I would work at the studio all day, then try to find ideas for Paramount at night when I came home."

The first "Felix" cartoon was produced by Sullivan in 1916, and became an instant success. "I was fiddling around and came up with a little cat. I thought he could be a pet who lived in different homes, and who would also act as a mascot for various explorers. I wanted the cat to do good deeds instead of the usual running around. I created a simple, realistic black cat, because many of the cartoons featured animals dressed up in clothing and I didn't like that. That was my first step.

"As Felix developed he became very pleasant and was more human-like in his expressions than the other animals I had created. He acted like a human being. He lived kindly and did good deeds. A typical 'Felix' story went like this: Felix fishes in a little pond and catches a small fish on a hook. When he sees the fish is crying, he doesn't have the heart to eat him, and throws him back in the water. Later on, Felix is in a storm on the ocean and some nasty shark threatens his life. The small fish who has grown up by now, sees Felix in trouble, remembers his good deed and thinks to himself, 'You saved me, now

"Felix," off on another adventure. ■ (Illustration courtesy of the Museum of Modern Art/Film Still Archive.)

I'll save you.' Through some trickery, he knocks the shark off, says 'Jump on my back,' and gives Felix a lift to shore. Stories like this make kids feel good. I knew children were watching and I figured the good deeds could make an impression on them. I noticed through fan mail that Felix was making a big hit, so I featured him. He ws named by Paramount. 'Felix' is taken from 'feline' and 'felicity.' The good luck cat.''

Because Messmer was working for a studio, he wasn't credited with the creation of Felix. "For many years I had to do all the work and sign Pat Sullivan's name. They claimed it had a value, the same value as calling something a Walt Disney cartoon. I created the cartoons, and the studio received one–half of the proceeds. I didn't get the other half, because Sullivan just regarded me as a working man, on salary. I was paid about $300.00 a week, which I considered a very good salary. In those days, it sure was good, but now we have copyright laws. Nowadays, I would be a wealthy man. But given the economic circumstances in those days, I'm thankful to Pat Sullivan for taking me on."

Messmer was assigned by Universal Films to the Australian–born cartoonist, Pat Sullivan of Sullivan Studio, creating both

"Felix" was created by Pat Sullivan and Otto Messmer around 1916. ■ (From *The World Encyclopedia of Cartoons*, edited by Maurice Horn.)

"Fearless Freddy" and "20,000 Laughs under the Sea" before joining the signal corps and serving in World War I. In France, Messmer won an award for his designs in the Victory Carnival. "In 1917 I was drafted. That put a halt on things. I didn't join the infantry because I didn't want to kill. I went into the signal corps for two years on the front—right on the front in France. Radio wasn't invented yet. Messages were all in Morse code—dots and dashes. That was very exciting."

1919. Returned to France. Worked on "Charlie Chaplin" cartoons for Pat Sullivan with animators Earl Hurd, Frank Moser, and John Terry as well as "Silly Hoots" (a pun on silhouettes) for the Paramount Screen Magazine. "We made all kinds of cartoons which were very popular. In all of the theaters in New York they ran a cartoon before every movie."

1921. The "Felix" cartoons were syndicated by Margaret Winker and later by Pat Sullivan's lawyer with the financial backing of Educational Films. Sullivan Studios began producing one "short" every ten days. "My days were so busy. You have so many more drawings in animation than in comics. If a character has to walk, it takes five drawings for him to take one step. A one-minute cartoon is an incredible amount of work. It takes twenty-four drawings for each second. Most of our cartoons were six minutes long—so figure that out! I was lucky to have a lot of assistants. But when I got home I had to worry about stories for the next day. It was quite a lot of pressure to keep coming up with new gags and ideas."

1922. Created a "Felix" comic strip which ran in the *London Illustrated News,* though he was still obligated to sign Sullivan's name. "The 'Felix' cartoons were a rage, a hit in London, so the *London Illustrated News* asked for a double-fold center page comic, which would run once a week."

August 14, 1923. "Felix" featured as a Sunday comic by King Features Syndicate. "The New York newspapers asked Pat for a Sunday page which he handed over to me. It bothered me for awhile to remain anonymous, but I felt it was better than nothing. At least I was doing it. I was glad to see Felix's popularity anyway."

1927. King Features assumed the copyright to "Felix," and ran the comic as a daily strip.

1933. Sullivan died. "The years went by. I was always under the name Pat Sullivan. Even after he died the newspaper insisted that I sign Pat Sullivan's name."

Messmer maintained a personal friendship with Walt Disney. "Disney was a great fan of Felix. When he first started, he wanted me to come out West with him to help open his studios. But I had just married and had my family here, my mother and father and the children. I had too many ties, and Felix was starting to click. I couldn't take Felix with me, he belonged to Pat Sullivan. But Walt [Disney] went to California and made a big hit with the aid of a lot of other cartoonists. Whenever he came to New York, we would take our wives out to dinner and shows. We had good times together.

"After Sullivan died I worked with Douglas Leigh, the advertiser. I did the first electric light animation for him. That was terrific. I worked with him until I was 86 years old. We made signs all over the world—in Mexico City, Spain, Japan."

1944-1945. Worked on storyboards for "Popeye" and "Little Lulu," as well as "Snuffy Smith" and other animated cartoons. "I worked a lot with Bill Turner at Paramount. I didn't mind working on other people's creations at all. They were nice characters to work with."

In **1945,** Pat Sullivan's nephew re-opened the Sullivan Studio and formed the "Felix the Cat" Corporation with New Jersey animator Joe Oriolo.

1954. "Felix" was relinquished to Joe Oriolo who syndicated him in 1960. "Pat Sullivan missed the boat. He was inexperienced and just gave the copyright away. Oriolo got control of Felix—all of him—for a few bucks. They lost the character when they revived him. He was cartoon-type silly. He wasn't popular and he wasn't cute."

Messmer quit the Sunday papers, but continued executing occasional drawings until his retirement in 1973.

1967. A team of Canadian researchers, preparing an exhibit for the World's Fair of early animation, uncovered Messmer as the true creator of "Felix." "Two men came from the Montreal World's Fair to the United States and discovered the truth about several animators who had been unrecognized over the years. They invited my wife and me to Montreal, where I was honored at the Fair along with three other animators. It was quite a thrill after so many years of anonymity.

"Ever since then I have had so many requests from schools and universities to speak. I have also been featured in a film about the history of animation. It's bringing in an awful lot of fan mail. I can't handle it. I answer as much as I can, but it's quite a strain now."

"Felix's" magic bag of tricks originated in the television version of "Felix the Cat." The syndicated half-hour series premiered in 1960. Copyright by Joe Oriolo Productions.

Messmer celebrates his ninetieth birthday with friends.

1977. The Museum of Modern Art and the Whitney Museum ran simultaneous Felix Film festivals. Messmer appeared on television's "To Tell the Truth," and was invited to judge an International Film Festival in Zagreb, Yugoslavia, but declined for health reasons.

October 28, 1983. Died of a heart attack at his home in New Jersey. "I worked up until a few weeks ago on my fan mail. My eyesight started to give a little bit, but I still give a sketch with the letters I send. I want to get my eyes straightened out so I can answer the mail. I have quite a few letters here.

"I don't know about the modern comic strips. I can't quite get them. They're a little bit fantastic—a little out of my line. The cat was realistic. And in that sense, people could relate to him. But the modern stuff is weird. I think the old cartoons and comics were better, of course,—I was one of the creators.

"Now that they have schools that teach animation, my advice to anyone interested in a career would be to check in and see if you have any ability in drawing or writing. Take those courses, then get help. We never had the opportunity to get professional training. We had to do it ourselves."

FOR MORE INFORMATION SEE: "Otto Messmer and Felix the Cat" (motion picture; also video cassette), Phoenix Films, 1978; Maurice Horn, editor, *The World Encyclopedia of Cartoons,* Volume 1, Gale, 1980. Obituaries: *Facts on File,* October, 1983; *Variety,* November 2, 1983.

METOS, Thomas H(arry)   1932-

PERSONAL: Born June 14, 1932, in Salt Lake City, Utah; son of Harry G. (a lawyer) and Grace (Milner) Metos; married Marilyn Oberg, September 3, 1955; children: Jeffery, Melissa. *Education:* University of Utah, B.S., 1954, M.S., 1958, Ph.D., 1963. *Home:* 1427 North Sunset Dr., Tempe, Ariz. 85281. *Office:* College of Education, Arizona State University, Tempe, Ariz. 85281.

CAREER: History teacher at public schools in Salt Lake City, Utah, 1954-62, curriculum supervisor, 1962-63; University of Utah, Salt Lake City, assistant professor of education, 1963-64; San Diego County Department of Schools, San Diego, Calif., curriculum coordinator in social studies, 1964-65; Arizona State University, Tempe, assistant professor, 1965-67, associate professor, 1967-71, professor of educational administration, 1965—, director of Research Services of Bureau of Educational Research and Services, 1965-78. Consultant to government agencies. *Member:* American Educational Research Association, National Conference of Professors of Educational Administration, Western Psychological Association. *Awards, honors:* Joint committee of National Science Teachers Association and Children's Book Council named *Exploring With Metrics* an outstanding science book for children in 1975, and named *Exploring With Solar Energy* in 1978.

WRITINGS—All for children: (With C. D. Montgomery) *Workbook: The Free and the Brave,* Rand McNally, 1967, 3rd

THOMAS H. METOS

edition, 1977; (with Montgomery) *Workbook: The Adventure of the American People,* Rand McNally, 1968; (with Gary Bitter) *Exploring With Metrics,* Messner, 1975; (with G. Bitter) *Exploring With Pocket Calculators,* Messner, 1977; (with G. Bitter) *Exploring With Solar Energy,* Messner, 1978; *Robots A Two Z,* Messner, 1980.

Contributor: E. T. Demars, editor, *Utah School Organization and Administration,* University of Utah Press, 1964; Locke Bowman, editor, *Education for Volunteer Teachers,* Scottsdale, Ariz., 1971.

Co-author of film scripts: "Using the Pocket Calculator," Centron Corp., 1978; "Introducing the Pocket Calculator," Centron Corp., 1978; "Using the Pocket Calculator," Centron Corp., 1978. Contributor to school surveys and education journals. Editor of *Arizona Professor,* 1969-72; member of editorial review board of *Louisiana Education Research Journal,* 1977—.

WORK IN PROGRESS: A book on the impact of automation and automatic devices on society, publication by Messner.

SIDELIGHTS: "My interest in writing for children has evolved over a long period of time. Though being a professor causes one to write from time to time on professional subjects, I first became interested in writing for children while an undergraduate in college. One of my friends' mothers was a very prolific author who wrote for children as well as adult fiction and nonfiction. We had many long talks about writing and since that time I have had a real interest in writing for children.

"However, I did not pursue this interest until recently, except for some work done for students in American history several years ago. It was almost by chance that I got started in writing nonfiction for children. This chance and an excellent, sympathetic editor has helped me to continue publishing in the field.

"All of my writings for children have been in the areas of mathematics, science, and technology. I have no real background in these areas since my educational background is in political science, history, and education. However, I have become fascinated in writing about scientific subjects and enjoy immensely doing the research about them. Even more enjoyable has been the correspondence and contact with individuals active in the particular field that I am writing about. For example, when gathering pictures and information for the book about robots, I came into contact with individuals who literally had spent their lives developing and building a robot and their enthusiasm rubbed off on me. This enthusiasm and excitement is important to me and I hope it will continue to motivate me."

MINER, Jane Claypool 1933-
(Jane Claypool; Veronica Ladd, a pseudonym)

BRIEF ENTRY: Born April 22, 1933, in McAllen, Tex. Teacher and author of young adult books. A graduate of California State University, Miner taught at various schools between 1956 and 1981 before becoming a full-time writer. She has written both fiction and nonfiction for several series, including "Floweromance," "Crisis," "Wildfire," "Jem High-Interest-Low-Reading Level," and "Impact." Her ten books in the "Crisis" series (all under name Jane Claypool; all published by Crestwood, 1982) depict teenagers overcoming problems in their lives. The *High/Low Report* found these books "quality high/low fare that provides interesting characters, situations teens can relate to and writing that does not talk down to poor readers." *Catholic Library World* noted their "realistic heroes and heroines that most adolescents can identify with." Other books by Miner include *Senior Class* (Scholastic Book Services, 1982), *A Love for Violet* (under name Jane Claypool; Westminister, 1982), *For Love of Lori* (under pseudonym Veronica Ladd; Simon & Schuster, 1982), *Alcohol and Teens* (under name Jane Claypool; Messner, 1983), and *Working in a Hospital* (under name Jane Claypool; Messner, 1983). She is currently at work on more young adult novels for Simon & Schuster under the pseudonym Veronica Ladd. *Home:* 103 Dawes Ave., Pittsfield, Mass. 01201. *For More Information See: Berkshire Eagle,* April 14, 1981; *Contemporary Authors,* Volume 106, Gale, 1982.

MOORE, Ray (S.) 1905(?)-1984

OBITUARY NOTICE: Born about 1905, in Montgomery City, Mo.; died following a stroke, January 13, 1984, in Kirkwood, Mo.; cremated. Cartoonist. Moore attended Washington University Art School in St. Louis and was the co-creator of the comic strip "The Phantom" with Lee Falk. The strip featured a masked hero, clad in purple tights, opposing injustice and villainy. *Obituaries: Facts on File,* January, 1984; *Washington Post,* January 16, 1984; *Chicago Tribune,* January 17, 1984; *New York Times,* January 17, 1984; *Newsweek,* January 30, 1984; *Variety,* February 8, 1984.

MORRISON, Bill   1935-

BRIEF ENTRY: Born in 1935. Educator, author and illustrator of books for children. A teacher of illustration, Morrison has illustrated over thirty books for children written by others and has received several awards in National Exhibitions held by the Society of Illustrators. He has also written and illustrated three of his own books: *Squeeze a Sneeze* (Houghton, 1977), *Louis James Hates School* (Houghton, 1978), and *Simon Says* (Little, Brown, 1983). *School Library Journal* has described his work as "light–hearted [and] fast moving . . . [with] . . . amusing watercolor illustrations with pen–and–ink details. . . ." In *Squeeze a Sneeze,* Morrison employs colorful cartoons and nonsense rhyme to create what *Publishers Weekly* called an "exuberant book" in which he "snares the eye and ear easily with his exercise in buffoonery." Among his illustrated works are *Finding Out about Shapes* (McGraw-Hill, 1969) by Mae Freeman; *Where's Izzy?* (Follett, 1972) by Jeannette McNeely; *Too Fat to Fly* (Garrard, 1973) and *Gus Gets the Message* (Garrard, 1974), both by Adelaide Hall; *Know about Alcohol* (McGraw-Hill, 1978) by Margaret O. Hyde; a series of "Oz" books adapted by C. J. Naden, including *L. Frank Baum's Dorothy and the Wicked Witch* (Troll Associates, 1980); *The Bloodhound Gang in the Case of Princess Tomorrow* (Random House, 1981) and *The Bloodhound Gang in the Case of the 264-Pound Burglar* (Random House, 1982), both by Sid Fleischman; and *Morning* (Four Winds Press, 1983) by Maria Polushkin. *Residence:* Massachusetts.

JILL MURPHY

MUNRO, Eleanor   1928-

PERSONAL: Born March 28, 1928, in Brooklyn, N.Y.; daughter of Thomas B. (an editor and educator) and Lucile (Nadler) Munro; married Alfred M. Frankfurter (an editor and writer), May 29, 1960 (divorced December, 1964); married E. J. Kahn, Jr. (staff writer for *The New Yorker),* June 31, 1969; children: (first marriage) David, Alexander. *Education:* Smith College, B.A., 1949; Columbia University, M.A., 1965. *Home:* 1095 Park Ave., New York, N.Y.

CAREER: Art News Magazine, associate editor, 1953-58; *Art News Annual,* managing editor, 1956-59; free-lance art critic, writer, and lecturer.

WRITINGS: Encyclopedia of Art, Western Publishing, 1964; *Through the Vermilion Gates,* Pantheon, 1971; *Originals: American Women Artists,* Simon & Schuster, 1979. Contributor of articles to magazines and newspapers.

WORK IN PROGRESS: Books and articles.

MURPHY, Jill   1949-

PERSONAL: Born July 5, 1949, in London, England; daughter of Eric Edwin (an engineer) and Irene (Lewis) Murphy. *Education:* Attended Chelsea, Croydon, and Camberwell art schools. *Agent:* A.P. Watt Ltd., 26/28 Bedford Row, London WC1R 4HL, England.

CAREER: Free-lance writer and illustrator, 1976—. *Awards, honors:* Kate Greenaway Award commendation from the British Library Association, 1981, for *Peace at Last.*

WRITINGS—All self-illustrated: *The Worst Witch* (juvenile), Allison and Busby, 1974, Schocken Books, 1980; *The Worst Witch Strikes Again* (juvenile), Schocken Books, 1980; *Peace at Last,* Dial, 1980; *A Bad Spell for the Worst Witch* (juvenile), Kestrel, 1982; *On the Way Home,* Macmillan, 1982; *What Next, Baby Bear!* Dial, 1984.

ADAPTATIONS: "The Worst Witch," BBC-TV, 1978; "Peace at Last," BBC-TV, second showing, 1984.

SIDELIGHTS: "I was lucky; I inherited the ability to draw from my father and I had a mother who *liked* being a mother. She encouraged me to be observant and to write from the age of three. I have drawn and written little books stapled together ever since I can remember. I always had a difficult time at school because I never wanted to do anything except write stories and draw pictures, which drove my teachers to distraction. When I look back at books written when I was six years old with perfect spelling, and original stories, I would have thought any teacher would be rejoiced! However, my mother rejoiced, and I feel it is because of her trust in my being different that I knew I would be a writer/illustrator in the end whatever else I had to trudge through. It never occurred to me that I would be anything else. Now I write and draw because I always have. It was a choice of making a success of it or working in a shop. I can't think of a more satisfying career and feel very fortunate that I am able to do it."

Murphy commented about her illustrating and writing. "Apart from my black and white illustrations which I do with a rapidograph, I always use coloured pencils. You can get lovely light effects very softly with coloured pencils. Also I hate all the mess of paints and inks and I always seem to knock things over! I always write by hand in an exercise book exactly the same as when I was a child. In fact I still work as I did when

. . .On the floor amid shattered teacups and pools of milk, Mildred saw to her dismay that she had hurled herself into Miss Hardbroom's private study. ■ (From *The Worst Witch Strikes Again* by Jill Murphy. Illustrated by the author.)

I was ten, only now my imagination isn't as good! I always point this out when I'm visiting schools.

"I get on very well with kids. I worked in a children's home, off and on, for five years; I also worked as a nanny for a little boy. Being with children and listening to them keeps me in touch with what they like and what their problems are.

"I have an amazing dog who is used in television commercials. We have great fun together, and last year she earned enough money to buy us a car! I have lived in small villages in Ghana and Togo, and have traveled all over Europe."

FOR MORE INFORMATION SEE: Washington Post Book World, February 14, 1982.

MURPHY, Jim 1947-

PERSONAL: Born Septmeber 25, 1947, in Newark, N.J.; son of James K. (a certified public accountant) and Helen Irene (a bookkeeper and artist; maiden name, Grosso) Murphy; married Elaine A. Kelso (a company president), December 12, 1970. *Education:* Rutgers University, B.A., 1970; graduate study, Radcliffe College, 1970. *Home and office:* 138 Wildwood Ave., Upper Montclair, N.J. 07043.

CAREER: Seabury Press, Inc., juvenile department (later Clarion Books), New York, N.Y., 1970-77, began as editorial secretary, became managing editor; free-lance author and editor, 1977—. *Member:* Asian Night Six Club (founding member). *Awards, honors: Weird and Wacky Inventions* was a "Children's Choice" of the International Reading Association, 1979.

Harold went to the park
and sat on a rock.
"No more BIG Plans," he said.
"BIG Plans are stupid!"

■ (From *Harold Thinks Big* by Jim Murphy. Illustrated by Susanna Natti.)

WRITINGS—All for children: *Weird and Wacky Inventions* (nonfiction; self-illustrated), Crown, 1978; *Rat's Christmas Party* (fiction; illustrated by Dick Gackenbach), Prentice-Hall, 1979; *Harold Thinks Big* (fiction; illustrated by Susanna Natti; Junior Literary Guild selection), Crown, 1980; *Death Run* (ALA Notable Book; fiction), Clarion Books, 1982; *Two Hundred Years of Bicycles*, Harper, 1983; *The Indy 500*, Clarion Books, 1983; *Tractors: From Yesterday's Steam Wagons to Today's Turbo-Charged Giants,* Lippincott, 1984; *Baseball's All-Time All-Stars,* Clarion Books, 1984; *The Custom Car Book,* Clarion Books, 1985; *Guess Again: More Weird and Wacky Inventions,* Four Winds Press, 1985; *The Pinto Man* (tentative title), Clarion Books, 1985. Also contributor of articles to *Cricket*.

WORK IN PROGRESS: Siege, a fictional account of the siege of a thirteenth-century castle for Lippincott; *The Snow Wolf,* a young adult fiction for Clarion Books.

SIDELIGHTS: "I was raised in Kearny, N.J., a nice enough suburban town, made up largely of Scots, Irish, and Italians. My friends and I did all the normal things—played baseball and football endlessly, explored abandoned factories, walked the railroad tracks to the vast Jersey Meadowlands, and, in general, cooked up as much mischief as we could. And since Kearny was close to both Newark and New York City, we would often hop a bus or train to these cities. We loved wandering through those places, so much different than our comfortable, tree-lined streets, watching the people and eating strange and usually greasy foods.

"Oddly enough, I wasn't a very big reader back then. In fact, I hardly cracked a book willingly until a high school teacher announced that we could 'absolutely, positively NOT read' Hemingway's *A Farewell to Arms.* I promptly read it, and every other book I could get a hold of that I felt would shock my teacher. I also began writing, mostly poetry, but with an occasional story or play tossed in there.

"Now this doesn't mean that I abandoned physical activity completely. I ran track while in school and was part of national championship teams for the 440 and mile relays. I was also ranked somewhere in the top ten of high school sprinters. In addition, I had a series of strange jobs, including repairing boilers, tarring roofs, putting up chain link fences, operating a mold injection machine, and doing maintenance for two apartment buildings. The highlight, however, was a stint as a tin knocker on several New York City construction jobs.

"It wasn't too long after this that I landed an editorial job in the juvenile department (later named Clarion Books) of Seabury Press. I stayed there seven years, going from editorial secretary to managing editor. It was during this time that I realized that many of my earlier experiences could be of value in my writing.

"I thoroughly enjoy my work. The nonfiction projects let me research subjects that I'm really interested in; they provide an opportunity to tell kids some unusual bits of information. The fiction lets me get out some of the thoughts and opinions that rattle around in my head."

NEIMARK, Paul G.   1934-

BRIEF ENTRY: Born October 13, 1934, in Chicago, Ill. A free-lance writer and author of books for adults and children, Neimark graduated from Roosevelt University. He has contributed more than four thousand articles to newspapers and periodicals, including the *New York Times* and *Readers Digest*. In 1971 he received an M. K. Cooper Award for best human relations book. Covering a variety of topics, many of his books were written in collaboration with professionals in a given field. For adults these include *Blackthink: My Life as Black Man and White Man* (with Jesse Owens; Morrow, 1970), *Confessions of a Divorce Lawyer* (with Herbert A. Glieberman; Regnery, 1975), *Good-bye Loneliness* (with Jay H. Schmidt; Stein & Day, 1979), and *The Berkowitz Diet Switch* (with Gerald Berkowitz; Arlington House, 1981). His books for children include *The Jesse Owens Story* (with Owens; Putnam, 1970), *Cycle Cop: The True Story of Jack Muller, the Chicago Giant Killer Who Feared No Evil* (Putnam, 1976), and *Getting Along: How to Be Happy with Yourself and Others* (with Schmidt; Putnam, 1979). He is also the author of the "Wilderness World" series for children, published by Children's Press in 1981. These books explore basic guidelines, equipment, and techniques in *Camping and Ecology, Fishing, Hiking and Exploring*, and *Survival*.

NOBLE, Trinka Hakes

BRIEF ENTRY: An author and illustrator of children's books, Noble studied illustration under artist Uri Shulevitz at his Advanced Workshop in Greenwich Village. She has written four books and illustrated three more by other authors. The first book she wrote and illustrated, *The King's Tea* (Dial, 1979), was praised by *Publishers Weekly* for its use of ". . . the snowballing effects that children love. . . ," while *Horn Book* called it ". . . an attractively designed book." In 1980 Noble teamed up with noted illustrator Steven Kellogg who provided the pictures for *The Day Jimmy's Boa Ate the Wash* (a Junior Literary Guild selection; Dial), the comic tale of a young girl's field-day trip to a farm. It was described by *School Library Journal* as ". . . fine, funny, and full of pep." Its sequel is *Jimmy's Boa Bounces Back* (Dial, 1984). *Hansy's Mermaid*

(Dial, 1983), is a fantasy that Noble wrote and illustrated. *Publishers Weekly* called her work ". . . distinctive, warm, and gently humorous. . . ," adding that her ". . . paintings are realistic [and] beautiful. . . ." Noble also illustrated *Will You Take Me to Town on Strawberry Day?* by Marilyn Singer, *The Witch Who Lost Her Shadow* by Mary Calhoun, and *Karin's Christmas Walk* by Susan Pearson. *Residence:* Upper Montclair, N.J.

NÖSTLINGER, Christine   1936-

BRIEF ENTRY: Born in 1936, in Vienna, Austria. Journalist, author of books for children and novels for young adults. Although Nöstlinger attended art school with the intention of becoming a painter, marriage and two children led her to abandon that career. She later became a journalist and works now on one of Vienna's daily newspapers. She has written numerous books in her native German language, over ten of which have been translated into English by Anthea Bell and published both in England and the United States. These include several novels for young adults, the first of which was *Fly Away Home* (F. Watts, 1975). In this autobiographical story of a young girl caught in the nightmare of World War II, Nöstlinger relates her own struggle for life as a child in Vienna during the occupation of both the Nazi and Russian troops. *Publishers Weekly* described the book as ". . . richly humorous, boisterous, angry and (above all) painfully moving," while the *Times Literary Supplement* labeled it ". . . a kaleidoscope of a story with shifting patterns and colours, and vivid concrete impressions. . . ." Nöstlinger's other novels include *Girl Missing* (F. Watts, 1976), *Four Days in the Life of Lisa* (Abelard, 1977), *Marrying Off Mother* (Andersen Press, 1978), and *Luke and Angela* (Harcourt, 1981). Although these books are set in more contemporary times, they nonetheless deal with the problems of young adults in the same realistic, straightforward manner evident in *Fly Away Home*, with an overlay of humor and satire. *Junior Bookshelf* commented: "To compare her books with those of Judy Blume is to realise how different the approach can be to the same problems."

Nöstlinger's translated works for children include *The Cucumber King: A Story with a Beginning, a Middle, and an End, in Which Wolfgang Hogelmann Tells the Whole Truth* (Abelard, 1975), *The Disappearing Cellar: A Tale Told by Pia Maria Tiralla, a Viennese Nanny* (Abelard, 1975), *Fiery Frederica* (Abelard, 1975), *Konrad* (F. Watts, 1977), and *Mr. Bat's Great Invention* (Andersen Press, 1978). She is the recipient of numerous awards, including the Friedrich-Bödecker Prize which she received in 1972 for her contribution to children's literature. The following year she was awarded the German Youth Literature Prize for the original German edition of *The Cucumber King*. In 1977 she received the Mildred L. Batchelder Award for *Konrad*, and in 1981 *Luke and Angela* was selected as an ALA Notable Book. Nöstlinger's other awards include the Buxtehuder Bulle, 1973, for *Maikaefer flieg!* (title means "Fly Away, Mayfly!"); the Oesterreichischer Staatspreis fuer Kinder-und Jugendliteratur, 1975, for *Achtung, Vranek sieht ganz harmlos aus* (title means "Careful: Vranek Seems to be Totally Harmless"), and 1979, for *Rosa Riedl, schutzgespenst* (title means "Rosa Reidl, Guardian Ghost"). *For More Information See: Fifth Book of Junior Authors and Illustrators*, H. W. Wilson, 1983.

OAKES, Vanya   1909-1983

OBITUARY NOTICE—See sketch in *SATA* Volume 6: Given name originally Virginia; born September 13, 1909, in Nutley, N.J.; died November 2, 1983, in Los Angeles, Calif. Journalist, librarian, and author. Oakes served as a correspondent in China and Southeast Asia for magazines and newspapers from 1932 until 1941. At that time she became a public lecturer in the United States and began writing a series of juvenile works based on her stay in China. Oakes taught journalism and world affairs at Los Angeles City College during the 1940s and 1950s. In 1959 she joined the staff of the Los Angeles Public Library as a reference and young adult librarian, retiring in 1975. Her books for young people include *By Sun and Star, Footprints of the Dragon, Roy Sato,* and *Challenging Careers in the Library World. For More Information See: Authors of Books for Young People,* 2nd edition, Scarecrow, 1971; *Wilson Library Bulletin,* June, 1972; *Who's Who in the West, 1976-77,* 15th edition, Marquis, 1976. *Obituaries: Los Angeles Times,* November 23, 1983.

OANA, Katherine D.   1929-
(Kay D. Oana)

BRIEF ENTRY: Born August 29, 1929, in Akron, Ohio. An educator and author, Oana received both a B.S. and M.S. from the University of Akron. She has taught school since 1951, working also as a counselor and part-time instructor at the University of Akron. Oana, an associate editor of Oddo Publishing Inc., is a member of numerous organizations, including the Society of Children's Book Writers. All of Oana's children's stories involve animals. In *The Little Dog Who Wouldn't Be* (Oddo, 1978), an unsatisfied pup experiences life on "the other side of the fence" as he is changed into a variety of animals. However, his adventures convince him that life as a dog is the best choice after all. *Shasta and the Shebang Machine* (Oddo, 1978), is a story about a mischievous pet that involves a new typewriter and a too-curious kitten. *School Library Journal* noted that "everything in the book is pretty and cute from the heroine with bouncy hair to the rag doll whose expression changes with the action to the background of flowered wallpaper." Other children's books by Oana include *Robbie and Raggedy Scarecrow* (Oddo, 1978), *Timmy Tiger and the Masked Bandit* (Oddo, 1980), *Bobbie Bear Goes to the Beach* (Oddo, 1980), *Bobbie Bear and the Blizzard* (Oddo, 1980), *Leonard the Leopard* (Ideals Publishing, 1982), *Harry the Horse* (Ideals Publishing, 1982), and *Gertrude the Goat* (Ideals Publishing, 1982). For adults she has written *Opportunities in Guidance and Counseling* (National Textbook Co., 1979), and *Women in Their Own Business* (National Textbook Co., 1982). *Office:* Riedinger Middle School, Akron, Ohio 44311. *For More Information See: Contemporary Authors,* Volume 108, Gale, 1983.

Yasuo Ohtomo with children.

No,
but I've got a kiss for you.

(From *Where's My Daddy?*, adapted from a story by Shigeo Watanabe. Illustrated by Yasuo Ohtomo.)

OHTOMO, Yasuo 1946-

PERSONAL: Born March 24, 1946, in Saitama, Japan; son of Isaburo (a forwarding agent) and Haru Ohtomo; married Noriko (a writer), 1967; children: Masanori, Sakutaro, Saburo. *Education:* Attended Setsu Mode Seminar, and Kodansha-Famous School. *Religion:* Catholic. *Home:* 733 Hirobakama-cho, Machida-shi, Tokyo 194, Japan.

CAREER: Illustrator. *Member:* Artists' Union for Juvenile Illustrated Publication.

WRITINGS—All self-illustrated: *Araiguma to Nezumi-tachi* (title means "The Mice and the Raccoon Family"), Fukuinkan, 1977; *Momoko to Goro no Okurimono* (title means "A Present from Momoko and Goro"), Doshinsha, 1978; *Otōto nanka Daikirai* (title means "I Don't Like My Younger Baby Brother"), Doshinsha, 1979.

Illustrator: Yuhi Takesaki, *Dabu Dabu Sabuchan* (title means "Sabu Likes Bigger Things"), Kaiseisha, 1974; Masao Tsurumi, *Tabemono A-I-U-E-O* (title means "Introduction to A-I-U-E-O"), Kaiseisha, 1974; Tomiko Inui, *Saburo To Himitsu No Umi* (title means "Saburo and His Secret Sea"), Doshinsha, 1975; Shigeo Watanabe, *Oisha-san nanka Kowakunai* (title means "I Dare to See a Doctor!"), Akane-Shobo, 1976; T. Inui, *Taranoki Hakase Wa Sencho-san* (title means "Dr. Taranoki Was a Captain"), Dai-Nippon Tosho, 1976; Kiyoshi Soya, *Yamaguni Hoikuen* (title means "Nursery School in a Small Village"), Fukuinkan, 1977; S. Watanabe, *Dōsureba Iinokana*, Fukuinkan, 1977, published in English as *How Do I Put It On?: Getting Dressed,* Philomel, 1979; S. Watanabe, *Okaimono Daisuki* (title means "I Love to Go Shopping"), Akane-Shobo, 1978; Noriko Ohtomo, *Mousugu Oniichan* (title means "I'll Be a Big Brother Soon"), Doshinsha, 1978; T. Inui, *Ayumi to Himitsu no Otomodachi* (title means "Ayumi and Her Lovely Friend"), Iwanami, 1979; T. Inui, *Nagai Nagai Penguin no Hanashi* (title means "Long Story about Penguins"), Iwanami, 1979; N. Ohtomo, *Megumi wa Iina!* (title means "If I Were Megumi . . ."), Fröbel-kan, 1979; S. Watanabe, *Boku Pato-car ni Nottanda!* (title means "I Rode in a Police Car"), Akane-Shobo, 1979; S. Watanabe, *Boku Oyogerunda!* (title means "I Can Swim Well!"), Akane-Shobo, 1979; S. Watanabe, *Ice-Cream ga Futtekita* (title means "Ice-Cream Has Fallen"), Akane-Shobo, 1979; S. Watanabe, *Itadaki-maasu,* Fukuinkan, 1980, published in United States as *What a Good Lunch!,* Philomel, 1980; S. Watanabe, *Kon'nichiwa,* Fukuinkan, 1980, published in United States as *Where's My Daddy?,* Philomel, 1982; S. Watanabe, *Boku maigo ni nattanda* (title means "I Got Lost in the Crowd"), Akane-Shobo, 1980; S. Watanabe, *Kumata-kun no Orusuban* (title means "Kumata Looks after the House While Parents Are Away"), Akane-Shobo, 1980; S. Watanabe, *Yōi Don!,* Fukuinkan, 1980, published in United States as *Get Set, Go!,* Philomel, 1981; S. Watanabe, *Boku Shin'kansen ni Nottanda* (title means "Fun on the Shin'kansen Line"), Akane-Shobo, 1981; S. Watanabe, *Boku Camp ni Ittanda* (title means "Nice Camping"), Akane-Shobo, 1981; S. Watanabe, *Doronko, Doronko* (title means "Fun in the Mud"), Fukuinkan, 1981, published in United States as *I'm the King of the Castle!*, Philomel, 1982; S. Watanabe, *Boku Unten Dekirunda*, Fukuinkan, 1982, published in United States as *I Can Ride It!*, Philomel, 1982; S. Watanabe, *Boku Ouchi o Tsukurunda*, Fukuinkan, 1982, published in United States as *I Can Build a House!*, Philomel, 1983; S. Watanabe, *Kiiroi Taxi* (title means "The Yellow Taxi Cab"), Fukuinkan, 1982; S. Watanabe, *I Can Ride It!: Setting Goals*, Philomel, 1982; S. Watanabe, *I Can Take a Walk*, Philomel, 1984.

SIDELIGHTS: "In my youth I was very fond of cartoon and caricature and wanted to be a caricaturist. I enjoyed reading many magazines of caricature and at the same time it was my great pleasure to read picture books such as *Babar, The Little House* and so on.

"One day my eldest son brought a book, *Guri and Gura* (by Rieko Nakagawa, illustrated by Yuriko Omura, and published by Fukuinkan), from his nursery school. When I read it with him, I got an inspiration that I might be able to create picture books. This was a turning point in my life.

"In the future I would like to make picture books of folktales, in which, I think, there are lively spirits of people."

OSGOOD, William E(dward) 1926-

PERSONAL: Born March 24, 1926, in Nashua, N.H.; son of Horace E. (a contractor) and Ethel (Trow) Osgood; married Thelma Slabaugh (a librarian), June 18, 1949; children: Kathleen, Deborah. *Education:* University of New Hampshire, B.A., 1951; Simmons College, M.L.S., 1952. *Home:* Mill Hill, Northfield, Vt. 05663. *Office:* Center for Northern Studies, Wolcott, Vt. 05680.

CAREER: Tuscarawas County Library, New Philadelphia, Ohio, county librarian, 1952-53; Dartmouth College, Hanover, N.H., reference assistant, 1953-55; Free Public Library Services, Montpelier, Vt., adult services librarian, 1955-56; Goddard College, Plainfield, Vt., librarian, 1957-72; Center for Northern Studies, Wolcott, Vt., librarian, editor of *The Northern Raven*, director of seminar series, 1975—. Northfield observer for National Weather Service; Nordic Patrol advisor, Northern Vermont Region, National Ski Patrol, 1980; director, Tenth Mountain Division Association, 1980. Member, Vermont Governor's Advisory Panel on Scenery and Historic Sites, 1963. *Military service:* U.S. Army, 1944-46. *Member:* American-Scandinavian Foundation (fellow), Vermont Academy of Arts and Sciences (incorporator and former trustee), Northfield Historical Society (incorporator; president, 1974-75).

WRITINGS: (With Leslie J. Hurley) *Ski Touring: An Introductory Guide* (illustrated by Grace A. Brigham), Tuttle, 1969, 2nd edition, 1974; (with L. J. Hurley) *The Snowshoe Book: A Complete Guide to How, Why, When, and Where*, Stephen Green Press, 1971, 3rd edition, 1983; *How to Earn a Living in the Country without Farming*, Garden Way Publishing, 1974; *Wintering in Snow Country*, Stephen Greene Press, 1977. Contributor to *Vermont Life*.

WORK IN PROGRESS: A Book of Sleds, publication expected fall, 1985, and a book about North American Indian agriculture, both with Grace A. Brigham.

SIDELIGHTS: "I have always been fascinated by outdoor life, especially in the wintertime, and I'm sure that this fascination

William E. Osgood, building a spruce bough shelter in the Vermont winter forest.

was somehow conveyed to me by my parents who often took me on their winter excursions. I used one of these recollections in *The Snowshoe Book* for a brief section entitled 'New England Family Outing.'

"Some of my earliest memories are of skis, snowshoes, skates, and sleds. Perhaps this is why I like to write about these things.

"A high school teacher named Martha Cramer encouraged my early writing efforts and I enjoyed doing writing projects during my college years. But it was Walter Hard, long-time editor of *Vermont Life* magazine, who first got me into print with a piece on bee hunting in 1957. I've written a number of articles for *Vermont Life* since that first one.

"Les Hurley and I got to talking one day in the early sixties about the real enjoyment of ski touring and we were puzzled that there was no book on the subject. So we decided to write one ourselves. He provided most of the material, based in large part on his experience with mountain and cold weather training at Norwich University. We pooled our joint experiences with the ski and mountain troops during World War II, and I tried to put it all together, adding portions on the real joys of cross-country skiing as I had experienced it. Grace Brigham is an avid ski tourer and she made the wonderful drawings. We worked well together. But we had no publisher and the rejection

...After fifteen or twenty minutes they stop to check bindings, tighten or loosen pack straps ... and enjoy the view across pastures and fields to the mountains over the valley. ▪ (From *Ski Touring: An Introductory Guide* by William E. Osgood and Leslie J. Hurley. Illustrated by Grace A. Brigham.)

slips piled up until, purely by a stroke of good luck, I found a sympathetic reader at the Rutland, Vermont office of the Charles Tuttle Co. Getting that first contract with a five hundred dollar advance was quite a thrill.

"While the ski touring book was being set up at the Tokyo office of the Tuttle Co. I was spending a sabbatical year with my family in Finland. Correspondence and galley proofs went around the world. During the 1968-69 Finland year I spent quite a bit of time in the far North as well and made a long and mostly solitary hike right through the heart of Lapland. That Finnish year was a marvellous one, and it provided me with a huge amount of background material and experience of life in the North. I used some of this for my book, *Wintering in Snow Country.*

"Back in Vermont after the sabbatical year, I continued my work as a college librarian and began to write another book. This became *The Snowshoe Book.* Stephen Greene asked me to do this one and Les Hurley and Grace Brigham helped me with it. Of all the things I've written, *The Snowshoe Book* has been the most successful. The book has also been translated into French and a publisher in Milan has paid for rights to translate it into Italian.

"In 1972 I decided to try writing full time. It was then that I began work on the wintering book and also another one called *How to Earn a Living in the Country without Farming.* I also wrote a number of magazine articles but I found that this writer couldn't earn enough money to live in the country (or anywhere else for that matter). My wife brought in the bacon during those pinched years. I was fortunate to obtain part-time work as the librarian at the Center for Northern Studies in Wolcott, Vermont in the middle seventies. Since then the work has expanded there and I edit their quarterly publication, *The Northern Raven,* and organize a seminar series in addition to the library work. Modest income is a help to our budget; moreover the work is very interesting and I still have some time to do some writing.

"My current project is a book about sleds. Grace Brigham has agreed to do the illustrations and this will be an important feature of the book.

"I really enjoy writing and I also like doing background research. I get a wonderful feeling of satisfaction when I see my books in libraries and bookstores and when people write to me about them from all over the world. Another satisfaction is the opportunity to work at home in the midst of a delightful rural environment. I think these have been my chief rewards from writing."

PARR, Letitia (Evelyn) 1906-

PERSONAL: Born January 5, 1906, in Sydney, Australia; daughter of John Lile Lewis (a shopkeeper) and Elizabeth Christina Forsyth; married Harold George Parr (an optometrist), 1927; children: Patricia Lovell, Geoffrey, Susan Woods. *Education:* Attended girls' high school in Sydney, Australia. *Politics:* "On the side of mankind, not machines." *Religion:* "Christian, I hope." *Home:* Greenway, Flat CO5, Milsons Point, New South Wales 2061, Australia.

CAREER: Worked as a stenographer until 1927; Christian Education Home Correspondence Sunday School, Sydney, Australia, organizing secretary, 1964-68; writer, 1968—. Helped to establish free library at local community center; worked in after-school care at local primary school. *Member:* Australian Society of Authors, Australian Women's Writers. *Awards, honors: Green Is for Growing* was included in "Best of the Best" by United Nations Educational, Scientific and Cultural Organization's International Youth Library, 1969; Design award from Australian Book Publishers Association, 1969, for *Green Is for Growing.*

WRITINGS—Children's books: *Green Is for Growing* (illustrated by John Watts), Angus & Robertson, 1968; *When Sea and Sky Are Blue* (illustrated by J. Watts), Scroll Press, 1970; *Seagull* (photographs by son, Geoffrey Parr), Angus & Robertson, 1970; *Dolphins Are Different* (illustrated by Patricia Mullins), Angus & Robertson, 1972; *Flowers for Samantha*

LETITIA PARR

**When the water is low,
the green moss shows. . .
and the sea shells glisten
in the sunlight.**

■ (From *When Sea and Sky Are Blue* by Letitia Parr. Illustrated by John Watts.)

(illustrated by P. Mullins), Methuen of Australia, 1975; *Getting Well in Hospital* (illustrated by Nyorie Bungey), Methuen of Australia, 1977; *Grandpa Pearson* (illustrated by Sandra Laroche), Metheun of Australia, 1979.

Work represented in anthologies, including *Stuff and Nonsense,* Collins, 1974, and *Stories to Share,* Hodder & Stoughton, 1983. Stories and poems have been broadcast on "Kindergarten of the Air," by Australian Broadcasting Commission. Contributor to *Australian Author.* Also contributor of a story to *Once upon a Time,* A.B.C., 1983.

WORK IN PROGRESS: A book for young children tentatively titled *Fly Away Verses,* illustrated by Noela Young, to be published by Collins; a children's book, *Mr. Moriarty's Mate* with illustrations by P. Mullins; research for a biography of John Cadman, a convict, for elementary school children.

SIDELIGHTS: "I appreciate the importance of the early years to the whole of life and I have a natural empathy with children. In the main, my stories are about perceptions.

"My first story was written for my grandson, Timothy, who lives in Tasmania. I'd seen him only twice and had planned to visit the family, but I became ill and couldn't go. I decided that at least I could write Timothy a story, which I did. It created interest but, having no pictures, it was only half a story

for a child of four years. . . . A year later I sent a copy to the publisher Angus & Robertson. To my surprise I was told that they were interested but I had two stories in one. I would need to separate the story about the sea wall from the one about the park, and then they'd like to see the results. I called the story about the park 'Green Places,' but the editor said that wouldn't do at all—asked me to please think about it. I used to wake at night sometimes and I'd ask myself what the story was really about. It happened, one night; the idea of *Green Is for Growing* popped up and I knew it was right. The story about the sea wall was published soon afterwards as *When Sea and Sky Are Blue.*

"*Dolphins Are Different* was written when Sheila, a zoo dolphin, died. Actually she choked on all sorts of things lying at the bottom of the pool. The director of the zoo was reported as saying that they would probably be unable to have any other dolphins because the creatures, when in captivity, have a depraved appetite. Because they are out of their natural habitat where they can chase their food, they swallow anything that comes along, including handkerchiefs and ribbons and lollies and bits of string that fall into the pool. When I visited the zoo to talk to the keeper, Mr. Boness, he was in a wet suit down in the pool throwing the fish so the last dolphin could leap for it. He talked to me about the creatures and it was obvious that he cared very much about them. He told me about a book of stories about dolphins way back in the times of Greece and Rome. All this resulted in my book, *Dolphins Are Different.*

"*Flowers for Samantha* was the outcome of an editorial request for a story dealing with death. *Grandpa Pearson* expresses my belief that the old and the young are accepting of each other."

PARTRIDGE, Jenny (Lilian) 1947-

BRIEF ENTRY: Born July 25, 1947, in Romford, England. An artist, author, and illustrator of books for children, Partridge attended South East Essex Technical College from 1963 to 1968. Beginning in 1967 she worked as a photographic retoucher at Presentation Colour Ltd. in London until 1972, when she founded Romany Studio Workshop in Ebley, England. She is the author and illustrator of the "Oakapple Wood Stories," a series of ten books originally published in England by World's Work and later in the United States by Holt. The books are anthropomorphic in nature and reveal Partridge's affinity with wildlife. They feature *Mr. Squint* (1980), a mole, *Colonel Grunt* (1980), a vole, *Peterkin Pollensnuff* (1980), a woodmouse, *Hopfellow* (1980), a frog, *Grandma Snuffles* (1981), a hedgehog, and others. According to *School Library Journal,* these are "personified animals who lead happy, secure lives in a cozy English countryside setting." *Publishers Weekly* called Partridge's illustrations "enchanting pictures in the colors of springtime. . . ." while *School Library Journal* noted that they "are detailed and meticulous. . . . [and] depict an attractive world with touches of warmth and humor. . . ." In 1981 she was the recipient of the Critici in Erba prize from the Bologna Children's Book Fair for *Mr. Squint.* The other books in the series are *Dominic Sly, Harriet Plume,* and *Lop-Ear,* all published in 1981, *Oakapple Wood Stories* (1982), and *A Tale of Oakapple Wood* (1983). *Home and office:* Westend Cottage, 319 Westward Rd., Ebley, Gloucestershire, England. *For More Information See: Contemporary Authors,* Volume 109, Gale, 1983.

PASCAL, Francine 1938-

BRIEF ENTRY: Born May 13, 1938, in New York, N.Y. Pascal graduated from New York University with a degree in journalism. She wrote various humor and travel articles for *Ladies' Home Journal* and *Cosmopolitan.* In the late 1960s, Pascal wrote a soap opera as well as television script adaptations. With her husband, newspaper columnist John Pascal, she wrote the script for the Broadway musical "George M!" and later adapted it for television. In her realistic fiction for young adults, Pascal typically explores the everyday problems of teenagers. *Hangin' Out with Cici* (Viking, 1977), Pascal's first book for young adults, has been on the New York Public Library's "Books for the Teenage" list for six consecutive years. It was also adapted for television and aired as an ABC-TV "After School Special." In a review of the book *Booklist* commented that ". . . the time-travel situation is intriguing, the troubled mother-daughter relationship is appropriate to today's scene, and the story is fertile ground for teenage reader identification." *The Hand-Me-Down Kid,* one of Pascal's most popular books, focuses on the meaning of self-respect and personal determination. *Booklist* observed that it ". . . could easily work as an assertiveness training manual for preteens." Like many of her books, *My First Love and Other Disasters* is

written in the first-person, a narrative style that adds credence to the realistic fiction she writes. Other young adult books by Pascal include *Power Play* (Bantam, 1984), *Dangerous Love No. 6* (Bantam, 1984), and *About Face* (Bantam, 1984). She has also written two adult books, *The Strange Case of Patty Hearst* (New American Library, 1974), and a novel, *Save Johanna!* (Morrow, 1981). *Residence:* Manhattan, N.Y. *For More Information See: Fifth Book of Junior Authors and Illustrators,* H. W. Wilson, 1983.

PAYNE, Donald Gordon 1924-
(Ian Cameron, Donald Gordon, James Vance Marshall)

PERSONAL: Born January 3, 1924, in London, England; son of Francis Gordon and Evelyn (Rogers) Payne; married Barbara Back, August 20, 1947; children: Christopher, Nigel, Adrian, Alison, Robin. *Education:* Corpus Christi College, Oxford, M.A., 1949. *Religion:* Church of England. *Home:* Pippacre, Westcott Heath, near Dorking, Surrey, England. *Agent:* John Johnson (Authors' Agents) Ltd., Clerkenwell House, 45/47 Clerkenwell Green, London EC1R OHT, England; and Harold Ober Associates, Inc., 40 East 49th St., New York, N.Y. 10017.

CAREER: Christopher Johnson Publishers Ltd., London, England, trainee, 1950-53; Robert Hale Ltd. (publishers), London, editor, 1953-56; full-time writer. *Military service:* Royal

(From the movie "Island at the Top of the World," starring David Hartman, based on the novel *The Lost Ones* by Ian Cameron. Copyright © 1974 by Walt Disney Productions.)

(Promotion still for "The Golden Seal," which introduced ten year old Torquil Campbell. Copyright © 1983 by The Samuel Goldwyn Co.)

(Steve Railsback and Penelope Milford in a scene from the movie "The Golden Seal," based on the novel _A River Ran Out of Eden_ by James Vance Marshall. Produced and released by The Samuel Goldwyn Co., 1983.)

(From the movie "Walkabout," starring Jenny Agutter, based on the novel by James Vance Marshall. Copyright © 1971 by Twentieth Century-Fox Film Corp.)

Naval Volunteer Reserve, Fleet Air Arm pilot, 1942-46; became lieutenant. *Member:* Veterans Lawn Tennis Club of Great Britain.

WRITINGS—Under pseudonym Ian Cameron: *The Midnight Sea* (fiction), Hutchinson, 1958; *Red Duster, White Ensign* (story of Malta convoys), Muller, 1959, Doubleday, 1960; *The Lost Ones* (fiction), Hutchinson, 1961, Morrow, 1968, reprinted as *The Island at the Top of the World*, Avon, 1974; *Wings of the Morning* (story of Fleet Air Arm in World War II), Hodder & Stoughton, 1962, Morrow, 1963; *Lodestone and Evening Star* (history of sea exploration), Hodder & Stoughton, 1965, Dutton, 1966; *The Impossible Dream: Building of the Panama Canal*, Morrow, 1971; *The Mountains at the Bottom of the World: Novel of Adventure*, Morrow, 1972; *Magellan and the First Circumnavigation of the World*, Saturday Review Press, 1973; *Antarctica: The Last Continent*, Little, Brown, 1974; *The White Ship*, Scribner, 1975; *The Young Eagles* (fiction), St. Martin's, 1980; *To the Farthest Ends of the Earth* (non-fiction), Dutton, 1980; *Mountains of the Gods* (nonfiction), Century, 1984; *Exploring Antarctica*, Longman, 1984; *Exploring Africa*, Longman, 1984.

Under pseudonym Donald Gordon: *Star-Raker*, Morrow, 1962; *Flight of the Bat*, Hodder & Stoughton, 1963, Morrow, 1964; *The Golden Oyster*, Hodder & Stoughton, 1967, Morrow, 1968; *Leap in the Dark*, Morrow, 1971.

Under pseudonym James Vance Marshall; all fiction: *The Children*, M. Joseph, 1959, published as *Walkabout*, Doubleday, 1961; *A River Ran Out of Eden*, Hodder & Stoughton, 1962, Morrow, 1963; *My Boy John That Went to Sea* (illustrated by Lydia Rosier), Hodder & Stoughton, 1966, Morrow, 1967; *A Walk to the Hills of the Dreamtime*, Morrow, 1970; *The Wind at Morning*, Morrow, 1973, large print edition, G. K. Hall, 1974; *Still Waters*, Morrow, 1982.

WORK IN PROGRESS: Another novel and another nonfiction project.

ADAPTATIONS—Motion Pictures: "Walkabout," starring Jenny Agutter, Twentieth Century-Fox, 1971; "Island at the Top of the World," starring David Hartman, Walt Disney Productions, 1974; "The Golden Seal" (based on *A River Ran Out of Eden*), Samuel Goldwyn Co., 1983.

SIDELIGHTS: Payne writes under pseudonyms because he dislikes publicity. He chose the name Ian Cameron because it was the name of his godfather. He chose the name James Vance Marshall because the late J. V. Marshall provided much of the material of the Australian outback for his novel *Walkabout*. His books have sold over twenty-one million copies and have been translated into fourteen languages.

Payne lives with his family on the slopes of Leith Hill in Surrey, England, in a house surrounded by National Trust Land.

HOBBIES AND OTHER INTERESTS: Gardening, tennis, and writing.

POORTVLIET, Rien 1933(?)-
(Marien Poortvliet)

BRIEF ENTRY: Born about 1933. Dutch artist, author, and illustrator. Poortvliet is probably best known for his illustrations for the book *Gnomes* by Wil Huygen. In *Gnomes*, Huygen

describes the lifestyle, physical characteristics, and historical background of these imaginary creatures. Poortvliet's illustrations, which reviewers found reminiscent of Maurice Sendak, also appeared in Huygen's sequel, *Secrets of the Gnomes*, in which Huygen and Poortvliet are portrayed as gnome-size and travel through Siberia and Lapland with the help of gnome guides. Several of Poortvliet's books for children have been translated from the Dutch, including *The Living Forest: A World of Animals* (Abrams, 1979) and *The Farm Book* (Abrams, 1980). Poortvliet is also the illustrator of Jaap ter Haar's *Het wereldje van Beer Ligthart* ("Beer Ligthart's Little World"), which received a Golden Plaque from the Committee for General Promotion of the Dutch Book in 1974. Other juvenile works illustrated by Poortvliet include *Boris* and *King Arthur* by ter Haar, *The Sea Lord* by Alet Schouten, and *Teeny Tiny Gnome Tomes*, adapted from *Gnomes* by Bill Nygren. *For More Information See:* Rien Poortvliet, *Dutch Treat: The Artist's Life, Written and Painted by Himself*, translated by Maria Milne, Abrams, 1981.

POWLEDGE, Fred 1935-

PERSONAL: Born February 23, 1935, in Nash County, N.C.; son of Arlius Raymond (an auditor) and Pauline (Stearns) Powledge; married Tabitha Morrison, December 21, 1957; children: Pauline Stearns. *Education:* University of North Carolina, B.A., 1957; Columbia University, Russell Sage fellow,

FRED POWLEDGE

Armando, a member of one of the most famous circus families in history, has been a performer since he was three years old. ■ (From *Born on the Circus* by Fred Powledge. Photograph by the author.)

1966-67. *Home and office:* 271 Degraw St., Brooklyn, N.Y. 11231. *Agent:* Virginia Barber, 353 West 21st St., New York, N.Y. 10011.

CAREER: Associated Press, editor-writer in New Haven, Conn., 1958-60; *Atlanta Journal*, Atlanta, Ga., reporter, 1960-63; *New York Times*, New York, N.Y., reporter, 1963-66; free-lance writer, 1966—. Lecturer, New School for Social Research, New York, N.Y., 1968-69. *Military service:* U.S. Army Reserve, 1957-63.

WRITINGS: Black-Power—White Resistance: Notes on the New Civil War, World Publishing, 1967; *To Change a Child*, Quadrangle, 1968; *Model City, A Test of American Liberalism: One Town's Efforts to Rebuild Itself*, Simon & Schuster, 1970; *Mud Show: A Circus Season*, Harcourt, 1975; *Born on the Circus*

(self-illustrated with photographs) Harcourt, 1976; *The Backpacker's Budget Food Book*, McKay, 1977; *Journeys through the South*, Vanguard, 1979; *So You're Adopted: A Book about the Experience of Being Adopted*, Scribner, 1982; *Water: The Nature, Uses, and Future of Our Most Precious and Abused Resource*, Farrar, 1982; *A Forgiving Wind*, Sierra Club, 1983; *Fat of the Land*, Simon & Schuster, 1984. Contributor to periodicals including, *New Yorker, Esquire, Penthouse*, and *The Nation*.

WORK IN PROGRESS: Research and writing on the environment and food.

SIDELIGHTS: ''A more recent interest in environmental matters grows out of the realization that air, water, and earth need recognition of their rights, just as people do.''

FOR MORE INFORMATION SEE: New York Review, February 29, 1968.

PRIDEAUX, Tom   1908-

PERSONAL: Born May 9, 1908, in Hillsdale, Mich.; son of William and Rolla (Robards) Prideaux. *Education:* Yale University, Ph.D., 1930.

CAREER: Worked as a theater and amusements editor for *Life*, New York, N.Y., until 1972; author. *Military service:* U.S. Army Air Forces, World War II; became captain; received Legion of Merit. *Member:* Delta Kappa Epsilon, Elizabethan Club (Yale), Skull and Bones, Coffee House (New York City).

WRITINGS—For young people; with the editors of Time-Life: *The World of Delacroix, 1798-1863* (biography), Time-Life, 1966; *The World of Whistler, 1834-1903* (biography), Time-Life, 1970; *Cro-Magnon Man*, Time-Life, 1973.

Other: (Editor with Josephine Mayer) *Never to Die: The Egyptians in Their Own Words*, Viking, 1938; *World Theatre in Pictures, From Ancient Times to Modern Broadway*, Greenberg, 1953; *Love or Nothing: The Life and Times of Ellen Terry* (biography), Scribner, 1975.

Plays: ''Another Man's Poison,'' first produced in Tamiment, Pa., summer, 1934; ''Gallivanting Lady,'' first produced at Farragut Playhouse in Rye Beach, N.H., July 26, 1938. Also author of teleplay, ''The Milwaukee Rocket.''

PUNER, Helen W(alker)   1915-

PERSONAL: Born June 18, 1915, in New York, N.Y.; daughter of Michael (a businessman) and Ida (Liebert) Walker; married Samuel Paul Puner (chairman of the board of Educational Audio-Visual, Inc.), July 6, 1936; children: Nicholas, Margaret Levin, Polly Puner-Richter. *Education:* Barnard College, B.A. (honors), 1934. *Politics:* Independent. *Religion:* Jewish. *Home:* 157 Pinesbridge Rd., Ossining, N.Y. 10562.

CAREER: Fortune, New York City, 1935-44, began as researcher, became editor; free-lance writer, 1945-56; *Parents Magazine*, New York City, special editor, 1956-62; New School for Social Research, New York City, instructor, 1969-70, associate director of Human Relations Work-Study Center, 1970-74. Went to Israel as guest of the government, 1957. *Member:*

Helen W. Puner in Paris, 1978.

Authors League of America, Poetry Society of America. *Awards, honors:* Yaddo summer residency, 1960; Child Study Association of America Children's Book Award, 1966, for *The Wonderful Story of How You Were Born*.

WRITINGS: Daddies: What They Do All Day (illustrated by Roger Duvoisin), Lothrop, 1945, reprinted, 1966; *Freud: His Life and His Mind,* Howell, Soskin, 1947; *The Sitter Who Didn't Sit,* Lothrop, 1949; (ghost-writer) Sidonie M. Gruenberg, *The Wonderful Story of How You Were Born,* Doubleday, 1952, revised edition, 1970; *Not While You're a Freshman,* Coward, 1965; *I Am Big, You Are Little,* Young Scott Books, 1973. Also author of pamphlets for Public Affairs, Science Research Associates, and Child Study Association. Contributor of articles to *Harper's, McCall's, Vogue, Mademoiselle,* and other periodicals, and of light verse to *Harper's* and *New York Times Magazine.*

WORK IN PROGRESS: Articles; a book.

SIDELIGHTS: "I wrote my first books for children because I had children of my own and was engaged and fascinated by their interests, questions, and general way of being. My first children's book, *Daddies: What They Do All Day,* was triggered into being by a question from my three-year-old son (at the time). After my husband went off to work one morning, he asked me: 'What do daddies do all day?' The book was easy after that."

Puner comments about her biography of Freud as, "a very early, pioneering one. It has led a vital underground life, being referred to in most other books on Freud that have come out

since. . . . I have also learned that there is correspondence about the book between Anna Freud and Ernest Jones, before Jones wrote his official biography. This correspondence is said to be in the Freud Archives, sealed in the Library of Congress for fifty or a hundred years. There is, apparently, good reason to believe that Jones would not have written his biography had it not been for mine.

"I gave up writing when I had a serious illness a few years back, and was struggling with a piece of writing I'd never tried before and decided I didn't have to continue the lonely struggle at the typewriter. I have become a book collector instead, and a book dealer. It is different than writing, but it is fun and very much related to my lifelong passion for good printed words."

HOBBIES AND OTHER INTERESTS: "My avocations are the usual ones; gardening, travel, good conversation where and when I can find it, grandchildren (who are far more interesting than sealed archives), friendships, feeble tennis, spying. Also, reading. There are some fine young women writers coming up and I am cheering them on silently—or verbally, when I meet them. I love the idea that the climate for women writers is so much more benign than it was when I was a young writer. (Lionel Trilling dismissed my Freud book in the Sunday *New York Times Book Review* by saying that I was a woman and had no appreciation of the male heroic spirit. A gross misstatement of the true facts.)

"Another avocation is reading friends' and relatives' works in progress. They ask me to. It is a difficult, trying, but welcome experience. I very much like the feeling of younger writers asking older ones for advice and criticism. In the novel of a young friend who has already written at least one unforgettable novel, she thanks me at its end for my help."

RABOFF, Ernest Lloyd

BRIEF ENTRY: Born in Atlantic City, N.J. Raboff, who studied art at the Meschini Institute in Rome and the Académie Julien in Paris, has maintained a close relationship with the art world for over thirty years. He has worked as a lecturer in American art at the U.S. Embassy in Sweden as well as an art critic, dealer, auctioneer, collector, and gallery owner. He is the author of fifteen books in the "Art for Children" series published by Doubleday. Described by *Publishers Weekly* as "a satisfying reading and visual experience," each book in the series provides a brief biography of a master artist accompanied with full color reproductions of the individual's work. The titles include: *Marc Chagall, Pablo Picasso,* and *Paul Klee,* all published in 1968; *Albrecht Dürer, Harmensz van Rijn Rembrandt,* and *Henri de Toulouse-Lautrec,* all published in 1970; *Michelangelo Buonarroti,* 1971; *Frederic Remington,* 1973; *Paul Gauguin* and *Vincent Van Gogh,* both published in 1974.

I know a funny little man,
   As quiet as a mouse,
Who does the mischief that is done
   In everybody's house!
There's no one ever sees his face,
   And yet we all agree
That every plate we break was cracked
   By Mr. Nobody.

—Anonymous

GWYNEDD RAE

RAE, Gwynedd   1892-1977

PERSONAL: Born July 23, 1892, in London, England; died November 14, 1977; daughter of George Bentham (a stock broker) and Mary Victorine (Thompson) Rae. *Education:* Attended Manor House School, Brondesbury, London, 1907-09, and Villa St. George's School, Paris, France, 1909-10. *Politics:* Conservative. *Religion:* Anglican. *Home:* Tott Close, Burwash, Sussex, England. *Agent:* Laurence Pollinger Ltd., 18 Maddox St., London W1R OEU, England.

CAREER: Social worker for Girls Diocesan Association, Invalid Children's Association, and East End clergy, in London, England. Author, 1930-77. *Wartime service:* Member of Voluntary Aid Detachment in Kent during World War I. *Member:* National Book League, Voluntary Aid Detachment Club.

WRITINGS—"Mary Plain" series of children's books: *Mostly Mary,* E. Mathews & Marrot, 1930, Morrow, 1931, reprinted, Avon, 1972; *All Mary,* E. Mathews & Marrot, 1931, Avon, 1972; *Mary Plain in Town,* Cobden-Sanderson, 1935; . . . *on Holiday,* Cobden-Sanderson, 1937; . . . *in Trouble,* G. Routledge & Sons, 1940; . . . *in Wartime,* G. Routledge & Sons,

1942, published as *Mary Plain Lends a Paw,* 1949; *Mary Plain's Big Adventure,* G. Routledge & Sons, 1944; *Mary Plain Home Again,* Routledge & Kegan Paul, 1949; . . . *to the Rescue,* Routledge & Kegan Paul, 1950; . . . *and the Twins,* Routledge & Kegan Paul, 1952; . . . *Goes Bob-a-Jobbing,* Routledge & Kegan Paul, 1957; . . . *Goes to America,* Routledge & Kegan Paul, 1957; . . . , *V.I.P.,* Routledge & Kegan Paul, 1961; *Mary Plain's "Who-dunit,"* Routledge & Kegan Paul, 1965; *Mary Plain Omnibus,* Routledge & Kegan Paul, 1976.

Adult novels: *And Timothy Too,* Blackie & Son, 1934; *Leap Year Born,* Blackie & Son, 1935. Also author of *Lovely Heritage* (family history), privately printed.

WORK IN PROGRESS: An autobiography.

SIDELIGHTS: Rae's ever popular series, "Mary Plain," is about a bear who lives in the famous pit in Bern, Switzerland. Rae explained the inspiration for the series: "In the 30's I had to spend two years at Dr. Kocher's Clinic in Bern for a thyroid treatment and while there I visited the bear pit, which has been in existence since 1513, almost daily. . . ." Many critics believe the success of her series is in large part due to her accurate observations of both animal and human behavior. "All the children in my books are either my own nieces and nephews or those of my friends, and the Owl Man [Mary Plain's human friend who wears glasses] is my brother. This fact, and that of Mary being a real bear has, I think, greatly contributed to the success of the books through 45 years.

"I was immensely lucky in being one of the few juvenile writers whose books survived World War II. Considering the rising costs and the general climate of affairs, both hardbacks and paperbacks did quite well and I continued to receive a fair amount of fan mail, which is very heartening."

Rae commented about the "Teddy Bears Picnic," held on June 19, 1976, at Hartfield, Sussex, England to commemorate the fiftieth anniversary of the death of A. A. Milne, author of the "Winnie the Pooh" series of books. "I myself have a lovely Teddy Bear, given to me by my nieces and nephews when I dedicated *All Mary* to them. I took her with me, with her name 'Mary Plain,' and address 'The Bear Pits, Bern, Switzerland,' printed on a placard fixed on her back. We had, alas, the first rain for months, which fell heartily all the afternoon and spoilt all the plans made for entertainments, but bears from all over the world were there.

"I was sitting in my car when there came a tap on the window and a lady said, 'I have come from America with Christopher Robin's original bear and we fly back tomorrow, but he wants to shake Mary Plain's paw, please.' So the two bears solemnly did this."

The first five books in the series have been read on the "Children's Hour" BBC-Radio program and they, with others, have appeared on the children's television program "Jackanory" in England.

Rae traveled extensively in Europe, "in Italy, France, Holland, Germany, Austria, and Belgium but, best of all I loved the winter skating holidays in Switzerland whose mountains and scenery I adore." In 1955 she made her first visit to the United States to do research in Pennsylvania and California for her family genealogy.

FOR MORE INFORMATION SEE: Brian Doyle, *The Who's Who of Children's Literature*, Schocken Books, 1968.

REGEHR, Lydia 1903-

PERSONAL: Born November 29, 1903, in Russia; came to United States in 1923; daughter of Gerhard P. (a minister) and Maria (Siemens) Regehr. *Education:* Attended North West Bible School, 1936; University of Minnesota, B.S., 1942; University of Washington, Seattle, graduate study, 1949-50, summers, 1956-57. *Home:* 6339 34th S.W., No. 413, Seattle, Wash. 98126.

CAREER: Social worker in Minneapolis, Minn., 1936-46, and Seattle, Wash., 1946-53; substitute teacher of English, German, and Russian in high schools and colleges in Los Angeles, Calif., 1961-66. *Member:* National League of American Pen Women (vice-president of San Fernando Valley branch, 1966-71), American Translators Association. *Awards, honors:* Certificate from Washington State Federation of Women's Clubs, 1957, for poem "Tribute to Washington."

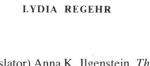
LYDIA REGEHR

WRITINGS: (Translator) Anna K. Ilgenstein, *The Story of Martin Luther for Young People*, Eerdmans, 1955; *The Morning Star of Wittenberg*, Review & Herald, 1956; (translator) *Finist the Falcon Prince: A Russian Folk Tale* (juvenile; illustrated by Mary Chagnon), Carolrhoda Books, 1973; *Bible Riddles of Birds and Beasts and Creeping Things*, Bible Memory Association International, 1982. Author of hymn, "Justified through Faith," Willis Music Co.; translator of German hymns. Contributor of translations to *NRTA Journal*, a play to *Religion Teacher's Journal*, and poems to *Instructor, Arizona Highways, Modern Maturity, Queen, Child Evangelism, The Catholic Digest, Vista, Helper, On the Line* (juvenile), *World Vision, Der Bote* (Canada), *Phoenix Gazette*, and *Pen Women*.

WORK IN PROGRESS: Transport to the King's Court, a picture book in verse for children; a textbook of twenty bilingual (English and German) animal poems; a juvenile story about Franz Gruber; a three-act play "Make Me Your Handmaid, Lord," about Kaethe von Bora, wife of Martin Luther; "Living in the Shadows of Revenge," a short story; a play on "Silent Night"; two comedies, "Mr. Shark Goes to Court" and "The String Quartet," both based on two of Krylov's fables; a script, "Mathilda Wrede of Finalnd: She Visited Those in Prison"; a religious drama, "Abraham, the Man of Faith."

SIDELIGHTS: "A 'Late Bloomer,' I had never planned to become a writer, translator, or poet. Who starts at age fifty?

"When I arrived here from Russia as a refugee in 1923, malnourished, poorly-dressed, English a foreign language, my first obligation was to pay for the journey across, offering to my

The oldest two were lazy and did not care to work. ■ (From *Finist the Falcon Prince: A Russian Folk Tale*, translated by Lydia Regehr. Illustrated by Mary Chagnon.)

father, on whose passport I had come, to contribute my share and part of my mother's.

"In Russia I had been educated in a parochial school, supported by the German Mennonites of the Ukraine, instruction in both languages, Russian and German. My favorite subjects were German grammar and poetry. We had to stand on our feet and recite the latter which I greatly enjoyed. After five years I entered a Russian Gymnasium, and took German as a foreign language along with Latin and French. An avid reader, I had read a German edition of *Little Women* entitled *Kleine Frauen*. My education was interrupted in the sixth grade, due to the Civil War following the 1917 Russian Revolution.

"After World War II I had sent some care packages to bombed-out Germany. The recipients, unknown to me, sent me a book on the wife of Martin Luther for Christmas that year. This led me to the translation of Kaethe von Bora, since, due to poor health, I had to resign from my position as a social worker. When I had completed the draft of my script, hundreds of rhyming words, from the beginning in English and German, seemed to be at my disposal. Anna Katterfeld, the German author, had quoted some of Luther's poetry throughout the book, a few lines here and there, which really had presented a problem at first. I acquired rhyming dictionaries, English and German, and pursued my newly-discovered area of writing. Later, my students in California enjoyed hearing my bilingual poems such as 'Proposal with a Kiss, Der Antrag Mit Dem Kuss,' and 'Lucy, Lucie.'

"At this time I find that due to lack of physical strength, it is easier for me to write poetry, in English the greater part, and also bilingually, since it does not require the typing of long manuscripts."

FRANK H. RHODES

RHODES, Frank H(arold Trevor) 1926-

PERSONAL: Born October 29, 1926, in Warwickshire, England; came to United States, 1968; naturalized U.S. citizen, 1976; son of Harold Cecil (an executive) and Gladys (Ford) Rhodes; married Rosa Carlson, August 16, 1952; children: Jennifer, Catherine, Penelope, Deborah. *Education:* University of Birmingham, B.Sc., 1948, Ph.D., 1950. *Home:* 603 Cayuga Heights Rd., Ithaca, N.Y. 14850. *Office:* Office of the President, Cornell University, Ithaca, N.Y. 14853.

CAREER: University of Durham, Durham, England, lecturer in geology, 1951-54; University of Illinois, Urbana, assistant professor, 1954-55, associate professor of geology, 1955-56, director of Wyoming field station, 1956; University of Wales, Swansea, professor of geology and head of department, 1956-68, dean of faculty of science, 1967-68; University of Michigan, Ann Arbor, professor of geology and mineralogy, 1968-77, resident associate of Museum of Paleontology and dean of College of Literature, Science, and the Arts, 1971-74, vice-president for academic affairs, 1974-77; Cornell University, Ithaca, N.Y., university president and professor of geology and mineralogy, 1977—. Director of first international field studies conference, National Science Foundation-American Geological Institute, 1961; editor of geological series, Commonwealth Foundation, 1965-66; chairman of curriculum panel, Counsel for Educational Geological Science, 1970-71; trustee, Carnegie Foundation for the Advancement of Teaching, 1978—; visiting professor and lecturer at various universities, including University of Illinois, 1951-52 (summers), 1959, Cornell Uni-

versity, 1960, Ohio State University, 1966, University of Michigan, 1976.

MEMBER: Geological Society of London (fellow; council member, 1963-66), Palaeontological Association (vice-president, 1963-68), British Association for the Advancement of Science, Geological Society of America, American Association of Petroleum Geologists, Society of Economic Paleontologists and Mineralogists, Phi Beta Kappa (honorary). *Awards, honors:* Fulbright scholarship, University of Illinois, 1950-51; Daniel Pidgeon Fund Award, Geological Society (London), 1953; D.Sc., University of Birmingham, 1963, and University of Wales, 1981; Bigsby Medal, Geological Society of London, 1967; LL.D., College of Wooster (Ohio), 1976, and Nazareth College (Rochester, N.Y.), 1979; L.H.D., from Colgate University, 1980, Johns Hopkins University, 1982, Wagner College, 1982, Rensselaer Polytechnic Institute, 1982, and Hope College, 1982; D.Litt., from University of Nevada, Las Vegas, 1982.

WRITINGS—For young people; all "Golden Guide" series, published by Golden Press: (With others) *Fossils: A Guide to Prehistoric Life* (illustrated by Raymond Perlman), 1962; *Geology* (illustrated by R. Perlman), 1972; *Evolution* (illustrated by Rebecca Merrilees and Rudolph Zallinger), 1974.

Other: *The Evolution of Life,* Penguin Books, 1962, 2nd edition, 1976; *Language of the Earth,* Pergamon Press, 1981. Also author of essays and pamphlets on geographical geology, paleontology, and education.

IAN RIBBONS

RIBBONS, Ian   1924-

PERSONAL: Born August 20, 1924, in London, England; son of Harold (a journalist) and Annie Alexandra (Storm) Ribbons; married in 1950 (marriage ended); married Laura Vasini (a poet and interpreter), 1963; children: (first marriage) Alexander Mortimer; (second marriage) Shannon, Dhana. *Education:* Attended Beckenham School of Art and Royal College of Art; received degree in graphic design and illustration.

CAREER: Author and illustrator of books for young people, and painter. Art instructor at Guildford College, Brighton College, and Hornsey College of Art, London; part-time lecturer in illustration at St. Martin's School of Art, London. Served on Children's Writers Group Committee for four years. *Military service:* British Army, Royal Artillery, World War II; served in India and Burma. *Member:* Society of Authors. *Awards, honors: The Battle of Gettysburg, 1-3 July, 1863* was a runner-up for the Carnegie Medal, 1974.

*WRITINGS—*For young people: all self-illustrated; all published by Oxford University Press, except as noted: *Monday, 21 October 1805: The Day of Trafalgar,* David White, 1968; *Tuesday, 4 August 1914: The First Day of World War I,* David White, 1970; *The Island,* 1971; *The Battle of Gettysburg, 1-3 July 1873,* 1974; *Mr. McKenzie Painted Me,* 1975; *Waterloo, 1815,* Kestrel, 1982.

Illustrator; all published by Oxford University Press, except as noted: Smith, *Knave-Go-By,* 1951; Meynell, *Under the Hollies,* 1954; Elizabeth Goudge, *Linnets and Valerians* (ALA Notable Book), Coward, 1964; Penelope Farmer, *The Sea Gull,* Brockhampton, 1964, Harcourt, 1966; Philip Turner, *Sea Peril,*

1966; Ronald Welch, *The Bowman of Crecy,* 1966, Criterion, 1967; Ivan Southall, *The Fox Hole,* St. Martin's, 1967; Rosemary Weir, *High Courage,* Farrar, Straus, 1967; Roger L. Green, compiler, *Ten Tales of Detection,* Dutton, 1967; I. Southall, *Let the Balloon Go,* St. Martin's, 1968; Martha Edith Almedingen, *Fanny,* Farrar, Straus, 1970; Hesba Fay Brinsmead, *Who Calls from Afar?,* 1971; I. Southall, *Over the Top,* Methuen, 1972; Frederick Grice, *Young Tom Sawbones,* 1972; Rudyard Kipling, *Twenty-one Tales,* Folio Society, 1972; Robert Leeson, *Beyond the Dragon Prow,* Collins, 1973; John Ridgway, *Gino Watkins,* 1974; Robert Louis Stevenson, *Treasure Island,* 1974; Peter Carter, *Under Goliath,* 1979; Alain Foumier, *Le Grand Meaulnes,* Folio Society, 1979; E. M. Forster, *A Passage to India,* Folio Society, 1983.

SIDELIGHTS: As a child, Ribbons escaped his somewhat dismal environment in South London by immersing himself in books of the Impressionists and discovering the existence of a world different from his own. It is this sense of detachment that he strives to incorporate into his historical books for young people, focusing on a particular date and event, and bringing the reader into his writings as a "first-eye" viewer.

Utilizing pen and ink, brush, and splatterwork, Ribbons visually recreates a time in history, accompanied by thoroughly researched writings. He concerns himself with key turning points in history, such as the first day of World War I and the Battle of Gettysburg. His aim is not to present a "pretty" picture of events, but rather an accurate one.

"In my nonfiction books, particularly *Waterloo,* my main concern is to look at *all* available contemporary primary source material (letters, diaries, etc.; I am always astonished at how much unused material there is still available), then to edit extracts in such a way as to gain, I hope, an overall but immediate picture of an observer's viewpoint who might have witnessed it. I am rigorous in inventing nothing—even weather, time of sunrise, coach departure time, etc., are all thoroughly checked. The text is mainly factual. That allows me to make the drawings, although based on accurate research, as lively and perhaps impressionistic as I like."

HOBBIES AND OTHER INTERESTS: Music and travel.

FOR MORE INFORMATION SEE: Lee Kingman and others, compilers, *Illustrators of Children's Books: 1957-1966,* Horn Book, 1968; *New York Times Book Review,* January 17, 1969, May 3, 1970; *Illustrators of Books for Young People,* 2nd edition, Scarecrow, 1975; Doris de Montreville and Elizabeth D. Crawford, editors, *Fourth Book of Junior Authors and Illustrators,* H. W. Wilson, 1978; Lee Kingman and others, compilers, *Illustrators of Children's Books: 1967-1976,* Horn Book, 1978.

Cock crows in the morn,
    To tell us to rise,
And he who lies late
    Will never be wise.
For early to bed,
    And early to rise,
Is the way to be healthy
    And wealthy and wise.

—Nursery rhyme

**It was said that ancient Britons had lived up there on the top of the hill. . . .He could imagine
their ghosts still dancing there. ■** (From *The Sea Gull* by Penelope Farmer. Illustrated by Ian
Ribbons.)

IVY RUCKMAN

RUCKMAN, Ivy 1931-

PERSONAL: Born May 25, 1931, in Hastings, Neb.; daughter of Joy Uberto (a tree surgeon) and Lena Chloe (Osgood) Myers; married Edgar Baldwin Heylmun, December 17, 1955 (divorced, 1963); married Stuart Allan Ruckman (a dentist), June 6, 1965 (died, 1983); children: Kimberly Sue, William Bret, Stuart Andrew. *Education:* Hastings College, B.A., 1953; University of Utah, graduate study, 1963-65. *Home and office:* 3698 Golden Hills Ave., Salt Lake City, Utah 84121.

CAREER: Natrona County High School, Casper, Wyo., English teacher, 1953-57, Skyline High School, Salt Lake City, Utah, English teacher, 1962-65, creative writing instructor, 1970-72; author, 1974—. *Member:* Society of Children's Book Writers, Southeastern Advocates of Literature for Young People, Utah Children's Literature Association, Friends of the Salt Lake County Library System, Manuscripters. *Awards, honors:* First place, Utah Fine Arts Contest, 1982, for *What's an Average Kid Like Me Doing Way Up Here?;* Utah Children's Book Award nomination, 1982, for *Melba the Brain;* Hastings College Outstanding Alumni Award, 1984.

WRITINGS—All for young people: *Who Needs Rainbows?,* Messner, 1969; *Encounter,* Doubleday, 1978; *Melba the Brain* (illustrated by Ruth Van Sciver), Westminster, 1979; *What's an Average Kid Like Me Doing Way Up Here?,* Delacorte, 1983; *In a Class By Herself,* Harcourt, 1983; *The Hunger*

Scream, Walker, 1983; *Night of the Twister,* Harper, 1984. Edited television play for the ABC-TV series "Room 222." Contributor of short stories to the periodicals *Jack and Jill, Cricket,* and *Ranger Rick.*

SIDELIGHTS: "As often happens in a family, two children may develop such an affinity that they seem to think interchangeably. This was true for my brother William and me. We were children during the Depression years, a fortunate time for us: make-believe was all the pleasure we could afford. We were poor in material things, but we didn't know or care. We had each other and considered ourselves the best company. While our parents and the five older children dealt with dust storms, drought, and anxiety, our whole existence was play. Left to our own devices, unhampered by balls or trikes, we entered imaginary worlds yet to be invaded by televison or comic books.

"On a typical afternoon an upended stool became a ship's parapet, a rag mob displayed the colors. The longest stirring spoon in the kitchen stood by for an oar. The Captain and his First Mate, thus grandly appointed, rolled out to sea with solemn purpose—the capture of pirates. Together William and I built igloos in the Arctic tundra, stalked big game in steaming jungles while black panthers stalked us; we performed daring feats on a slender bar and did acrobatics on the broad-backed workhorses who always looked astonished to find themselves

There was Astrocat in his flashing silver space suit, fussing and fuming like always, his tail in a nervous twitch. ■ (From *Melba the Brain* by Ivy Ruckman. Illustrated by Ruth Van Sciver.)

the dappled darlings of the circus ring. Christmas opulence, our contemporaries will remember, consisted of one or two gifts and a sack of nuts and candy from church. One year the two of us exchanged Woolworth 'diamond' rings, then spent the entire holidays slinking about the house as jewel thieves.

"If our shoes didn't always fit during those magic years, we nonetheless had books. Our mother read *Robinson Crusoe* to us before I was old enough to understand it. Our real bonanza, however, was to be found in the trash that our father hauled from people in town who owned and discarded books. A broad sampling came our way—everything from an ancient copy of Washington Irving to a volume called *White Slavery in America*. We also salvaged bookkeeping ledgers from the trash pile if they contained empty pages for drawing or writing, and once, heavy medical tomes from a doctor's effects, accompanied by a human foot preserved in a specimen jar which Daddy locked in the shed. This treasure was ultimately viewed by every skeptical kid in the neighborhood and, as I remember, became something of a status symbol for my brother and me.

"When three older brothers joined the Navy and World War II became a reality to our family, William and I took matters into our own hands. We rolled out a huge map on the cellar floor and located Germany. (Later we repeated the process with Japan). 'They won't win,' William assured me. 'See? They're smaller than we are.' I believed him, the way I always did. As far as I was concerned, the war was as good as won.

"Later, during our teens, we took a serious turn, devoting our energies to saving the drunken and downtrodden. We joined the Salvation Army. We played in the band and testified on the street corner. I learned the beat of the gospel tunes and solicited souls through the piano and the street organ. We gave our lives to God. It was William, I recall, who paid for my first black Salvation Army bonnet so that I could look as holy as I felt. I couldn't say, now, which of us outshone the other in piety.

"Though we continued to share interests in biology and Shakespeare, by the time we received degrees from Hastings College we had different goals. For the first time, we went separate ways. William became a cardiovascular surgeon; I became a high school English teacher. However, nothing has contributed so much to my 'writer's reservoir' as those early years spent skipping along after my creative and capricious brother.

"Now I have my own family, Kim, Bret, and teenager Stuart, who is my toughest critic. Their interests and enthusiasms naturally contribute to my work. The characters in my books take on many of their mannerisms, much of their speech, and end up usurping most of their activities.

"Today I am writing for children full time, specializing in middle-grade and young adult novels. By habit I have become a peripatetic, which means I never stay put. I have a desk and a home office, but I end up writing everywhere—in the car, at auto repair shops, cross-legged on the porch swing. Once, even, while lunching out. I do my best thinking and planning in the bath tub or the swimming pool. It's while writing those first drafts that my portable is forever on the go. My husband, Allan, built a deck for me alongside our stream because I enjoy writing outdoors so much. There, of course, I can't hear the phone, the doorbell, the stereo, or the kids' power struggles. Also, for some reason, the properties of water seem to free my mind for creative thinking.

"For me, the writing itself is very difficult. If I can produce two to four pages of prose in a day, I feel I've done well (at top speed one day I wrote thirteen pages of a novel; another time, creeping like a snail, I produced one paragraph). Because the *sound* of one's writing is so important, I rely heavily on my 'ear' for realistic dialogue, for the flow of my prose, for the sentence balance I want to achieve. I may spend hours searching for the right word or an apt metaphor. The hardest part of writing, as I see it, is getting a story to work in the first place; the revising, or 'fine tuning,' is the most enjoyable. First and foremost, however, I want my characters to live. I want the reader to care about what happens to them, to laugh at their foolishness and cry over their sorrows. I become very much involved in the lives of my fictional 'children.' I succeed as a writer, I feel, only to the extent readers share my involvement.

"If I'm not writing or busy being a housewife, I'm probably packing a lunch or a suitcase or a backpack (you name it, I've packed it!). Having married an ardent mountain climber and being mother of three young adults who regard higher elevations as their natural habitat, I live an exciting and suspenseful life purely by association. My own recreational preferences run to swimming and skiing, but I live in a tent every chance I get.

"Though my travels have taken me as far as Europe and Mexico, now when I pack I'm more often accompanying my family on one of their expeditions. While they climb, I set up my portable table in a clump of aspen, not too far from the fire and coffeepot, and indulge myself in writing books for kids."

RUCK-PAUQUÈT, Gina

BRIEF ENTRY: Born in Cologne, Germany. Now an author of picture books for children, Ruck-Pauquèt has worked in advertising and as a photo-journalist as well as a model. She began her writing career as a poet, later concentrating on books for children. More than ten of her books have been translated from her native German into English and have been published both in England and the United States. Like Aesop's tales, her stories characteristically center around the simple adventures of animals and are accented with a moralistic twist. *Publishers Weekly* described her writing as "ginger-sharp" and "sparkling," while the *New York Times Book Review* took note of the "definite foreign flavor" which pervades her work . . . "rather old-fashioned and severe—though not disagreeably so. . . ." In 1967 she was awarded the Oesterreichischer Staatspreis fuer Kinder-und Jugendliteratur in the youth book category for *Joschko* (Breitschopf, 1967). Ruck-Pauquèt's translated works include *Little Hedgehog* (Hastings House, 1959), *Ghosts Don't Eat Sausages* (Thomas Nelson, 1964), *Aunt Matilda and the Baby Seal* (Hart, 1968), *Oh, That Koala* (McGraw-Hill, 1979), *Mumble Bear* (Putnam, 1980), and *The Singing Elephant* (Hodder & Stoughton, 1983).

O you that are so strong and cold,
O blower, are you young or old?
Are you a beast of field or tree,
Or just a stronger child than me?
 O wind, a-blowing all day long,
 O wind, that sings so loud a song!

—Robert Louis Stevenson

RUE, Leonard Lee III   1926-

PERSONAL: Born February 20, 1926, in Paterson, N.J.; son of Leonard Lee (a marine engineer) and Mae (Sellner) Rue; married Beth Castner, May 6, 1945 (divorced, 1976); children: Leonard Lee IV, Tim Lewis, James Keith. *Education:* Educated in Belvidere, N.J. *Religion:* Methodist. *Home and office:* RD3, Box 31, Blairstown, N.J. 07825.

CAREER: Free-lance writer and photographer. Summer guide for canoe trips in Canada, gamekeeper for hunt club, teacher of outdoor subjects, lecturer, photographer, former camp ranger. Has made several appearances on radio and television and talk shows for the Upjohn Company. *Member:* Society of American Mammalogists, National Parks Society, Wilderness Society, National Wildlife Federation, Audubon Society, Wildlife Society, Masons. *Awards, honors:* Received eleven book awards from New Jersey State Association of English; New Jersey Institute of Technology award, 1963, for *The World of the White-Tailed Deer* and 1966 for *Cottontail;* New Jersey Institute of Technology golden award, 1979; inducted to New Jersey Literary Hall of Fame, 1979.

WRITINGS: Animals in Motion, Doubleday, 1956; *Tracks and Tracking,* Doubleday, 1958; *The World of the White-Tailed Deer,* Lippincott, 1962; *The World Picture Guide to American Animals,* Arco, 1962; (with Dorothy Knight) *The World of the Beaver,* Lippincott, 1963; *The World of the Raccoon,* Lippincott, 1964; *New Jersey Out-of-Doors,* privately printed, 1964;

Cottontail, Crowell, 1965; *Pictorial Guide to the Mammals of North America,* Crowell, 1967; *Sportsman's Guide to Game Animals,* Outdoor Life, 1968, revised edition published as *Game Animals of North America,* 1981; *The World of the Red Fox,* Lippincott, 1969; *Pictorial Guide to Birds,* Crowell, 1970; *The World of the Ruffed Grouse,* Lippincott, 1973; *Games Birds of North America,* Outdoor Life, 1973; *The Deer of North America,* Outdoor Life, 1978; *Furbearing Animals of North America,* Crown, 1981; *When Your Deer Is Down: Preparing the Meat,* Winchester, 1982; (with William Owen) *Meet the Opossum* (illustrated with photographs), Dodd, 1983; *How I Photograph Wildlife and Nature,* Norton, 1984; *Meet the Moose,* Dodd, 1984. Contributor of monthly nature columns to *American Hunter, Petersen's Hunting Deer,* and *Deer Hunting;* also contributor of articles and photographs to more than a thousand publications in forty-two countries.

Illustrator: John Bailey, *Our Wild Animals,* T. Nelson, 1965. Also illustrator of *American Animals,* Ridge Press, 1965.

WORK IN PROGRESS: Tracks and Tracking, Reading Sign in North America; Turkey Hunting Methods of the Pros.

SIDELIGHTS: Rue is a prolific writer whose work appears in over fifty magazines each month. He is also the most published wildlife photographer in North America. "I've often been asked how long it takes me to write a book. A lifetime! All of my life I have been preparing for this and every other book I've written or hope to write. All of my life I have been watching,

Fawn's dappled coat helps it "disappear" in leaves and tall grass. ■ (From *Our Wild Animals* by John Bailey. Photograph by Leonard Lee Rue III.)

Leonard Lee Rue III and a black-capped chickadee.

studying, living with, and reading about wildlife, and my hope is that I can spend the rest of my life watching, studying, living with, and reading about wildlife.

"I've always considered myself most fortunate to have been raised on a farm; my roots are in the soil. Even today, no matter where I travel throughout the world, I am always checking the livestock, crops, water, and soil from a farmer's point of view—and calculating how those components of the ecosystem affect wildlife.

"Times were rough on the farm during the last years of the Depression, and the work was hard. The life was a good one, though, and if I had my early life to live over I wouldn't change it at all. I'm thankful that I haven't forgotten how to do hard manual work, although I'm equally thankful I don't have to work that physically hard today. Every moment that I could spare from my work (and some that I couldn't) I roamed the wooded hills and valleys and along the streams and rivers. I lived for the hours I could spend in such surroundings, and I still do. Not much of a formal education ever rubbed off on me, but my thirst for knowledge about everything in the outdoors was unquenchable. It remains so today. I've looked for the beauty of God's work that surrounds us on all sides, and I have found it.

"I've lived among deer all my life. I've watched them, studied them, photographed them, hunted them, eaten them. For more than two decades I was chief gamekeeper of Coventry Hunt Club, the largest such club in New Jersey. I've seen a hundred and eighty-three deer in one night, in one hour's time, within five miles of my home. I can still see deer most days just by looking out of my windows. I've crisscrossed the continent, east to west, north to south, more times than I can recall to study and photograph deer and other wildlife. I read everything I can get my hands on about deer. My personal library—my pride and joy—has over nine thousand bound volumes, and I have bulging file cases of clippings and research reports." [Leonard Lee Rue III, *The Deer of North America*, Outdoor Life, 1978.]

SABERHAGEN, Fred (Thomas)   1930-

PERSONAL: Born May 18, 1930, in Chicago, Ill.; son of Frederick Augustus and Julia (Moynihan) Saberhagen; married Joan Dorothy Spicci, June 29, 1968; children: Jill, Eric, Thomas. *Education:* Attended Wright Junior College, 1956-57. *Residence:* Albuquerque, N.M. *Agent:* Eleanor Wood, Spectrum Literary Agency, 225 West 34th St., New York, N.Y. 10122.

CAREER: Motorola, Inc., Chicago, Ill., electronics technician, 1956-62; free-lance writer, 1962-67; assistant editor, *Encyclopaedia Britannica*, 1967-73; free-lance writer, 1973—. *Military service:* U.S. Air Force, 1951-55. *Member:* Science Fiction Writers of America.

WRITINGS: The Golden People, Ace Books, 1964; *Water of Thought*, Ace Books, 1965; *The Broken Lands* (also see below), Ace Books, 1967; *Black Mountains* (also see below), Ace Books, 1970; *Changeling Earth* (also see below), DAW Books, 1973; *Book of Saberhagen* (collection), DAW Books, 1975; *Specimens*, Popular Library, 1975; *Love Conquers All* (first published in *Galaxy* magazine, 1974-75), Ace Books, 1978; *Mask of the Sun*, Ace Books, 1978; *The Veils of Azlaroc*, Ace Books, 1978; *The Ultimate Enemy* (collection), Ace Books, 1979; *Empire of the East* (based on *The Broken Lands, Black*

Mountains, and *Changeling Earth*), Ace Books, 1979; (editor) *A Spadeful of Spacetime* (collection), Ace Books, 1980; (with Roger Zelazny) *Coils*, Tor, 1980; *Octagon*, Ace Books, 1981; *Earth Descended* (collection), Tor, 1981; *The First Book of Swords*, Tor, 1982; *A Century of Progress*, Tor, 1982; *The Second Book of Swords*, Tor, 1983.

"Berserker" series: *Berserker*, Ballantine, 1967; *Brother Assassin*, Ballantine, 1969; *Berserker's Planet*, DAW Books, 1975; *Berserker Man*, Ace Books, 1979; *Berserker Wars* (collection), Tor, 1981.

"Dracula" series: *The Dracula Tapes*, Warner Paperback, 1975; *Holmes-Dracula File*, Ace Books, 1978; *An Old Friend of the Family*, Ace Books, 1979; *Thorn*, Ace Books, 1980; *Dominion*, Tor, 1981.

WORK IN PROGRESS: Berserker Base for Tor.

SANDAK, Cass R(obert)   1950-

BRIEF ENTRY: Born May 4, 1950, in Johnstown, Pa. Author of books for children. Sandak received his B.A. summa cum laude from Union College in 1972 and completed two years of graduate study at the University of Pennsylvania. From 1974 to 1976 he worked as a civilian management analyst for the U.S. Army in Fort Hamilton, N.Y., and then as a public relations consultant and medical editor in New York City. Since 1978 he has been employed as a technical writer for General Electric in Schenectady, N.Y. "As an author," Sandak has said, "I am drawn to children's nonfiction because I still find the world a vast, incomprehensible, and exciting place to live. And it is both fun and helpful to know how and why people do the things they do. . . ." This attitude has led him to write over twenty books for children on a variety of topics, such as *Christmas, Thanksgiving, The White House, Museums, Football, Bridges, Dams,* and *Skyscrapers.* Sandak also believes that "writers and artists have the mission to keep alive and pass along the values that have informed civilization throughout the ages. . . ." With Susan Purdy he has written several books that exemplify this tradition, including *Ancient Egypt, Ancient Rome, Aztecs,* and *North American Indians.* He is currently working on fiction for both children and adults and is considering the possibility of book illustration as well. Also a poet, Sandak received a prize from the Academy of American Poets in 1971 for his poem "The Garden of the Mint Green Unicorn." For Sandak, "writing . . . is a chance to share a unique vision of life, a pattern of existence, a perspective, a point of view. . . ." *Home:* 145 Seeley St., Scotia, N.Y. 12302. *For More Information See: Contemporary Authors*, Volume 108, Gale, 1983.

SCHOENHERR, John (Carl)   1935-

PERSONAL: Born July 5, 1935, in New York, N.Y.; son of John F. and Frances (Braun) Schoenherr; married Judith Gray, September 17, 1960; children: Jennifer Lauren, Ian Gray. *Education:* Attended Art Students League; Pratt Institute, B.F.A., 1956. *Home:* R.D. 2, Box 260, Stockton, N.J. 08559.

CAREER: Free-lance illustrator, with work appearing in magazines and books for children and adults. Began illustrating for science fiction magazines in 1956, and has gradually come

JOHN SCHOENHERR

to do nature illustration almost exclusively; member, South Hunterdon Juvenile Conference Committee, 1968—. Paintings were exhibited in one-man shows, Bronx Zoo, New York, 1968, and Carson Gallery of Western American Art, Denver, 1983, and are included in a number of private collections. *Member:* Society of Illustrators, Society of Animal Artists, American Society of Mammalogists. *Awards, honors:* First prize, National Speleological Society Salon, 1963; recipient of citations, Society of Illustrators, 1964, 1966, 1967, 1968, 1969, 1970, 1972, 1973, 1974, 1976, 1979, 1980, 1981; World Science Fiction Award, 1965, for best science fiction artist of the year; author award, New Jersey Council of Teachers of English, 1969, for *The Barn;* illustrated Jean Craighead George's *Julie of the Wolves* which won the Newbery Award, 1973; *Simon Underground* was selected for the Children's Book Showcase, 1977.

WRITINGS: The Barn (juvenile; self-illustrated; ALA Notable Book), Little, Brown, 1968.

Illustrator; all for children: Sterling North, *Rascal: A Memoir of a Better Era* (*Horn Book* honor book; ALA Notable Book) Dutton, 1963 (published in England as *Rascal: The True Story*

of a Pet Raccoon, Hodder & Stoughton, 1963); Walter Morey, *Gentle Ben,* Dutton, 1965; Robert William Murphy, *The Golden Eagle,* Dutton, 1965; Berniece Freschet, *Kangaroo Red,* Scribner, 1966; Daniel P. Mannix, *The Fox and the Hound,* Dutton, 1967; Era Zistle, *The Dangerous Year,* Random House, 1967; Adrien Stoutenburg, *A Vanishing Thunder: Extinct and Threatened American Birds,* Natural History Press, 1967; Arthur Catherall, *A Zebra Came to Drink,* Dutton, 1967; A. Stoutenburg, *Animals at Bay: Rare and Rescued American Wildlife,* Doubleday, 1968; Harry Harrison, *Man from P.I.G.,* Avon, 1968; Jean Craighead George, *The Moon of the Chickarees,* Crowell, 1968; Julian May, *The Big Island,* Follett, 1968; S. North, *The Wolfling: A Documentary Novel of the 1870s,* Dutton, 1969.

Allan W. Eckert, *Incident at Hawk's Hill,* Little, Brown, 1971; Ferdinand N. Monjo, *The Jezebel Wolf,* Simon & Schuster, 1971; Charles G. Roberts, *Red Fox,* Houghton, 1972; J. C. George, *Julie of the Wolves* (*Horn Book* honor book; ALA Notable Book), Harper, 1972; Theodore Clymer, *The Travels of Atunga,* Little, Brown, 1973; Harold Keith, *Susy's Scoundrel,* Crowell, 1974; Alison Morgan, *River Song,* Harper, 1975; John A. Giegling, *Black Lightning: Three Years in the Life of*

(From *Rascal* by Sterling North. Illustrated by John Schoenherr.)

country in 1914—my mother from Hungary and my father from Germany—and German was what they'd taught me. A couple of houses down from us lived a little boy my own age who chattered away in Chinese, and around the corner Italian prevailed. I was a virtual mute in that polyglot precinct until the day I got so desperate to communicate that I grabbed up a pencil and *drew*. Later I learned English from the comic strips, but I still kept drawing all the time.'' [Frances Traher, ''John Schoenherr,'' *Artists of the Rockies and the Golden West*, summer, 1983.¹]

At the age of eight, Schoenherr was given his first set of watercolors. At the age of thirteen he was taking Saturday classes at the Art Students League in New York City. Besides art, Schoenherr was fascinated with stone as a young boy, and used to explore caves, later learning how to rock climb. ''Climbing made me aware of the tactility of stone. You almost climb with the feel of each hold to your fingers. Of late years I've become aware again of the influence that Edward Weston had as a photographer, with his monumental stones and simplicity and elegance and strength of composition, the way he

a Fisher, Coward, 1975; Faith McNulty, *Whales: Their Life in the Sea*, Harper, 1975; Joanne Ryder, *Simon Underground*, Harper, 1976; Jane Annixter and Paul Annixter, *Wapootin*, Coward, 1976; Nathaniel Benchley, *Kilroy and the Gull*, Harper, 1977; Randall Jarrell, *A Bat Is Born* (poetry; excerpted from Jarrell's *The Bat-Poet*), Doubleday, 1977; J. C. George, *The Wounded Wolf*, Harper, 1978; Colin Thiele, *Storm Boy*, Harper, 1978; Lee Harding, *The Fallen Spaceman* (illustrated with son, Ian Schoenherr), Harper, 1980.

All written by Miska Miles; all published by Little, Brown: *Mississippi Possum*, 1965; *The Fox and the Fire* (*Horn Book* honor book; ALA Notable Book), 1966; *Rabbit Garden*, 1967; *Nobody's Cat* (ALA Notable Book), 1969; *Eddie's Bear*, 1970; *Hoagie's Rifle-Gun* (Junior Literary Guild selection),1970; *Wharf Rat*, 1972; *Somebody's Dog*, 1973; *Otter in the Cove*, 1974; *Beaver Moon*, 1978.

WORK IN PROGRESS: Paintings and graphics.

SIDELIGHTS: Schoenherr was born in New York City in 1935. ''. . . When I was four years old . . . I made the unsettling discovery that nobody out in the street where we lived in Queens could understand a word I said. My parents had come into the

He looked up, startled, and found himself face to face with an enormous badger. . . . ■ (From *Incident at Hawk's Hill* by Allen W. Eckert. Illustrated by John Schoenherr.)

She watched him board his little boat and head slowly down the coast. ■ (From *Otter in the Cove* by Miska Miles. Illustrated by John Schoenherr.)

would reduce things to the minimum that would work and thereby produce a significant image that would move some people.

"But there were also scientists among my boyhood heroes, and I seriously considered becoming a biologist."[1]

His love for art superseded his love of biology, and he opted to study at Pratt Institute in Brooklyn after high school instead of studying biology. During the summers Schoenherr returned to the Art Students League, where he studied under Frank Reilly, an illustrator closely devoted to the old French Academy style. "I appreciated certain skills that style engendered, and the perception it produced for seeing values and colors and changes in your subject—but I learned that I had to work out my organization on the painting itself. A too-rigid method wasn't for me. Organization itself, though, I liked. And early on, strong shapes and strong colors. Those qualities—and going for the overall look instead of the detailed thing."[1]

By 1956, at the age of twenty-one, Schoenherr was becoming recognized as a successful illustrator with work appearing in science fiction magazines. "I did a great deal of science fiction, and every one of those magazines had at least one of my illustrations. John Campbell, the editor of *Astounding Science Fiction,* which has since become *Analog,* I found always demanding, always forgiving. I'll always be proud of the 'genuine aliens' I designed for the stories Campbell published. Never were they humans with insect antennae. For beings from a heavy planet, I always managed to work out the structural support that logically their existence would have required."[1]

During the years that Schoenherr was working as an illustrator

for magazines, he was also busy raising a family on a farm in rural New Jersey. The countryside surrounding his farm gave Schoenherr an interest in animals and nature which gradually led him to doing nature illustration almost exclusively. His neighbor's barn became the idea for his children's book, *The Barn,* published in 1968. "A little skunk that I watched waddle up to that barn and disappear inside it became the central figure in the one children's book I have written myself and, of course, illustrated: *The Barn,* published by Atlantic-Little, Brown."[1]

Pursuing his interest in nature and in larger and more exotic animals, Schoenherr has traveled to many countries and extensively in the United States. "It was my travels back and forth through northern Arizona and around Albuquerque, and exploring caves in the non-developed areas of the Black Hills, Yellowstone and Montana, that taught me what my great love really is. It's structure. Back East, everything is covered with trees—whereas it's stone and dirt that I love. Deep down, I probably want to be a desert dweller. And yet, our New Jersey place is a tree farm. Not for growing them, but for enjoying them. And I have made so much preparation for painting animals. I like raccoons with their robber or carnival masks. I never can decide which it is they wear. And bears! I tend to be more sympathetic with the larger monochromatic animals that I can use a big brush on. Bears, as I say, have a nice form. It's solid. And moose, I like. They look so awkward in an artificial situation; but I've seen a moose go through a cedar swamp over fallen, twisted tree trunks and matted growth without wrestling anything. A moose can be a dynamic, controlled, solid mass in movement.

"When I have been painting animal shapes for a long time I find I need to freshen my perceptions. Oddly enough, my theme

Ben stretched his neck, closed his eyes, and grunted like a pig, in pure ecstasy. Mark leaned back against Ben's solid side. . . . ■ (From *Gentle Ben* by Walt Morey. Illustrated by John Schoenherr.)

may still be 'shape,' but for my subjects I like to turn to woodworking tools from around the 1870s. Shape-*makers!* Sometimes I work a piece of old cedar myself with one of my models that isn't currently part of a still life. Some of the tools have wooden thumbscrews that you just turn and unlock, and press in the nicely-fitting pieces to change the tension and the depth of cut. I find wood comfortable to work with.'''

Schoenherr is renowned as a painter as well as an illustrator. His paintings have been exhibited in a one-man show at the Bronx Zoo and, most recently, at The Carson Gallery of Western American Art in Denver, Colorado. Presently he is working exclusively as a painter and graphic artist. ''I think what I've grown to try to get in my paintings is a presence. By putting a lot of myself into a painting, something inside the frame comes to exist by itself—almost like another person. The test is, has the painting enough content so that you can react to it in many different ways; can you see it differently when you're sad than when you're happy? Then the painting is not illustration, not a literal record of something—it's an existence. Whether I'm painting a stone or a barrel or a bear, I want to make it exist!'''

FOR MORE INFORMATION SEE: Lee Kingman and others, compilers, *Illustrators of Children's Books: 1957-1966,* Horn

Book, 1968; Diana Klemin, *The Illustrated Book,* Clarkson Potter, 1970; *Contemporary American Illustrators of Children's Books,* Rutgers University Art Gallery, 1974; Doris de Montreville and Elizabeth D. Crawford, editors, *Fourth Book of Junior Authors and Illustrators,* H. W. Wilson, 1978; Lee Kingman and others, compilers, *Illustrators of Children's Books: 1967-1976,* Horn Book, 1978; Frances Traher, ''John Schoenherr,'' *Artists of the Rockies and the Golden West,* summer, 1983.

SEWALL, Marcia 1935-

PERSONAL: Born November 5, 1935, in Providence, R.I.; daughter of Edgar Knight and Hilda (Osgood) Sewall. *Education:* Rhode Island School of Design; Pembroke College, B.A., 1957; Tufts University, M.Ed., 1958. *Religion:* Unitarian Universalist. *Residence:* Boston, Mass.

CAREER: Children's Museum, Boston, Mass., staff artist, 1961-63; teacher of art in Winchester, Mass., 1967-75. Participant in Boston adult literacy program. *Awards, honors: Come Again in the Spring* was named one of *New York Times* ''Outstanding Books of the Year'' and was selected for the American Institute of Graphic Arts Book Show, both 1976; notable book citation, American Library Association, 1978, for *Little Things; The Nutcrackers and the Sugar-Tongs* named one of best picture

MARCIA SEWALL

"The moment I come looking where you are, you're off to where I'm finished being." ■ (From *The Story of Old Mrs. Brubeck and How She Looked for Trouble and Where She Found Him* by Lore Segal. Illustrated by Marcia Sewall.)

books, *New York Times*, 1978; *The Leprechaun's Story* was selected for the American Institute of Graphic Arts Book Show, 1979; *The Story of Old Mrs. Brubeck and How She Looked for Trouble and Where She Found Him* named one of best picture books, *New York Times*, 1981; *Song of the Horse* selected for exhibition at Bratislava International Biennale, 1983.

WRITINGS—Adapter; all self-illustrated: *Master of All Masters: An English Folktale*, Little, Brown, 1972; *The Wee, Wee Mannie and the Big, Big Coo: A Scottish Folktale*, Atlantic-Little, Brown, 1977; *The Little Wee Tyke: An English Folktale*, Atheneum, 1979; *The Cobbler's Song*, Dutton, 1982.

Illustrator: Richard Kennedy, *The Parrot and the Thief*, Atlantic-Little, Brown, 1974; P. C. Asbjornsen, *The Squire's Bride: A Norwegian Folktale*, Atheneum, 1975; Joseph Jacobs, *Coo-My-Dove, My Dear*, Atheneum, 1976; R. Kennedy, *The Porcelain Man*, Atlantic-Little, Brown, 1976; R. Kennedy, *Come Again in the Spring*, Harper, 1976; Anne Laurin, *Little Things*, Atheneum, 1978; Drew Stevenson, *Ballad of Penelope Lou . . . and Me*, Crossing Press, 1978; Edward Lear, *The Nutcrackers and the Sugar-Tongs*, Atlantic-Little, Brown, 1978; Anne Elito Crompton, *The Lifting Stone*, Holiday House, 1978; R. Kennedy, *The Rise and Fall of Ben Gizzard*, Atlantic-Little, Brown, 1978; R. Kennedy, *The Leprechaun's Story*, Dutton,

1979; Paul Fleischman, *The Birthday Tree*, Harper, 1979; Phyllis Krasilovsky, *The Man Who Tried to Save Time*, Doubleday, 1979; R. Kennedy, *Crazy in Love*, Dutton, 1980; John Reynolds Gardiner, *Stone Fox*, Crowell, 1980; Nancy Willard, *The Marzipan Moon*, Harcourt, 1981; R. Kennedy, *Song of the Horse* (ALA Notable Book) Dutton, 1981; Lore Segal, *The Story of Old Mrs. Brubeck and How She Looked for Trouble and Where She Found Him*, Pantheon, 1981; Clyde Robert Bulla, *Poor Boy, Rich Boy*, Harper, 1982; Lyn Littlefield Hoopes, *When I Was Little*, Dutton, 1983; P. Fleischman, *Finzel the Farsighted*, Dutton, 1983; Walter Wangerin, *Thistle*, Harper, 1983.

SIDELIGHTS: Sewall was reared in Providence, Rhode Island. "I think of my mother as a very creative person. When I was growing up she was always knitting and sewing and painting. My father was from Maine and all his family had a real love of storytelling. He could just reel off yarns, especially Holman Day's comical poems. I loved to listen."

She received her bachelor's degree from Pembroke College at Brown University, and then took a Masters Degree in Education at Tufts University. "One wonderful summer I studied at the Rhode Island School of Design. It was an intensive program with the freshman year squeezed into a summer. I never worked so hard in my life, and I learned a tremendous sense of discipline there. It was the first extremely structured art training I'd had. I needed it, and loved it.

"Before becoming a children's book illustrator, I primarily taught art to high school students and worked at the Children's Museum in Boston. When I was there, it was a very small museum and although I had the elegant title of 'Staff Artist,' I did everything from taking tickets at the door, to running a little Saturday art class, and helping with exhibits."

Sewall's first published book was *Master of All Masters: An English Folktale*. "I was drawn to the joyfulness of those funny, eccentric words.

"When I first receive a manuscript, I walk through the story and divide it into pictures. If it's to be a thirty-two page book then I am limited to about thirteen double-page spreads. I begin to immediately struggle with the sense of character, the movement of character, and then on to the transformation of that flat surface into a believable space. An author gives me clues as to person and place and then it's a matter of sorting them out. The illustrator often makes decisions about the period and costuming. I next try to capture the rhythm and movement of the story in the dummy book.

"Although I may not immediately 'see' a character, I have to believe that it's within me to see him or her. On reading and rereading a manuscript, a sense of person begins to emerge and it is that which I try to capture in my initial sketches. It took a stack of paper and lot of drawing of *Old Mrs. Brubeck*

"NOOOOOoooooooooo!" Death bellowed. He flung his arms about hysterically, splattering ink, then screamed out again.... ■ (From *Come Again in the Spring* by Richard Kennedy. Illustrated by Marcia Sewall.)

(From *The Squire's Bride* by P. C. Asbjörnsen. Illustrated by Marcia Sewall.)

before she would materialize for me. At first I had difficulty with her as a personality. She worried too much! Then I thought, 'My gosh, she's me and she's everybody I know!' I began to feel that there was humor about her, and then she just took shape. I thought if I gave her wooden shoes we would not only see but could hear her move about the house in her search for 'Trouble,' and, as a final statement, I distilled her anxious movements in silhouettes against the endpapers.''

Sewall has illustrated seven books for author, Richard Kennedy. ''Sometimes I know immediately how a book must look. As I read the manuscript for the *Song of the Horse*, I visualized the story in scratchboard. Scratchboard is a black ink surface over a white gessoed board. Instead of putting a black line down on white paper you scratch a white line away from a black surface. It is sort of electrical, magnetic. It has a vibrancy that seemed appropriate for that particular story.''

The Cobbler's Song (1982) was Sewall's first full-color book. ''What an absolute joy it was to sit down and paint, and use colors that seemed to express the changing moods of the story. I used gouache which is an opaque watercolor paint not unlike

poster paint. The story is a variation of the old rich man, poor man theme. It deals with feelings, so it made sense to use full-color and to put paint on expressively.

''I don't think you can force a book. If a manuscript seems natural and comfortable and appealing, I accept it readily. You work so hard for three or four months on the material that you must be comfortable with it. I love the wisdom, the character, and the tradition in folk people, so I often choose books with that sort of quality.

''I have always enjoyed the sensation of movement—dance, athletic activity of all kinds—and that has really helped me with moving figures about a page. My characters are not based on real people, though I notice when I illustrate a book that sometimes people I know will appear. Months later, it will occur to me that I have illustrated the boy in the corner market, or I discover that one of my figures sits like someone I know. I think an artist is constantly taking in visual impressions, but not always consciously. And you don't deliberately pull them out. They come.

"I work on a book for about three months. It isn't a nine to five process for me, but intense portions of every day are spent working on illustrations."

Sewall lives and works in Boston, Massachusetts. "The view from my window is of a rugged city. I have mused on that because the view on my paper is usually of a nice old horse, a country gentleman or a rolling hill.

"For relaxation I enjoy reading and I've been doing some landscape paintings. Two authors I've always admired are Carl Sandburg and Nathaniel Hawthorne. Hawthorne for his sense of New England character, and Sandburg for his great feeling for people and earth."

She presently teaches a college level course in children's book illustration at a local art school. "I want my students to have the experience of actually preparing a children's book for publication; to go through the same process that I do with every book, making similar decisions. I hope these students will develop their own individuality. Illustrations that I enjoy most have a real personality about them, and somehow I feel the unique quality of the people who created them. Honoré Daumier, the French satirist, and Beatrix Potter are two of my many favorite illustrators.

"I do love to translate words into pictures. I love to draw out of my imagination people and places. I somehow think that my strong desire to illustrate children's books made it possible for me to become an illustrator."

FOR MORE INFORMATION SEE: Lee Kingman and others, compilers, *Illustrators of Children's Books: 1967-1976*, Horn Book, 1978.

HAROLD SHERMAN

SHERMAN, Harold (Morrow) 1898-

PERSONAL: Born July 13, 1898, in Traverse City, Mich.; son of Thomas Henry and Alcinda E. (Morrow) Sherman; married Martha Frances Bain, September 26, 1920; children: Mary Alcinda (Mrs. Bernard J. Kobiella), Marcia Anne (Mrs. Wendell R. Smith). *Education:* Attended University of Michigan, 1918-19. *Politics:* Independent. *Religion:* "Nonsectarian." *Home:* Highway 5, South Mountain View, Ark. 72560. *Office:* ESP Research Associates Foundation, 1660 Union National Plaza Building, Little Rock, Ark. 72201.

CAREER: Marion Chronicle, Marion, Ind., reporter, 1921-24; free-lance writer, 1924—; CBS-Radio, writer and commentator of "Your Key to Happiness" in New York, N.Y., 1935-36, and Chicago, Ill., 1943; ESP Research Associates Foundation, Little Rock, Ark., founder, president, and director, 1964—, also director of annual workshop. Investigator, experimenter, and lecturer on extra-sensory perception. Co-developer of Blanchard Springs Caverns. *Member:* Authors Guild of Authors League of America (life member), Dramatists Guild, Lions.

*WRITINGS—*Fiction: *Fight 'em, Big Three*, Appleton, 1926; *Mayfield's Fighting Five*, Appleton, 1926; *Touchdown!*, Grosset, 1927; *Beyond the Dog's Nose*, Appleton, 1927; (with Hawthorne Daniel) *Cameron MacBain, Backwoodsman*, Appleton, 1927; *Get 'em, Mayfield*, Appleton, 1927; *Hit by Pitcher*, Grosset, 1928; *Block That Kick!*, Grosset, 1928; *Bases Full!: "Ernie Challenges the World"*, Grosset, 1928; *Safe!*, Grosset, 1928; *Over the Line*, Goldsmith Publishing, 1929; *Don Rader,*

Trailblazer, Grosset, 1929; *Flashing Steel*, Grosset, 1929; *Hit and Run!*, Grosset, 1929.

Hold That Line!, Grosset, 1930; *Flying Heels and Other Hockey Stories*, Grosset, 1930; *Ding Palmer, Air Detective*, Grosset, 1930; *Batter Up!: A Story of American Legion Junior Baseball*, Grosset, 1930; *Number Forty-Four and Other Football Stories*, Grosset, 1930; *Shoot That Ball!, and Other Basketball Stories*, Grosset, 1930; *The Land of Monsters*, Grosset, 1931; *It's a Pass!*, Goldsmith Publishing, 1931; *Slashing Sticks and Other Hockey Stories*, Grosset, 1931; *Strike Him Out!*, Goldsmith Publishing, 1931; *Goal to Go!*, Grosset, 1931; *Interference, and Other Football Stories*, Goldsmith Publishing, 1932; *Down the Ice, and Other Winter Sport Stories*, Goldsmith Publishing, 1932; *Double Play! and Other Baseball Stories*, Grosset, 1932; *Crashing Through!*, Grosset, 1932; *Under the Basket, and Other Basketball Stories*, Goldsmith Publishing, 1932; *The Tennis Terror, and Other Tennis Stories*, Goldsmith Publishing, 1932; *Let Freedom Ring!: A Novel of These Turbulent Times*, N. H. White, Jr., 1932; *Tahara among African Tribes*, Goldsmith Publishing, 1933; *Tahara: Boy King of the Desert*, Goldsmith Publishing, 1933; *Tahara: Boy Mystic of India*, Goldsmith Publishing, 1933; *Tahara in the Land of Yucatan*, Goldsmith Publishing, 1933.

Call of the Land: A Novel of High Adventure in 4-H Club Work, M. A. Donohue, 1948; *The Green Man and His Return* (science-fiction), Amherst Press, 1979. Also author of *One Minute to Play* (novelized from the photo play), 1926.

Nonfiction: *Your Key to Happiness*, H. C. Kinsey, 1935; (with George Hubert Wilkins) *Thoughts through Space*, Creative Age Press, 1942; *Your Key to Married Happiness*, Putnam, 1944; *Your Key to Youth Problems*, Putnam, 1945; *Your Key to Ro-*

mance, Pegasus Books, 1948; *You Live after Death*, Creative Age Press, 1949; *You Can Stop Drinking*, Creative Age Press, 1950, reprinted as *Anyone Can Stop Drinking (Even You!)*, C. & R. Anthony, 1959; *Know Your Own Mind: An Amazing Revelation of Your Inner Consciousness*, C. & R. Anthony, 1953; *The New TNT: Miraculous Power within You*, Prentice-Hall, 1954, revised edition, 1966; *Adventures in Thinking*, Master Publications, 1956; (with Claude Myron Bristol) *TNT, The Power within You: How to Release the Forces inside You and Get What You Want!*, Prentice-Hall, 1957; *How to Turn Failure into Success*, Prentice-Hall, 1958; *How to Use the Power of Prayer*, C. & R. Anthony, 1958.

How to Make ESP Work for You, DeVorss, 1964; *How to Solve Mysteries of Your Mind and Soul: A Way to Find a Philosophy of Life that Meets the Needs of Today*, DeVorss, 1965; *Wonder Healers of the Philippines*, DeVorss, 1967; *Your Mysterious Powers of ESP: The New Medium of Communication*, World Publishing, 1969; *How to Foresee and Control Your Future*, Fawcett, 1970; *How to Take Yourself Apart and Put Yourself Back Together Again*, Fawcett, 1971; *The Harold Sherman ESP Manual*, Human Development Associates, 1972; (with Ambrose Worrall and Olga Worrall) *Your Power to Heal: How to Work with the God Power within You to Regain Health of Body and Mind*, Harper, 1972; *You Can Communicate with the Unseen World*, Fawcett, 1974; *How to Know What to Believe*, Fawcett, 1976; *How to Picture What You Want*, Fawcett, 1978; *The Dead Are Alive: They Can and Do Communicate with You*, privately printed, 1981.

Other: "Her Supporting Cast" (play), 1933; "The Little Black Book" (play), 1935; "The Adventures of Mark Twain" (screenplay), Warner Brothers, 1942.

Contributor to *Boy's Life, American Boy, Target, Top Notch,* and *Ropeco*.

WORK IN PROGRESS: ESP research and lectures.

SIDELIGHTS: Sherman began his writing career as a reporter for the *Marion* (Indiana) *Chronicle* then moved to New York where he lived for seventeen years. During that time he wrote over sixty sports and adventure novels. He also wrote two plays which were produced on Broadway and had his own personal philosophy radio show, "Your Key to Happiness."

During this time Sherman also developed an interest in extrasensory perception (ESP) which grew and led to his becoming an eminent lay authority on ESP. "[I have] gained firsthand knowledge through personal experience and through the study of the psychic phenomena occurring in the lives of thousands of other men and women and young people."

Thoughts through Space is a book Sherman wrote to describe mind-to-mind communication experiments conducted between New York City and the Wilkins expedition three thousand miles to the north, in which he claims seventy per cent accuracy as a receiver of thoughts. Since then, his entire career has been devoted to psychic research and has gone beyond simple mind-to-mind communication experiments. He has conducted research on psychic surgery in the Philippines on two occasions, and *Wonder Healers of the Philippines* is one of the results of his studies.

Sherman believes that everyone possesses at least a latent extrasensory perception ability, and through his foundation and his books (which have been translated and published abroad), he attempts to open up new areas for research and bring the information to the general reader.

Sherman and his wife, Martha, live in the Ozark Mountains in Arkansas where he writes. His writing now deals with ESP and he frequently lectures on the topic. He is founder of the Research Associates Foundation.

He has made three record albums, "How to Develop ESP," 1964, "Advanced Techniques of ESP," 1964, and "How to Foretell Your Future," 1964, and two cassette series, "Know Your Own Mind" and "The Big Fight and How You Can Win" (formerly "Anyone Can Stop Drinking").

SHIELDS, Brenda Desmond (Armstrong) 1914-

PERSONAL: Born November 26, 1914, in Mount Morgan, Queensland, Australia; daughter of Kenneth and Lucy (Calcutt) Armstrong; married Geoffrey F. Beck (a medical practitioner), 1937 (died, 1945); married Gordon Henderson Shields, August 4, 1950 (died, 1972); children: (first marriage) Terence, Sandra (Mrs. Ian Whelan), Geoffrey Brendan, Christine (Mrs. Anton Iseli); (second marriage) Bronwyn, Katrina. *Education:* St. Vincent's Hospital, Melbourne, certificate of dietetics; special courses at Emily McPherson Domestic College, University of Melbourne. *Home:* "Rhyme," 4 Stawell St., Dromana, Victoria, Australia.

CAREER: Geelong Hospital, Victoria, Australia, dietitian, 1936-37, 1955-59; Health Department, Maternal and Child Welfare Branch, Melbourne, Victoria, dietitian, 1958-63, teacher in education department, 1963-66; Science Teachers' Association of Victoria, executive officer, 1967-75.

BRENDA DESMOND SHIELDS

WRITINGS: Tezza, the Coral Trout (juvenile; illustrated by John Derrick), Blair, 1962; *Nutrition during Pregnancy,* Pitmans (Australia), 1980.

WORK IN PROGRESS: The Birds That Danced; Diary of a Babysitter; The Value of Age.

SIDELIGHTS: "I wrote *Tezza, the Coral Trout* after a holiday on the Great Barrier Reef because I felt all children would be fascinated by the wonderful variety of reef life, its brilliant colors and great beauty. The story is woven around the life on the reef, the fish and other creatures who populate it and the coral polyps who made it. Information is basically correct but the story is fantasy. John Derrick carefully studied scientific details before using his imagination with paint for the illustrations.

"I have always realized the value of story telling and hope to give more time to this in the future. Since I love travelling I have spent more time overseas than at home since 1975. I have lived in England for over three years and in Holland for six months."

SIEGAL, Aranka 1930-

BRIEF ENTRY: Born June 10, 1930, in Beregszasz, Hungary. In her autobiographical book for young adults, *Upon the Head of the Goat: A Childhood in Hungary, 1939-1944* (Farrar, Straus, 1981), Siegal recalls the chilling events of Hitler's Jewish persecution that eventually led to her imprisonment in the concentration camp at Auschwitz in 1944. Siegal, the fifth girl in a family of seven, and one of her sisters were the only members of the family to survive the horrors of Auschwitz. Following her liberation by the British First Army in April, 1945, she spent several years in Sweden before immigrating to the United States at the age of eighteen. After marrying and raising two children, Siegal earned a degree in social anthropology at Empire State College. *Upon the Head of the Goat* chronicles her life before her actual deportation to Auschwitz: the food rationing and curfews, the compulsory Star of David insignia, relatives who were snatched away or simply disappeared, the struggle to endure the hardships of ghetto life. *Newsweek* observed: "The story is familiar and so is the scapegoat theme, but a few pages into . . . [this] fine memoir . . . you feel the power and interest of her particular experience and remember that this story cannot be told too often." The *New Yorker* noted that it is "written with love and dignity . . . [and] can convey to young readers a sense of the Holocaust while stopping short of the ultimate horrors." In 1981 the book won the Janusz Korczak literary competition in which it was cited the work that best exemplified selflessness and human dignity. It was also selected a Newbery Honor Book in 1982 and that same year received the *Boston Globe-Horn Book* Award for nonfiction. *For More Information See: Newsweek,* January 18, 1982; *Fifth Book of Junior Authors and Illustrators,* H. W. Wilson, 1983.

SIROF, Harriet 1930-

PERSONAL: Born October 18, 1930, in New York, N.Y.; daughter of Herman (a dress manufacturer) and Lillian (Miller) Hockman; married Sidney Sirof (a psychologist), June 18, 1949; children: Laurie, David, Amy Sirof Bordiuk. *Education:* New School for Social Research, B.A., 1962. *Home and office:* 792 East 21st St., Brooklyn, N.Y. 11210.

CAREER: Remedial reading teacher at elementary schools in Brooklyn, N.Y., 1962-76; St. John's University, Jamaica, N.Y., instructor in creative writing, 1978—. Instructor at South Shore Adult Center, 1977—, Long Island University, 1978-79, and Brooklyn College of the City University of New York, 1980-81, 1984—. *Member:* International Women's Writing Guild, Authors Guild, Authors League of America, League of Women Voters (past president of Brooklyn branch), Forum of Writers for Young People, Society of Children's Book Writers.

WRITINGS—Juveniles: *A New-Fashioned Love Story* (novel), Xerox Education Publications, 1977; *The IF Machine* (novel), Scholastic Book Services, 1978; *The Junior Encyclopedia of Israel,* Jonathan David, 1980; *Save the Dam!* (novel; illustrated by Jan Albrecht), Crestwood, 1981; *That Certain Smile* (young adult novel), Xerox Education Publications, 1982.

Work represented in anthologies, including *Voices of Brooklyn,* edited by Sol Yorick, American Library Association, 1973; *The Switch and Other Stories,* edited by Mary Verdick, Xerox

"Look how near the dam we are," Beth said. "Is this where you saw the diver?" ■ (From *Save the Dam!* by Harriet Sirof. Illustrated by Jan Albrecht.)

HARRIET SIROF

Education Publications, 1976; *Remember Me and Other Stories,* edited by M. Verdick, Xerox Education Publications, 1978; *Triple Action Play Book* (contains "Itchy Feet," a one-act play for children), edited by Jeri Schapiro, Scholastic Book Services, 1979.

Author of "Your Child," a column in *Flatbush News,* in *Kings Courier,* in *Bay News,* and in *Canarsie Digest,* all 1962-65. Contributor of stories and articles to magazines for adults and young people, including *North American Review, Descant, Highlights for Children, Rainbow, Maine Review, Alive, More, Merry-Go-Round, Read, Know Your World,* and *Alpha.*

WORK IN PROGRESS: A young adult novel, tentative title, "Where It's At"; a juvenile historical novel based on the second-century Bar-Kokba revolt in Judea.

SIDELIGHTS: "My father taught me to read when I was four years old and I have been hooked on books ever since.

"One of the delights of my childhood was to fill up my library card. In those days, library cards had lines front and back on which the librarian stamped the date you borrowed a book and returned it. When all the lines were filled, you were issued a new card. It was a point of honor with me to get a new card as often as possible. The library frustrated me by only permitting two books out at a time. I responded by bringing my books back for new ones the day I finished them. It never occurred to me to read thin books so they would go faster. That would have been cheating.

"Since I loved to read, it seemed natural to write as well. I wrote stories at home and compositions in school. I enjoyed doing both—until my sixth grade teacher decided to teach us to organize our writing. First she told us to construct an outline complete with Roman numerals I and II and large and small 'a.' Then, after she corrected the outline, we were to write a composition exactly as outlined. I simply could not do it. I finally solved the problem by writing whatever popped into my head and then constructing an outline from the finished composition.

"I still have not learned to 'organize' my writing. I begin a story or a book with a vague idea: for example, a girl who can't help embroidering the truth. The main character begins to grow in my mind and gradually the other people in her life appear along with the specific situation she finds herself in. I make notes on slips of paper (most of which I eventually throw away) and do research on the story's background. Finally one morning I wake up with the first sentence of the book in my head. I go to the typewriter and begin to write. I keep writing to find out what happens to my characters who by this time are as real to me as my own family.

"I came to writing late. After many years devoted to being a mother and teacher, I began to write short stories for adults. Sales to the literary quarterlies and the interest of an agent persuaded me to attempt an adult novel. It took me nearly two years and two thousand discarded pages to discover that it was not for me.

"Deeply discouraged, I was considering giving up writing when I received a letter from Scholastic (for whom I had previously written some educational materials) looking for novels for children with reading problems. I tried one and found to my surprise that I loved writing it. I have since published four novels and one nonfiction book for young adults and am now working on a historical novel for nine- to twelve-year-olds.

"My life is representative of many women of my generation. At the age of ten, sure that I would be a famous writer when I grew up, I dictated stories to my friend Boopsie who planned to be a secretary. When I entered college at seventeen I still held onto the dream of writing someday, but was persuaded to train for something practical like teaching English. I married at eighteen, left school to plunge wholeheartedly into domesticity, and soon had three small children. Although writing had been relegated to the status of an abandoned adolescent fantasy, I began to feel that something was missing in my life. I returned to school, earned a scholarship, wrote term papers while the children watched 'Romper Room' on television, and graduated first in my class. Teaching was the next obvious step for a woman whose own children were entering school, so I taught reading.

"I don't know what eventually reactivated the old dream of being a writer—probably a combination of the ideas of the women's movement and my own personal growth. In any case, I hauled out the old term-paper typewriter and began. At first it seemed necessary to reject the years of child rearing and child teaching and to assume a new identity by writing adult literature. Only gradually did it dawn on me that those years had not been wasted, that I had spent so much time with children because I liked them, and that I really wanted to write for children.

"I write primarily for older children and young adults with an occasional adult short story for variety. I have also written for 'reluctant' readers. My science fiction novel, *The IF Machine,* was designed for junior high school students reading on a second or third grade level. The book is used in school remedial reading programs and I am always delighted when I receive a letter from a youngster saying it is the first book he or she ever read all the way through.

SNOW, Richard F(olger) 1947-

BRIEF ENTRY: Born October 28, 1947, in New York, N.Y. A magazine editor and author, Snow received his B.A. from Columbia University in 1970. That same year he joined the staff of *American Heritage* magazine, becoming an associate editor, 1972-77, senior editor in book division, 1977-78, and, presently, managing editor. He is the author of *Freelon Starbird* (Houghton, 1976), a novel for young adults which was cited by *New York Times Book Review* as one of the outstanding juvenile books of 1976. *Publishers Weekly* called the book a ''. . . rare treat . . . witty, instructive, altogether splendid. . . .'' Told through the eyes of a soldier in George Washington's army, it has been well-received by critics as an unadorned rendition of the American Revolution. *School Library Journal* observed that ''. . . the book's strength is in its unglorified picture of military life with the added appeal . . . of exposing the 'underside' of events in 1776.'' *Horn Book* further added: ''The ribald, often coarsely outspoken narrative is lusty in the manner of Leon Garfield's heartily realistic stories of the eighteenth century.'' Snow's second book for young adults, *The Iron Road: A Portrait of American Railroading* (Four Winds Press, 1978), is an historical account of the development of the railroad in the United States. *Horn Book* described it as ''fascinating as it is informative . . . [with] . . . insight into the reasons why railroads have so insinuated themselves into the American imagination. . . .'' In 1979 it was selected as a nonfiction honor book by the *Boston Globe* and *Horn Book*. Snow's other writings include *The Funny Place* (J. Philip O'Hara, 1975), a book of poetry, and *The Burning* (Doubleday, 1981), an historical novel for adults. *Home:* 490 West End Ave., New York, N.Y. 10024. *For More Information See: Contemporary Authors,* Volume 106, Gale, 1982.

SOKOL, William 1923-
(Bill Sokol)

PERSONAL: Born November 21, 1923, in Warsaw, Poland; brought to United States in 1930; naturalized U.S. citizen; married wife, Camille (an author and artist); children: two daughters. *Education:* Attended American University, Biarritz, France, and Art Students League.

CAREER: Illustrator of children's books, 1956—. Early in career, worked as free-lance designer and art director, Montreal and Quebec, 1946-49; and as experimental designer for advertising agencies in New York City for two years; worked in promotion departments for periodicals in New York City, including *Esquire,* 1950-51, *Look,* 1950-51, and *New York Times,* 1951-59, became associate art director. Work has been included in one-man exhibitions in Montreal, 1947, 1948, and New York City, 1953, 1956, and is in numerous private collections, museums, and libraries throughout the United States, including the Library of Congress, Washington, D.C. Chairman, American Institute of Graphic Arts Children's Book Show, 1963-64. *Awards, honors:* Recipient of medal from Art Directors Club of New York, 1956, for press advertising designs; *Cats, Cats, Cats, Cats, Cats* was chosen as a *New York Herald Tribune* honor book, 1958; *All Aboard: Poems* was cited by the *New York Times* as one of the Best Illustrated Children's Books of the Year, 1958, and received Boys' Club Junior Book Award, 1959; citation of merit, Society of Illustrators, 1959; gold medal, Delgado Museum of New Orleans, 1959, for graphic prints.

WRITINGS—Under name Bill Sokol: *A Lion in the Tree* (juvenile; self-illustrated), Pantheon, 1961; *The Fable of Profitt, the Fox* (juvenile; self-illustrated), Holt, 1964.

Illustrator; all for children; all under name Bill Sokol: Beatrice Schenk deRegniers, *A Child's Book of Dreams,* Harcourt, 1957; Mary Britton Miller, *All Aboard: Poems,* Pantheon, 1958; B. S. deRegniers, *Cats, Cats, Cats, Cats, Cats,* Pantheon, 1958; Hans Christian Andersen, *The Emperor and the Nightingale,* Pantheon, 1959; Franklyn M. Branley, *Rockets and Satellites,* Crowell, 1961, revised edition, 1970; Clifford B. Hicks, *Al-*

A smile of welcome crossed his face. "Hi, Daphne!"

"Could you help me, Sergeant Ellsworth? . . ."

■ (From *Alvin's Swap Shop* by Clifford B. Hicks. Illustrated by Bill Sokol.)

vin's Secret Code, Holt, 1963; written by wife, Camille Sokol, *Dis-moi*, Holt, 1963; C. Sokol, *La Pluche*, Holt, 1963; Lloyd Alexander, *Time Cat: The Remarkable Journeys of Jason and Gareth*, Holt, 1963; C. B. Hicks, *Alvin Fernald, Foreign Trader*, Holt, 1966; C. Sokol, *The Lucky Sew-It-Yourself Book*, Four Winds, 1966; Dana Bruce, editor, *Tell Me a Joke*, Platt, 1966; Barbara K. Bate, *The Fun and Games Book, Starring Leon the Lion*, Platt, 1967; Alexandre Dumas, *The Count of Monte Cristo*, Platt, 1968; C. Sokol, *How to Be Mother's Helper*, Platt, 1968; C. B. Hicks, *Alvin Fernald, Mayor for a Day*, Holt, 1970; C. B. Hicks, *Alvin Fernald, Superweasel*, Holt, 1974; C. B. Hicks, *Alvin's Swap Shop*, Holt, 1976; Edward Edelson, *Great Movie Spectaculars*, Doubleday, 1976; Molly Cone, *Mishmash and the Sauerkraut Mystery*, Archway, 1979.

SIDELIGHTS: Sokol was born in Warsaw, Poland, and immigrated to the United States when he was seven years old. He has drawn since early childhood. One of his most significant memories is of a fourth-grade teacher at P.S. 39 in New York City who encouraged him to draw large motifs in colored chalk on the classroom blackboard.

Sokol is a self-taught artist, although he studied for a short time at the American University in Biarritz and the Art Students League in New York. He has worked as an advertising director, graphic arts director, easel painter and illustrator and has received recognition for his work from museums in New York, the Art Directors Club of New York, the American Institute of Graphic Arts, and *Graphis* magazine. His works are included in private collections, various museums, and libraries in the United States and in the Kerlan Collection at the University of Minnesota.

FOR MORE INFORMATION SEE: Graphis, March, 1958.

SOREL, Edward 1929-

BRIEF ENTRY: Born March 26, 1929, in New York, N.Y. An artist and illustrator of books for children, Sorel received his diploma from Cooper Union College in 1951. That same year he joined the staff of *Esquire* magazine where he worked until 1953 when he and two former classmates founded Push Pin Studios, an innovative commercial and graphic arts enterprise located in New York. After leaving Push Pin in 1956, Sorel worked as director of promotional art at CBS-TV. Later Sorel's free-lance work brought him into the first rank of political cartoonist-illustrators. From the late 1960s to early 1970s, he was the creator of "Sorel's News Service," a syndicated political feature in which he reflected a style reminiscent of nineteenth-century cartoonists such as Thomas Nast and Frank Bellew. He has received awards from the Society of Illustrators and Art Directors Club of New York as well as the Augustas St. Gauden's medal from Cooper Union and, in 1981, the George Polk award for satiric drawing.

Sorel is widely recognized not only as a caricaturist, but also as an illustrator of children's books. Both *Pablo Paints a Picture*, 1959, and *Gwendolyn and the Weather Cock*, 1963, were selected as one of the *New York Times* best illustrated books of the year. In 1961 *Gwendolyn the Miracle Hen* received the Spring Book Festival Award; in 1972 Jay Williams' *Magical Storybook* was selected as one of the American Institute of Graphic Arts fifty books of the year as well as for its Children's Book Show. Included among Sorel's other illustrated works for children are *King Carlo of Capri: Freely Adapted from "Riquet with the Tuft of Hair"* by Charles Perrault, *What's*

Good for a Five-Year-Old? by William Cole, and *The Pirates of Penzance*, adapted by Ward Botsford. Many of his caricatures and cartoons have been published in several collections for adults, such as *How To Be President: Some Hard and Fast Rules, Making the World Safe for Hypocrisy*, and *Superpen*. He is also a contributor to national magazines, including a weekly cartoon in *The Village Voice*. *For More Information See: American Artist*, May, 1960; *Graphis*, January, 1963; *Illustrators of Children's Books: 1957-1966*, Horn Book, 1968; *Contemporary Authors*, Volumes 9-12, revised Gale, 1974; *The World Encyclopedia of Cartoons*, Gale, 1980.

SRIVASTAVA, Jane Jonas

BRIEF ENTRY: Specialist in elementary school mathematics education and author of books for children. Srivastava, a graduate of Swarthmore College, received her masters degree from Harvard University. Once an elementary school teacher, she also worked on several mathematics curriculum projects before becoming a housewife and free-lance writer. Her seven books in the "Young Mathematician" series deal with math concepts, each book giving a simple explanation of the topic and offering suggestions for related activities. Her books are *Weighing and Balancing* (illustrated by Aliki; Crowell, 1970), *Computers* (illustrated by James McCrea and Ruth McCrea; Crowell, 1972), *Statistics* (Crowell, 1973), *Area* (Crowell, 1974), *Averages* (illustrated by Aliki; Crowell, 1975), *Number Families* (Crowell, 1979), and *Spaces, Shapes and Sizes* (Crowell, 1980). *Residence:* West Vancouver, British Columbia, Canada.

STANLEY, Diane 1943-
(Diane Zuromskis)

PERSONAL: Born December 27, 1943, in Abilene, Tex.; daughter of Onia Burton Stanley, Jr. (a U.S. Navy captain) and Fay (a writer; maiden name, Grissom) Stanley; married Peter Zuromskis, May 30, 1970 (divorced, 1979); married Peter Vennema (a corporation president), September 8, 1979; children: (first marriage) Catherine, Tamara; (second marriage) John Leslie. *Education:* Trinity University, B.A., 1965; attended Edinburgh College of Art, 1966-67; Johns Hopkins University, M.A., 1970. *Politics:* Democrat. *Religion:* Episcopalian. *Home and office:* 2120 Tangley, Houston, Tex. 77005.

CAREER: Author and illustrator of books for children. Free-lance medical illustrator, 1970-74; Dell Publishing, New York, N.Y., graphic designer, 1977; G. P. Putnam's Sons and Coward, McCann & Geoghegan, New York, N.Y., art director of children's books, 1977-79. *Awards, honors: The Farmer in the Dell* was a children's choice book in a selection sponsored by the International Reading Association, 1979.

WRITINGS: Fiddle-I-Fee: A Traditional American Chant (Junior Literary Guild selection; self-illustrated), Little, Brown, 1979; The Conversation Club (Junior Literary Guild selection; self-illustrated), Macmillan, 1983.

Illustrator; all for children: (Under name Diane Zuromskis) *The Farmer in the Dell*, Little, Brown, 1978; (under name Diane Stanley Zuromskis) Verna Aardema, *Half-a-Ball-of-Kenki: An Ashanti Tale Retold*, F. Warne, 1979; Tony Johnston, *Little Mouse Nibbling*, Putnam, 1979; M. Jean Craig, *The Man Whose Name Was Not Thomas*, Doubleday, 1981; Toni Hormann,

Onions, Onions, Crowell, 1981; Giambattista Basile, *Petrosinella, a Neopolitan Rapunzel,* translated by John E. Taylor, F. Warne, 1981; Jane Yolen, *Sleeping Ugly* (Junior Literary Guild selection), Coward, 1981; Jean Marzollo and Claudio Marzollo, *Robin of Bray,* Dial, 1982; Joanne Ryder, *Beach Party,* Warne, 1982; James Whitcomb Riley, *Little Orphant Annie,* Putnam, 1983; Samuel Marshak, *The Month Brothers: A Slavic Tale,* translated by Thomas P. Whitney, Morrow, 1983; James Skofield, *All Wet! All Wet!* (Junior Literary Guild selection), Harper, 1984.

WORK IN PROGRESS: A Country Tale for Macmillan.

SIDELIGHTS: "I always loved to draw and paint. I remember the awe I felt when I saw my first fine art museum (the National Gallery) when I was sixteen. But I didn't consider art as a career until after college. Looking for a field that was appropriate to my detailed, realistic, miniaturist approach to art, I chose medical illustration. One of my art instuctors strongly urged against it. He said it wasn't creative enough, but I saw no place for my skills in the mainstream of fine art.

"My training in Scotland, and later at Johns Hopkins, was oriented towards classical drawing and painting. At Hopkins we did pen-and-ink work using fine cross-hatching and 'eyelashing.' We used a delicate dry brush watercolor technique which I later used in *Petrosinella.* After several years of freelancing as a medical illustrator, I discovered the world of children's books—through my own baby daughter. I was so impressed by the exciting variety and fine craftsmanship in the field. I remembered my love for books as a child. I knew exactly what I wanted to do, and haven't had a doubt since. I spent a year preparing an appropriate portfolio, and got my first book contract in 1976, from Little, Brown. I have been busy with books ever since.

"I try to approach each new book in a manner which suits the story. Consequently, my books are quite different from one another. This is also because I'm still experimenting with new styles and techniques. I think my best work has a sentimental quality to it. As a child I loved fantasy—but mine was more a fantasy of things as they ought to be. I don't think sentimentality needs to be patronizing, though it is often simplistic. It comes of a desire for order and beauty in the world, and is a mild sort of fantasy. It does not have to be trite. I love drawing characters (the witches in *Petrosinella,* the animated mush in *Kenki,* the trolls in *Robin of Bray*). I have a difficult time with 'ideal beauty,' which has no character to grasp on to.

"I often wish I had had a picturesque upbringing, instead of a modern suburban one. I have to do a lot of research for my

(From *Fiddle-I-Fee: A Traditional American Chant.* Illustrated by Diane Stanley.)

DIANE STANLEY

books, which invariably have a country, period setting. Whenever I travel I try to observe such things as how thatched roofs are put together, how period houses are furnished, etc. I love beautifully designed books and enjoy such extras as ornaments and initial caps. I basically love my work—though it is lonely at times. I feel lucky to earn a living doing something so full of delight!''

SUGARMAN, Tracy 1921-

PERSONAL: Born November 14, 1921, in Syracuse, N.Y.; son of David (a lawyer) and Golda (Sophian) Sugarman; married June Feldman (a worker in inter-group relations), September 24, 1943; children: Richard Steven, Laurie Ellen. *Education:* Syracuse University, B.F.A., 1943. *Politics:* Democrat. *Religion:* Jewish. *Home:* 21 Owenoke Park, Westport, Conn. 06880. *Office:* Rediscovery Productions, Inc., 2 Halfmile Common, Westport, Conn. 06880.

CAREER: Free-lance illustrator, beginning in 1945, work has appeared in many national magazines, including *Ladies' Home Journal, McCall's, Esquire,* and *Saturday Evening Post;* also illustrator for William Morrow and Co., Simon & Schuster, Doubleday & Co., and other publishing houses, pictorial reportage for American industry and governmental agencies; Rediscovery Productions, Inc. (educational documentary film producers), Westport, Conn., co-founder, writer, and producer, 1969—. *Military service:* U.S. Navy, 1943-45; small-boat officer in Normandy Invasion; became lieutenant junior

grade. *Member:* Society of Illustrators, American Association for the United Nations (past president, Westport chapter), Westport Artists Association (past president).

WRITINGS: Stranger at the Gates, Hill & Wang, 1966.

Illustrator: Emma Gelders Sterne, *I Have a Dream,* Knopf, 1965; Marilyn Sachs, *Amy and Laura,* Doubleday, 1966; Carol F. Drisko and Edgar A. Toppin, *The Unfinished March,* Doubleday, 1967; Joan Gill, *Hush, Jon!,* Doubleday, 1968; Philip Sterling and Maria Brau, *The Quiet Rebels,* Zenith, 1968; Ann McGovern, *Robin Hood of Sherwood Forest,* Scholastic Book Services, 1970; Alberta Eiseman and Nicole Eiseman, *Gift from a Sheep: The Story of How Wool Is Made,* Atheneum, 1979.

Also illustrator of six documentary films for CBS-TV, including "How Beautiful on the Mountains," and more than thirty documentary films for Rediscovery Productions, including "Never Turn Back, The Life of Fannie Lou Harner," PBS-TV, 1983, and "The Time Has Come," PBS-TV, 1983. Contributor of articles to *American Artist, Vista Volunteer,* and U.S. Information Agency publication.

Daisy Bates nodded silently. She was trying to decide on the next move. The "Battle of Little Rock" was just beginning. ■ (From *I Have a Dream* by Emma Gelders Sterne. Illustrated by Tracy Sugarman.)

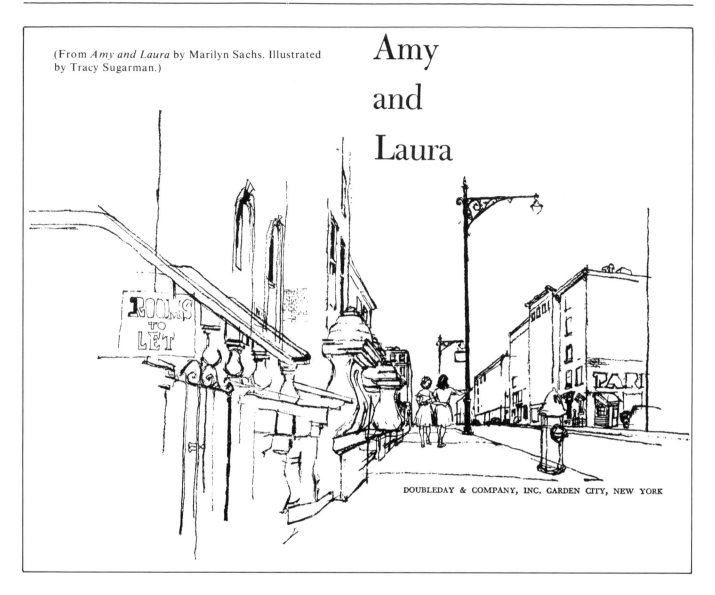

(From *Amy and Laura* by Marilyn Sachs. Illustrated by Tracy Sugarman.)

Amy
and
Laura

DOUBLEDAY & COMPANY, INC. GARDEN CITY, NEW YORK

SIDELIGHTS: Sugarman participated in the Mississippi Summer Project in 1964, and has since been "deeply involved" in the civil rights movement as a lecturer and worker.

SUTHERLAND, Zena B(ailey)   1915-

PERSONAL: Born September 17, 1915, in Winthrop, Mass.; daughter of Jacob and Lena (Baum) Karras; married Roland Bailey, December 19, 1937 (marriage ended, 1961); married Alec Sutherland (employed by British Broadcasting Corp.), July 30, 1964; children: Stephen, Thomas, Katherine (Mrs. Thomas Linehan). *Education:* University of Chicago, B.A., 1937, M.A., 1966. *Politics:* Independent. *Religion:* Unitarian-Universalist. *Home:* 1418 East 57th St., Chicago, Ill. 60637. *Office:* 1100 East 57th St., Chicago, Ill. 60637.

CAREER: Bulletin of the Center for Children's Books, Chicago, Ill., editor, 1958—; University of Chicago, Chicago, lecturer, 1972-77, associate professor of library science, 1977—. Consultant to National Broadcasting Co. (NBC), 1968-71, and Museum of Science and Industry. *Member:* International Research Society for Children's Literature, International Reading Association, International Board on Books for Young People,

Women's National Book Association, American Library Association (member of board of directors, 1977-80), National Council of Teachers of English, Authors League of America, Mensa, Children's Reading Round Table, Children's Literature Association, Authors Guild, University Women's Club of London, Colony Club, University of Chicago Service League, Society of Midland Authors, Beta Phi Mu, Quadrangle Club (member of board of directors, 1976-79). *Awards, honors:* Phi Delta Kappa award, 1973, and Pi Lambda Theta award for best educational book, 1974, both for *Children and Books;* annual award from Children's Reading Round Table, 1978, for contributions in the field of children's literature; Zena Sutherland Lectureship Fund established, at the University of Chicago, 1981.

WRITINGS: History in Children's Books, McKinley Publishing, 1967; (with May Hill Arbuthnot and Dianne L. Monson) *Children and Books* (illustrated by Charles Mikolaycak), 4th edition (Sutherland was not associated with earlier editions), Scott, Foresman, 1972, 6th edition, 1981; (editor) *The Best in Children's Books: The University of Chicago Guide to Children's Literature, 1966-1972,* University of Chicago Press, 1973; (editor) *The Arbuthnot Anthology of Children's Literature* (illustrated by M. Arbuthnot), 4th edition (Sutherland was not associated with earlier editions), Scott, Foresman, 1976;

(From *Children and Books,* sixth edition, by Zena Sutherland, Dianne L. Monson and May Hill Arbuthnot. Illustrated by Charles Mikolaycak.)

ZENA B. SUTHERLAND

(editor) *Burning Bright*, Open Court, 1979; (editor) *Close to the Sun*, Open Court, 1979; (editor) *Spirit of the Wind*, Open Court, 1979; (editor) *The Arbuthnot Honor Lectures*, American Library Association, 1980; (compiler) *Nursery Rhymes, Songs and Stories* (juvenile), Lodestar Books, 1980; (editor) *The Best in Children's Books: The University of Chicago Guide to Children's Literature, 1973-1978*, University of Chicago Press, 1980; *Children and Libraries*, University of Chicago Press, 1981; (editor with Myra C. Livingston) *The Scott, Foresman Anthology of Children's Literature* (juvenile), Scott, Foresman, 1983.

Contributor to *World Book Encyclopedia, Britannica Junior, American Library Association Yearbook, Children's Books International, International Board on Books for Young People Congress Proceedings*, and *Compton Encyclopedia Yearbook*. Contributor to magazines for adults and children, including *Modern Realistic Stories for Children and Young People, Children's Literature in Education*, and library journals. Contributing editor of *Saturday Review*, 1972-77; children's book editor of *Chicago Tribune*, 1977—.

WORK IN PROGRESS: A history of American children's literature for Rabén & Sjögren; *Children and Books*, 7th edition.

SIDELIGHTS: "One of my major interests is making *good* films from *good* books; I am now consultant for a Britannica program to that end. I am also interested in the exchange and

translation of international children's literature. I have served on international juries which honor books for children, traveling to many European countries and Iran. I consider *Children and Books* my major work. My co-author [May Hill Arbuthnot] died many years ago and the book carries her name (always will), but it expresses all my passionate concern and my ideas about what ought to be taught at the college level about children's literature."

TANNEN, Mary 1943-

PERSONAL: Born June 2, 1943, in New London, Conn.; daughter of Matthew W. (an educator) and Doris (Beal) Gaffney; married Michael Tannen (a lawyer), June 25, 1965; children: Catherine, Noah. *Education:* Attended William Smith College, 1961-63; Barnard College, B.A., 1965. *Home and office:* 90 Riverside Dr., New York, N.Y. 10024.

CAREER: Men's Wear, New York City, copy writer, 1965; *Popular Mechanics*, New York City, in promotion, 1965-66; *Show*, New York City, copy writer, 1966-67; Avon Products, New York City, copy writer, 1967-70.

WRITINGS: The Wizard Children of Finn (juvenile; illustrated by John Burgoyne), Knopf, 1981; *The Lost Legend of Finn* (juvenile; illustrated by Michael Hostovich), Knopf, 1982;

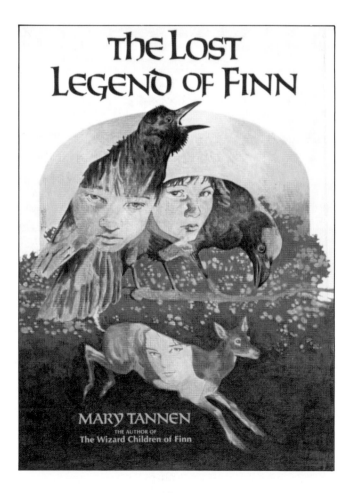

(Jacket painting by Troy Howell from *The Lost Legend of Finn* by Mary Tannen.)

MARY TANNEN

Huntley Nutley and the Missing Link (illustrated by Rob Sauber), Knopf, 1983.

WORK IN PROGRESS: A contemporary novel; a juvenile book.

SIDELIGHTS: "Although I've lived most of my adult years in the heart of New York City, I grew up in a country town in western New York State. Because the town was small and our family was large, I had the good fortune of not being looked after too closely. By the age of five, I could walk to school, to the playground, uptown to get a popsicle, and best of all, down to the wild ravine at the end of our backyard. There, the Oatka Creek ran through what was probably a few acres of scrub brush. To me, it looked like miles of untracked wilderness. It was the memory of this wild ravine that inspired me to write *Huntley Nutley and the Missing Link*.

"Coming from a long line of recorders on both sides of my family, (genealogists, historians, teachers, and preachers), I inherited the urge to write. Writing is my way of saving bits and pieces of life. When I write, impressions from childhood—the sound of a screen door slamming on a summer night, the feel of a frog in the palm of the hand, the whispers of children hiding in the hedges—come back with strangely disproportionate power.

"My work habits are probably as bad as anyone's. I'm at the typewriter whenever I have time, usually a few hours every day. Most of what I put down is between me and the waste-basket, as I do countless numbers of drafts.

"I think anyone who wants to write should go ahead and do it. It's a way of responding to life, like dancing, or throwing

pots, or spinning deals. I wasted many years not daring to write because I was afraid I wouldn't like what I wrote. Finally, the urge to join my voice to the great babble of humanity overcame my fear or modesty. Now I'm so happy at my work that I think only old age and debilitating infirmities will stop me.

"I do have strong beliefs, but I'm not given to aphorisms. I guess that's why I enjoy writing fiction, because the ideas I hold most sacred can seep up out of the story, to be recognized, or not, by the reader. In fact, I'm often surprised myself by what comes to the surface.

"*The Wizard Children of Finn* and *The Lost Legend of Finn* were written purely to entertain children. It was only after I had finished them that I realized the books had to do with a family: the relationships of the members to each other, and the ties that bind them to their ancestors."

TESTER, Sylvia Root   1939-

BRIEF ENTRY: Born October 6, 1939. A free-lance writer and author of over forty children's books, Tester attended Cincinnati Bible College and Elgin Community College. She began her career in publishing as an assistant editor for Standard Publishing Co. from 1959 to 1960. In 1963 she went to David C. Cook Publishing Co. where she eventually became school products editor in 1968. She left publishing to write free-lance between 1974 and 1977, returning again in 1977 as an editor with The Child's World Inc. A born-again Christian, Tester has written books dealing with her faith. Her early works include *Jesus Lives* (Standard Publishing, 1963), *God's Children Help* (David Cook, 1964), and *But I Can't See Him* (David Cook, 1966). She also wrote *The World into Which Jesus Came* (Child's World, 1982), which describes the people, customs, laws, and politics of the Jewish people of Jesus's time. Other books by Tester are *My Friend the Doctor* (David Cook, 1967), *Billy's Basketball* (Children's Press, 1976), *Opposite Odelia: A Book of Antonyms* (Children's Press, 1978), *We Laughed a Lot: My First Day of School* (Children's Press, 1979), *Magic Monsters Learn about Weather* (Child's World, 1980), and *Learning about Ghosts* (Child's World, 1981). *Home:* 1001 Cedar St., Elgin, Ill. 60120. *For More Information See: Contemporary Authors, New Revision Series*, Volume 8, Gale, 1983.

THAYER, Marjorie

BRIEF ENTRY: Author of children's plays and novels. Prior to writing for children, Thayer worked as promotion director of Knopf's juvenile department from 1951 to 1955 and as juvenile editor for Prentice-Hall beginning in 1955. She was also associated with Funk & Wagnalls and Doubleday, and owned and operated a bookstore in Whittier, Calif., among other jobs. Her eight books for young people include the plays *The Halloween Witch* (Golden Gate, 1976), *The Valentine Box* (Golden Gate, 1977), *The First Day of School* (Golden Gate, 1977), *The April Foolers* (illustrated by Don Freeman; Golden Gate, 1978), and *A Mother for Mother's Day* (Golden Gate, 1980). Among her juvenile novels are *Climbing the Sun: The Story of a Hopi Indian Boy* (written with Elizabeth Emanuel and illustrated by Anne Siberell; Dodd, 1980) and *The Youngest* (illustrated by Dale Payson; Dodd, 1982). The latter is the "almost all real" story of nine-year-old Margie Thornton, a tom-boy growing up on a California ranch during World War

I. Thayer also wrote *The Christmas Strangers* (illustrated by Don Freeman; Golden Gate, 1976). *Residence:* Los Angeles, Calif. *For More Information See: Publishers Weekly,* October 29, 1955.

TROUGHTON, Joanna (Margaret)   1947-

PERSONAL: Born September 9, 1947, in London, England; daughter of Patrick (an actor) and Margaret Troughton. *Education:* Hornsey College of Art, N.D.A.D. (first class honors), 1969. *Residence:* London, England. *Agent:* B. L. Kearley Ltd., 13 Chiltern St., London W1M 1HE, England.

CAREER: Free-lance illustrator for advertising, television, magazines, and books, 1969—; Harrow School of Art, Middlesex, England, teacher of illustration, 1975—. Part-time teacher of graphics at Barnet College of Art, 1979. *Awards, honors:* Kate Greenaway Medal commendation, 1976, for *How the Birds Changed Their Feathers.*

WRITINGS—All for children; all published by Blackie & Son, except as noted: (Reteller) *Sir Gawain and the Loathly Damsel,* Dutton, 1972; *Soldier, Soldier, Won't You Marry Me?,* 1972; *Spotted Horse,* 1972; (reteller) *Why Flies Buzz: A Nigerian Folk Tale,* 1974; (adapter) *The Story of Rama and Sita,* 1975, British Book Center, 1978; (reteller) *How the Birds Changed Their Feathers,* 1976; (reteller) *What Made Tiddalik Laugh,* 1977; *How Rabbit Stole the Fire,* 1979; *Tortoise's Dream,* 1980; *The Magic Mill,* 1981; *The Wizard Punchkin,* 1982; *Blue-Jay and Robin,* 1983; *Mouse-Deer's Market,* 1984.

Illustrator; all for children: Greta James, *The Bodhi Tree,* Geoffrey Chapman, 1971; *The Little Mohee: An Appalachian Ballad,* Dutton, 1971; Kevin Crossley-Holland, *The Sea Stranger,* Heinemann, 1972, Seabury, 1974; Barbara S. Briggs, *Cookery Corner Cards,* Mills & Boon, 1973; Geoffrey Trease, *Days to Remember: A Garland of Historic Anniversaries,* Heinemann, 1973; Jenny Taylor and Terry Ingleby, *The Scope Storybook* (illustrated with Andrew Sier and Barry Wilkinson), Longman, 1974; K. Crossley-Holland, *The Fire-Brother,* Seabury, 1975; Elizabeth Kyle (pseudonym of Agnes Mary Robertson Dun-

lop), *The Key of the Castle,* Heinemann, 1976; K. Crossley-Holland, *The Earth-Father,* Heinemann, 1976; Sheila K. McCullagh, *The Kingdom under the Sea,* Hulton, 1976; James Reeves, reteller, *Quest and Conquest: "Pilgrim's Progress" Retold,* Blackie & Son, 1976; Richard Blythe, *Fabulous Beasts* (illustrated with Fiona French), Macdonald Educational, 1977, published as *Dragons and Other Fabulous Beasts,* Grosset, 1980; Julia Dobson, *The Smallest Man in England,* Heinemann, 1977; John D. Lincoln, *Montezuma,* Cambridge University Press, 1977; J. D. Lincoln, *The Fair-Skinned Strangers,* Cambridge University Press, 1977; Wendy Body, *Clay Horses,* Longman, 1979; Robert Nye, *Out of the World and Back Again,* Collins, 1979; Adele Geras, *A Thousand Yards of Sea,* Hodder & Stoughton, 1979; Gillian Wrobel, reteller, *Ali Baba and the Forty Thieves,* Macdonald Educational, 1979; Michael Pollard, *My World* (illustrated with Kim Blundell), Macdonald Educational, 1979; J. Taylor and T. Ingleby, *Ganpat's Long Ride [and] Shanti and the Snake,* Longman, 1979; Anna Sproule, reteller, *Warriors,* Macdonald Educational, 1980; A. Sproule, *Villains,* Macdonald Educational, 1980; Patricia Daniels, reteller, *Ali Baba and the Forty Thieves,* Raintree, 1980; Gail Robinson, *Raven the Trickster: Legends of the North American Indians,* Chatto & Windus, 1981, Atheneum, 1982.

ADAPTATIONS: "What Made Tiddalik Laugh," was produced as a film for the "Words and Pictures" series for the British Broadcasting Corp. (BBC).

SIDELIGHTS: "From an early age I always wanted to be an illustrator. At seventeen I went to Hornsey College of Art to study graphic design, where I took the National Diploma in Art and Design with First Class Honours. After leaving college, I became a free-lance illustrator. So far I have written and illustrated . . . picture books, and I have also done a variety of illustrative work for advertising, magazines and publishing. I also teach illustration one day a week at Harrow School of Art in Middlesex. My main interest is mythology, folklore and fairy tales, from which I obtain most of my ideas for picture books. Apart from this, my other great interest is in the theater. My father and two brothers are all actors." [Lee Kingman and others, compilers, *Illustrators of Children's Books: 1967-1976,* Horn Book, 1978.]

As he dodged and darted through the forest of legs he met with a number of hazards. ■ (From *The Smallest Man in England* by Julia Dobson. Illustrated by Joanna Troughton.)

"Although I retell myths and legends from all around the world, my favorite areas for stories are North and South America. I'm not sure if this is because the myths were collected in these areas at just the right time, that is before they became too 'civilized,' or whether it is simply that the Indians' stories are so good! They also have the best 'trickster' stories in the world—a group of myths that particularly fascinates me. I suppose that mythology inspires me because it is made up of 'archetypes.' And the study of mythology leads to other areas that interest me—ethnology, ethology, anthropology, etc. I am also very inspired by 'primitive' art.

"The medium I work in is watercolor; I may use other bits and pieces with this (for example, crayon and gouache), but watercolor is my favorite. For line work, I use pen and change the nib size to suit the illustration."

HOBBIES AND OTHER INTERESTS: Reading, talking, and walking.

TUNIS, John R(oberts)   1889-1975

PERSONAL: Born December 7, 1889, in Boston, Mass.; died February 4, 1975, in Essex, Conn.; son of John Arthur (a parson) and Caroline Greene (a teacher; maiden name, Roberts) Tunis, married Lucy Rogers. *Education:* Harvard University, A.B., 1911. *Home:* Stanford Hill Rd., Essex, Conn.

CAREER: Sportswriter, *New York Evening Post,* 1925-32, Universal Service, 1932-35; broadcaster of tennis matches for National Broadcasting Co., 1934-42; writer. *Military service:* Served in France during World War I. *Awards, honors: New York Herald Tribune* Spring Book Festival Award, 1938, for *The Iron Duke,* honor book, 1940, for *The Kid from Tomkinsville,* 1948, for *Highpockets,* and 1949, for *Son of the Valley;* Child Study Children's Book Award, 1943, for *Keystone Kids;* Junior Book Award from Boys' Club of America, 1949, for *Highpockets.*

*WRITINGS—*For young readers: *The Iron Duke* (illustrated by Johann Bull), Harcourt, 1938; *The Duke Decides* (illustrated by James MacDonald), Harcourt, 1939; *Champion's Choice* (illustrated by Jay Hyde Barnum), Harcourt, 1940; *The Kid from Tomkinsville* (illustrated by J. H. Barnum), Harcourt, 1940; *World Series,* Harcourt, 1941; *All-American* (illustrated by Hans Walleen), Harcourt, 1942; *Million-Miler: The Story of an Air Pilot,* Messner, 1942; *Keystone Kids,* Harcourt, 1943; *Rookie of the Year,* Harcourt, 1944; *Yea! Wildcats!,* Harcourt, 1944; *A City for Lincoln,* Harcourt, 1945; *The Kid Comes Back,* Morrow, 1946; *Highpockets* (illustrated by Charles Beck), Morrow, 1948 (also see below); *Son of the Valley,* Morrow, 1949; *Young Razzle,* Morrow, 1949.

The Other Side of the Fence, Morrow, 1953; *Go, Team, Go!,* Morrow, 1954 (also see below); *Buddy and the Old Pro* (illustrated by J. H. Barnum), Morrow, 1955; *Schoolboy Johnson,* Morrow, 1958; *Silence over Dunkerque,* Morrow, 1962; *His Enemy, His Friend,* Morrow, 1967; *Two by Tunis: Highpockets* [*and*] *Go, Team, Go!,* Morrow, 1972; *Grand National,* Morrow, 1973.

Other: *$port$, Heroics, and Hysterics,* John Day, 1928; *American Girl* (novel), Brewer & Warren, 1930; *Was College Worth While?,* Harcourt, 1936; *Choosing a College,* Harcourt, 1940; *Sport for the Fun of It,* A. S. Barnes, 1940, 2nd revised edition,

JOHN R. TUNIS

Ronald, 1958; *Democracy and Sport,* A. S. Barnes, 1941; *This Writing Game: Selections from Twenty Years of Free-Lancing,* A. S. Barnes, 1941; *Lawn Games,* A. S. Barnes, 1943; *The American Way in Sport,* Duell, Sloan & Pearce, 1958; *A Measure of Independence* (autobiography), Atheneum, 1964.

Contributor of more than two thousand articles to magazines, including *Collier's, Esquire, Reader's Digest, New Yorker,* and *Saturday Evening Post.*

ADAPTATIONS: "Hard, Fast and Beautiful" (movie), RKO.

SIDELIGHTS: **December 7, 1889.** Born in Boston, Massachusetts. "I am the product of a parson and a teacher. Any such person is forever trying to reform or to educate, himself if nobody else. This is an overwhelming inheritance, and a wonderful inheritance, too. My parents gave me faith, that strange, elusive thing. Faith has always been a part of me, faith in the great land of my birth, faith in Jefferson's dream of a democratic society, but especially faith in the individual, faith that man is free to shape his own destiny.

"It was a clear, sunny morning, so I've been told by my mother, when I was born in the large, yellow, two-family house on Harvard Street, Cambridgeport, where my father had charge of the Unitarian parish. The parson was an important figure in those days, and folks were sincerely and acutely interested in him and in his family.

"'Tomorrow is your birthday,' my mother wrote me many years later. 'You had an auspicious beginning. Never did a child come into this world with more rejoicing. We put you in your bassinet in a room, your Auntie Tite at the door, while a steady stream of callers walked around you for three days. There are just a few moments which bring back my past so vividly. This is one of them. Life seemed so full of hope and promise. If your father and I had been magicians, we would not have wished nor planned more for you.'

"My father, my mother, my grandfather Roberts—this was our household at my birth. Although I cannot reconstruct the life of my parents, I do know their background and part of their story. When my mother later wrote in her letter that 'life seemed so full of promise and hope,' I know this was the way she felt toward life. For she and my father had a vast store of courage and a cheerful, undaunted faith. If I am sure of anything it is the happiness of that small household." [John Tunis, *A Measure of Independence*, Atheneum, 1964.[1]]

1896. Father died. "Death is a difficult acquaintance for a six-year-old boy to make. My brother and I looked at my mother. She looked back at us, and as she wrote many years afterward, 'It was you and Roberts who had lost more than I. That was my most poignant thought as I held you there on my knees that morning. My own loss was as nothing compared with yours.'

"We sat there, thinking, wondering. Our father dead? Then we would never see him again, we asked my mother. No, never, she replied, her tearless eyes staring at us with sorrow and affection. No, we would never see him again. Suddenly we both began to cry, for he was real and close to us, especially to me.

"Although I know little about my father and remember less, I do know he was a good person and a devoted priest. . . .

"If my mother gave me many things, my father must have bequeathed me his zeal for independence in life, for making his way as he wished. He was himself an independent operator. When he made a mistake, he did not in the least mind admitting it publicly. My experience is most men are able to resist this temptation.

"Some years after, as a boy in Boston, I was with my mother at a reception when we were introduced to Bishop William Lawrence of Massachusetts. He caught my mother's name. 'Tunis?' he asked. 'Ah . . . the widow of John Tunis, that wonderful man!'

"Most older persons who had known my father were more fatuous. Usually they made the same remark, always addressed to the small boy or the embarrassed young man in his teens: 'I hope you'll be as good a man as your father.'

"Quite obviously there was no answer. This highly unoriginal remark, usually uttered in an unctuous manner, not merely filled me with loathing, but silenced me completely. Inwardly I determined not to be as good as my father, but to be thoroughly bad. I later found both these ambitions difficult of achievement."[1]

Fall, 1896. ". . . We moved from Millbrook to New York City where my mother had obtained a position teaching in the Brearley School for girls on the East Side. . . . So our household was my mother, grandfather, my brother and myself. We lived mostly on the third floor of the house. After teaching all morning my mother returned to more work, with three persons to look after. Each day after lunch she taught us our lessons, and insisted we do certain assigned work in the mornings. . . .

"Before her marriage my mother had, as a teacher, read about and studied the Montessori method. Dr. Maria Montessori, the first Italian woman doctor and perhaps the first of the so-called progressive educators, was the exponent of new ways of instructing young children, a method depending upon the self-motivation of the pupil. After studying by this method for only a few months we had no trouble with words, and reading became simple. One just read, that was all.'"[1]

1899. Moved to Cambridge, Massachusetts. "My mother had two articles of faith; first, that we should be brought up in the church of our father, and second, attend Harvard, his college. The flaw in this was that the Episcopal Church had not always been his, and that City College in New York was the real foundation of his intellectual life. However, inconsistencies of this sort never bothered her in the least.

"Perhaps her one fixation about us was that we should be educated. Education was her whole being, she believed in it with a passion that not many persons have for anything today. It was a source with her. She held it with both hands, cherished it. That we should receive an education also was her principal aim in life, all her energies were bent toward that goal, to this end she dedicated her tremendous determination. Of course we were going to college! Of course we were going to Harvard! The only question was how.

"With this aim in view . . . she packed our shaggy furniture and along with her father and her two sons moved to Cambridge. There, she felt sure, we would be near the well of education and all its advantages. Without hesitation she rented half a frame house at 47A Irving Street. Irving was a wide, tranquil street in those days, shaded with elms and maples, and the small house of six rooms was a ten- or fifteen-minute walk from the Harvard Yard. There was a reason for this proximity. She planned to support us all by setting up an eating house.

"Obviously with the boarding house to run, the marketing to do with my grandfather—he also assisted the colored girl with the cooking—she had little time to devote to her sons. For she was feeding in all from thirty to forty hungry undergraduates three times a day, which meant constant and unremitting labor. I can see her standing in the hall greeting most of them by name as they entered in a whirl of snow, tossing hats and coats on the big table at one side. During meals she was continually in and out of the kitchen, for she was a good cook herself and knew food as well as anyone.

"My mother's busy existence threw our education into disarray. After some thought, she hit upon an idea to educate us at no cost to herself. The trick was simple. She was located at the fount of learning; why not take advantage of it? By offering three meals daily in her eating house, which was acquiring a reputation for excellent, low-priced food, she found herself in a position to secure competent tutors for her two sons. It is true, these tutors were mostly impecunious young men studying for a master's or a doctorate at the College, and were carefully chosen by the help of the Dean's office.'"[1]

1904. "The family fortunes were not . . . on an upward curve. Except for Mr. Cesar Ritz and Mr. Conrad Hilton, nobody since time was has ever made more than a stingy living out of an eating house. Since my mother dispensed good food, she was no exception to the general rule. . . .

"Accordingly we went downhill from 47A Irving to a cheaper house in a brick block on Kirkland Street nearby, then after a year to a three-story walk-up at 23 Wendell Street, above and on the wrong side of Harvard Square. In those days it was important to live on the right side of the Square, although

What would he do in the pitcher's place—shoot it over, of course. This was the one, the one to hit.... ■ (From *The Kid from Tomkinsville* by John R. Tunis. Illustrated by Jay Hyde Barnum.)

naturally it was a matter of indiffence to our family. The house was a wooden structure, and in the flat below four nurses shared bedrooms when off duty and resting between cases. Occupying the ground floor was an elderly couple who must often have shuddered as my brother and I banged the front door and raced up the hard wood stairs to the top floor. There the shaggy furniture was getting shaggier. . . . Of course my brother and I couldn't have cared less, but I realize now we were certainly not in the money those days.

"Because the steady income from the Grotonians was finished, my mother turned again to teaching. As New York was the largest Jewish city on earth, Boston was at the time the largest Irish city, and the public schools were in the hands of the politicians, among whom was John F. (Honey Fitz) Fitzgerald, grandfather of former President John F. Kennedy. My mother passionately denounced these politicians who milked the schools.

"Boston did not then recognize a New York teaching certificate. Therefore she was unable to receive a regular appointment, something that would have happened automatically had she known the right people. But nobody helped her or realized or perhaps even knew she was a widow with two boys and an old man to support. Consequently she did a full day's work as a substitute teacher in different grades and different classes, in different schools as far away as the outskirts of Dorchester and South Boston, never knowing one week where she would be teaching, or whom, the next week. Worst of all, as a substitute she received less pay than regularly appointed teachers.

"The regime of the tutors having ended, my brother Roberts and I, then perhaps twelve and fourteen, were entered in the Cambridge Latin School, a free public high school, filled up with smart, eager boys and girls. In geography, reading and history we were far ahead of our classmates. But in Latin and English we were nowhere, and we couldn't multiply seven by nine correctly. I was having my teeth straightened, and was suffering, and to make everything worse we both lacked any discipline in work. We simply did not know how to apply ourselves. The standards of Cambridge Latin like those of Boston Latin were high; therefore Roberts and I faced a stern test in class. There was also an amount of homework that presented unsurmountable difficulties."[1]

1907. ". . . I was . . . ready for college—or let me put it correctly; I had been admitted to Harvard with a condition in freshman English. . . .

"Why did my mother's feverish desire for an education as well as her vast and consuming intellectual curiosity never rub off on me? It is hard to say. Yet I had been brought up in an atmosphere of books and exposed to learning from an early age. One must admit that I stubbornly resisted all attempts at that period to educate me. . . . I possessed no intellectual disciplines, being ignorant, lazy and uninterested. I seldom applied myself seriously, nor indeed did I know how. Moreover, I was immature, shy, all too often, I realize, frightened of my professors. . . .

"What did interest me in college? Two things, athletics and the theater, in which I had been indoctrinated by my mother as a boy. Once on my own the theater became a passion. It opened up a new world, the world then termed 'frenzied finance,' the world of romance and love, the world of girls and songs and make-believe. In those days anyone who visited the Boston theater could hardly lose. For 25 cents you had an excellent seat in the front row of the second balcony, or, if your feet were as good as mine, stood in the rear of the theater. Many times after standing three hours through a long musical, I trudged back to Cambridge in rain or snow because of lack of carfare. Often I went without breakfast, occasionally without warm clothes, but during those four years I managed to visit the world of the theater two or three times weekly.

"During those early years as an undergraduate I grew slowly apart from my brother, and we never recaptured that closeness of our early years. Perhaps this was inevitable. He entered with the class of Robert Whittemore, our boyhood friend, when I was a junior. Later on, he became a private in the army; I was an officer. Afterward he stayed in Boston; I left. I married, he remained a bachelor. He never changed his politics, but stayed a conservative and a Republican, whereas I deserted the party in which I had been reared. We were ever close, affectionate and loving; but we began to see life differently and never felt those ties of boyhood again."[1]

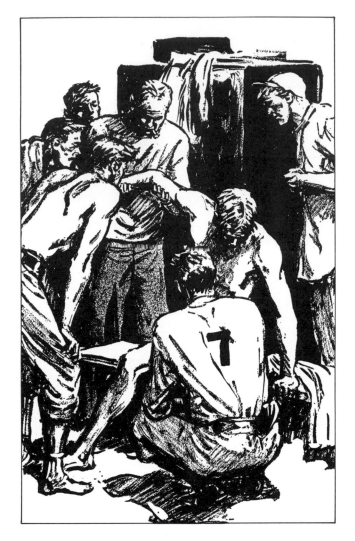

"Is it okay, Doc? Is it okay?" ■ (From *The Kid from Tomkinsville* by John R. Tunis. Illustrated by Jay Hyde Barnum.)

1911. Received an A.B. degree from Harvard. "Picture a young man with no training, no business experience, without any special talent or ability trying to obtain work in a city such as Boston where little existed even for those with something to offer. I was of no use to any prospective employer, and most employers had the good sense to realize this on sight. Inasmuch as I recognized it myself, I had no confidence or assurance facing businessmen. I did not know how one went about securing a job, where to turn next, who to see, even what business, if any, I wanted to enter.

"Finally, thanks to the Reverend Prescott Evarts, the rector of Christ Church, Cambridge, I secured a place in a cotton mill in Newburyport, Massachusetts, north of Boston. The cotton business was flourishing at the time in New England, and this position was regarded as letting me in on a particularly good thing. The general idea was that I should 'learn the business from the ground up.' Thirty-five years later, John P. Marquand was to use Newburyport as the setting for one of his most famous books, *Point of No Return.*

"After about a year and a half of Newburyport and the mill, it slowly penetrated that I would be no asset to the cotton

business, nor did I really want to be. So . . . I started looking for work in Boston."[1]

1913. "I entered the Boston University Law School the middle of the year. About the only thing I got there was an acute interest in a Vassar graduate with nice ankles named Lucy Rogers."[1]

Tunis eventually married Lucy Rogers. During World War I he was called into active service in the Army. "My next few years were spent in and out of the Army of the United States. I did not enjoy them. When this country entered the war I went to the Plattsburg Training Camp, where I received a commission. Following a summer at Camp Upton, Long Island, and a winter in Jacksonville, Florida, I was ordered to France. Although I finally persuaded Lucy Rogers to marry me, I could not find time in which to get married. When I took that transport in Hoboken I had been married less than a week.

"My service in the Army was surely undistinguished. . . ."[1]

1919. "By mid-summer . . . the war over, I had returned to the United States, and Lucy and I were living in an old, white-painted clapboard house on top of a hill in a town called Winchendon, Massachusetts, close to the New Hampshire line.

"Immediately I began to write in earnest. . . . Brash, ignorant, unaware of magazine requirements, of editors' needs or anything else, I flooded the United States mails with rafts of the impossible stuff every beginner does and must. I hated the post office in town where I was regarded with amusement by the staff.

"As P. G. Wodehouse remarks, 'I have always felt that the glamour of rejection slips wears off; when you have seen one, you have seen them all.' My rejection slips soon filled a bottom drawer, yet I kept on. My assets: ignorance, consummate nerve, plus that selfish singleness of purpose all writers must have. What made me think I could succeed? Or ever become a writer? Anyhow I pushed along, and whenever a scribbled pencil comment appeared on a rejection slip, my day was made.

"Then after several months the impossible happened. *Life,* the ancient, humorous weekly, sent me a check for $5.62, in payment for some sketch I had sent in. There! Now I felt certain I would be a writer. Or so, anyhow, that check seemed to say. Here was visual proof one might earn money by writing. It was my first check—and of course, the most important.

"Of course I was writing furiously every spare moment, encouraged by my wife—quietly—and my mother—openly. I even took a thirteen-dollar correspondence course from some mail-order house in St. Louis, which had been advertised in a writer's magazine. If this did nothing else, it kept me completing the weekly assignments, because my New England background prevented me from stopping when I had paid for the course. In 1920, I made $81, better than the $19 for the last half of the year previous, and sold short pieces to the Boston *Globe* and the Boston *Transcript.* Not much, true, yet that $80 kept alive the spark of hope that some day I might become a professional writer. With the meager returns, plus the $17 weekly wage from the factory, plus my wife's careful managing, we existed."[1]

1922. Moved to Rowayton, Connecticut, to be near the literary markets in New York City. "Both Lucy and I liked Rowayton, an unpretentious town and as far from Greenwich and Scarsdale socially as the desert of Sahara. We also liked our neighbors, mostly commuters taking the 7:54 from the New Haven station across the street. There was no keeping up with the Joneses because there were no Joneses in Rowayton to keep up with. Until 1928, we had no car. . . .

"Keeping abreast of the bills those days necessitated considerable pavement pounding in New York. I had changed from the timid writer, afraid to see the editor of *Collier's* or *Liberty*, and was learning the hard way how to be a salesman. Naturally I made many mistakes, but I also made many sales. It was like working for the Fuller Brush Company, and in many magazine offices I must have been no more welcome. To my amazement I discovered that many editors were deficient in imagination. Therefore I began writing or rather typing out ideas in a few sentences on a small, white card. This ploy seemed to work. Often, too, I presented a one- or two-page outline of the idea, although usually this was a second step in my selling approach."[1]

1929. Wrote first novel. "With the unbelievable stupidity of the inexperienced writer, I plunged ahead and started a novel called *American Girl*, meant to be a study of a feminine tennis champion. The book appeared in the summer . . . and received a press that publishers, especially small and unimportant ones such as mine, dream about. Since the book came out in the early days of August, before the full flood of fall books had reached the market, it was lavishly reviewed. Like most inexperienced writers I was vain enough to subscribe to a clipping bureau. For five or six weeks reviews poured in from newspapers and magazines all over the country. (It is staggering to see the number of those clippings today and realize how much space in our press was once devoted to books.)

"The firm that brought out the book, two young and charming innocents, was in ecstasy. Within a fortnight the novel was on the best-seller list, for we had reached Labor Day and the National Singles Championships at Forest Hills was under way. Interest in the novel flared, so did my imagination. I had visions: a juicy Hollywood contract, publishers fighting to take me to lunch in the Oak Room of the Plaza and asking for my next book, and a truck backing up to our cellar door in Rowayton and shoveling gold nuggets in beside that new furnace we had just installed.

"The National Singles came and went, Bill Tilden won the title for the last time and Helen Wills the women's title. New and better books soon crowded mine off the best-seller list. The edition of three thousand five hundred copies sold out (I later discovered this wasn't bad for a first novel), and naturally the publishers did not reprint, although they concealed this fact. Nobody invited me to the Oak Room of the Plaza for lunch, no publisher pursued me for another book. In fact the firm that brought it out went bankrupt several months later, doubtless assisted to that regrettable ending by my small contribution.

"Exactly twenty years later, Collier Young, who had been attached to the Brandt office when the book appeared, remembered this yarn about a tennis star and offered me several thousand dollars for the movie rights. I accepted. It was sold through RKO and called 'Hard, Fast and Beautiful.' I made the mistake every writer does, and went to the picture. A professional author who sees his book made into a Hollywood film by persons whose one aim is to keep solvent has the same feeling as a mother who finds her son in prison garb: What have I done to deserve this?"[1]

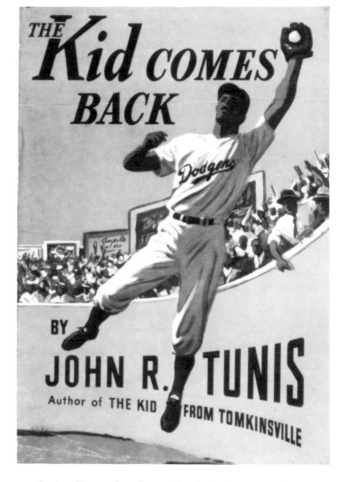

(Jacket illustration from *The Kid Comes Back* by John R. Tunis.)

1938. *The Iron Duke* published. ". . . During the next winter I sandwiched in time to write a novel. In it I tried to describe the reactions of a boy from a Middle Western high school, who comes east and gets lost in the big world of Harvard. A firm believer in going to the top, I sent the book to Mr. Alfred Harcourt, the genius and founder of Harcourt, Brace.

"Ten days later a letter arrived saying that he liked the novel and asking me to come in and see him. He was businesslike and came directly to the point. The book was excellent. They would be happy to publish it as a juvenile.

"I was shocked, rocked, deflated. What on earth was a juvenile? I stuttered and sputtered. He paid no attention. Taking me firmly by the arm, with my manuscript under his other arm, he hustled me down the hall to a tiny cubicle where sat an alert, attractive, brown-eyed woman. Introducing her as Mrs. Hamilton, he dropped the book on her desk as though it might explode, and fled. In business, whenever there is an unpleasant job to do, executives are most happy to have a smart woman at hand.

"Naturally my boiling point had been reached. What did I know or care about juveniles? My book was a book. Patiently the brown-eyed lady explained there was a large and continuing market for such a story. Further, she suggested that the New York *Tribune* was inaugurating a prize for the best book of the kind published in the spring. She felt mine stood a chance.

Disconsolate, I suggested she could throw it out on 45th Street, signed a contract and left the office.

"Six months later, the book was published. It did win the _Tribune_ prize. Over the years in hard cover it has sold sixty thousand copies and still brings me in a fertile annuity of $1,000 a year."[1]

1940. "In mid-winter . . . I sat adding up bills and looking hard at my resources. There had been months, too often of late, when no checks came in; after twenty years of steady work it was frightening. My slowly declining curve from writing was only too apparent. If the magazines were harder to sell, why not? I had nothing to offer them. Nervously I glanced at the list of pieces scheduled ahead, which I kept on the wall before me. It was painfully small.

"Though I didn't realize it, the end of free-lancing, for me at any rate, was in sight. Since the Depression many smaller magazines I had been selling regularly had folded year by year. New and prosperous ones were emerging, but they were mostly staff written and no help to a free-lance writer. Earlier that winter I had sold the _Saturday Evening Post_ and received the exact sum they had paid me for my first piece fifteen years previously. _Collier's_ gave me $400 that winter for a story; I had been paid the same in 1925.

". . . By the winter of 1940, the winter of the Phony War in Europe, I had two boys' books published and selling steadily, bringing in an income of about $1,200 a year. If I could hold out until eight or ten were published, a fairly consistent income was in sight. There were risks. But with luck I might make it. Besides, what choice lay before me?

"The next morning I piled in to see Mrs. Hamilton, my editor at Harcourt, Brace. Would she, I asked, be interested in a big league baseball story? Again good fortune intervened. She must have been one of the few junior book editors in New York, and surely the only Phi Beta Kappa from Vassar, who had regular seats behind the plate at the Polo Grounds each week. She nodded to my question, immediately agreed on an advance of $200, with which I hoped to pay my own way south to the baseball training camps in Florida. Without hesitation she gave me that vote of confidence every writer needs at such a moment.

"A few years later when a number of these books were published and selling, and I had time to breath, I decided to take a six-week summer course at St. John's College in Annapolis, determined to spend a while studying and steeping myself in the classics, never looking at newspapers or listening to the radio. Mrs. Hamilton listened while I explained our new book would be delayed because I was spending a month and a half reading Thucydides and the Greek dramatists. As an editor, she might have pointed out that it would be more profitable to sit home and work. She didn't.

"A decade or so later I had written twenty books for Elisabeth Hamilton. As suggested earlier, she stretched and challenged me like Fred Allen. If years before he taught that the future belongs to the optimists and that the pessimists are merely along for the ride, Elisabeth Hamilton helped me at critical moments, enabled me to say things I wanted to about the land of my birth, showed me how to say them simply and directly so any boy—or girl—would understand."[1]

During a writing career that spanned over fifty years, Tunis wrote numerous sports books for boys. He was considered by many critics and readers to be the dean of the American juvenile sports novel. "A book written for my audience doesn't have to be merely as good as a book for adults; it must be—or should be—better. Not only does youth deserve the best, but also no youths read a book because it is on the best-seller list. There is no best-seller list. Nor do they read it because it has a huge advertising budget, or is well reviewed; they read it for one reason alone, they want to. They find it says something to them in an area they know and understand. These readers are important, perhaps the most important audience in the country today. . . ."[1]

1947. Mother died. "Inasmuch as everything had been paid for in advance, she left not the smallest burden for my brother and myself. Her tiny inheritance ended at her death. So did the small pension from the City of Boston. There was nothing saving a couple of faded black dresses, that envelope with the card and on the back a single line in her firm handwriting.

"Roberts, I leave you John. John, I leave you Roberts."[1]

1949. Received a Junior Book Award from the Boy's Club of America. ". . . Looking back, my basic beliefs about American sport and leisure-time activities have been consistent over the years. The moment our athletics become subservient to the cash nexus, a shift in emphasis from a game to a business was inevitable. Obviously sportsmanship is and must be a joke in our organized sport today."[1]

1973. Last sports book, _Grand National_, published. "Often, nowadays, I ask myself whether it is better to be old and rich or young and poor. Both have advantages; also disadvantages. Mine is an ordinary American story, but a happy one, chiefly because I was able to do what I wanted to do in life, and make a living so doing. Looking back I realize nobody could have lived a fuller life. I was rare among my contemporaries to be permitted freedom of choice. Without consciously trying for it, I achieved that measure of independence which, above all, was necessary for me to exist.

"Not many writers or artists have been so lucky. Blessed with a good constitution from Yankee forebears with a conservatively reared wife who never worried because we took chances, I worked and competed through many exciting years. In that work and in outside activities such as politics I made friends, and also acquired a feeling of having taken a tiny part in the forward movement of my country. What more can a man ask?"[1]

February 4, 1975. Died in Essex, Connecticut. "We do not have to indoctrinate our young peole, or claim our system is perfect. We need only to show the system with its drawbacks and defects, and hope our young people of today will do something later to change it."[1]

FOR MORE INFORMATION SEE: John Tunis, _A Measure of Independence_, Atheneum, 1964; Miriam Hoffman and Eva Samuels, _Authors and Illustrators of Children's Books_, Bowker, 1972; _Horn Book_, December, 1977; D. L. Kirkpatrick, _Twentieth-Century Children's Writers_, St. Martin's Press, 1978; _Contemporary Literary Criticism_, Volume 12, Gale, 1980. _Obituaries: New York Times_, February 5, 1975; _AB Bookman's Weekly_, February 24, 1975, _Publishers Weekly_, March 24, 1975.

The school system has much to say these days of the virtue of reading widely, and not enough about the virtues of reading less but in depth.

—John Ciardi

UNTERMEYER, Louis 1885-1977

PERSONAL: Born October 1, 1885, in New York, N.Y.; died December 18, 1977, in Newtown, Conn.; son of Emanuel (a manufacturing jeweler) and Julia (Michael) Untermeyer; married Jean Starr (a poet), January 23, 1907 (divorced); married Virginia Moore (a poet), November, 1926 (divorced); married Esther Antin (a lawyer), 1933 (divorced); married Bryna Ivens (an editor), July 23, 1948; children: (first marriage) Richard (deceased), Lauren S., Joseph Louis; (second marriage) John Moore. *Education:* Left high school before graduating; awarded high school diploma, 1965. *Residence:* Newtown, Conn.

CAREER: In manufacturing jewelry business with father and uncle, Untermeyer-Robbins Co. and Charles Keller & Co., 1901-23, became vice-president and manager of factory at Newark, N.J., resigned, 1923; writer, editor, anthologist, poet, lecturer, 1923—. Amherst College, Amherst, Mass., Henry Ward Beecher Lecturer, 1937; Knox College, Galesburg, Ill., Honnold Lecturer, 1937; poet-in-residence at University of Michigan, Ann Arbor, 1939-40, University of Kansas City, Kansas City, Mo., 1939, Iowa State College, Cedar Falls, 1940. U.S. Office of War Information, publications editor, 1942; Armed Services Editions, editor, 1944; Decca Records, New York, N.Y., publications editor, 1945-58; Library of Congress, consultant in English poetry, 1961-63. U.S. representative at conferences in India, 1961; conducted seminars in American poetry, in Japan, 1962. *Member:* National Institute of Arts and Letters, Phi Beta Kappa. *Awards, honors:* Gold Medal, Poetry Society of America, 1956, for services to poetry; selected Phi Beta Kappa poet at Harvard, 1956; Sarah Josepha Hale Award, 1965; Golden Rose, New England Poetry Society, 1966; D.H.L., Union College, 1967.

*WRITINGS—*Of interest to young readers: *The Forms of Poetry: A Pocket Dictionary of Verse* (textbook), Harcourt, 1926, reprinted, Darby Books, 1982, latest revised edition, 1954; *The Donkey of God* (short stories; illustrated by James MacDonald) Harcourt, 1932; *Chip: My Life and Times, As Overheard by Louis Untermeyer* (fiction; self-illustrated with Vera Neville), Harcourt, 1933; *The Last Pirate: Tales from the Gilbert and Sullivan Operas* (illustrated by Reginald Birch), Harcourt, 1934; (with Clara Mannes) *Songs to Sing to Children,* Harcourt, 1935; (reteller) *The Wonderful Adventures of Paul Bunyan* (illustrated by Everett Gee Jackson), Heritage, 1945; (reteller) Charles Perrault, *French Fairy Tales* (illustrated by Gustave Doré), Didier, 1945; (reteller) C. Perrault, *All the French Fairy Tales* (illustrated by G. Doré), Didier, 1946; (reteller) C. Perrault, *More French Fairy Tales* (illustrated by G. Doré), Didier, 1946; *The Kitten Who Barked* (fiction; illustrated by Lilian Obligado), Golden Press, 1962; *The World's Great Stories: Fifty-Five Legends That Live Forever* (illustrated by Mae Gerhard), Evans, 1964, published as *The Firebringer and Other Great Stories: Fifty-Five Legends That Live Forever,* 1968; *The Second Christmas* (illustrated by Louis Marak), Hallmark Cards, 1965; *The Paths of Poetry: Twenty-Five Poets and Their Poems* (illustrated by Ellen Raskin), Delacorte, 1966; *Plants of the Bible* (illustrated by Anne O. Dowen), Golden Press, 1970; *Cat o'Nine Tales* (fiction; illustrated by Lawrence Di Fiori), Heritage, 1971.

Other: *The New Era in American Poetry* (essays), Holt, 1919, reprinted, Scholarly Press, 1970; *Heavens* (parodies), Harcourt, 1922; *American Poetry Since 1900* (essays; based on *The New Era in American Poetry*), Holt, 1923, reprinted, Folcroft, 1977; *Collected Parodies,* Harcourt, 1926; *Moses* (novel), Harcourt, 1928; *Blue Rhine, Black Forest: A Hand-and-Day Book* (travel book), Harcourt, 1930; (with Carter Davidson)

Caricature of Louis Untermeyer by William Gropper.

Poetry: Its Appreciation and Enjoyment, Harcourt, 1934; *Heinrich Heine: Paradox and Poet,* two volumes, Harcourt, 1937; (with others) *Doorways to Poetry* (textbook) Harcourt, 1938; *Play in Poetry* (Henry Ward Beecher lectures), Harcourt, 1938, reprinted, Arden Library, 1980; *From Another World: The Autobiography of Louis Untermeyer,* Harcourt, 1939; *A Century of Candlemaking, 1847-1947,* privately printed, 1947; *Makers of the Modern World* (biography), Simon & Schuster, 1955; *Lives of the Poets: The Story of 1000 Years of English and American Poetry,* Simon & Schuster, 1959; *Edwin Arlington Robinson: A Reappraisal,* Library of Congress, 1963; *Robert Frost: A Backward Look,* Library of Congress, 1964; *Bygones: The Recollections of Louis Untermeyer,* Harcourt, 1965; *The Pursuit of Poetry: A Guide to Its Understanding and Appreciation* (young adult), Simon & Schuster, 1969; *Said I to Myself, Said I: Reflections and Reappraisals, Digressions and Diversions,* privately printed, 1978.

Poetry: *The Younger Quire* (parodies), Mood Publishing, 1911; *First Love,* French, 1911; *Challenge,* Century, 1914; *—and Other Poets* (parodies), Holt, 1916; *These Times,* Holt, 1917; *Including Horace,* Harcourt, 1919; *The New Adam,* Harcourt, 1920; *Roast Leviathan,* Harcourt, 1923, facsimile reprint, Arno, 1975; (with son, Richard Untermeyer) *Poems,* privately printed, 1927; *Burning Bush,* Harcourt, 1928; *Andirondack Cycle,* Random House, 1929; *Food and Drink,* Harcourt, 1932; *First Words before Spring,* Knopf, 1933; *Selected Poems and Parodies,* Harcourt, 1935; *For You with Love* (juvenile; illustrated by Joan Walsh Anglund), Golden Press, 1961; *Long Feud: Selected Poems,* Harcourt, 1962; *One and One and One* (juvenile; illustrated by Robert Jones), Crowell-Collier, 1962; *This Is Your Day* (juvenile; illustrated by John Johnson), Golden

American and English poets meet at Astor Hotel, New York to honor John Masefield. Standing from left to right: Laurence Housman, Witter Bynner, Percy MacKaye, Edwin Markham, G. Y. Rice, Louis Untermeyer, Vachel Lindsay. Sitting from left to right: Amy Lowell, Josephine Daskam Bacon, John Masefield, and Alfred Noyes. ■ (Photograph courtesy of The Bettmann Archive, Inc.)

Press, 1964; *Labyrinth of Love,* Simon & Schuster, 1965; *Thanks* (juvenile; illustrated by Joan Berg Victor), Odyssey, 1965; *Thinking of You* (juvenile), Golden Press, 1968; *You* (juvenile; illustrated by Martha Alexander), Golden Press, 1969.

Editor; all poetry, except as indicated: *Modern American Verse,* Harcourt, 1919, published as *Modern American Poetry,* 1921, latest revised editon, 1969; *Modern British Poetry,* Harcourt, 1920, latest revised edition, 1969; *Modern American and British Poetry,* Harcourt, 1922, 9th revised edition, 1962; *Walt Whitman,* Simon & Schuster, 1926; *Emily Dickinson,* Simon & Schuster, 1927; *Conrad Aiken,* Simon & Schuster, 1927; *A Critical Anthology: Modern American Poetry, Modern British Poetry,* Harcourt, 1930 (contains revised editions of *Modern American Poetry* and *Modern British Poetry*); *American Poetry from the Beginning to Whitman,* Harcourt, 1931; *The Book of Living Verse: English and American Poetry from the Thirteenth Century to the Present Day,* Harcourt, 1932, revised edition published as *The Book of Living Verse: Limited to the Chief Poets,* Harcourt, 1939, text edition, 1949; *The New Treasury of Verse,* Odhams Press, 1934; *A Treasury of Great Poems: English and American,* Simon & Schuster, 1942, revised and enlarged edition, two volumes, 1955, also published as *A Concise Treasury of Great Poems: English and American,* Permabooks, 1953; Edgar Allan Poe, *Complete Poems,* Heritage, 1943; Henry W. Longfellow, *Poems,* Heritage, 1943; Robert Frost, *Come In, and Other Poems,* Holt, 1943, revised and

enlarged edition published as *The Road Not Taken: An Introduction to Robert Frost,* 1951; *Great Poems from Chaucer to Whitman,* Editions for the Armed Services, 1944.

Ralph Waldo Emerson, *Poems,* Heritage, 1945; (and author of introduction) *The Pocket Book of Story Poems,* Pocket Books, 1945, revised and enlarged edition published as *Story Poems: An Anthology of Narrative Verse,* Washington Square Press, 1957; John Greenleaf Whittier, *Poems,* Heritage, 1945; (and author of foreword) *The Love Poems of Elizabeth Barrett Browning and Robert Browning,* Rutgers University Press, 1946; *A Treasury of Laughter* (and prose), Simon & Schuster, 1946; (with others) *The Pocket Treasury* (prose selections), Pocket Books, 1947; William Cullen Bryant, *Poems,* Heritage, 1947; Omar Khayyam, *Rubaiyat,* Random House, 1947; *An Anthology of the New England Poets from Colonial Times to the Present Day,* Random House, 1948; *The Love Poems of Robert Herrick and John Donne,* Rutgers University Press, 1948; *The Pocket Book of American Poems from the Colonial Period to the Present Day,* Pocket Books, 1948; *The Inner Sanctum Walt Whitman* (prose), Simon & Schuster, 1949.

(With R. E. Shikes) *The Best Humor of 1949-50* (and prose selections), Holt, 1951; (with R. E. Shikes) *The Best Humor of 1951-52* (and prose selections), Holt, 1952; Emily Dickinson, *Poems,* Heritage, 1952; *Early American Poets,* Library Publishers, 1952, reprinted, Books for Libraries, 1970; *The*

Book of Wit and Humor (prose selections), Mercury Books, 1953; (and author of commentary) *A Treasury of Ribaldry*, Hanover House, 1956; (and author of commentary) *The Britannica Library of Great American Writing* (prose selections), two volumes, Britannica Press, 1960; (and author of commentary) *Lots of Limericks, Light, Lusty and Lasting*, Doubleday, 1961; *The Letters of Robert Frost to Louis Untermeyer*, Holt, 1963; *An Uninhibited Treasury of Erotic Poetry*, Dial, 1963; *Love Sonnets*, Odyssey, 1964; *Love Lyrics*, Odyssey, 1965; *Men and Women: The Poetry of Love*, Heritage, 1970; *Treasury of Great Humor: Including Wit, Whimsy and Satire from the Remote Past to the Present*, McGraw, 1972; (and author of commentary) *Fifty Modern American and British Poets, 1920-1970*, McKay, 1973.

Editor; for young readers: *This Singing World*, Harcourt, Volume I: *An Anthology of Modern Poetry for Young People* (illustrated by Florence Wyman Ivins), 1923, Volume II: *Junior Edition* (illustrated by Decie Merwin), 1926, Volume III: *For Younger Children*, 1926; *Yesterday and Today: A Comparative Anthology of Poetry*, Harcourt, 1926, revised edition published

**Serenity is everywhere,
Except within man's heart.**

■ (From "The Chart" by Michael Lewis in *Stars to Steer By*, edited by Louis Untermeyer. Illustrated by Dorothy Bayley.)

"Listen, children, listen, won't you come into the night?. . ." ■ (From "Who Calls?" by Frances Clarke in *Stars to Steer By*, edited by Louis Untermeyer. Illustrated by Dorothy Bayley.)

as *Yesterday and Today: A Collection of Verse (Mostly Modern) Designed for the Average Person of Nine to Nineteen and Possibly Older* (illustrated by Edna Reindel), Harcourt, 1927; (with Clara Mannes and David Mannes) *New Songs for New Voices* (poems; illustrated by Peggy Bacon), Harcourt, 1928; *Rainbow in the Sky* (poems; illustrated by Reginald Birch), Harcourt, 1935; *Stars to Steer By* (poems; illustrated by Dorothy Bayley; ALA Notable Book), Harcourt, 1941.

The Magic Circle: Stories and People in Poetry (illustrated by Beth Krush and Joe Krush), Harcourt, 1952; *The Golden Treasury of Poetry* (illustrated by Joan Walsh Anglund), Golden Press, 1959; (and adapter) *Aesop's Fables* (illustrated by Anne Provensen and Martin Provensen), Golden Press, 1965; *Merry Christmas: Legends and Traditions in Many Lands* (illustrated by Joan Berg Victor), Golden Press, 1967; *Songs of Joy: Selections from the Book of Psalms* (illustrated by J. B. Victor), World Publishing, 1967; *A Friend Indeed*, Golden Press, 1968; *Lift Up Your Heart*, Golden Press, 1968; *Poems* (illustrated by J. W. Anglund), Golden Press, 1968; *Tales from the Ballet* (illustrated by A. Provensen and M. Provensen), Golden Press, 1968; *Favorite Classics*, Golden Press, 1968; *Your Lucky Stars*, Golden Press, 1968; *Tales and Legends*, Golden Press, 1968; *A Time for Peace: Verses from the Bible* (illustrated by J. B.

**Jack fell down
And broke his crown
And Jill came tumbling after.**

■ (From "Jack and Jill" by Mother Goose in *Rainbow in the Sky,* edited by Louis Untermeyer. Illustrated by Reginald Birch.)

Victor), World Publishing, 1969; *The Golden Book of Fun and Nonsense* (poems; illustrated by A. Provensen and M. Provensen), Golden Press, 1970; *More Poems* (illustrated by J. W. Anglund), Golden Press, 1970; *Roses: Selections* (poems; illustrated by Anne O. Dowden), Golden Press, 1970; *The Golden Book of Poems for the Very Young* (illustrated by J. W. Anglund), Golden Press, 1971; *The Golden Treasury of Animal Stories and Poems,* Golden Press, 1971.

Editor with wife, Bryna Untermeyer; all published by Golden Press, except as indicated: *Big and Little Creatures* (illustrated by Elizabeth Jones and others), 1961; Jakob Ludwig Karl Grimm and Wilhelm Karl Grimm, *Fairy Tales: The Complete Household Tales of Jakob and Wilhelm Grimm* (illustrated by Lucille Corcos), Limited Editions Club, 1962; *Old Friends and Lasting Favorites* (illustrated by William Dugan and others), 1962; *Fun and Fancy* (illustrated by Lilian Obligado and others), 1962; *Wonder Lands* (illustrated by Joan Winslow and others), 1962; *Unfamiliar Marvels* (illustrated by Hans Helweg and others), 1962; *Beloved Tales* (illustrated by L. Obligado and others), 1962; *Creatures Wild and Tame* (illustrated by Charles Harper and others), 1963; *Legendary Animals* (illustrated by A. Prov-

ensen and M. Provensen and others), 1963; *Adventures All* (illustrated by Gordon Laite and others), 1963; *Tall Tales* (illustrated by Charles Dolesch and others), 1963; *Creatures All,* 1963; *The Golden Treasury of Children's Literature,* 1966 (published in England as *The Children's Treasury of Literature in Colour,* Hamlyn, 1966); *Animal Stories,* 1968; *Words of Wisdom,* 1968; *Stories and Poems for the Very Young,* 1973; (and author of commentary) *A Galaxy of Verse,* Evans, 1978.

Compiler: *Miscellany of American Poetry,* Harcourt, 1920, 1922, 1925, 1927, reprinted, Granger, 1976, 1977, 1978; *The Book of Noble Thoughts,* American Artists Group, 1946.

Translator: Heinrich Heine, *Poems,* Harcourt, 1923; (and adapter) Gottfried Keller, *Fat of the Cat, and Other Stories,* Harcourt, 1925; H. Heine, *Poetry and Prose,* Citadel, 1948; Edmond Rostand, *Cyrano de Bergerac,* Limited Editions Club, 1954; (and editor) H. Heine, *The Poems of Heinrich Heine,* Limited Editions Club, 1957.

Also editor of *The Poems of Anna Wickham,* 1921; contributing editor, *The Liberator,* 1918-24; co-founder and contributing

"Will you awake him?" "No, not I;
For if I do, he'll be sure to cry."

■ (From "Little Boy Blue" by Mother Goose in *Rainbow in the Sky*, edited by Louis Untermeyer.
Illustrated by Reginald Birch.)

editor, *Seven Arts;* poetry editor, *American Mercury,* 1934-37; editorial consultant, "Prose and Poetry" series of recordings, L. W. Singer Co., 1963. Contributor to periodicals, including *New Republic, Yale Review, Saturday Review,* and others.

ADAPTATIONS—Recordings: "A Treasury of Great Poetry," read by Alexander Scourby, Bramwell Fletcher, and Nancy Wickwire, Listening Library, 196?; "A Golden Treasury of Poetry," read by A. Scourby, Golden Record, 1962; "Dis-

"Who are you, aged man?" I said.
"And how is it you live?"

■ (From "The White Knight's Song" by Lewis Carroll in *The Golden Treasury of Poetry,* selected by Louis Untermeyer. Illustrated by Joan Walsh Anglund.)

covering Rhythm and Rhyme in Poetry," read by Julie Harris and David Wayne, Caedmon, 1967; "A Treasury of Ribaldry," read by Martyn Green, Riverside, c. 1957; "The Democratic Vistas of Walt Whitman," based on *Makers of the Modern World,* Norton, c. 1974; "Magnificent Misfit: Vincent Van Gogh," based on *Makers of the Modern World,* Norton, c. 1974; "Mark Twain: The Eternal Boy," based on *Makers*

of the Modern World, Norton, c. 1974; "Paradox of Henry Ford," based on *Makers of the Modern World,* Norton, c. 1974; "American Thought: A Literary Critic," Encyclopedia Americana/CBS News Audio Resource Library, 1975.

SIDELIGHTS: **October 1, 1885.** "I was born in a New York City apartment. Two years later, when my sister Pauline was born, we acquired a 'Fräulein,' a combination governess and seamstress, and moved to a house on Lexington Avenue near Ninety-first Street. It was a four-story brownstone-fronted house; the rooms were large and furnished in the elegantly furbelowed taste of the 1890s. Although not wealthy, my parents were well-to-do. My mother's family was upper middle class and my father's prospering jewelry firm, of which he was the youngest member, enabled them to travel frequently to Europe.'' [Louis Untermeyer, *Bygones: The Recollections of Louis Untermeyer*, Harcourt, 1965.[1]]

1895. "At ten I fancied myself a storyteller; my brother was a rewarding listener. Our beds were in the front room on the third floor—the cook and 'upstairs maid' had two rooms in the back—and every night I would tell Martin another episode in the saga which was not so much an invention as a plagiarized improvisation. Growing in action and complexity as I went along, it was a hodgepodge of everything I could lay my mind on—the Arabian Nights, the Rover Boys, Jason and the Golden Fleece, Oliver Optic's Onward and Upward series, King Arthur and Lancelot, the Three Musketeers, the historical juveniles of G. A. Henty—a violently romantic serial in which I was the invincible adventurer, the long-awaited lover, the full–blooded but unblemished boy-knight who rose from rags to riches. I talked Martin to sleep and myself into dreams that were extensions of my fantasies.

"It was fantasy that led to my discovery of poetry. Mother had read Longfellow to me when I was a child; but 'Paul Revere's Ride' and 'King Robert of Şicily' and 'Hiawatha' had been read as tales, and it was as tales that I had listened to them. Almost as soon as I could read by myself I was transported to another and higher level of storytelling. On a large table in the living room were several oversize volumes which attracted me partly because of their size and partly because they were all illustrated in a way that was fantastic yet, somehow, realistic. They were Coleridge's *Rime of the Ancient Mariner*, La Fontaine's *Fables*, Tennyson's *Idylls of the King*, and Dante's *Inferno*. All were illustrated by Gustave Doré and I was spellbound by the elaborate designs, the swirling draughtsmanship, and the bravura conceptions, brilliantly romantic and, at the same time, bizarre. I began to read the text, not so much for its own sake as for clarification of the pictures. I read every page, not skipping the many lines I could not understand and, knowing nothing about the poets, found, unawares, I was reading poetry—something that, like the Doré illustrations, was fantastic yet, somehow, realistic.

"Fantasy was the most important part of my boyhood—at least it is the only part I remember. There was school, of course, but I cannot recall a single companion or an interesting classroom incident. I excelled in nothing, not even in 'compositions' supposed to reveal a latent creative talent. I was educationally torpid and physically clumsy. I mishandled the simplest apparatus; any problem in mathematics discomfited me. I am still helpless when anything goes wrong with fuses, furnaces, refrigerators, wiring, storm windows, dishwashers, can openers (machinery has always conspired against me), and I still cannot solve Euclid's most elementary theorem—an amusing irony since my three sons are mechanically as well as mathematically adept. At all events, including the athletic ones, my imagination was not stirred and certainly never stimulated by anything taught at P.S. 6. My soul, as a minor American poet put it, was far away, sailing the blue Vesuvian bay, or turning Ivanhoe into another installment or nightly self-glorification.

"My memories of high school are somewhat clearer than those of the grade school through which I floundered. Not that I

stopped floundering. On the contrary, I remained an inept student, not really rebellious or even recalcitrant, but dully resigned. At fifteen my mind went to sleep during the routine instruction and woke only after school. I read insatiably and indiscriminately. I had three cards from the Aguilar Free Library—one in my own name and one each in my brother's and sister's—and each week I unconsciously educated myself by bringing home volume after volume of Dumas, Dickens, Thackeray, Verne, and Hugo—I had not discovered the Russians. The curriculum at Boys' High, later renamed De Witt Clinton High School, seemed a long-drawn-out trial and the classroom a compelled exile to one who wanted to live in the multiple worlds of D'Artagnan, David Copperfield, Pendennis (a blood-brother, for he too was lovingly spoiled by his mother), Captain Nemo, and Jean Valjean. Far from bringing me closer to any of these worlds, the English course textbooks (in which the selections were followed by inane questions, childish explana-tions, and vocabulary tests) alienated me from them. I could not wait to escape from Thirteenth Street and Sixth Av-

Let others share your toys, my son,
Do not insist on *all* the fun.
For if you do it's certain that
You'll grow to be an adult brat.

■ (From "Let Others Share" by Edward Anthony in *The Golden Treasury of Poetry*, selected by Louis Untermeyer. Illustrated by Joan Walsh Anglund.)

**Why
Is the sky?**

■ (From "Questions at Night" in *The Golden Treasury of Poetry*, selected by Louis Untermeyer. Illustrated by Joan Walsh Anglund.)

enue into the sewers of Paris, the purlieus of London, and the new dimensions of time and space which were being disclosed by H. G. Wells.''[1]

1898. Editor of summer camp newspaper. ''Until I was old enough to have a home of my own I was away from home only three summers, twice at a school camp in Highmount in the Catskill Mountains, once at a lakeside camp in central Maine. It was at the former that, at thirteen, I saw my name in print for the first time. There was a camp paper and, since I shirked every sport except swimming and every game except tennis, I was appointed one of the editors. I took advantage of my position to become the little weekly's most constant contributor. I composed sentimental verses, sentimental descriptions of the scenery, and sentimental accounts of hikes down to Pine Hill and up to Grand Hotel.

''My parents were only slightly disgruntled when I refused to return to the classroom at Boys' High. They were mollified when I told them I thought I could get into Columbia University without having to finish high school. Toward that end I took various and curiously uncoordinated Regents' examinations ranging from music to history, both of which I could play by ear. I did well in those I took. Thanks to widely scattered and somewhat precocious reading, my marks were far beyond my grade in literature and, since I had acquired conversational freedom via our old Fräulein in German, I received a second-year-college 80 per cent in that language. But I declined to struggle with any papers on mathematics, and was discomfited when I learned that Columbia's doors were not open to students who could not show passing marks in algebra and plane geometry. I was, as I say, discomfited, but not dismayed. I had no love for any kind of curriculum, and I assured myself that I could 'learn from life,' even life in the jewelry business.''[1]

1901. Began working in father's jewelry business. ''I was not quite sixteen when I learned how to wrap parcels, seal envelopes, and pack boxes in the shipping room of Keller and Untermeyer, soon to be enlarged into the twin firms of Charles Keller and Company, which produced gold link buttons, brooches, scarfpins, lockets, lavalieres, watch chains, fobs, and every other conceivable item of jewelry except rings, and Untermeyer-Robbins Company, which manufactured rings only. Later I was permitted to arrange the drawers in which the articles were kept, to check the goods as they arrived from the factory, and gradually to take charge of the stock.

''. . . Until I was eighteen it never occurred to me that I might be a writer. I had an entirely different career in mind; my only uncertainty was whether I would be a concert pianist or a composer. I had been taking piano lessons ever since I was eight, and I could (and, at any opportunity, would) perform Schumann's *Carnival,* Grieg's A-Minor Concerto, Schubert's Impromptus, and a few of Liszt's bravura showpieces. Studying harmony and counterpoint, I began writing songs, using the lyrics of Shelley, Poe, and the Rossettis. I also constructed a sonata or two, so full of echoes from the dead past that (as I have said somewhere) I was not composing but decomposing.

''I was nineteen, a junior traveling salesman whose 'territory' was the East—not the Orient, but north to Boston and south to Washington—a dilettante who felt he had given up some kind of creative career, although it was not apparent that anything had been sacrificed. I was too well aware of my musical borrowings to continue composing; instead I had been experimenting with the writing of lyrics and light verse. However, I still played the piano with enthusiasm. I had given up all thoughts of concertizing—I had neither the time nor the tem-

perament to discipline myself to practicing—but I joined little groups of semiprofessional musicians and played the piano part in trios, quintets, and sonatas for violin and piano by Grieg, Franck, and Mozart.''[1]

1907. Married Jean Starr. Their son Richard was born the following year. ''The satisfactions of domestic life were increased by my self-satisfaction in becoming a 'professional' poet. In my late teens and early twenties I had written two or more poems a week . . . some of the . . . verses managed to get published. Published, I should add, without being paid for. They appeared in little journals which . . . gave credit but withheld the cash. . . . I was, however, still very much of an amateur when some of my short poems began to appear fairly regularly in *The Forum.* They were purportedly 'serious,' but they were as artificial as the light verse I had produced so glibly. They were, as someone is supposed to have said, the kind of thing one should go to the trouble of not writing.

''Far from being a prodigy, I was twenty-four before anything of mine appeared in a book. My so-to-speak debut was in *The Younger Choir,* a pseudo-vellum-bound, gold-leaf-encrusted anthology of (obviously) younger poets. The book was the outgrowth of one of the ephemeral magazines, *Moods,* to which I contributed a monthly article of—there was no one to stop me—music criticism entitled 'Chords and Discords.'''[1]

1911. First volume of verse privately published. ''*First Love* was scarcely a lucrative piece of merchandise—the seventy-two cents profit—but I was a published poet with my name printed on catalogue cards in public libraries. I was twenty-five; I had entered the lists (the publishers' lists) and I was one of those young men rising in America, ready 'to carry on the apostolate of poesy.'

''My life was now divided into three uneven parts. There was the life of the junior traveling salesman, showing his samples of jewelry, entertaining his customers or being entertained by them when the sample cases were closed. There was the home life of the young married man, the time spent with an only child, the hours shared with a wife earnest about music, books, and the state of the world, the evening's endless, inconclusive, but self-satisfying discussions, and the midnight's wordless rapture. There was the life of the 'budding' poet, a life of conventional unconventionality, of sporadic forays into bohemianism, intermittent and innocent flirtations with the avant garde of Greenwich Village.''[1]

1915. Met Robert Frost who became a life-long friend. ''Perhaps it was Robert [Frost] who made me discontented with being a businessman; perhaps I was temperamentally unfit for mercantile life. At any rate, I grew increasingly dissatisfied with business routine although, for almost twenty years, I followed it doggedly and, at times, conscientiously. . . .

''I was not unhappy. Until I was in my late thirties, I went nonchalantly back and forth from various residences on upper Broadway into the West Side subway and, until the Hudson Tubes were in operation, by ferry to the three busy floors on Mulberry Street. I drew sketches of lockets, link buttons, brooches, barrettes, pendants, fobs, tie-clasps, and scarfpins which our employees, German-American craftsmen who had learned their skill abroad, improved and made marketable. I leaned over the workers' benches and inspected the die-struck patterns with critical remarks that were expected of me. Occasionally I adjusted salaries, but I had nothing to do with the bookkeeping, which was done in the New York office. My hours were largely my own, and I employed many of them to further my extracurricular career as poet. There was always a sheet of half-finished rhymes in the drawer of my desk camouflaged with work slips, cost cards, and packets of semiprecious stones.

"I was devoting many hours to parody, and at thirty I had ready a volume which Henry Holt and Company, Frost's publishers, issued in 1916. Entitled —and Other Poets, it consisted of lampoons, burlesques, and buffooneries, some of which I hoped were critical exposures. Flattering myself with the assumption that parody is the poet's half-holiday, I ventured to 'modernize' a batch of nursery rhymes by showing how Mother Goose might have been advantageously rewritten by Frost, Masefield, Yeats, Abercrombie, De la Mare, Robinson, Lindsay, and twenty other poets of the day. I was taking poetry as lightly as I was taking my work."[1]

1917-1919. Began editing and compiling poetry collections in additon to his writing. ". . . Within two years after Holt had issued my parodies in —and Other Poets Harcourt published a volume of my more serious poems, These Times, dedicated to Robert Frost, and followed it with The New Era in American Poetry, a series of impressionistic chapters which, purporting to be critiques, were essentially pronunciamentos celebrating a new, native tone of voice and calling for the extension of a fresh idiom to match a fresh poetic point of view. . . .

"When Alfred Harcourt left Holt to form his own firm of Harcourt, Brace and Howe, Inc., it was this volume which made him think I was the person to put together a more or less pioneering collection of modern American verse. . . ."[1]

1923. ". . . Now that I had an independent income, I no longer had to be tied to the office routine; I determined to give my undivided time to writing."[1]

January, 1923-December, 1924. "We were in Austria for almost two years. The first year was an uninterrupted pleasure for both of us. Jean sang, and I wrote. . . ."[1]

1926. Divorced wife, Jean. Married Virginia Moore.

1927. Second marriage ended. Returned to first wife, Jean. "In a state of emotional and mental turmoil I wrote to Virginia's father explaining as well as I could what had been happening. When John [son by the second marriage] was a few months old, Mr. Moore came over to take charge and I went to Germany to resume a life with Jean. Looking back, I cannot believe that any man could have been so irresponsible, so unrealistic. The only excuse I can give is that I was out of my mind."[1]

Moved to the country to get away from the turmoil of the city. ". . . I had to get away from New York. . . . I . . . longed for a home in the hills. A few months later Jean and I were living in the Adirondack Mountains, two miles outside of Elizabethtown, a little east of Lake Placid and a little south of Ausable Chasm.

"It was an old-fashioned farmsite. Three miles out of the village, it had enough of a Currier and Ives quality to have a bell above the kitchen to summon the farm hands at mealtime, a plank bridge over a brook, and a battered but still serviceable watering trough."[1]

Son, Richard, hanged himself while a student at Yale University. "I had lost two sons, one by death, the other by separation, and I longed to compensate for the loss. Jean agreed,

and we adopted an infant, Joseph. However, I did not want to repeat the pattern of the one and only child, so I prevailed upon her to adopt another boy, Larry [Lauren S.]. We took much pleasure in them but, until they were ready for school, I must admit they were brought up less by us than by an incongruous pair: Edith, an English nanny, and Kelly MacDougall, a local hired man.

"The lecture platform has claimed me for a portion of each year [beginning in 1915]. For one thing, it has served as a kind of compensation for my failure to achieve a formal education; it is a pleasant irony that I have become a part-time teacher. I have been 'poet in residence' at various universities—Michigan, Knox, Kansas City, Dayton, Amherst, among others— and have addressed audiences in every state of the Union except Hawaii and Alaska. At the request of the State Department, I have lectured in India and have conducted seminars in Japan. . . ."[1]

1933. Left Jean; married Esther Antin. "It was on a lecture tour that, in Toledo, Ohio, I met Esther Antin. She was a lawyer who had briefly been a magistrate and was now in private practice. . . ."[1]

1941. "A few months after the United States entered the war I joined the New York branch of the Office of War Information. My motives for making the move were not pure. I was impelled by a genuine desire to do what I could to end the unremitting horrors of a universal madness, and I used the situation as an excuse to separate myself from Esther. Things were made easy for me by the government. [In 1942] I was appointed senior editor of publications and given an imposing desk. I was surrounded by writers who had been or soon became my friends. I lived in a hotel in the West Forties and made occasional trips to 'Stony Water' while the boys, now in high school, came for visits and excitement to the city."

1945-1958. At Decca Records Untermeyer worked as editor of publications assisting in the production of recordings of poetry and plays. "After the end of the Second World War the Armed Services Editions was no longer a necessity. When it was discontinued I thought of free-lancing. But I was worried about the mounting cost of living or, as someone speaking of separation and alimony payments put it, the high cost of leaving. I felt I needed a steady source of supply, a dependable income, in short, a regular salary. . . .

"Other ventures led to albums of dramatized stories and legends: Moby Dick with Charles Laughton, Treasure Island with Thomas Mitchell, The Pied Piper of Hamelin with Ingrid Bergman, The Selfish Giant with Fredric March, The Cask of Amontillado with Sydney Greenstreet, master of horror. I was even urged to adapt Bulfinch, which I did by turning out Tales of the Olympian Gods for Ronald Colman. . . ."[1]

1948. Separated from Esther; married Bryna Ivens.

1950. Charter member of the panel of CBS-TV show "What's My Line?"

1960. "We had come to hate the metropolis, but we were not quite ready to give up the income we derived from it. We managed to persuade our respective employers to let us come to the office only three days a week. Even that was too much, at least for me. Although Bryna continued to edit the fiction for Seventeen magazine, she induced me to devote all my time to writing and . . . I finally closed my desk at Decca Records.

"The time has come," the Walrus said,
"To talk of many things. . . ."

■ (From "The Walrus and the Carpenter" by Lewis Carroll in *The Magic Circle: Stories and People in Poetry,* edited by Louis Untermeyer. Illustrated by Beth and Joe Krush.)

". . . The next few years passed pleasantly, varied by rewarding spells of work at my desk in Newtown [Connecticut] and equally rewarding vacations in Europe. . . ."[1]

1961-1963. Accepted a position at the Library of Congress as a consultant in poetry.

"I was facing my late seventies when I returned to Connecticut, facing them resignedly though not regretfully. Like Landor I had warmed both hands before the fire of life; unlike him, I was not ready to depart. There were things to be done, and done by me alone. One of the first things I did was to give up a post that few people knew I had held for almost a quarter of a century: chairman of the Pulitzer Prize Poetry Jury.

"The decision was hard to make, but the work of judging was harder. I was not always chairman of the jury; in the early 1940s I was the junior member of an advisory committee. . . .

". . . I was spending too much time appraising the products of other writers. I had also spent too many days in too many other activities and in too many places. It was late but not, I hoped, too late. I determined to spend the rest of my life concentrating on my own writing in a place and in a role that were, as long as fate would grant it, my own.

". . . It is in the actual process of writing that I am most myself. At my desk I feel (instinctively rather than intellectually) that I am doing what I am supposed to do: fulfilling my function whether I write in the role of biographer, storyteller, editor of anthologies, impressionistic critic, or, occasionally, poet.

"The poet's lot has seldom been a happy one. Never simple and rarely secure, his position today is the more hazardous and

(From "The Great and Little Fishes" in *Aesop's Fables*, selected and adapted by Louis Untermeyer. Illustrated by Alice and Martin Provensen.)

complicated because, attempting to hold a clouded mirror up to nature, he cannot help but reflect in distorted images the complexities of everyday existence. On the one hand he hopes to express what is hopeful; acknowledging that 'life is real, life is earnest,' he also wants to show it is meaningful. On the other hand he is faced with a world torn by fears, tensions and hatreds, a world where the favorite medium of time-wasting presents a daily televised riot of crime and cruelty, where children are entertained by pistol-packing, trigger-happy untouchables, and where murder is a half-hour pastime.

"It is not easy to hear a poet's voice in such a world. Nevertheless, the poet somehow manages to make himself heard, chiefly because people want to hear him. They listen, sometimes inattentively, sometimes hopefully, and, in times of greatest stress, desperately. For poetry is the great renewer, the freshener of the commonplaces by which we live: joy, grief, hunger, faith, longing, 'mixing memory and desire.' It is not a statement about life but an insight into it, an illumination, a provocation."[1]

December 18, 1977. Died in Newtown, Connecticut, at the age of ninety-two.

FOR MORE INFORMATION SEE: Louis Untermeyer, *From Another World* (autobiography), Harcourt, 1939; *Publishers Weekly,* January 19, 1946; *Time,* June 12, 1950; Loring Holmes Dodd, *Celebrities at Our Hearthside,* Dresser, 1959; L. Untermeyer, *Bygones: The Recollections of Louis Untermeyer,* Harcourt, 1965; *Books for Children, 1960-1965,* American Library Association, 1966; Nancy Larrick, *A Teacher's Guide to Children's Books,* Merrill, 1966; *Current Biography,* January, 1967; N. Larrick, *A Parent's Guide to Children's Read-*

ing, 3rd edition, Doubleday, 1969; Haviland and Smith, *Children and Poetry,* Library of Congress, 1969; *New York Times,* October 1, 1970.

Obituaries: *New York Times,* December 20, 1977; *Washington Post,* December 20, 1977; *Detroit Free Press,* December 20, 1977; *Time,* January 2, 1978; *Newsweek,* January 2, 1978; *Current Biography Yearbook,* 1978; *Contemporary Authors,* Volumes 73-76, Gale, 1978.

VAN ALLSBURG, Chris   1949-

PERSONAL: Born June 18, 1949 in Grand Rapids, Michigan. *Education:* Received a B.F.A. from the University of Michigan and an M.F.A. from the Rhode Island School of Design. *Residence:* Providence, R.I.

CAREER: Sculptor and author and illustrator of children's books. Teaches illustration at the Rhode Island School of Design, Providence, R.I., 1977—. *Exhibitions:* Work has been shown at the Whitney Museum of American Art, New York, N.Y. and in one-man exhibitions at Allan Stone Gallery, New York City. *Awards, honors:* Eight awards, including *New York Times* best illustrated children's book of the year choice, 1979, *Boston Globe Horn Book* Award for illustration, 1980, Irma Simonton Black Award, 1980, Caldecott honor book, 1980, and selection for the International Board on Books Honor List for illustration, 1982, for all *The Garden of Abdul Gasazi; Boston Globe Horn Book* honor book for illustration, 1981, *New York Times* best illustrated children's book of the year choice, 1981, and Caldecott Medal for illustration, 1982, all for *Jumanji; Ben's Dream* selected as one of *New York Times* ten best illustrated books of the year, 1982.

WRITINGS—All juvenile; all self-illustrated; all published by Houghton: *The Garden of Abdul Gasazi*, 1979; *Jumanji*, (*Horn Book* honor list) 1981; *Ben's Dream*, 1982; *The Wreck of the Zephyr*, 1983.

WORK IN PROGRESS: A novel, tentatively titled *Harris Burdock's Pictures.* "It's about an illustrator who brings in fourteen drawings to show an editor and then disappears without a trace.

"The actual story begins some thirty years after this strange event. I appear in my own persona, having been asked to write an introduction for a book of the drawings. That preface both sets forth the known facts about the mysterious artist, and conjectures, based on clues in the art work, about the probable content of the missing stories."

SIDELIGHTS: **1950(?).** Born in Michigan, the artist grew up in Grand Rapids. ". . . In my elementary school we had art twice a week. I loved those days. Children often use a slight fever as an excuse to stay home from school, drink ginger ale, and eat ice cream in bed. Once, in the second grade, I felt feverish at breakfast but concealed it from my mother because it was an art day. Midway through the morning art class, my teacher noticed that I looked a little green. Ordinarily it wouldn't be unusual, but paint wasn't being used that day. She took me out into the hall where we children left our coats and boots and asked if I felt O.K. I said I felt fine and then threw up into Billy Marcus's boots. I was profoundly embarrassed. The teacher was very comforting. She took me to the nurse's office, and my mother was summoned. I went home, drank ginger ale, and ate ice cream in bed.

"There was another occasion when my physical health and my passion for art collided. When I was eight, my friend Russell and I became voracious stamp collectors. I loved those tiny

From the kitchen came the sounds of banging pots and falling jars. ■ (From *Jumanji* by Chris Van Allsburg. Illustrated by the author.)

little pictures. We wanted all our relatives to take a vacation in the Ukraine and write us lots of letters. After three weeks of looking at nothing but stamps, I got a fever–the flu again. In my delirium, all I could see was a stamp picturing the Lewis and Clark expedition. I was there, too, with Lewis and Clark, standing in front of a timber fort with our Indian guides, but we never went anywhere. When I pulled out of the fever, I gave all my stamps to Russell. To this day I'm a terrible letter-writer, no doubt because of my lasting aversion to stamps.

"There was a great deal of peer recognition to be gained in elementary school by being able to draw well. One girl could draw horses so well, she was looked upon as a kind of sorceress. (Everyone else's horses looked like water buffalo.) Being able to draw cartoon characters was a good trick, too. Pluto and Mickey always impressed friends. I specialized in Dagwood Bumstead, a little too sophisticated, perhaps, to be widely appreciated.

"But the status gained by these skills wanes as one gets older. Certain peer pressures encourage little fingers to learn how to hold a football instead of a crayon. Rumors circulate around the schoolyard: Kids who draw or wear white socks and bring violins to school on Wednesdays might have cooties. I confess to having yielded to these pressures. Sixth grade was the last time I took art in public school. My interests went elsewhere.

"Then, in college I enrolled in art classes as a lark. At that time I was quite naive about the study of art. As a freshman I received a form that listed the courses I would have, their times and places, and the necessary materials. One course, described simply as 'Fgdrw,' met at eight o'clock in the morning. I did not know what Fgdrw meant, but the materials required were newsprint and charcoal. I went to the appointed room and was surprised to see an older woman wearing a terry-cloth robe and slippers. I thought, 'What?' Does she live here or something? Maybe we're here too early, and she hasn't had time to dress.' Then she took off her bathrobe, and I deduced the meaning of Fgdrw.

"During that year the art classes I took as a lark became more important and involving than any of my other classes. In fact, it took me five years to get my undergraduate degree because I never let liberal arts courses get in the way of making art. Going to classes like philosophy and French upset my rhythm, my pace. So I just skipped them, which upset my credit re-

Six times Miss Hester's dog Fritz had bitten dear cousin Eunice. ■ (From *The Garden of Abdul Gasazi* by Chris Van Allsburg. Illustrated by the author.)

CHRIS VAN ALLSBURG

quirements (and my parents, too). It was clear I had a fever again. The fever to make art.

"Actually, fever may be a misleading description of my own rather deliberate approach, but there is a constant urge to create. I am fascinated by the art of making something real that at one point is only an idea. It is challenging and beguiling to sense something inside, put it on paper (or carve it in stone), and then step back and see how much has got lost in the process. The inevitability of losing some of the idea in trying to bring it to life is what keeps me working. I am always certain that next time, I'll lose less.

"Ideas themselves have varied origins. In writing and illustrating *Jumanji*, the inspiration was my recollection of vague disappointment in playing board games as a child. Even·when I owned Park Place with three hotels, I never felt truly rich, and not being able to interrogate Colonel Mustard personally was always a letdown. Another motivating element for *Jumanji* was a fascination I have with seeing things where they don't belong. The pictures in newspapers of cars that have run amok and crashed into people's living rooms always get my attention. There's the room, almost normal: sofa, TV, amused homeowner, end tables, and the front half of an Oldsmobile. It occurred to me that if an Oldsmobile in the living room looked that good, a herd of rhinoceros could have real possibilities.

"I am surprised now that my fairly recent discovery of the illustrated book was a way of expressing ideas did not happen earlier. It is a unique medium that allows an artist-author to deal with the passage of time, the unfolding of events, in the same way film does. The opportunity to create a small world

between two pieces of cardboard, where time exists yet stands still, where people talk and I tell them what to say, is exciting and rewarding." [Chris Van Allsburg, "Caldecott Medal Acceptance," *Horn Book,* August, 1982.[1]]

Van Allsburg's entry into the world of children's books began when wife, Lisa, began working as a grade-school teacher. "Lisa would bring home children's books from time to time and tell me I could do as well.

"What makes book illustration distinct from other illustration is that it isn't thrown out after a month, or even two, like an illustration for a story in a magazine. It stays around; it endures." [Selma G. Lanes, *"Story behind the Book: The Wreck of the Zephyr,"* Publishers Weekly, April 9, 1983.[2]]

Of his technique in *The Wreck of the Zephyr,* Van Allsburg explains, "In *Zephyr,* I used Rembrandt pastels—crayons as thick as a finger—for broad passages and well-sharpened pastel pencils for the details. If I had thought color drawing would be easier in pastel than other alternatives I've since learned from colleagues—and experience—that that medium is just about the hardest one I could have chosen.

"So far I haven't spent more than a half-year on any of my books. That was how long *Ben's Dream* took, because it was technically the hardest. For both *Gaszai* and *Jumanji,* the finished drawings required only about 10 days."[2]

"It is also rewarding to receive mail from people who appreciate your work. The first letter I received as a result of having a book published came from a man in Cleveland. I don't remember his name, so I'll use a pseudonym. His letter was written with red Magic Marker on tissue paper. 'Dear Mr. Van Allsburg,' he wrote, 'I love your work. Do you think life as we know it will exist in the year 2000? Yours truly, Frank Selmer.' More recently, I received a letter from Alexandra Prinstein (her real name) from Delaware: 'Dear Mr. Van Allsburg. I love the books you write. I am so glad your books are so weird because I am very weird. I think you are weird but great. I wish a volcano and flood would be in my room when I am bored. I am happy I am only five because I have lots more years to enjoy magical gardens and crazy games in books by you. Love Alexandra. P.S. I have a younger brother Peter too.'"[1]

FOR MORE INFORMATION SEE: Horn Book, August, 1982; *Publishers Weekly,* April 9, 1983, *Children's Literature Review,* volume 5, Gale, 1983.

WADE, Theodore E., Jr. 1936-

PERSONAL: Born June 28, 1936, in Pueblo, Colo.; son of Theodore E. (a doctor) and Zola (a nurse; maiden name, Talbott) Wade; married Karen A. Peterson (a certified public accountant), July 8, 1956; children: Timothy, Dorothea, Melvin. *Education:* Union College, Lincoln, Neb., B.A., 1958; University of Nebraska, M.A. (physics), 1962, Ph.D. (education), 1970. *Religion:* Seventh-Day Adventist. *Home and office:* Gazelle Publications, 5580 Stanley Dr., Auburn, Calif. 95603.

CAREER: John Nevins Andrews School, Takoma Park, Md., teacher, 1972-73; Home Study Institute, Washington, D.C., director of studies, 1973-79; Weimar College, Weimar, Calif., professor of education, 1980—. *Member:* Association for Su-

This game is similar to "alphabet signs." Here the players look for objects beginning with each of the letters of the alphabet. For example, A irplane, B arn, C ow, and so on. ∎ (From *Fun for the Road* by T. E. Wade, Jr. Illustrated by Michael Baptist.)

pervision and Curriculum Development, National Home Study Council.

WRITINGS—For children: (Editor) *With Joy: Poems for Children* (illustrated by Harold Munson and others), Gazelle, 1976, revised edition, 1980; *Fun for the Road* (illustrated by Michael Baptist and Wendel Hill), Gazelle, 1978.

Other: *School at Home: How Parents Can Teach Their Own Children,* Gazelle, 1980, revised edition published as *The Home School Manual: A Guide for Parents' Teaching Their Own Children,* 1984. Also author of several home study course guides for Home Study International.

SIDELIGHTS: "Soon after completing studies for my master's degree, I and my family went to Rwanda, Africa, to serve as

missionaries. We studied French in France for five months en route. When we returned, I continued my studies and received my doctorate. Then we served a term in Haiti. Both assignments were in education. The idea of publishing for the fun of it occurred as I considered the many people who like to write poetry but find very little market. I screened and edited from many who sent in poems for my first book. It never really made money, but I learned a lot. Someday I want to do another one.

"Having some knowledge and experience in home schooling, I wrote my first book in that field to sell for over a dollar. Although addressed to a narrow population segment, it was successful. Now it's replacement, *The Home School Manual,* is gaining momentum. God has blessed me and I give Him the credit."

THEODORE E. WADE, JR.

WAKIN, Edward 1927-

PERSONAL: Born December 13, 1927, in Brooklyn, N.Y.; son of Thomas Najem and Josephine (Aziz) Wakin; married, November 11, 1952; married second wife, December 3, 1967; children: Daniel. *Education:* Fordham University, B.A., 1948; Northwestern University, M.S.J., 1950; Columbia University, M.A., 1962; Fordham University, Ph.D., 1973. *Office:* Fordham University, Bronx, N.Y. 10458.

CAREER: Buffalo Evening News, Buffalo, N.Y., assistant city editor, 1950-52; *New York World-Telegram,* New York, N.Y., variously night city editor, feature editor, and Brooklyn city editor, 1952-59; Fordham University, Bronx, N.Y., 1960—, began as assistant professor, currently professor in communications department. United States Information Service lecturer in Africa, the Middle East, and the Far East, 1971 and 1973. Consulting education editor, WCBS-TV, 1966-69; consultant to numerous corporations and government agencies. *Member:* International Press Institute, American Association of University Professors, Association for Education in Journalism, American Sociological Association, Sigma Delta Chi. *Awards, honors:* George Polk Memorial Award for Journalism, 1957; mass media fellowship, Fund for Adult Education, 1959-60.

WRITINGS: A Lonely Minority: The Modern Story of Egypt's Copts, Morrow, 1963; *The Catholic Campus,* Macmillan, 1963; *At the Edge of Harlem: Portrait of a Middle-Class Negro Family,* Morrow, 1965; (with J. F. Scheuer) *The De-Romanization of the American Catholic Church,* Macmillan, 1966; *Controversial Conversations with Catholics,* Pflaum Press, 1969.

(With Christiane Brusselmans) *A Parents' Guide: Religion for Little Children,* Our Sunday Visitor Publications, 1970, revised edition, 1977; *Black Fighting Men in U.S. History,* Lothrop, 1971; (with James DiGiacomo) *We Were Never Their Age,* Holt, 1971; *The Battle for Childhood,* Abbey Press, 1973; *Jobs in Communication,* Lothrop, 1974; *Children without Justice,* NCJW Books, 1975; *Enter the Irish-American,* Crowell, 1976; *The Immigrant Experience,* OSV Books, 1977; *Communications: An Introduction to Media,* American Book Co., 1978; (with Richard Armstrong) *You Can Still Change the World,* Harper, 1978; (with Frank J. McNulty) *Should You Ever Feel Guilty,* Paulist/Newman, 1978; *Monday Morality: Right and Wrong in Daily Life,* Paulist/Newman, 1980; (with James DiGiacomo) *Understanding Teenagers,* Argus, 1983.

Contributor of more than 100 articles to magazines, including *Saturday Review, Harper's, Nation, Science Digest,* and *Commonweal.*

EDWARD WAKIN

All told, 200,000 black soldiers were sent overseas, making up one out of ten soldiers in The American Expeditionary Force. ■ (From *Black Fighting Men in U.S. History* by Edward Wakin. Illustration courtesy of the U.S. Signal Corps.)

WALLACE, Robert A.   1932-

BRIEF ENTRY: Born January 10, 1932, in Springfield, Mo. Professor of English, poet, and author. A summa cum laude graduate of Harvard College, Wallace also received bachelor's and master's degrees from St. Catharine's College, Cambridge. A teacher of English since 1957, Wallace became a full professor of English at Case Western Reserve University in 1974. Wallace has also been a reader for Book-of-the-Month Club and for Educational Testing Service. His poetical works for

young people are *Critters* (Bits Press, 1978), *Charlie Joins the Circus* (Bits Press, 1979), and for young adults, *Swimmer in the Rain* (Carnegie-Mellon University Press, 1979). Wallace has received the William Rose Benét memorial award from Poetry Society of America in 1957 and the Bragdon Prize from *Approach* magazine in 1965. He wrote *Writing Poems* (Little, Brown), in 1982. *Home:* 2199 Delaware Dr., Cleveland, Ohio 44106. *For More Information See: Contemporary Authors,* Volumes 13-16, revised, Gale, 1975; *Who's Who in America, 1982-83,* 42nd edition, Marquis, 1982; *Directory of American Poets and Fiction Writers, 1983-84,* Poets & Writers, 1983.

WALTRIP, Mildred 1911-

PERSONAL: Born October 4, 1911, in Nebo, Kentucky; daughter of Walter and Coralee (Payne) Waltrip. *Education:* Attended School of the Art Institute of Chicago, New School of Design, Northwestern University, New York University, and Monterey Peninsula College. *Home:* 130 Grand Ave., 4D, Englewood, N.J. 07631.

CAREER: Pioneer Instrument Co., Teterboro, N. J., visualizer, 1943-44; Grey Advertising Agency, New York, N.Y., layout artist, 1944-47; free-lance illustrator, 1947—; *Encyclopaedia Britannica,* Palo Alto, Calif., art director, 1962; Boxwood Press, Pacific Grove, Calif., artist and designer, 1972-76. *Military service:* Artist/illustrator in civil service during World War II, Signal Corps Lab., Ft. Monmouth.

ILLUSTRATOR: Irving J. Lee, *Language Habits in Human Affairs,* Harper, 1951; Brandwein and others, *Science for Better Living,* Harcourt, 1950, revised edition, 1962; Ruchlis and Lemon, *Exploring Physics,* Harcourt, 1952, revised edition, 1959; George Barrow, *Your World in Motion,* Harcourt, 1956; Brinckerhoff and others, *The Physical World,* Harcourt, 1958, revised edition, 1962; Nicholson, *The Question and Answer Book of Stars,* Golden Press, 1958; Milgrom, *The Question and Answer Book of Weather,* Golden Press, 1959; M. O. Hyde, *This Crowded Planet,* McGraw, 1961; M. O. Hyde, *Molecules Today and Tomorrow,* McGraw, 1963; (contributor) *"Yellow" Biology,* Harcourt, 1963; (contributor) Gregory and Goldman, *Biological Science for High School* (with workbook), Ginn, 1964; Yoho, *Health for Today,* Allyn & Bacon, 1967; Schneider, *Health and Growth,* Allyn & Bacon, 1967; Ralph Buchsbaum, *Animals without Backbones,* 2nd revised edition (Waltrip was not associated with earlier editions), University of Chicago Press, 1975.

MILDRED WALTRIP

The ability to present tricks with numbers so that the audience "sits up and takes notice" is called showmanship. ■ (From *Entertaining with Number Tricks* by George Barr. Illustrated by Mildred Waltrip.)

"First Book of" series; all published by F. Watts: Joseph B. Icenhower, *First Book of Submarines,* 1957; O. Irene Sevrey, . . . *the Earth,* 1958; Francis S. Smith, . . . *Water,* 1959; Patricia Markum, . . . *Mining,* 1959; . . . *Indian Wars,* 1959.

"Young Scientist" series; all written by George Barr; all published by McGraw: *Research Ideas for Young Scientists,* 1958; *More Research Ideas for Young Scientists,* 1961; *The Young Scientist and Sports: Featuring Baseball, Football, Basketball,* 1962; *The Young Scientist Looks at Skyscrapers,* 1963; *Research Adventures for Young Scientists,* 1964; *Show Time for Young Scientists,* 1965; *Young Scientists and the Fire Department,* 1966; *The Young Scientist and the Police Department,* 1967; *Fun and Tricks for Young Scientists,* 1968; *The Young Scientist and the Doctor,* 1969; *The Young Scientist and the Dentist,* 1970; *Entertaining with Number Tricks,* 1971.

Also illustrator of mathematical diagrams and charts for books about home economics, and for *Men, Money and Market.*

Contributor of illustrations to *New World of Chemistry* by Jaffe, published by Silver Burdette, and *Book of Popular Science,* published by Grolier.

WORK IN PROGRESS: Invertebrate Zoology for University of Chicago Press; *Basic Ecology* for Boxwood Press.

SIDELIGHTS: "I had a good basic four-year education in art, which I recommend for anyone who wants to be an illustrator, except for such people who seem born knowing how to draw.

"The most valuable habit I formed was carrying a sketchbook and drawing whatever interested me, wherever I went. This develops power of observation, speed, and accuracy. Self-taught artists also recommend this practice.

"Art school introduced me to different media; I was expected to handle water color, oil, acrylic, etc. I especially enjoyed etching and lithography.

"My first eight years as a professional artist were spent mostly as a mural artist, on the WPA art project, and private jobs. I also did illustration design and display.

"World War II ended my 'mural' career, and left me in New York City where I became a commercial artist, and later a free-lance illustrator. I believe that I was able to make that switch because I had the fundamental skills. Illustration requires the ability to work from other people's ideas, as contrasted with painting from one's own idea.

"Eventually I specialized in science illustration, largely because my lifelong friends Ralph and Mildred Buchsbaum are biologists, and because science education relies on pictures almost as much as it does on text to teach.

"My chief hobbies for forty years have been ceramics and photography, which is an adjunct to sketching.

"I'm not sorry that I worked so hard and studied a great deal to prepare myself for my work because it enriches my enjoyment of nature and life."

WANGERIN, Walter, Jr. 1944-

BRIEF ENTRY: Born February 13, 1944, in Portland, Ore. Wagerin received a B.A. from Concordia Senior College (now Concordia Theological Seminary) in 1966, an M.A. from Miami University of Ohio in 1968, and an M.Div. from Christ Seminary in 1976. He has worked as a migrant peapicker, lifeguard, ghetto youth worker, radio announcer, producer, and instructor in English literature. Wangerin is currently a minister as well as a writer whose books have received much attention from the public and critics. *The Book of the Dun Cow* (Harper, 1978) has been described as a religious allegory, a metaphysical fable, and a book "for all ages," although it has been classified as a children's story. It won the National Religious Book Award (children/youth category) in 1980, and the American Book Award for paperback science fiction in 1981. *The Book of the Dun Cow* appeals to every reading level, touching the youngest reader through fantasy and the oldest reader through a much deeper level of meaning. The *Times Literary Supplement* observed, ". . . The book has parallels with the New Testament. These parallels are not contrivances designed to lend a bogus aura to a simple tale, but the natural projections of a deeply religious mind." *Publishers Weekly* added, "Wangerin's fable eludes classification by age grouping or any other method. The writing is baroque; the plot is intricate; and the animal characters are cleverly individualized. This is one book sure to be noticed." *Thistle*, a story about the child of potato farmers, is another of Wangerin's books for children that has met with favorable critical attention. *Publishers Weekly* said, ". . . The author presents a second novel, different from his animal allegory but with the same earthy and spiritual qualities." Other children's books by Wangerin include *The Glory Story* (Concordia, 1974), *God, I've Gotta Talk to You* (Concordia, 1974),

written with A. Jennings, *A Penny Is Everything* (Concordia, 1974), *The Baby God Promised* (Concordia, 1976), and *My First Book about Jesus* (Rand McNally, 1983). *Residence:* Evansville, Ind. *For More Information See: Contemporary Authors,* Volume 108, Gale, 1983.

WARTSKI, Maureen (Ann Crane) 1940- (M. A. Crane)

BRIEF ENTRY: Born January 25, 1940, in Ashiya, Japan. High school English teacher and author of award-winning children's books. Wartski began her career as a reporter for the *English Mainichi* in Kobe, Japan, in 1957. Eleven years later she was teaching at public schools in Sharon, Mass., where she later taught high school history and English. Her first book for young people, *My Brother Is Special* (Westminster, 1979), is the story of Noni Harlow and her attempts to make her retarded brother a winner in the Special Olympics. *Kliatt* called it "a heartwarming story," while *Interracial Books for Children* commented that her treatment of family and peer attitudes and relationships were "accurately conveyed . . . real and legitimate." According to Wartski, "Too often, young people . . . feel that courage is shown by winners, by people who are physically strong, or who get there first. I wanted to show that true courage means a great deal more." Her second book for children, *A Boat to Nowhere* (Westminster, 1980), deals with the plight of three Vietnamese children and an old man struggling to stay alive as boat people. It won the Annual Book Award of the Child Study Committee at Bank Street College of Education in 1980. Its sequel, *A Long Way from Home* (Westminster, 1980), was named a Child Study Committee honor book. Her latest book, *The Lake Is on Fire* (Westminster, 1981), was described by *Publishers Weekly* as "a moving story of courage and hope battling with despair." *Home:* 15 Francis Rd., Sharon, Mass. 02067. *For More Information See: Contemporary Authors,* Volumes 89-92, revised, Gale, 1980.

WATERTON, Betty (Marie) 1923-

PERSONAL: Born August 31, 1923, in Oshawa, Ontario, Canada; daughter of Eric Williams and Mary Irene (Hewson) Wrightmeyer; married Claude Waterton (a pilot in the Royal Canadian Air Force), April 7, 1942; children: Eric, Julia, Karen (Mrs. James Alexander Maxwell). *Education:* Attended Vancouver School of Art. *Religion:* Fundamentalist. *Home:* 10135 Tsaykum Rd., R.R.1, Sidney, British Columbia, V8L 3R9, Canada.

CAREER: Vancouver Sun, Vancouver, British Columbia, retoucher, 1957; free-lance caricaturist, early 1960s; KVOS Television, Vancouver, animator, mid-1960s; also taught at School District 63, Sidney, British Columbia, as adult education teacher of art. *Member:* Canadian Society of Children's Authors, Illustrators, and Performers. *Awards, honors:* Runner-up for children's book of the year award, Canadian Library Association, 1979, Amelia Frances Howard-Gibbon Medal, Canadian Library Association, 1979, and Canada Council Children's Literature Prize, 1979, all for *A Salmon for Simon.*

WRITINGS: A Salmon for Simon (juvenile; illustrated by Ann Blades), Douglas & McIntyre, 1978, Atheneum, 1980; *Pettranella* (juvenile; illustrated by A. Blades), Vanguard Press, 1981; *Mustard* (juvenile); Scholastic Tab, 1983.

Long ago in a country far away lived a little girl named Pettranella. ▪ (From *Pettranella* by Betty Waterton. Illustrated by Ann Blades.)

BETTY WATERTON

WORK IN PROGRESS: An anthology, *The Cat of Quinty,* for Nelson Canada; *The White Moose,* for Ginn; *The Fribble,* for Annick Press; *Quincy Rumpel,* for Douglas & McIntyre.

SIDELIGHTS: "A seventh-generation Canadian, I have lived most of my life on the West Coast. My father had been, from time to time, a writer of short stories—all, unfortunately, unpublished. I was an early versifier, and once earned a dollar for a poem in the *Vancouver Sun.* After this triumph I quite disappeared from the literary scene until somewhere in mid-life, when I began to write for children."

WEST, (Mary) Jessamyn　　1902(?)-1984

OBITUARY NOTICE: Born July 18, 1902 (some sources cite 1907), near North Vernon, Ind.; died of a stroke, February 23, 1984, in Napa, Calif. Author. West graduated from Whittier College in 1919 and taught in a one-room schoolhouse in California before entering the graduate school of the University of California at Berkeley. Just before her twenty-ninth birthday, she was stricken with tuberculosis and spent the following two years in a sanitarium. While convalescing at home, West received the inspiration for a collection of related short stories based on her own Quaker ancestry and centering on Indiana farmers during the nineteenth century. Published in 1945 under the title *The Friendly Persuasion,* the stories met with instant critical acclaim. In the following years she wrote over five novels and several collections of short stories, as well as screenplays, plays, poetry, and autobiographies.

The Friendly Persuasion remained her most popular book and was successfully adapted to film in 1956. Its sequel, *Except for Me and Thee,* was published in 1969. Most of West's works focus on either her Quaker heritage or the lives of early California settlers, such as *South of the Angels, Leafy Rivers, The Massacre at Fall Creek,* and *Cress Delahanty.* She was the recipient of the Thurmod Mosen Award in 1958, the Janet Kafke Prize in 1976, and several honorary degrees, including those from Whittier College, Mills College, Swarthmore College, and Indiana University. *For More Information See:* Jessamyn West, *To See the Dream* (journal), Harcourt, 1957; Jane Muir, *Famous Modern American Women Writers* (juvenile), Dodd, 1959; Alfred S. Shivers, *Jessaymn West,* Twayne, 1972; West, *Hide and Seek: A Continuing Journey* (autobiography), Harcourt, 1973; *Contemporary Authors,* Volumes 9-12, revised, Gale, 1974; West, *The Woman Said Yes: Encounters with Life and Death, Memoirs,* Harcourt, 1976; *Contemporary Literary Criticism,* Volume 7, Gale, 1977; *Current Biography 1977,* H. W. Wilson, 1978; Diana Gleasner, *Breakthrough: Women in Writing* (juvenile), Walker, 1980; West, *Double Discovery: A Journey* (autobiography), Harcourt, 1980; *Contemporary Novelists,* third edition, St. Martin's, 1982. *Obituaries: New York Times,* February 24, 1984; *Variety,* February 29, 1984; *Newsweek,* March 5, 1984; *Time,* March 5, 1984; *Publishers Weekly,* March 9, 1984.

WILLARD, Nancy　　1936-

PERSONAL: Born June 26, 1936, in Ann Arbor, Mich.; daughter of Hobart Hurd (a chemistry professor) and Marge (Sheppard) Willard; married Eric Lindbloom (a photographer), 1964; children: James. *Education:* University of Michigan, B.A.,

NANCY WILLARD

When the rabbit showed me my room,
I looked all around for the bed.
I saw nothing there
but a shaggy old bear
who offered to pillow my head.

■ (From "A Rabbit Reveals My Room" in *A Visit to William Blake's Inn: Poems for Innocent and Experienced Travelers* by Nancy Willard. Illustrated by Alice and Martin Provensen.)

1958, Ph.D., 1963; Stanford University, M.A., 1960; studied art in Paris and Oslo. *Home:* 133 College Ave., Poughkeepsie, N.Y. 12603. *Agent:* Jean V. Naggar Literary Agency, 336 E. 73rd St., Suite C, New York, N.Y. 10021. *Office:* Department of English, Vassar College, Poughkeepsie, N.Y.

CAREER: Writer. Lecturer in English at Vassar College, Poughkeepsie, N.Y. Bread Loaf Writers' Conference, teacher, summers. *Awards, honors:* Hopwood Award, 1958; Woodrow Wilson fellowship, 1960; Devins Memorial Award, 1967, for *Skin of Grace; Sailing to Cythera and Other Anatole Stories* was selected as one of the Fifty Books of the Year by the American Institute of Graphic Arts, 1974; National Endowment for the Arts Award and Creative Artists' Public Service Award, both 1976, both for poetry; Lewis Carroll Shelf Award, 1977, for *Sailing to Cythera and Other Anatole Stories* and 1979, for *The Island of the Grass King: The Further Adventures of Anatole;* Art Books for Children Citation from the Brooklyn Museum and the Brooklyn Public Library, 1978, for *Simple Pictures Are Best;* Newbery Medal, Caldecott honor book, and Association of American Publisher's American Book Award nomination, all 1982, all for *A Visit to William Blake's Inn: Poems for Innocent and Experienced Travelers.*

WRITINGS: *Things Invisible to See,* Knopf, 1964; *In His Country: Poems,* Generation (Ann Arbor, Mich.), 1966; *Skin of Grace* (poetry), University of Missouri Press, 1967; *A New Herball: Poems,* Ferninand-Roter Gallerias, 1968; *The Lively Anatomy of God* (short stories), Eakins, 1968.

Testimony of the Invisible Man: William Carlos Williams, Francis Ponge, Rainer Maria Rilke, Pablo Neruda, University of Missouri Press, 1970; *Nineteen Masks for the Naked Poet: Poems,* Kayak, 1971, reprinted, Harcourt, 1984; *Childhood of the Magician,* Liveright, 1973; *The Carpenter of the Sun: Poems,* Liveright, 1974; *The Merry History of a Christmas Pie: With a Delicious Description of a Christmas Soup* (juvenile), Putnam, 1974; *Sailing to Cythera and Other Anatole Stories* (juvenile; illustrated by David McPhail), Harcourt, 1974; *All on a May Morning* (juvenile; illustrated by Haig Shekerjian and Regina Shekerjian), Putnam, 1975; *The Snow Rabbit* (juvenile; illustrated by Laura Lydecker), Putnam, 1975; *Shoes without Leather* (juvenile; illustrated by L. Lydecker, Putnam, 1976; *The Well-Mannered Balloon* (juvenile; illustrated by H. Shekerjian and R. Shekerjian), Harcourt, 1976; *Simple Pictures Are Best* (juvenile; illustrated by Tomie de Paola; Junior Literary Guild selection), Harcourt, 1977; *Stranger's Bread* (juvenile; illustrated by D. McPhail), Harcourt, 1977; *The Highest Hit* (juvenile; illustrated by Emily McCully), Harcourt, 1978; *The Island of the Grass King: The Further Adventures of Anatole* (juvenile; illustrated by D. McPhail), Harcourt, 1979; *Papa's Panda* (juvenile; illustrated by Lillian Hoban; Junior Literary Guild selection), Harcourt, 1979.

The Marzipan Moon (juvenile; illustrated by Marcia Sewall), Harcourt, 1981; *A Visit to William Blake's Inn: Poems for Innocent and Experienced Travelers* (juvenile; illustrated by Alice Provensen and Martin Provensen), Harcourt, 1981; *Household Tales of Moon and Water* (poetry), Harcourt, 1982; *Uncle Terrible: More Adventures of Anatole* (juvenile; illustrated by D. McPhail), Harcourt, 1982; *Angel in the Parlor: Five Stories and Eight Essays,* Harcourt, 1983; *The Nightgown of the Sullen Moon* (illustrated by D. McPhail), Harcourt, 1983.

Illustrator: John Kater, *The Letter of John to James,* Seabury, 1981; J. Kater, *Another Letter of John to James,* Seabury, 1982.

Contributor to *Cricket, Esquire,* and *Redbook.*

ADAPTATIONS: "A Visit to William Blake's Inn" (filmstrip), Miller-Brody.

SIDELIGHTS: Willard was raised in Ann Arbor, Michigan, where her father, an internationally-known chemist, taught at the University. "I grew up in a lively house with all sorts of characters in it. It was a little like William Blake's Inn."

"As for guests, nobody could ask for a greater variety than ours. On the third floor lived my grandfather, whose room held

his clothes, his chewing tobacco, and the books he counted among his special friends: the Bible, *Pilgrim's Progress,* treatises and beekeeping and osteopathy, and the work of Edgar Allan Poe. When I came home from school, I could hear his voice rolling through the house, breathing life into the raven, Annabel Lee, and the tintinnabulation of the bells.

"From morning till evening, my grandmother talked to herself, and to the living and the dead. At night, her English slipped away and she recited prayers in German and dreamed herself back on her father's farm in Iowa, and that country church where the women sat on the left side and the men on the right and heard about the wages of sin, while an occasional wise cow waited outside like a visitor from a more peaceable kingdom." ["Newbery Medal Acceptance," *Horn Book* Magazine, August, 1982.[1]]

"I especially remember the part of my childhood in a small town in Michigan where we spent the summer in our cottage on Stony Lake. By today's standards I guess it would be considered a very simple life. My sister and I had to walk down the road to a well to get our drinking water.

"The first story in *Sailing to Cythera* is set there. The nearest town is Oxford and in one of the pictures in the book the child is wearing a T-shirt that says: 'Oxford, Michigan, Gravel Capital of the World.' We still have that cottage. And now my sister and I go out there for summer reunions with our children."

"I often wrote there. I made books as presents for people on Christmas and birthdays—stories with little pictures including elaborate borders made of hundreds of figures and flowers on parchment. I almost went blind trying to imitate the crosshatchings I found in old engravings in the family library. I didn't know the drawings had been reduced. I thought artists simply drew things that small." [Nancy Willard, *Angel in the Parlor,* Harcourt, 1983.[2]]

"I think my parents encouraged my creativity. They certainly didn't do anything to stop it. My mother used to give me shelf paper which came in huge rolls. You could draw and draw and never reach the end of the paper. I used to draw all the neighborhood children. They'd come around and I'd tell them stories and they'd let me draw them. Of course, I had to work fast. They didn't sit still." ["Meet the Newbery Author: Nancy Willard," Random House/Miller Brody, 1983.[3]]

"My parents gave us lots of books. I liked George Macdonald stories, and I loved the 'Oz' books. I went through almost all of those. There was a college bookshop in Ann Arbor and every June they held a big sale. You could buy any book for ten cents. My sister and I would carry books home by the arm loads. Sometimes I would pick the books by their covers and they were awful—terrible sermons, books of manners. But once in awhile, I'd find something good. We would take these books out to the cottage in Oxford and read them all summer.

"When people asked me, 'What do you want to do when you grow up?' I answered: 'I want to tell stories.' And they would always say, 'Oh, you want to work on a newspaper, do you?' So my mother suggested that [my older sister] Ann and I start our own newspaper."[3] Thus was born the "Stony Lake News." "It was a two person paper. The community was so small there wasn't any news, but I went door to door with a notebook. I'd knock at each door and say, 'Has anything happened?' Usually, nothing had happened. I remember one lady said, 'Well, I got up at eleven o'clock this morning.'"

They ate in silence, the tailor leaning forward on his stool, drinking tea with one hand and stroking Anatole with the other. ■ (From *Uncle Terrible: More Adventures of Anatole* by Nancy Willard. Illustrated by David McPhail.)

"...When he was ready to make his wish, he found Grandmother had fallen asleep." ■ (From *The Island of the Grass King* by Nancy Willard. Illustrated by David McPhail.)

"Of course, the real news wasn't what happened, it was the way people told what happened. Some of them were wonderful storytellers. I loved listening to them." [Barbara Lucas, "Nancy Willard," *Horn Book* Magazine, August, 1982.[4]]

"We'd also ask for want ads. And when we had enough news, which we stored in a shoebox under my bed, my sister would print it on a little press. I used these memories in my book *The Highest Hit*. The news items that are used in Kate's paper really came from the paper my sister and I ran."

"The books that I liked as a child were fantasy, and they had interesting girls as main characters. *Alice in Wonderland* was probably my favorite book as a child. Alice was a strong character—she must have been strong—she made it through Wonderland! All of the 'Oz' books featured Dorothy as a heroine. Those are books I still re-read."

When Willard was seven, one of her poems was published on the children's page of a Unitarian church magazine. Years later, her miniature book, "A Child's Star," which she had written as a high school senior, was published in *Horn Book* magazine. "A teacher of mine in high school encouraged me to send the book to *Horn Book*. It came out as an inset for their Christmas issue." She later received a letter from the editor, Bertha Mahony Miller, claiming that Mahony was so taken with one of the drawings that *Horn Book* wanted to use it for their Christmas card that year. "She sent me ten dollars! That was a fortune to me."

"At that time, I had practically no formal art training except in the art classes at school. The teacher let me draw as I pleased, so most of the time I worked in pen and ink."

"I wonder how many writers can remember the person or experience that called them to their craft. If you ask a dozen writers why they started writing, their answers will be as various as their work. It was neither a teacher nor a parent that called me. It was a dream. I was three years old and not yet going to school. As I could not write, I was forced to remember my dreams in greater detail than I do now. A few years later, when I learned to write, I set down my dream, feeling greatly relieved that I did not have to carry it around in my head any longer. And since that dream was the first story I ever wanted to write, I have always respected the strong connection between the process of dreaming and the process of writing."[2]

"While I was reading or drawing or doing my homework, I listened, and I wrote down whatever seemed worth saving; a fragment of speech, a line of poetry."[1] "If you want to write stories, that's a very good way to begin. You can just start eavesdropping."[3]

In 1958 Willard attended the University of Michigan. "I was in the honors English program. . . . It was very rigorous. I studied English literature, and I had one professor who had us memorize fifty lines of every poet we read. We all moaned and groaned but it was a wonderful thing to be asked to do, because those poets are now part of me. All those passages that I learned are part of me, too.

"Our Shakespeare teacher read aloud passages from the plays. I don't remember what he taught me about Shakespeare, but when I read those lines I hear his voice. He taught us to love the play and that, perhaps, is the mark of a really great teacher."

As an undergraduate, "I did a children's book with elaborate pen and ink drawings and hand-lettered text which came out as an inset in the student literary magazine at the University of Michigan." "When Marianne Moore visited the campus, someone gave her a copy and she later sent me five dollars wrapped in a pink Kleenex requesting another copy. I was very touched. I am sure I saved the Kleenex."[4]

"The first book that I published after I graduated was part of a student poetry series at the University of Michigan. It was called *In His Country*."

Willard has studied all over the world. "In Oslo I studied folk art. I spent a lot of time in museums studying a particular kind called rosemaling (rose painting). In Paris I took a graphic art workshop with Antonio Frasconi, whose woodcuts I like and many of whose books I have.

"I went to Mexico to learn Spanish because there are such wonderful things to read in that language. I like many of the Spanish poets—Neruda and Vallejo are great favorites of mine. I like to read in Spanish, but I'm not fluent enough to write in it. I also studied lithography in workshops there."

Her Ph.D. studies in medieval literature at Stanford helped to shape her sensibilities. "I wrote my thesis at Stanford on medieval folk songs, which were preserved in very accidental ways. We don't even know who wrote them. They are very old and some of them are very beautiful. When you start getting interested in the medieval period, it opens doors to all kinds of legends and stories and fantasies. I think for a writer—especially someone writing fantasy—it's a wonderful period to know something about.

"*The Merry History of a Christmas Pie* was inspired by my medieval studies. I looked at paintings and read a lot of folklore for the thesis and looked up the backgrounds on the carols. In the middle ages the carol was a dance form. There were carols for different seasons.

"Transformation has always occurred in fantasy. Especially people turning into animals and vice-versa. Sometimes I read fairy tales to my students, for example, *The Seven Ravens*, in which the children turn into ravens and fly off. I ask, 'Is this true? Do people really ever turn into animals?' First they look skeptical, and then they realize it's a metaphor. People can act like animals, and fantasy just pushes that a bit further. Of course, in dreams transformation happens all the time. In that sense, it's a very true part of our lives.

"In my work, when characters dream themselves into the story, I never want to end with 'And then she woke up.' That's one part of *Through the Looking Glass* I don't like. Wonderland is a dream-world. It's so vivid. There's no reason to apologize for it by saying, 'Oh, it was only a dream.' *Only?* Dreams are important!

"A lot of stories start with the question, 'What if?' 'What if this happened?' is really the question that the writer asks. I've always thought that questions are more interesting than answers. When my son was at the stage where he was asking a lot of questions, I wrote them down and made them into a little book so he would know that questions were important—as important as answers. One of the first questions he asked me was 'Where does the sun go at night?' I was just about to tell him the scientific answer when I thought, 'Maybe he's got a good one.' He had a wonderful answer which happens to resemble an Egyptian myth. There's no way he could have read that myth at age three.

". . .As the coach floated over the iron gates and the mule's hooves brushed the tops of the gravestones." ■ (From *Uncle Terrible: More Adventures of Anatole* by Nancy Willard. Illustrated by David McPhail.)

"In the Egyptian myth, the sun is on a boat and it's rowed into the earth and comes up on the other side. In my son's version, the sun got on a train, entered the dining car, ate orange pie to keep its color and then came out the other side of the earth. I made that answer into a little book for him because I wanted to show him that there are two kinds of truth—the scientific answer and the imaginative answer. And we need both of them.

"Themes are something that other people find in things. Writers probably don't start with the theme. They start with the 'What happened?' In the old Irish myth, somebody asks Fionn, 'What's the finest music in the world?' And Fionn says, 'The music of what happens.'"

Willard has written poetry and literary criticism as well as prose. "Sometimes I can hear it. You can always hear the difference between a story and a poem—though a lot of my poems do tell stories. Not until you've really sat down do you know exactly what it is. It surprises you. It's as if the thing you create really does have its own life. It starts with listening. *The Highest Hit* began with hearing Kate's voice, hearing how Kate would say things.

"Writing for adults and writing for children is a line that's gradually getting blurred. I've noticed that many adults like children's books. Lewis Carroll appeals to all ages. And there are plenty of children who, for good reasons, read about books. My son, James, is now thirteen and he reads both. I have learned what interests children partly from him. But I think it's important to remember that some of the best children's book writers don't have children. Lewis Carroll didn't, for example, but he spent time with children. Maurice Sendak doesn't have children, but he writes for the child in himself. It's important for a writer to keep in touch with the child within. Sometimes having children around can help."

Willard's book, *Pappa's Panda,* was based on a conversation she overheard between her husband, photographer Eric Lindbloom, and James. "I work with whatever is at hand, and if my family is at hand, I work them in. I think all writers draw on things in their own lives. But by the time it comes out in a book, it's pretty different. A little bit of this aunt, a little bit of that grandmother. It's a mix. It makes something new.

"I've done illustrations for several books that were not my texts. We know a local Episcopal priest of whom my son asked a lot of questions, big questions like: 'Where does God come from?' and 'What happens when you die?' These are topics that no one likes to discuss, but this minister sent my son a letter, and some of the answers were so interesting, so sensible that I wrote it out as a little book with pictures. It was published by Seabury Press.

"I prefer to have other people illustrate my books—though I love drawing and still do a lot of it. There are so many good illustrators who are much better than I am. But I often do a layout for my picture books. I submit them that way to help the editor see the possibilities. But I tell the artist never to be bound by anything I've drawn." *William Blake's Inn,* for which Willard won the 1981 Newbery Award, began with a model of the inn. "I constructed most of William Blake's Inn and the writing came out of that. If I have a character in my mind, sometimes I'll make something that belongs to him like his hat. You learn about the characters as you work on things that belong to them. That certainly happened with *William Blake's Inn.* I made all his companions before I ever found William Blake. But Blake was on my mind. Things came together:

For several minutes there was silence between them. ■
(From *Strangers' Bread* by Nancy Willard. Illustrated by David McPhail.)

listening to Blake's poetry on a record and making a lot of characters for the inn. Sometimes it's better to just work without examining too closely how it all happens. It is something you don't always control.

"The inn took several years to build. I started with cardboard boxes which are nice because they're cheap, so I wasn't inhibited about making mistakes. A friend of ours came over one night and was dubiously admiring this odd structure when our cat jumped into it and the whole house fell down. Fortunately, our friend was a carpenter and offered to copy it in wood. He took all the measurements and then disappeared. He returned several months later with the shell of the house made from scraps. I painted it, filled it with furniture and people, and it became 'William Blake's Inn.' The house still stands in our dining room."

Willard teaches creative writing at Vassar College. "I teach a course in writing poetry. There are two ways to approach writing poetry. One is through workshops, where you bring in the work that you do on your own and the students take a look at it. I teach it differently. I give assignments. Often the assignments are designed to give someone a new way of shaping an experience.

"Aside from teaching and writing, I read a lot of poetry. Not just contemporary poets, but translations and early work.

William, William, writing late
by the chill and sooty grate,
what immortal story can
make your tiger roar again?

■ (From "The Tiger Asks Blake for a Bedtime Story" in *A Visit to William Blake's Inn: Poems for Innocent and Experienced Travelers* by Nancy Willard. Illustrated by Alice and Martin Provensen.)

"Children should be encouraged from the moment they begin to write or tell stories. You meet so many adults who say, 'Gee, I was turned off by poetry, and I don't know what happened along the way.' I suppose there are things that people have to learn in standard curriculum, and poetry is probably not one of them. But I think it's important to hear poetry and enjoy it. Finally, what any teacher teaches is not simply grammar, not simply subject matter, but a love for literature. That's what the student really remembers.

"I would tell young people who want to be writers to read. And I would pass on the Henry James adage, 'Try to be a person on whom nothing is lost'—to value all the different kinds of experiences. I can remember an assignment that my son was given by a very good teacher in fourth grade. James was told to go and find somebody sixty or older and ask that person what it was like to grow up. Of course, it was a very different world.

"Young writers should talk to people and listen to people. The world is out there full of wonderful things to write about. In my case, there's not much difference between writing and recreation. I do a lot of crafts and gardening. But writing is fun. Writing is what I really prefer to do."

WILLIAMSON, Henry   1895-1977

PERSONAL: Born December 1, 1895, in Bedfordshire, England; died August 13, 1977, in Berkshire, England; son of William Williamson; married twice (divorced twice); children: seven. *Residence:* Berkshire, England.

CAREER: Became a journalist in London after World War I; writer, 1921-74. Served as a broadcaster on farming life in 1930's and was a farmer in Norfolk. *Military service:* British Army, World War I; infantryman and officer. *Member:* National Liberal Club, Savage Club, Chelsea Arts Club. *Awards, honors:* Hawthornden Prize, 1928, for *Tarka the Otter.*

WRITINGS—"The Flax of Dream" series: *The Beautiful Years,* Dutton, 1921, revised edition, 1929; *Dandelion Days,* Dutton, 1922, revised edition, 1930; *The Dream of Fair Women,* Dutton, 1924, revised edition, 1931; *The Pathway,* J. Cape, 1928, Dutton, 1929; tetralogy published as *The Flax of Dream,* Faber, 1936.

"A Chronicle of Ancient Sunlight" series; all published by Macdonald, except as noted: *The Dark Lantern,* 1951; *Donkey Boy,* 1952; *Young Phillip Maddison,* 1953; *How Dear Is Life,* 1954; *A Fox Under My Cloak,* 1955; *The Golden Virgin,* 1957, revised edition, Panther, 1963; *Love and the Loveless: A Soldier's Tale,* 1958; *A Test to Destruction,* 1960, revised edition, Panther, 1964; *The Innocent Moon,* 1961; *It Was the Nightingale,* 1962; *The Power of the Dead,* 1963, revised edition, Panther, 1966; *The Phoenix Generation,* 1965; *A Solitary War,* 1966; *Lucifer before Sunrise,* 1967; *The Gale of the World,* 1969.

Other works: *The Lone Swallows,* Collins, 1922, Dutton, 1926, revised edition published as *The Lone Swallows and Other Essays of Boyhood and Youth,* Putnam, 1933; *The Peregrine's Saga and Other Stories of the Country Green,* Collins, 1923, published as *Sun Brothers,* Dutton, 1925; *The Old Stag: Stories,* Putnam, (London), 1926, Dutton, 1927; *Tarka the Otter: Being His Joyful Water-Life and Death in the Country of the Two Rivers* (novel), Dutton, 1927, another edition, illustrated

by C. F. Tunnicliff, Merrimack Book Service, 1982; *The Linhay on the Downs* (short stories), Mathews & Marrot, 1929; *The Wet Flanders Plain* (war recollections), Dutton, 1929, revised edition, Faber, 1929; *The Ackymals* (short stories), Windsor Press, 1929.

The Patriot's Progress: Being the Vicissitudes of Private John Bullock (novel), Dutton, 1930, *The Village Book* (short stories), Dutton, 1930; *The Wild Red Deer of Exmoor: A Digression on the Logic and Ethics and Economics of Stag-Hunting in England Today,* Faber, 1931; *The Labouring Life* (short stories), J. Cape, 1932, published as *As the Sun Shines,* Dutton, 1933; *The Gold Falcon; or, The Haggard of Love: Being the Adventures of Manfred, Airman and Poet of the World War, and Later, Husband and Father, in Search of Freedom and Personal Sunrise, in the City of New York, and of the Consummation of His Life* (novel; published anonymously), Smith, 1933, revised edition published under own name, Faber, 1947; *The Star-Born,* Faber, 1933, revised edition, 1948, Chivers, 1973; *On Foot in Devon; or, Guidance and Gossip: Being a Monologue in Two Reels* (short stories), Maclehose, 1933; *The Linhay on the Downs and Other Adventures in the Old and New World* (short stories), J. Cape, 1934; *Salar the Salmon* (novel), Faber, 1935; *Devon Holiday,* J. Cape, 1935; (editor) *An Anthology of Modern Nature Writing,* Thomas Nelson, 1936; *Goodbye West Country,* Putnam (London), 1937, Little, Brown, 1938; (editor) *Richard Jefferies: Selections of His Work,* Faber, 1937; (editor) Richard Jefferies, *Hodge and His Masters,* Methuen, 1937; *The Children of Shallowford* (autobiography), Faber, 1939, revised edition, 1959.

As the Sun Shines: Selections, Faber, 1941; *The Story of a Norfolk Farm* (autobiography), Faber, 1941; *Genius of Friendship: "T. E. Lawrence",* Faber, 1941; (editor) L. R. Haggard, *Norfolk Life,* Faber, 1943; *The Sun in the Sands* (novel), Faber, 1945; *Life in a Devon Village* (short stories), Faber, 1945; *Tales of a Devon Village,* Faber, 1945; (editor) *My Favorite Country Stories,* Lutterworth, 1946; *The Phasian Bird* (novel), Faber, 1948, Little, Brown, 1950; *Scribbling Lark,* Faber, 1949; (editor) *Unreturning Springs: Being the Poems, Sketches, Stories and Letters of James Farrar,* William & Norgate, 1950.

Tales of Moorland and Estuary (short stories), Macdonald, 1953; *A Clear Water Stream* (autobiography), Faber, 1958, Washburn, 1959, revised edition, Macdonald, 1975; *In the Woods* (short stories), St. Albert's Press (Wales), 1960; (contributor) *A First Adventure with Francis Thompson,* St. Albert's Press, 1966; *Collected Nature Stories,* Macdonald, 1970; "The Vanishing Hedgerow" (television play), 1972; *The Scandaroon* (novel illustrated by Ken Lilly), Macdonald, 1972, Saturday Review Press, 1973; *Animal Saga* (short stories) Macdonald and Jones, 1974. Also contributor to *Some Nature Writers and Civilization,* 1960.

ADAPTATIONS: "Tarka the Otter" (adventure film), narrated by Peter Ustinov, Rank, 1979.

SIDELIGHTS: Williamson wrote autobiographies, essays, short stories, and novels, but was best known for his books on nature. Many of his nature books, particularly his early novels, appealed to children because he gave his animal characters unique personalities.

His most widely acclaimed animal book was entitled *Tarka the Otter,* based on the experiences of Williamson and an otter that he raised. The setting described in *Tarka the Otter* and several of his other books was Devon in the English countryside, where Williamson lived in the 1920s. "In several Devon

There, bewildered, it moved about with uncertainty until Sam Baggott, with a neat movement of one sea-boot, pinned the bird by a wing. ■ (From *The Scandaroon* by Henry Williamson. Illustrated by Ken Lilly.)

villages, during the period of ten years after the great War . . . I have heard and seen many things which interested me. Some were made immediately into stories, rapidly written while the impressions remained unworn by later and different thought. "The Badger Dig" and "The Ackymals" were two written immediately after the actual happenings. Many, however, were written some time afterwards; some have been left overlong until the desire to write—which always must first break through an indolence and distaste for writing—has gone. Those sketches which were not written spontaneously were written afterwards from the notes I made in various places; and looking over the pages of the note-books, the envelopes, the match-boxes, the letters and odd bits of paper on which they were jotted down, I see what many of the entries are short stories already—stories which are truly short. . . ." [Henry Williamson, *The Village Book*, Dutton, 1930.[1]]

Williamson was acclaimed as a gifted nature writer who advocated soil conservation and water conservation. Reviewers praised his books for their passages of pure literature. One reviewer called Williamson "a man who is trying to understand himself along with the rest of nature."

About his literary purpose and place in literature, Williamson remarked: "I am, or was, a wilderness writer; but I have had to unlearn what I learnt there. When I began to see the scape-goat-bones by the wayside, and the sanded horizon apparently melting in swooning air, yet remaining static in its barren leagues, I hurried back, hoping it was not too late to lose myself among the sheep once more.

"While yet in the wilderness of my illusions I began to write *The Village Book;* and although fatigued from the conception and writing of the four novels ending with *The Pathway*, I still felt I had the power to write a new truth, to transmute, by the ardour of vision, sand into air ascending. Now that I have finished the job—which, after all, was done by means of a pen and paper, and was pretty hard and often tedious work—I wish

that I had perceived before the only truth that I can now accept: the truth that Truth is not so much a vision of reformation as an understanding of things as they are." [Henry Williamson, *As the Sun Shines*, Dutton, 1933.[2]]

FOR MORE INFORMATION SEE: Saturday Review of Literature, January 3, 1925, May 21, 1927, December 21, 1929, July 19, 1930; *New York Tribune*, June 14, 1925; *New York World*, June 21, 1925, March 24, 1928, June 15, 1930; *New York Times*, April 17, 1927, March 4, 1928, December 8, 1929, July 13, 1930, March 27, 1938, October 15, 1950; *Springfield Republican*, April 21, 1929; *New York Herald Tribune Book Review*, September 8, 1929, July 20, 1930, April 10, 1933; *Spectator*, July 14, 1930; I. Waveny Girvan, *A Bibliography and a Critical Survey of the Works of Henry Williamson*, Alcuin Press (Gloucestershire), 1931; Henry Williamson, *As the Sun Shines*, Dutton 1933; H. Williamson, *The Children of Shallowford*, Faber, 1939, revised edition, 1959; H. Williamson, *The Story of a Norfolk Farm*, Faber, 1941; *Christian Science Monitor*, November 4, 1950, July 30, 1959; *Chicago Sunday Tribune*, November 5, 1950; H. Williamson, *A Clear Water Stream*, Faber, 1958, Washburn, 1959; *Times Literary Supplement*, June 27, 1958.

OBITUARIES: New York Times, August 14, 1977; *AB Bookman's Weekly*, October 1, 1977.

WITHAM, (Phillip) Ross   1917-

PERSONAL: Born April 11, 1917, in Stuart, Fla.; son of Paul N. (in U.S. Navy) and Lucille (Ross) Witham; married Mabel

ROSS WITHAM

Back to the sea. Note "crawl" left behind. ■ (From *Turtles: Extinction or Survival?* by Sarah R. Riedman and Ross Witham. Photograph by Dr. Archie Carr.)

Josephine Blasko (a teacher of the handicapped), May 27, 1945; children: Chester Randolph, Steven Paul, Timothy Dean, Julie Ann Witham Hartwigger. *Education:* University of South Florida, B.I.S., 1973; University of Oklahoma, M.L.S., 1976. *Home:* 1457 Northwest Lake Point, Stuart, Fla. 33494. *Office:* Florida Department of Natural Resources, P.O. Box 941, Jensen Beach, Fla. 33457-0941.

CAREER: U.S. Navy, Jacksonville, Fla., civilian aircraft mechanic, 1949-52; Public Health Foundation for Cancer and Blood Pressure Research, Inc., Stuart, Fla., supervisor of hydroponics, 1959-66; Florida Department of Natural Resources, St. Petersburg, biologist, researcher on sea turtles, and supervisor of field station in Jensen Beach, 1965—. Curator of marine activities for Martin County Historical Society, 1955-65; biological aide with Florida Board of Conservation, 1963-65. Member of Southeast Region Marine Turtle Recovery Team, of National Marine Fisheries Service and U.S. Fish and Wildlife Service, U.S. Army Corps of Engineers task force on sea turtles and dredging, and consutant for wider Caribbean sea turtle conservation network. *Military service:* U.S. Navy, aviation machinist's mate, 1934-44; served in Pacific theater.

MEMBER: American Institute of Biological Sciences, American Society of Zoologists, American Society of Ichthyologists and Herpetologists, American Institute of Fishery Research Biologists, Ecological Society of America, Izaak Walton League of America (past president of Martin County chapter), Ex-plorers Club (fellow), Pearl Harbor Survivors Association (life member), Disabled American Veterans (life member), Florida Academy of Sciences, Gulf and Caribbean Fisheries Institute.

WRITINGS: (With Sarah R. Riedman) *Turtles: Extinction or Survival?* (juvenile), Abelard, 1974. Contributor of more than fifteen articles to scientific journals, including *Sea Frontiers*.

WORK IN PROGRESS: Continuing research on sea turtles.

SIDELIGHTS: "I became interested in sea turtles following the discovery of a nearly dead hatchling on Hutchinson Island, Martin County, Florida; I had been walking along the beach as rehabilitation therapy following knee surgery. I became interested in sea turtles and spiny lobsters, and these interests led to employment by the state of Florida, first to research spiny lobsters and later sea turtles. Authorship followed as a matter of course because of the need to publish research findings, as I did with Sarah Riedman in *Turtles: Extinction or Survival?* My sea turtle research was featured on television programs, including 'Animals, Animals, Animals,' 'That's Incredible,' and 'Those Amazing Animals.'"

His studies were pursued but never effectually overtaken.

—H.G. Wells

WOLF, Bernard 1930-

BRIEF ENTRY: Born in 1930, in New York, N.Y. Photographer and author of children's books. Wolf began his career as an interior designer with various furniture manufacturers and eventually broke away from them to begin designing and photographing his own work. He later turned to travel photography, working in locations such as Madeira, Athens, Thailand, and Macau. His photographs have appeared in *House Beautiful, Travel and Camera, Camera 35, Fortune,* and *New York Magazine.* Wolf's books for children all deal with the everyday lives of real people. *Don't Feel Sorry for Paul* (Lippincott, 1974), *Connie's New Eyes* (Lippincott, 1976), and *Anna's Silent World* (Lippincott, 1977) all feature handicapped people. Wolf's other books for children include *The Little Weaver of Agato: A Visit with an Indian Boy Living in the Andes Mountains of Ecuador* (Cowles Book Co., 1969), *Tinker and the Medicine Man: The Story of a Navajo Boy of Monument Valley* (Random House, 1973), and *Firehouse* (Morrow, 1983). Several of Wolf's books have received awards, including *Adam Smith Goes to School* (Lippincott, 1978) which was named a Notable Children's Trade Book in the Field of Social Studies jointly by the National Council for the Social Studies and Children's Book Council in 1978. *Residence:* New York, N.Y. *For More Information See: Fifth Book of Junior Authors,* H. W. Wilson, 1983.

WOLKOFF, Judie (Edwards)

BRIEF ENTRY: Wolkoff was born in Montana and graduated from the University of Utah after attending schools in Mexico and Spain. She has taught primary grades in California and New York City. Her first book, *Wally* (Bradbury Press, 1977), is the story of a young boy who attempts to harbor a chuckwalla in his closet. Aimed at middle readers, the book was described by *School Library Journal* as "fast, fresh, and funny . . . replete with silliness and slapstick. . . ." Her other books, intended for young adults, are mainly realistic fiction into which she occasionally weaves humor to deal with the problems so common-place with that age group. In *Ace Hits the Big Time* (Delacorte, 1981), Wolkoff uses comedy to lighten her social commentary on peer pressure. ". . . Ace is a small triumph," *Horn Book* noted, "for the mild-mannered, peace-loving souls everywhere who spend their lives intimidated by more aggressive peers." In books like *Where the Elf King Sings* (Bradbury, 1980), Wolkoff demonstrates an ability to create realistic characters. *VOYA* observed that "Thanks to skillful characterization, the young adult reader can identify with the isolation and confusion the child of an acoholic parent feels." *Residence:* Chappaqua, N.Y.

ZIMELMAN, Nathan

BRIEF ENTRY: Zimelman became a full-time writer of children's books when he retired from business. As an author, he often uses animals as central characters, employing every species from dogs and cats to elephants and gorillas. Because of the antics of these animals, his stories usually overflow with soft humor. In *Positively No Pets Allowed,* a pet gorilla, Irving, is mistaken by an iceman for a human being. In *The Lives of My Cat Alfred,* illustrated by Evaline Ness, Zimelman recounts the many experiences Alfred may have had with important people in the past. Lighthearted comedy is a hallmark of Zimelman's other books, many of which center on the simple adventures and problems of young children. His books include *Beneath the Oak Tree* (Steck-Vaughn, 1966), *Once When I Was Five* (Steck-Vaughn, 1967), *So You Shouldn't Waste a Rhinoceros* (Steck-Vaughn, 1970), *Michael Allen Found a Dime* (Carolrhoda, 1972), *Cats of Kilkenny* (Carolrhoda, 1972), *Look Hiroshi!* (Aurora, 1973), *I Will Tell You of Peach Stone* (Lothrop, 1974), *Walls Are to Be Walked* (Dutton, 1977), *Mean Chickens and Wild Cucumbers* (Macmillan, 1983), and *How to Fly Like a Bird Even If You're Only a Boy* (Green Tiger Press, 1983). *Residence:* Sacramento, Calif.

CUMULATIVE INDEX TO ILLUSTRATIONS AND AUTHORS

Illustrations Index

(In the following index, the number of the volume in which an illustrator's work appears is given *before* the colon, and the page on which it appears is given *after* the colon. For example, a drawing by Adams, Adrienne appears in Volume 2 on page 6, another drawing by her appears in Volume 3 on page 80, another drawing in Volume 8 on page 1, and another drawing in Volume 15 on page 107.)

YABC

Index citations including this abbreviation refer to listings appearing in *Yesterday's Authors of Books for Children,* also published by the Gale Research Company, which covers authors who died prior to 1960.

Author Index

The following index gives the number of the volume in which an author's biographical sketch, Brief Entry, or Obituary appears.

This index includes references to all entries in the following series, which are also published by Gale Research Company.

YABC—*Yesterday's Authors of Books for Children: Facts and Pictures about Authors and Illustrators of Books for Young People from Early Times to 1960,* Volumes 1-2
CLR—*Children's Literature Review: Excerpts from Reviews, Criticism, and Commentary on Books for Children,* Volumes 1-6

Author Index

Author Index